67964

D1611457

Great Voyages
of Discovery

Jacques Brosse

Great Voyages of Discovery

Circumnavigators and Scientists, 1764–1843

Translated by Stanley Hochman

Preface by Fernand Braudel

Facts On File Publications
New York, New York • Oxford, England

Contents

To the memory of my brother,
Commander André Brosse, who,
when I was a child,
sailed the vast world.

Preface

Jacques Brosse's book offers us a triple delight. To begin with, we can sail across the immensity of oceans without leaving home; second, we can take passage aboard fragile wooden sailing vessels; and, finally, we can participate in the belated completion of the maritime discoveries taking place in the eighteenth century under the banner of disinterested scientific curiosity. The great maritime discoveries, those of the end of the fifteenth century and of the sixteenth century, had ended with the conquest of the planet's *useful* ocean routes. Two centuries later, the situation changes completely: The voyages around the world "had no other goal than to obtain new information about geography, the natural sciences, and the mores of different peoples."

It was, as a matter of fact, England's George III who initiated the change shortly after his country's victory over France (Treaty of Paris, 1763), when he organized the expedition of Commodore John Byron, who sailed from the Downs on June 21, 1764, for a first trip around the world with two ships: the frigate *Dolphin* and the sloop *Tamar*.

After that, expedition followed expedition, and Jacques Brosse describes them up to 1843, ending with the voyage of James Clark Ross, who took his two ships—the *Erebus* and the *Terror*—to the strange shores of the Antarctic.

Thus you have laid out before you the story of the voyages made during almost a century under the command of English, French, and "American" explorers. The most brilliant chapter is undoubtedly the one devoted to the marvelous island of Tahiti, which Cook explored in detail at the time of his first voyage, after it had been discovered by Wallis in 1767 and by Bougainville in 1768. Had Paradise been found?

As a reader, you will have the privilege, without risk, of sailing on board ships where life is difficult but from whose rails everything can be seen close up—the movement or the color of the sea water, the changing shades of the immense liquid plains, the flying fish, the friendly dolphins intent on following the ships, the schools of fish, and, finally, the shores that appear on the horizon. The anchor will be dropped only briefly—the time necessary to put in provisions of drinking water, wood, and fresh food to fight against scurvy—unless, of course, we linger to observe the strange, primitive populations of these universes outside the routes of great wealth: still unknown Australians, Polynesians, Melanesians, or Fuegians about whom we will bring back precious observations, some of which constitute true ethnographic studies.

These voyages are recounted to us with clarity and intelligence. We are given maps and marvelous pictures, the very ones that were made on the spot by artists accompanying these missions. There is a biographical dictionary of navigators and scientists; and a dictionary of ports of call, very necessary because the archipelagos have often changed names in the course of time. So come on board. You will be captivated, bewitched—but it will be a bewitchment from which you will draw profit and pleasure.

Fernand Braudel
Professor Emeritus
Collège de France

The
first voyages
around the world,
1519-1764

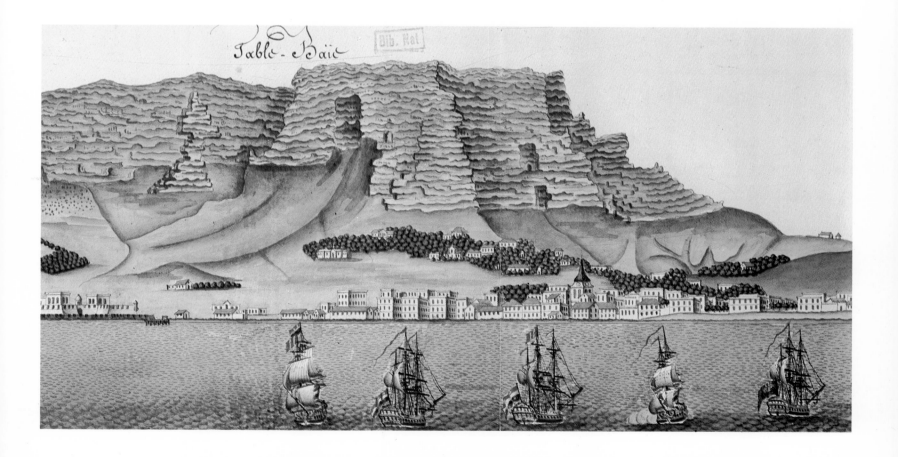

From Magellan to De Brosses

On September 8, 1522, the *Victoria,* a small 85-ton vessel commanded by Sebastian del Cano and carrying eighteen men, returned to Seville. They were the only survivors of an expedition that had left three years earlier with four other vessels that formed the flotilla of the Portuguese Fernão de Magalhães, who had been sent to seek a western route to the Indies. Skirting the recently discovered new continent, at the tip of South America the man we know as Magellan crossed through the strait to which he gave his name and, on November 28, 1520, entered the great ocean that he called the Pacific. By continually sailing west, Magellan had actually reached the Far East; he disembarked at the Philippines, where he died in a fight on Mactan on April 27, 1521.

Of the five ships and 239 men that had left, only one vessel and eighteen men had come back, but having "gone 14,460 leagues," they had, according to Pigafetta, the chronicler of the expedition, "sailed around the world from the Levant to the West" and made the first of the voyages circumnavigating the globe. Magellan and del Cano had demonstrated that Christopher Columbus had not discovered, as he believed, the northeastern coast of Asia, but, as the Florentine navigator Amerigo Vespucci insisted, a "New World"—the one the Saint-Dié printer Martin Waldseemüller, in the preface to his *Cosmographiae introductio* (1507), called America.

Magellan's voyage was a major episode in the Hispano-Portuguese rivalry for the conquest of the world and, especially, for the control of the Spice Route. Thanks to a Portuguese, Spain had discovered the Pacific, and its navigators explored it until the end of the sixteenth century. In 1528, Alvaro de Saavedra touched at the north coast of New Guinea and disembarked at Eniwetok in the Marshall Islands, but he died at sea. The two following expeditions, which also left from Mexico—that of Grijalva in 1537 and Villalobos in 1542—were disastrous. According to a probably untrue traditional story, the chronicler of Villalobos's voyage, an Italian named Juan Gaetano, landed on the Hawaiian Islands two hundred years before Cook.

These explorations of the Pacific, sporadic under Charles V, were continued in a much more methodical fashion by his son, Philip II, who undertook to expand the Spanish empire and preach

the true faith. In 1564–1565, Legaspi was sent from Mexico to the Philippines to colonize and evangelize them. One of his ships, commanded by Arellano, separated from the rest of the fleet and reached the Mariana Islands. Of greater importance was the voyage of Mendaña de Neira, who sailed from Callao, Peru, with two ships. This voyage had been undertaken at the urging of Sarmiento y Gamboa, the historian of the Incas, who had found mention in their traditions of a "Western Land" rich in silver and gold. Sarmiento concluded from this that there was a vast southern continent that perhaps corresponded to the far-off islands of Ophir and Tarshish, which according to the Bible had been discovered by King Solomon's ships. This *Terra australis nondum cognita,* represented on Ortelius's world map in 1570, was thought to occupy the entire southern part of the globe from Tierra del Fuego to Australia. Sarmiento and Mendaña never found it, but, in 1568, Mendaña explored an archipelago which he unhesitatingly named the Solomon Islands. It was not until 1595 that Mendaña obtained permission to colonize these islands, which he had discovered twenty-seven years earlier. Accompanied by the Portuguese pilot Pedro Fernandes de Queiros, he failed to relocate the Solomons but in-

Above: Magellan, in sight of Tierra del Fuego, discovers the strait that will bear his name (October 1520). Engraving by Jean-Théodore de Bry, about 1590. (Bibliothèque nationale, Paris. Photo © Bibl. nat./Photeb.)

Opposite: A full-rigged caravel. This type of fast ship was used in voyages of discovery from the end of the fifteenth to the sixteenth century. Illustration from Manuel de pilotage á l'usage des pilotes bretons *by G. Brouscon, 1548. (Bibliothèque nationale, Paris. Photo © Bibl. nat./Arch. Photeb.)*

Preceding page: View of the city of the Cape of Good Hope and Table Mountain, an indispensable stop on the route to the Far East. Watercolor by Lafitte de Brassier, 1786. (Bibliothèque nationale, Paris. Photo J.-L. Charmet © Arch. Photeb.)

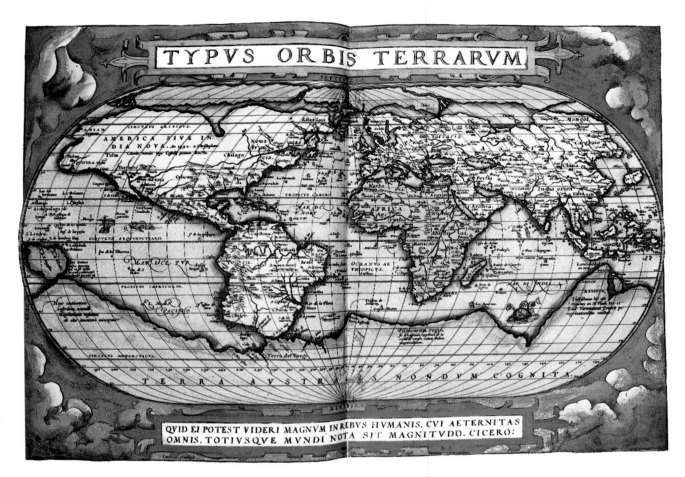

TYPVS ORBIS TERRARVM

QVID EI POTEST VIDERI MAGNVM IN REBVS HVMANIS, CVI AETERNITAS OMNIS, TOTIVSQVE MVNDI NOTA SIT MAGNITVDO. CICERO:

Map of the world by Abraham Oretelius, from his atlas Theatrum orbis terrarum, *1570. Notice the immense space given to the supposed southern continent. (National Maritime Museum, London. Photo © by the museum/Photeb.)*

stead discovered a portion of the Marquesas and the Santa Cruz Islands, where he died. Queiros, convinced of the existence of the *Terra australis,* again set off to look for it in 1605 with Luis Vaez de Torres. He reconnoitered several small islands in the Tuamotu Archipelago before disembarking in the New Hebrides on an island that he baptized *Tierra Australia del Espiritu Santo,* for he was convinced that it was a part of the looked-for continent. Separated afterward from Queiros, Torres found the strait that bears his name; New Guinea was therefore an island.

But because of inexact measuring procedures, all these scattered discoveries in the Great Ocean were so imprecisely charted that on the maps of the day they moved about like floating islands. For two centuries, explorers were to find new lands while looking for those already discovered and now untraceable; it sometimes also happened that they thought they had discovered new islands when these had actually already been reconnoitered by their predecessors.

Dutch, English, and French

After the beginning of the seventeenth century, Spanish navigators were to be slowly replaced by Dutch Protestants—former rebellious subjects of the Catholic kings, now resolved to take the place of the Portuguese, who were no longer able to fend them off. Between 1598 and 1603, thirteen Dutch fleets set out for the Indies. In 1602,

the powerful Dutch East India Company was established, and its navigators began to reconnoiter the coasts of the enormous land mass sighted by the Portuguese as early as the sixteenth century. After Willem Jansz explored its northern coast in 1605–1606, he called that land New Holland. In 1615–1616, Jakob Le Maire and Willem Schouten reconnoitered Cape Horn and, finding a new route to the Pacific by way of Le Maire Strait, they discovered several new islands there.

In 1642, Anthony Van Diemen, the governor-general of the Dutch East India Company, wanted more precise information about the possible relationship between New Holland and the *Terra australis;* he entrusted the mission of scientifically exploring the South Pacific to Abel Janszoon Tasman, an excellent cartographer. He discovered Van Diemen's Land (Tasmania) in 1642 and discovered the northwest Australian coast in 1644. Continuing on to the east, Tasman became the first European to reach the northwestern coast of New Zealand, thus demonstrating a skill that was not to be seen again until Cook. However, with the exception of Tasman, the Dutch navigators were interested only in commercial goals, and, to safeguard their monopoly, the Low Countries kept most of their discoveries secret.

The first English voyage around the world had taken place as early as 1577–1580. Sent by Queen Elizabeth to seek out lands not belonging to the Spanish crown, Sir Francis Drake sailed down the length of the eastern coast of South America; proved that Tierra del Fuego was an island; then, pillaging

Sir Francis Drake (1540–1596), the first of the great English circumnavigators. Anonymous painting from the end of the sixteenth century. (National Maritime Museum, London. Photo © by the museum/Photeb.)

Spanish ports and ships as he went along, sailed up the western coast as far as California, over which he affirmed English rights by calling it New Albion. Having been unable to find in the north of the American continent the hypothetical passage which was thought to link the Pacific and the Atlantic, Drake sailed to the Philippines, crossed the Indian Ocean, and returned to England by way of the Cape of Good Hope. Drake's exploit was duplicated in 1586–1588 by Thomas Cavendish, but, two other voyages having failed, the English did not return to the Pacific until a century later.

In 1683, the buccaneer William Dampier set out on a long voyage that took him to Chile, Peru, the Galapagos Islands, and Mexico, from which he left the following year for the Pacific. Dampier reached Guam in the Mariana Islands, then, by way of the Philippines, China. He was also the first Englishman to set foot on Australian soil. In 1699, Dampier made a new voyage of reconnaisance to Australia and discovered New Britain. In 1702–1707, he was again in the Pacific, this time with two ships. A mutinous crew abandoned the captain of the second ship and four of his men on an island of the Juan Fernàndez group off Chile in 1704. In 1708, Dampier was the pilot of Woodes Rogers's *Duke,* which put into this island and picked up the Scots sailor Alexander Selkirk, the only one to have survived the four years. Selkirk's story, reported by Rogers, aroused enormous interest in Great Britain. Inspired by it, the novelist Daniel Defoe wrote his *Robinson Crusoe,* which was published in 1719 and met with immediate success. Dampier himself related his adventures in four works that contained extremely lively descriptions of the places he had visited and the people he had encountered. They thus helped draw the attention of his compatriots to the South Seas and the possibilities they offered.

The French, too, had set off on long voyages, but they were in no position to dispute their conquests with powerful rivals, especially in the South Seas region. With few exceptions, the French expeditions were isolated undertakings, often carried out by pirates or buccaneers from St. Malo. If they made any discoveries, few traces of them remained. One of their reports, however, was to haunt the imaginations of French sailors for several centuries: the much-talked-about land discovered in January 1504 by Gonneville, a captain from Honfleur. His ship, the *Espoir,* reached a coast on which the inhabitants were extremely welcoming to the navigators, who remained there six months. When they left, they took with them Essomeric, the son of a local ruler. After a shipwreck in the English Channel, Gonneville returned to Honfleur with twenty-four survivors, among them Essomeric, who was baptized and founded a family in Normandy. It was not until the nineteenth century that Gonneville's Land was identified as probably being part of the South American coast; for two and a half centuries it was thought that Gonneville had reached the *Terra australis,* over which France would thus have had a prior claim.

The French began trading in the ports of Chile and Peru in 1695. Before the Spanish put a stop to their activities in 1720, the French had dispatched 168 ships on this profitable trade. Two scientists had accompanied these expeditions: Father Feuillée in 1707–1712, an astronomer and botanist, who published an interesting journal of his observations; and the military engineer Frézier in 1711–1714, who was responsible for the best contemporary map of South America and who wrote the enormously successful *Relation du voyage à la mer du Sud* (Account of the Voyage to the South Sea). His book served as a reference for the Dutch explorer Roggeveen. Frézier, who believed in the existence of a southern continent, lived until 1773 and was consulted by Louis Antoine de Bougainville.

At the beginning of the eighteenth century, the race for new lands had slowed down, the great maritime powers—especially Great Britain—being more concerned with taking over territories already conquered by their Portuguese and Spanish predecessors. Nevertheless, there were still enor-

Arrival of a Portuguese ship in the roads of Nagasaki in 1593. Detail from a pair of screens by the Japanese artist Kano Naizen. (Municipal Museum of Namban Art, Kobe. Photo L. Joubert © Arch. Photeb.)

BATAVIA

View of Batavia, island of Java. Founded in 1619, it became the capital of the Dutch settlements in the East Indies. Anonymous watercolor from the eighteenth century. (Bibliothèque nationale, Paris. Photo © Bibl. nat./Arch. Photeb.)

mous blanks on the map, as well as many unresolved questions. The most intriguing, as well as the most irritating, of these was that posed by the *Terra australis,* which the Dutchman Roggeveen and the Frenchman Bouvet set out to find.

Jacob Roggeveen was about sixty when he undertook a project his father had not been able to finish: to look for new islands, and especially for the southern continent, in the South Pacific. Leaving Texel Island on August 21, 1721, with three ships, Roggeveen rounded Cape Horn, failed to find the land supposedly reconnoitered by the Englishman Edward Davis in 1687, but discovered Easter Island on April 14, 1722. Crossing the Tuamotu Archipelago, he passed through the Society Islands, where he explored Bora Bora and Maupiti, and then several atolls in the Samoas, before reaching Batavia (Djkarta) in September 1722. However, his voyage was disavowed by the East India Company.

It was to look for Gonneville's Land that two ships set sail from Lorient on July 19, 1739, under the command of Captain Bouvet de Lozier, who was in the service of the French East India Company. On January 1, 1739, while their ships were surrounded by icebergs and floating blocks of ice, the navigators caught sight of the steep bluff of a snow-covered land at 54° S. Bouvet, who thought he was dealing with a tip of the southern continent, called it Cape Circumcision. The longitude he reported, however, was incorrect, which led to many difficulties in rediscovering this land. In any case, what he had sighted was an isolated island now identified on maps as Bouvet Island.

The voyages of Roggeveen and Bouvet were only private undertakings that had scarcely any echo in the spirit of the times; governments were prepared neither to encourage such expeditions nor even to profit from them. However, the expedition dispatched in 1740 by Great Britain, which a year earlier had declared war on Spain, had as its goal attacks on the enemy in its American colonies and, if possible, the capture of one of the galleons bringing gold and silver back to the mother country. From this point of view, the mission confided to Captain George Anson was a success, but otherwise it was a disaster. Leaving on September 18, 1740, with six ships manned by 1,955 men, Anson returned to Spithead on June 15, 1744, with a single ship; he had lost 1,051 men, almost all of them to scurvy. On the other hand, Anson had pillaged Paita on the coast of Peru, damaged numerous Spanish vessels, and above all captured the galleon *Nuestra Señora de Cobadonga,* thus bringing back £400,000 in coins and ingots. Needless to say, he was given a triumphal welcome. Followed by thirty-two wagons piled with Spanish booty, the crew paraded through the streets of London to the sound of fifes and drums.

The journal published by Anson sold well; it was translated into several languages and was kept in print for many years. His extremely vivid account brought together a host of new facts and exercised a great influence over the navigators who came later. In addition, the enormous number of deaths due to scurvy encouraged research into the disease, and, in 1753, James Lind dedicated to Anson a treatise on scurvy in which he recommended the use of lemons as a preventative. Appointed to the Admiralty in 1745, Anson remained a member until his death and finished his career as an admiral and First Lord of the Admiralty. The basic reforms he introduced to the British navy brought it to the height of its power and caused their author to be known as the "Father of the Navy."

The beginning of a new era

Shortly after 1750, there was a rapid change in the way people saw things. Scientific developments aroused more and more interest, and since

George Anson (1697–1762). Engraving by C. Grignion from a painting by A. Pond. (National Maritime Museum, London. Photo © by the museum/Photeb.)

the applications of science were expected to improve the conditions of life, there was the hope of limitless progress.

In Great Britain, the Royal Society, presided over by Isaac Newton for more than twenty years, represented this new spirit. The Kew Gardens had been founded in 1730, and new plants soon found their way there from everywhere in the world. In Paris, the collections of the Jardin du Roi (the King's Garden)—the future Museum of Natural History—grew richer year after year under the direction of Buffon and the Jussieu brothers, while the Academy of Sciences sent scientific missions all over the world, such as the one confided to Charles Marie de La Condamine in 1735. Thanks to these powerful institutions, the scientists were able to pool the results of their research. Science knew no nationality, and researchers from all over Europe corresponded with one another. The time had come to take stock of the knowledge that had been acquired and to see what remained to be done.

The Swedish botanist Carolus Linnaeus (Carl von Linné), who devoted his entire life to the elaboration of a rational classification of nature, had become the acknowledged world authority. In France, the same period saw the appearance of the thirty-three-volume *Encyclopédie,* a gigantic inventory of scientific and technical knowledge—the first volume of which was published in 1751–and of the *Histoire naturelle, générale et particulière* (Natural History, General and Particular). Buffon's work, the first volume of which came off the press in 1749 and was to be followed by thirty-five more, was not only a most ambitious scientific exposé—the author going so far as to propose a complete theory of the genesis of the Earth—but, like the *Encyclopédie,* was meant for the educated reader, who greeted it enthusiastically.

These great studies had aroused general interest. As Hubert Deschamps wrote at the time: ". . . heaven no longer monopolizes our concerns. Attention is turned toward the earth, which has to be explored; toward man, who has to be known." In 1746, Abbé Prévost, the author of *Manon Lescaut,* had begun publication of the *Histoire générale des voyages* (General History of Voyages), which was to comprise seventy-four volumes; the eleventh (1753) dealt with voyages to the Pacific. Natural history collections were in fashion, as were learned societies, which multiplied even in the provinces.

Dijon was a very active center, with its own Academy of Sciences and Letters, which in 1750 awarded a prize to Jean-Jacques Rousseau. Among its eminent members was the president of the Burgundy *parlement.* An extremely cultivated man who was curious about everything, Charles De Brosses published his *Histoire de la navigation aux terres australes* (History of Navigation to the Southern Lands) in 1756. It was the first detailed study of the subject.

De Brosses still believed in the equilibrium theory, which maintained that there must be in the southern hemisphere a land mass sufficient to counterbalance the weight of the continents in the northern hemisphere, though he acknowledged that it might be not a single land but a great number of islands. He was convinced that Gonneville's Land did exist; only ice floes had prevented Bouvet from

The Dutch navigators Le Maire and Schouten take part in a kava ceremony at the Horn Islands, an archipelago between the Samoas and the Fijis. Engraving from the Journal *of G. C. Schouten, 1619, Amsterdam. (Bibliothèque nationale, Paris. Photo by Michel Didier © Photeb.)*

15

tages to the sciences of a complete inventory of animal and vegetable life. In keeping with the spirit of his time, he rejected all notions of conquest. The new explorations were to bestow the advantages of progress on the peoples encountered—though it was certainly true that the future colonies could and should be great sources of wealth and power. They might also serve as places to which criminals and "guilty women" could be deported. The president foresaw settlements in which deportees could mend their ways and be given the opportunity to make new lives for themselves. Though this project did not arouse interest in France, thirty years later it was to be realized by the British, who dispatched convicts to settle the New South Wales discovered by Cook.

The value of the *Histoire de la navigation* was quickly recognized both in France and abroad. Among its enthusiastic readers was Alexander Dalrymple, who, having spent several years in the Orient in the employ of the British East India Company, had become interested in the exploration of the Pacific. Dalrymple got in touch with De Brosses, and the two men remained friends until the death of the president. His *Account of the discoveries made in the south pacific ocean previous to 1764* had an enormous influence in Great Britain and was in fact responsible for the Royal Society once again taking up the exploration of the Pacific—this time in a more systematic manner.

That work did not appear until 1768, only a few months before Cook's departure; De Brosses's work had appeared twelve years earlier. Bougainville consulted its author, and the *Histoire de la navigation*, according to A. C. Taylor, helped determine and orient the direction of English exploration. More important still, it had defined the new scientific and humanitarian spirit that was to preside over new expeditions, and it was to this spirit that not only Bougainville but Cook—who had read Dalrymple—and most of their successors conformed.

When President De Brosses's book was published in 1756, the world situation was not very promising. The Seven Years War had erupted, and put a stop to all projects of exploration. In 1763, that war ended with the Treaty of Paris: France lost Canada, Senegal, and several of the Antilles; she retained in India only a small number of isolated trading posts; and she also ceded Louisiana to Spain as a compensation for Florida, which the latter had turned over to Great Britain. At the height of its world expansion, Great Britain decided to pursue and complete the exploration of the Pacific, and to resolve the question of the southern continent. The regions visited were to provide the greatest possible number of observations on physics, hydrography, and navigation, as well as on flora, fauna, and—especially—on the inhabitants of these far-off lands. Great Britain was inaugurating the era of great scientific explorations.

A tarsier from Celebes Island, one of the first known prosimians. Engraving from Collection des animaux quadrupèdes classés par ordres et genres sur le système animal de Linné, *by Buffon. (Bibliothèque nationale, Paris. Photo © Bibl. nat./Arch. Photeb.)*

finding it in 1739. Like all his contemporaries, De Brosses did not believe that the sea could freeze over; he was convinced that the floes came from the fresh water of rivers. Theorizing like the navigators who came after him, he noted: "The more earth there is, the more ice there is; consequently, the more ice floes that are found, the more earth there must be." However, De Brosses felt that Bouvet's Cape Circumcision probably did not belong to Gonneville's Land, which as he saw it must be "south of the southernmost Moluccas, in a region I have called Australasia." It was, indeed, De Brosses who coined this name, still used today—just as he was the first to use the word Polynesia, created from two Greek words meaning a multiplicity of islands.

His book began with a long essay on the advantages that could be expected from future expeditions to the "austral lands." Echoing his friend Buffon, De Brosses insisted on the potential advan-

The discovery
of Tahiti,
1764-1769

The ships and the men

After 1764, voyages of circumnavigation were no longer haphazard attempts but carefully organized expeditions furnished with precise instructions and the best available equipment. They were entrusted to officers who had excellent scientific training and were accompanied by scientists—astronomers, physicists, and naturalists—as well as by painters and draftsmen capable of bringing back a truly iconographic documentation. Initially, of course, there was much trial and error, and the first voyages hardly corresponded with this ideal plan. This was only slowly realized—thanks mainly to one man, Captain Cook, who became a model for all his successors.

With some exceptions, the ships were more than 300 tons, and a few were over 600. Handling easily and carrying a great deal of sail, they were capable of withstanding all weather. Their holds had to be sufficiently large to contain supplies for several years; the problem of speed was less important—a ship had to be able to make the most of favorable winds but could provide merely tolerable speeds when sailing close-hauled. The type of vessel necessary for these long voyages was available only after 1750, when improvements in naval construction brought sailing ships to their apogee. The new vessels were increasingly sturdy and more and more spacious; the rigging had been improved, and the topgallant of the bowsprit—so dangerous to manipulate—had disappeared, the sail having been replaced by a jib during the Seven Years War. The sumptuous poop ornaments of the era of Louis XIV had already been abandoned, and soon all traces of useless luxury were suppressed. In about 1750, Great Britain began covering the keels of its ships with copper plates in order to provide protection against shipworms, but such sheathing was not adopted in France until the end of the century; clouting—covering the wood with nails—was used for the same purpose. Unfortunately, these techniques worked against a ship's sailing capability. In the holds, stone and sand ballast had been replaced by iron or lead, which provided better stability for the vessel and freed the storerooms; in addition, since iron was coveted by the people the ship visited, it often served as a means of exchange.

The ships placed at the disposition of the great expeditions were rarely new and often had serious defects. Many navigators had cause for complaint,

but the best vessels in the fleet could not be assigned to such risky ventures. In any case, there were still navigation problems. As soon as the ships left the known routes—and they had to, since their mission was to discover new lands—the officers no longer had reliable maps available, and one of their principal tasks was to work these up themselves. Sailing was entirely dependent on the winds, and the much-feared equatorial calms could often immobilize an expedition for weeks on a leaden sea, under enormous dark clouds, in suffocating heat, while sickness raged and fresh food and even drinking water were lacking.

Though it had long been possible—thanks to the octant and then the sextant—to calculate the distance from the equator and to establish the direction traveled, until the end of the eighteenth century it was impossible to reckon accurately the distance either east or west from the point of departure—in other words, to calculate the longitude. For lack of a better means, use was made of a log—a triangular piece of wood attached to a cord marked, by knots, into measured sections. Trailed in the wake of a ship, it roughly measured distance.

But the only shipboard means of establishing the time was the hourglass, and on distant voyages

From top to bottom: eighteenth-century English sextant. (Musée de la Marine, Paris. Photo by Jeanbor © Arch. Photeb.)
Leroy type of marine chronometer, about 1800.
Berthoud chronometer used in 1817. (Musée de la Marine, Paris. Photos by Michel Didier © Photeb.)

it became important to solve the difficult problem of conserving prime meridian time. Beginning in 1714, the British parliament offered a £20,000 reward to anyone who could contrive a chronometer that would make it possible to calculate longitude. The clockmaker John Harrison worked forty years before finally getting that prize in 1775, though after 1771 his fourth chronometer was given to Cook when he left on his second voyage. In France, Leroy had developed a maritime timepiece for which he was given a prize by the Academy of Sciences in 1766, but he was outdone by his rival, the Swiss Berthoud, whose superior invention was greeted with general enthusiasm in 1768.

The impossibility of establishing longitude had often led to the erroneous charting of newly discovered lands. Navigators reported that a given island or archipelago might often be marked on a map two or three times under a different name and longitude. The Solomon Islands discovered in 1568 by Mendaña could not be found again, and they disappeared from maps for almost two centuries. When they reappeared, their longitude varied from 180° to 170° E—a distance of from 300 to 700 sea leagues from their true position. In 1768, Dalrymple confused them with New Guinea. When, in that same year, Bougainville discovered the islands that were named Bougainville and Choiseul, he never suspected that these were the Solomons—nor did Surville, who in 1769 baptized them Land of the Arsacides, nor the Englishman Shortland, in 1788.

Even more serious were the many problems posed by lodging and feeding so many men in so small a space for several years. The most important was food. There was no way of preventing the water from eventually turning putrid, supplies from spoiling, and livestock from dying. Jurien de La Gravière, who was a *volontaire* on the d'Entrecasteaux expedition of 1791 and who ended his career as a vice admiral and a peer of France, wrote in his *Souvenirs d'un amiral* (Memoirs of an Admiral): "The biscuits were invaded by numerous grubs and insects, and, perforated every which way, they fell into dust as soon as they were touched . . . cockroaches multiplied so rapidly that the corvettes were infested in very short order." The problem was simplified when, in 1809, Nicolas Appert discovered a method for preserving food; after 1817, French circumnavigators were able to carry preserved foods, provided they recognized that these foods did not always tolerate tropical heat. As for drinking water, it had to be kept from going bad, something that was possible only with iron bins, first used by the British at the beginning of the nineteenth century; however, the water supply also had to be renewed—in other words, watering places had to be found on the way. In addition, it was necessary to put in a supply of wood for cooking purposes.

On board, most often only the commander had his own cabin, in which he took his meals; officers were grouped in twos and threes. The scientists were no better lodged, and having no place of their own

in which to do their work, they had to dry their specimens on the deck, where there was always the risk that sailors would throw this "filth" overboard. In addition, the deck was not only encumbered with various pieces of equipment but also with the steers, cows, goats, sheep, and poultry that made up the fresh meat supply, as well as with the cages and aviaries in which the naturalists kept their catches.

As for the crew, it was crowded betweendecks. After 1750, this area was at least ventilated by portholes and, once the ship was under way, cleared of cannon stored in the hold; the sailors also had lockers in which to store their clothes and personal belongings, and there were benches and folding tables. The officers saw to it that both the ship and the men were clean, but they were probably less demanding when water was rationed or lacking. It is unlikely that basic rules of hygiene were respected, and, as a result, sickness was a constant threat, especially in the tropics. The most feared scourge was scurvy. For a long time, sea air was thought responsible for this illness, and only when it was understood that scurvy was due to the lack of fresh food could steps be taken to prevent it. Until the beginning of the nineteenth century, scurvy often took a fearful toll of the crew. Almost as serious was dysentery, which was frequent in the tropics and made Batavia a dreaded port of call.

Conditions on the voyage made it very difficult to recruit sailors. Ruse and sometimes force had to be employed to make them embark, often without knowledge of their real destination. In addition to the bounties, the only attraction of such an expedition was the more or less assured advancement. This weighed most heavily with young officers eager to win their first stripes. In the French navy, until the Revolution, there was a distinction according to uniform color, the "red" officers being of noble origin, the "blue" officers not—and therefore unable to aspire to the higher ranks. This distinction was abolished in 1791, but with it went certain aspects of discipline, and this led to other complications. It was not until 1770 that future officers were required to pass examinations in mathematics and navigational theory, but more was required of those participating in long voyages of exploration: Most had real scientific training—they were hydrographers, cartographers, or astronomers, not to mention naturalists.

Life on board ship was naturally very monotonous, especially after 1815 when discipline became very strict. In 1840, Dupetit-Thouars summed up a French sailor's day as follows: A drum awoke the crew, generally at 6 o'clock; after the morning call to quarters and the stowing of hammocks came breakfast. The men were grouped into eights—into "platters," or messes, each of which had a water can, a goblet, and a tin platter for meat. The morning ration consisted of a half-pound of bread or six ounces of biscuit with which to make a bread soup, and a quarter of a liter of wine or a tot of brandy. At 7 o'clock, the ship was washed down. At half

Group of midshipmen aboard the Beagle *during the course of FitzRoy's voyage (1831–1836). Painting by Augustus Earle. (National Maritime Museum, London. Photo © by the museum/Photeb.)*

past eight, everybody got into the uniform of the day and the officers made an inspection. At 10 o'clock, there was gun drill. At 12, they had a meal of half a pound of bread, an equal amount of fresh beef or six ounces of salt pork, and a quarter liter of wine. From 2 to 4 o'clock, there was drill with the sails and weapons, and a half hour later came dinner: six ounces of biscuit and a soup of lima beans or other legumes, washed down with a quarter of a liter of wine. Then the men were free until the evening call to quarters, generally around sunset. Half the crew alternated with the night watch. Every day at sea was identical except for Sunday, when, after general inspection—and Mass, if there was a chaplain on board—the men were free. Entertainments were organized, and in the evening there was dancing.

To maintain order among these "semi-devils with rather rough ways," punishments were sometimes necessary. The most feared of these—not abolished until 1848—was ducking: The guilty man was suspended from ropes at the ends of the mainyard, weights were attached to his feet, and he was thrice plunged into the sea until almost suffocated. This was called wet ducking; in dry ducking, the victim's fall was arrested before he had touched the water; in keelhauling, the guilty man was passed under water from one side of the ship to the other. Clearly, this punishment was applied only in cases of serious infringements, but the whip was often used. The French Revolution forbade it in principle, but until 1830, cabin boys were still whipped; the practice continued for a considerably longer time in the British navy. It is therefore not surprising that the number of deserters was considerable, especially during the course of very long voyages. Some men, seduced by the ease of life in the Pacific islands, chose liberty; but most simply succumbed to the temptations of recruiters from other ships, who made extravagant promises in order to reassemble a full crew and who would often get the sailors drunk.

Commodore Byron, 1764–1766

The British were the first to set out. The Treaty of Paris had been signed on February 10, 1763. On June 21, 1764, the frigate *Dolphin*—one of the first ships to be sheathed in copper—set sail from the Plymouth Downs with 190 officers and men. With it went the sloop *Tamar* (named after David's daughter in the Bible), which had a crew of 115. The mission assigned to these ships was to find in the Atlantic Ocean, between the Cape of Good Hope and the Strait of Magellan, undiscovered lands situated at latitudes convenient for navigation and in climates conducive to the production of items useful in commerce. The leader of the expedition, John Byron, was the second son of the fourth Baron Byron, and he was to be the grandfather of Lord Byron, who would use the account of these adventures in his *Don Juan*.

At seventeen, John Byron had signed on as midshipman for the Anson expedition. In 1741, the *Wager* was shipwrecked on the west coast of Patagonia, and Byron and his fellow survivors were for a year subjected to harsh treatment from the Indians and then taken by them to Chile. There the Spaniards had kept them imprisoned before putting them aboard a St. Malo ship. On his return to England, four years after his shipwreck, Byron had published an account of the loss of the *Wager* that had caused a sensation.

After having put in to Madeira, the Cape Verde Islands, and Rio, Commodore Byron informed the crew—which had signed on for the East Indies—of the expedition's true destination, which had remained secret. The men were promised double pay, and this news was greeted with shouts of joy. The *Dolphin* and the *Tamar* remained at Port Desire on the Patagonian coast from November 24 to December 3. Shortly afterward, when a troop of Patagonians was sighted, Byron went on shore and advanced alone to meet these extraordinary men with painted faces, whom he took for giants. After discovering Port Famine in the Strait of Magellan, the expedition met a French ship; though Byron did not discover this until his return, it was the *Aigle*, commanded by Bougainville, who had just estab-

lished a colony in the Falklands. In January 1765, Byron reconnoitered the northern coasts of this archipelago, to which he laid claim in the name of the British crown.

In April 1765, having passed through the Strait of Magellan, the navigators entered the Pacific. In June, they reached two islands in the Tuamotus; no anchoring place was found, and for this reason they were called the Disappointment Islands. The British next disembarked at Takaroa and Takapoto, which were then named for King George. Byron's name was given to Nukunau in the Gilbert Archipelago. The expedition reached Batavia in November 1765 and then Cape Town in February 1766. On May 9, it was back in the Downs, from which it had sailed twenty-three months earlier. All in all, Byron's mission had not been successful. Three months later, on August 22, 1766, the *Dolphin* again left Plymouth, this time under the command of Samuel Wallis.

Wallis and Carteret, 1766–1769

The *Dolphin* was accompanied by the *Swallow*, a dilapidated thirty-year-old sloop whose command Carteret had accepted only after being promised that she would be exchanged at the Falklands for a frigate sheathed in copper. Byron's crew having suffered from scurvy and the rationing of food, this expedition was provided with the necessary remedies and escorted by a supply ship, the

"The Point of Honor." Engraving by the caricaturist George Cruikshank, 19th century. The use of the whip was long to continue in the British navy. (National Maritime Museum, London. Photo © by the museum/Photeb.)

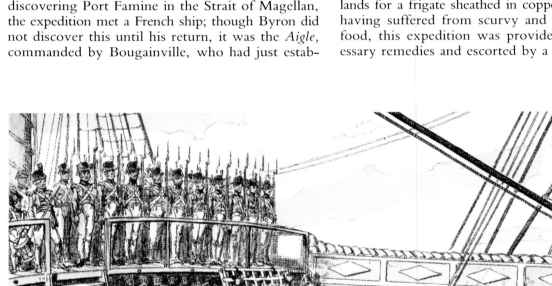

Prince Frederick. The promised frigate was not at the rendezvous, and, giving up hope of his vessel, Carteret suggested returning to Great Britain. Wallis refused and, to make sure that he did not lose Carteret, had the *Swallow* take the lead in passing through the Strait of Magellan, an operation that took four months (December 1766–April 1767). But just as they were about to enter the Pacific, the *Dolphin,* pushed by the current and a strong wind, moved ahead of the *Swallow* and was forced to continue on alone.

In June, Wallis reached the Tuamotus and visited several of the islands. On the night of June 18–19, a fog enveloped the ship, which had to heave to. When the sun came up, the sailors were amazed to see that they were surrounded by some hundred canoes. A few islanders came on board, and a goat that was on the deck butted one of them from the rear. Frightened by this angry animal, the like of which he had never seen, the man and his companions fled. The natives returned, however, while the sailors were looking for a place to anchor.

On the twenty-fourth, just as the *Dolphin* was preparing to drop anchor, the natives—who until then had been friendly—beseiged the ship in more than three hundred canoes and began to stone her. Several men on board were wounded, and it was decided to open fire; one native was killed and another wounded. The islanders attempted another attack. Then peace was made, and little by little Wallis and his men won the confidence of the inhabitants. The commander and his first lieutenant being sick, Second Lieutenant Tobias Furneaux took possession of the island in the name of the king and called it King George. It was Tahiti.

Queen Oberea came on board, then had Wallis taken to her house, where he was massaged by her attendants. The mountains and cool valleys of the island were overflowing with fruit, and the surrounding sea was thick with fish; pigs and poultry prospered. The Tahitians led a life of ease; the women and girls were most engaging and sold their favors in exchange for nails, the length of which varied according to their beauty. When the *Dolphin* left this enchanting spot on July 23, the queen could not restrain her tears—nor was she the only one.

After having traversed the Tonga Islands and stopped at Tinian, Wallis returned by way of Batavia, Cape Town, and St. Helena. The *Dolphin* reentered the Downs on May 19, 1768. In twenty-one months of sailing, Wallis had not lost a single man. His report was communicated to Captain Cook, who was preparing to leave.

As for Carteret, he had courageously decided to continue on his way aboard his old tub—and despite the worst conditions, in the midst of storms and served by an undernourished crew devastated by scurvy, his voyage was at least as profitable as

Wallis's. Carteret discovered a deserted island, Pitcairn; rediscovered Mendaña's Santa Cruz; and baptized as Gower—the name of his first lieutenant—an island he was unaware belonged to the Solomon archipelago. Disembarking at New Britain, he took possession of it in the name of his king and called the island to the north New Ireland. In the same archipelago, he discovered a third island, New Hanover, and called the group previously explored by Tasman the Admiralty Islands.

When, in November 1767, he reached Makasar, in the Celebes, the *Swallow* was in a pitiful state and half of her crew was dead or dying. Things did not improve until November 1768 in Batavia, where they had to spend four months while the ship was being repaired. As the *Swallow* approached the English coast, she was overtaken by a much faster French ship, whose commander had found the letter in a bottle left by Carteret at Ascension Island. A Frenchman came on board and informed Carteret that, after the *Dolphin* had returned to England a year earlier, two ships had been dispatched to look for him; he then asked all sorts of questions to which the Englishman replied reluctantly. This man, who did not reveal his identity, was Bougainville, and he was careful not to divulge that he himself had also just circumnavigated the globe. On March 20, 1769, the *Swallow* reached Spithead. She had lost more than half her men, but the thirty-one-month voyage, thanks to its commander's intrepid resolution, was to remain without equal in maritime history.

Queen Oberea welcomes Captain Wallis to Tahiti. Engraving by Godefroy, about 1780. (Archives Nationales, Paris. Photo by Michel Didier © Photeb.)

Heliotropium from New Zealand. Engraving from the Universal Conchologist *by Thomas Martyn, 1789. (Bibliothèque du Muséum d'histoire naturelle, Paris. Photo © Bibl. du Muséum/Photeb.)*

Bougainville

The Seven Years War had exhausted France, and henceforth Great Britain was in control. Though some people, like Voltaire, were unconcerned about the loss of Canada and India, others, particularly in the vanquished army, felt it was both dangerous and humiliating; among these was Louis Antoine de Bougainville.

A young and brilliant officer sprung from the *petite noblesse de robe,* he had been received into London's Royal Society at twenty-seven, thanks to his *Traité du calcul intégral* (Treatise on Integral Calculus), and he had served in New France as Montcalm's aide-de-camp. It was he who, as a colonel, after the fall of Quebec, had negotiated the surrender of the city and the evacuation of French troops. Returning to France so that he could urge French interests in America, he met only with official indifference. He then conceived the project of occupying one of the still available territories, which would simultaneously serve as a base from which any future British initiatives could be hindered and as a colony in which could be settled the unfortunate Acadians—who had remained French—deported by the British during the course of the war.

A reader of Anson, Frézier, and President De Brosses, whom he consulted, Bougainville chose southern islands that were deserted and so situated as to guard the route to the East Pacific. He managed to arouse the interest of St. Malo shipowners, who were always attracted by risky ventures, and obtained authorization from the Duc de Choiseul to found a settlement there. Aided by Pierre Nicolas Duclos-Guyot, a navy officer who had already sailed in those regions, and having traded his rank of colonel for that of captain, he had a frigate and a corvette—the *Aigle* and the *Sphinx*—built and outfitted.

On September 15, 1763, Bougainville left St. Malo with nineteen male Acadian colonists, five women, and three children, landing at the Falklands on January 31, 1764. He was accompanied by Dom A. J. Pernety, a chaplain who was also a naturalist. After putting together the first natural history collections made in the Falklands, Father Pernety published, in 1769, a *Journal du voyage fait aux îles Malouines* (Journal of a Voyage to the Falkland Islands).

Leaving the colony in the charge of his cousin, Bougainville returned to France and, in January 1766, came back with a new contingent of colonists. The settlement prospered, but Great Britain was keeping an eye on it. Aware of the importance of these islands—the French called them the Malouines—over which they could claim the rights of first discovery since they had been reconnoitered in 1592 by John Davis, the British had also sent Byron to explore them in 1765. The latter, visiting another part of the archipelago, probably did not notice the French settlements; but he did encounter Bougainville's ships, and the Admiralty sent Captain MacBride on the *Jason* with orders to take possession of the Falklands. The Spanish now entered the arena and claimed these lands as part of their American possessions. The French government, allied to Spain by the Family Compact, had to give way; they could neither alienate Spain nor risk another war with Great Britain.

The unfortunate Bougainville was given orders to negotiate this surrender. Sympathizing with his disappointment, Louis XV offered him the administration of the Ile de France and Bourbon Island, but Bougainville wanted further compensation. Since he had to go to the Falklands to cede them to the Spanish, why not continue on his way to the Great Ocean? The Duc de Praslin, a naval minister, immediately saw his point: it coincided with his own eagerness to increase the power of the French navy so that it could hold its own with the British navy.

The Boudeuse *and the* Etoile, *1766–1769*

In November 1766, Bougainville met in Nantes with Duclos-Guyot, who was busy equipping the frigate *Boudeuse.* She was to be joined in the Falklands by another vessel, the *Etoile,* fitted out in Rochefort. The *Etoile* was a sturdier ship than the frigate, which seemed hardly capable of such a voyage, and Bougainville therefore decided that, should the first ship be damaged, he would continue on the *Etoile.*

He made Duclos-Guyot second in command on the *Boudeuse,* since he had very little navigation experience himself and therefore needed someone he could rely on. Command of the *Etoile* was entrusted to Chesnard de la Giraudais, who had com-

Louis Antoine, Comte de Bougainville. Marble bust by F. J. Bosio. (Musée de la Marine, Paris. Photo by Michel Didier © Photeb.)

Bougainville's Ships and Crews

La *BOUDEUSE:* 550-ton frigate, 40 meters long and 26 cannons of 8, launched in the spring of 1766;
left from Nantes, 11/15/1766;
returned to St. Malo, 3/16/1769;
crew: 11 officers, 203 men;
deaths: 7.

Commander: Louis Antoine de Bougainville, captain.

Second: Pierre Nicolas Duclos-Guyot, fire-ship captain.

Ensigns: Chevalier de Bournand, made lieutenant commander, 8/18/1767; Chevalier d'Oraison; Chevalier du Bouchage, died of dysentery, 11/26/1768.

Gardes de la marine: Chevalier de Suzannet, made ensign, 8/18/1767; Chevalier de Kerhué, made ensign, 8/15/1768.

Merchant officer: Josselin Le Corre.

Volontaire: C. F. P. Fesche, disembarked at the Ile de France, 11/8/1768.

Writer: L. A. de Saint-Germain, similarly disembarked.

Chaplain: Reverend Father Lavaisse, similarly disembarked.

Surgeon: L. C. La Porte.

Passenger: Prince de Nassau-Siegen.

L'ETOILE: 480-ton storeship, 33.8 meters long;
left from Rochefort, 2/1/1767;
returned, 4/14/1769;
crew: 8 officers, 108 men;
deaths: 2.

Commander: F. Chesnard de La Giraudais, fire-ship captain.

Lieutenant: J. L. Caro L'Aîné, lieutenant commander of the East India Company.

Merchant officers: Donat, P. Landais, Fontaine, P. M. Lavary-le-Roi.

Volontaires: A. J. Riouffe, J. R. S. Lemoyne de Montchévry, died on the Ile de France, 11/15/1768.

Doctor and naturalist: Philibert Commerson, disembarked on the Ile de France, 11/8/1768.

Surgeon: F. Vivès, similarly disembarked.

Astronomer: C. F. P. Véron.

Cartographer: Charles Routier de Romainville, disembarked at the Ile de France in November 1768.

Writer: Michau.

---

manded the *Sphinx.* The expedition was prepared with the assistance of De Brosses and members of the Academy of Sciences; Buffon recommended Joseph Philibert Commerson as the naturalist.

"Ardent, impetuous, violent, and extreme in all things," Commerson had already acquired a solid reputation as a botanist. In 1766, he was thirty-nine years old, and his wife had died giving birth to a son. A landsman, Commerson found it hard to put up with the promiscuity in which he had to live aboard the *Etoile*—"that den in which reigned hatred, insubordination, bad faith, theft, cruelty, and disorders of all sorts"; in addition, he had a rival on board—F. Vivès, who unlike Commerson was not a doctor but only a surgeon and therefore always tried to place Commerson in the wrong. On the other hand, the botanist had a companion who helped him make his collections and hunted for him: the Prince of Nassau-Siegen. French by education and through his mother, this twenty-one-year-old had been living an extremely dissipated life and could escape his creditors only by going to sea. An intrepid man of proud appearance, he was to make a great impression on the inhabitants of the Pacific islands.

On November 15, 1766, the *Boudeuse* set sail from Nantes but had to put into Brest immediately, for a storm had broken her main mast. She left Brest on December 5 and arrived on January 31, 1767, in Montevideo, where she found the *Esmer-*

alda and the *Liebre,* the two Spanish frigates to which the Falklands were to be surrendered. The ceremony formalizing the transfer of the territory took place on April 1 and was marked by a twenty-one-gun salute. Bougainville read to the colonists a letter from the king that authorized them to remain under Spanish rule if they so desired. Some agreed to, but ten others embarked as seamen aboard the *Boudeuse* as replacements for the sick. For the next two months, Bougainville waited at the Falklands for the *Etoile,* without which he could not continue his voyage. Finally, his supplies about to give out, he headed for Rio, arriving on June 21—and there he found the *Etoile,* which had put in for repairs.

The Portuguese viceroy came to visit the French aboard their ships and showed himself well disposed; but, shortly afterward, relations with local authorities became so tense that Bougainville—who was waiting for the southern summer before traversing the Strait of Magellan—decided to go to Montevideo, where the French were sure of being better received. He stayed there from July 31 to November 14.

Commerson—who had found in the Falklands several species of unknown sea birds and even tried to take with him a king penguin, which did not survive—made important botanical findings in Rio and Montevideo. Among his specimens were "an admirable plant, with large blossoms of a sumptuous violet, which ornaments many houses" and

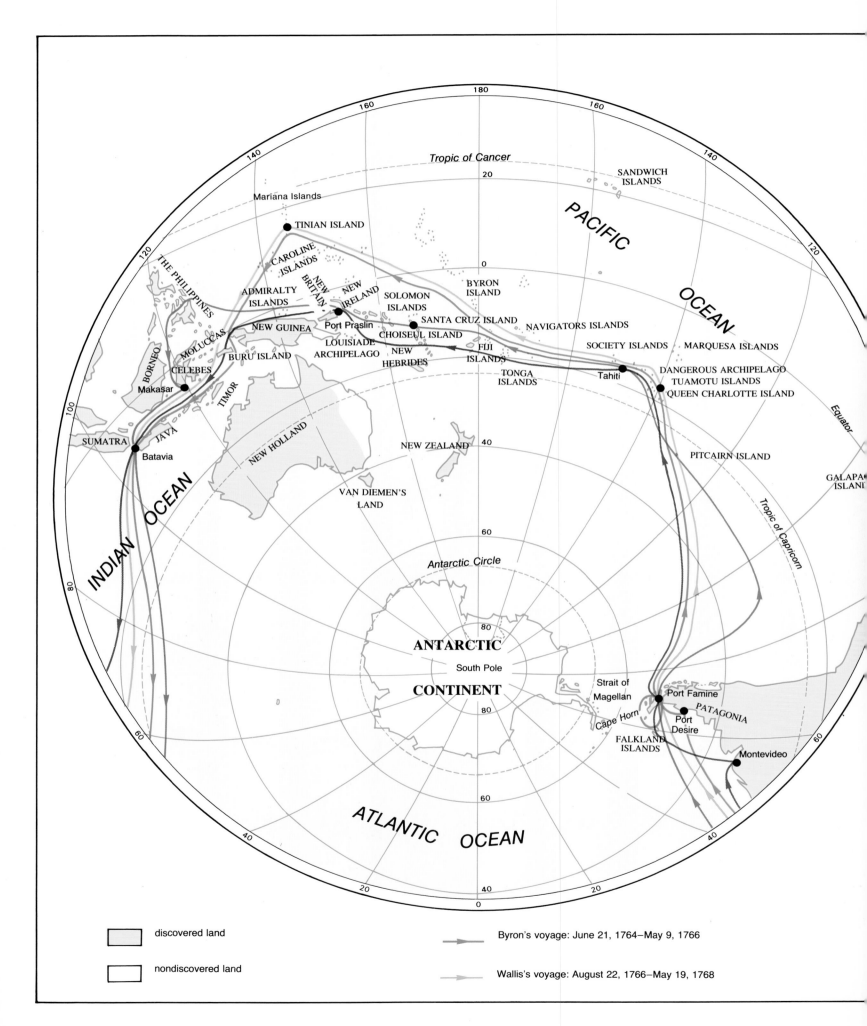

THE DISCOVERY OF TAHITI, 1764–1769

Tropic of Cancer

PACIFIC

OCEAN

SANDWICH
ISLANDS

Mariana Islands

TINIAN ISLAND

CAROLINE
ISLANDS

NEW
BRITAIN

NEW
IRELAND

ADMIRALTY
ISLANDS

THE PHILIPPINES

NEW GUINEA

Port Praslin

SOLOMON
ISLANDS

BYRON
ISLAND

SANTA CRUZ ISLAND

NAVIGATORS ISLANDS

CHOISEUL ISLAND

LOUISIADE
ARCHIPELAGO

NEW
HEBRIDES

FIJI
ISLANDS

SOCIETY ISLANDS

MARQUESA ISLANDS

BURU ISLAND

MOLUCCAS

CELEBES

TIMOR

TONGA
ISLANDS

Tahiti

DANGEROUS ARCHIPELAGO
TUAMOTU ISLANDS
QUEEN CHARLOTTE ISLAND

BORNEO

Makasar

SUMATRA

JAVA

Batavia

NEW HOLLAND

NEW ZEALAND

40

PITCAIRN ISLAND

Equator

GALAPA
ISLAND

INDIAN

OCEAN

VAN DIEMEN'S
LAND

60

Tropic of Capricorn

Antarctic Circle

ANTARCTIC

South Pole

CONTINENT

80

Strait of
Magellan

Cape Horn

FALKLAND
ISLANDS

Port Famine

PATAGONIA

Port
Desire

Montevideo

ATLANTIC   OCEAN

discovered land

nondiscovered land

Byron's voyage: June 21, 1764–May 9, 1766

Wallis's voyage: August 22, 1766–May 19, 1768

26

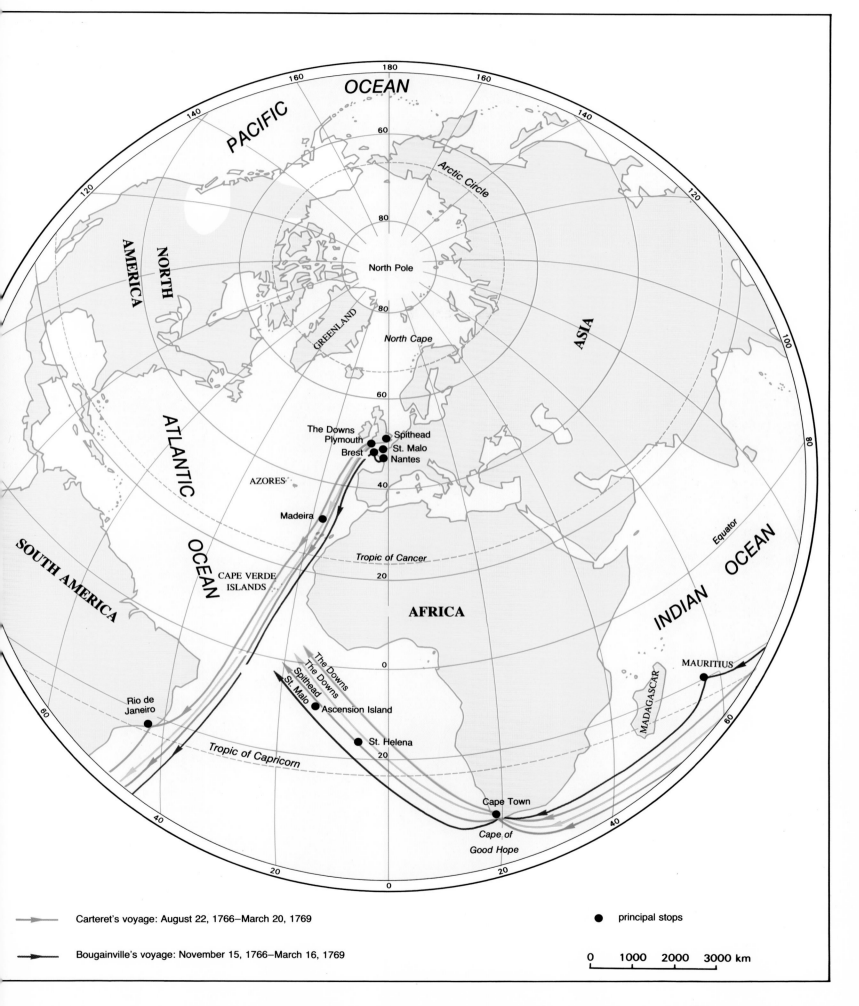

PACIFIC OCEAN

160   180   160   140

140

120

60

NORTH AMERICA

80

80

North Pole

GREENLAND

60

North Cape

ASIA

100

ATLANTIC OCEAN

40

The Downs   Spithead
Plymouth
Brest   St. Malo
             Nantes

AZORES

Madeira

Tropic of Cancer

20

CAPE VERDE
ISLANDS

AFRICA

Equator

INDIAN OCEAN

80

SOUTH AMERICA

80

MAURITIUS

The Downs
The Downs
Spithead
St. Malo   Ascension Island

MADAGASCAR

Rio de
Janeiro

St. Helena

20

Tropic of Capricorn

40

Cape Town

40

60

Cape of
Good Hope

20

20

0

Carteret's voyage: August 22, 1766–March 20, 1769

● principal stops

Bougainville's voyage: November 15, 1766–March 16, 1769

0   1000   2000   3000 km

27

which he named bougainvillea in honor of the expedition's leader; a bush with curiously shaped pointed leaves, *Colletia;* and a plant with leaves of two colors, *Caladium bicolor.* Along the coast he identified a black-and-white cetacean, which Lacépède was to name Commerson's dolphin.

On November 14, 1767, the *Boudeuse* and the *Etoile,* well provisioned, finally left for the great adventure. In December, they reached the Strait of Magellan. Though it was the middle of the austral summer, the weather was terrible, and it took them fifty-two days to traverse the strait. The officers "hydrographed" the gulfs and the channels; the astronomer Véron and Ensign du Bouchage calculated longitudes. In Bougainville Bay, already visited by him in 1765, Commerson, accompanied by Nassau, set out to botanize. He discovered a number of unknown plants, including a tree veronica, *Hebe elliptica,* and *Philesia magellanica,* with large reddish-pink blossoms, and saw a colpeo, or Magellan's wolf, which Byron had already observed. During numerous halts, they encountered friendly Patagonians. On January 26, 1768, wearied by continual hurricanes, the French finally set out to sea with both good weather and a favorable wind.

For a week, Bougainville looked for the land that the English privateer Davis claimed to have seen in 1686, but he finally decided that it didn't exist. On board the *Boudeuse,* a distilling machine had been set up, and it furnished a full barrel of fresh water every day. The first islands they encountered belonged to a very extended group; because of the reefs that bordered the low-lying lands, it was baptized the Dangerous Archipelago. It was the Tuamotus. The weather was horrible again, and scurvy had broken out. The crew needed a place to go ashore, and one soon presented itself. As they were nearing an island that Bougainville called Boudeuse Peak—it was Mehetia, which Wallis had seen in 1767 and named Osnaburgh—the navigators saw a wider stretch of land. Sailing along the coast, they stopped in Hitiaa Lagoon, which proved a very bad anchorage; if they had continued farther north, they would have found Matavai Bay, where Wallis had sojourned the previous year.

"Most of these nymphs were nude"

More than a hundred pirogues immediately surrounded the ships. They "were filled with women whose beauty was the equal of the majority of European women. Most of these nymphs were nude. . . . The men urged us to choose a woman and follow her ashore. . . . I ask you: given such a spectacle, how could one keep at work four hundred Frenchmen—young sailors who had not seen a woman in six months? Despite all our precautions, one young woman came aboard onto the poop and stood by one of the hatches above the capstan. This hatch was open to provide air to those who were working. The young girl casually allowed her pagne to fall to the ground and appeared to all eyes as Venus did to the Phrygian shepherd. She had the Goddess's celestial form. Sailors and soldiers hurried to get to the hatchway, and never was capstan heaved with such speed." On that day, April 6, 1768, the legend of Tahiti was born.

After a visit to the chief of the island, it was decided to set up a sick camp on land. At first, the natives objected, consenting only after the French promised to remain no more than nine days. There was, of course, much pilfering; though himself inclined to indulgence, Bougainville nevertheless took every precaution to avoid confrontations, and he sternly curbed the violence to which several of his men had yielded.

But what did these petty incidents matter when compared with the beauty of the surroundings—and of the women! "Several times I went on inland walks. I felt as though I had been transported to the Garden of Eden. . . . Everywhere reigned hospitality, peace, joy, and every appearance of happiness." On April 10, Bougainville noted in his journal: "The Chief offered me one of his women, young and fairly pretty, and the entire assembly sang the marriage hymn. What a country! What a people!" The nine days sped by. Eager to leave his hosts a useful souvenir, Bougainville had a garden prepared in which the French planted wheat as well as peas, beans, and other legumes, and he made the Tahitians a present of turkeys and geese. On April 12, "after having sent all the savages away," the French buried a plank on which was carved an Act

From top to bottom: bonita, a fish similar to the tuna. Original drawing by Philibert Commerson, from Histoire naturelle des Poissons. Bibliothèque du Muséum d'histoire naturelle, Paris. Photo © Bibl. du Muséum/Photeb.)

Halichoeris centiquadra (Lac.) Two examples of a species from the Ile de France shown in the "Herbier de poissons" done by Philibert Commerson. (Muséum d'histoire naturelle, Paris. Photo by Jeanbor © Photeb.)

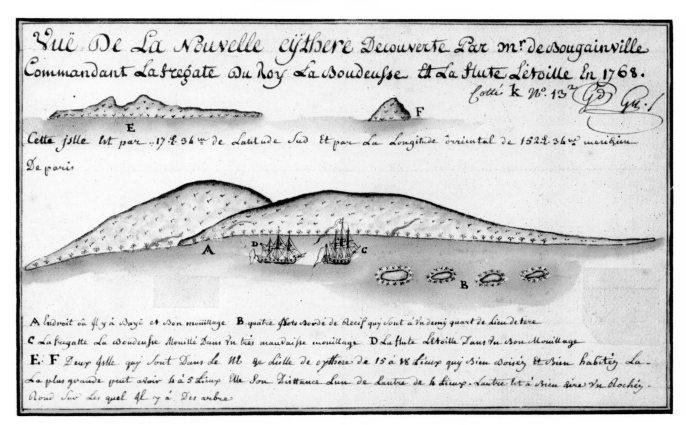

The "New Cythera." In foreground, the Boudeuse *and the* Etoile. *Anonymous watercolor from a drawing made on the site by A. Riouffe, volontaire in the Bougainville expedition. (Bibliothèque nationale, Paris. Photo © Bibl. nat./Arch. Photoeb.)*

of Possession by which the island was claimed for France and named New Cythera. The archipelago itself was given the name Bourbon. Bougainville knew nothing of Wallis's stay, but since there were obvious traces of a previous visit by Europeans, he did not claim to have discovered Tahiti.

Eleven difficult months

On April 16, 1768, the *Boudeuse* and the *Etoile* finally raised anchor in order to continue on their way. At dawn, when the Tahitians "saw that we were putting out sail," wrote Bougainville, "Ereti jumped into the first pirogue he found on the shore and came on board. When he arrived, he embraced us all, holding us for several moments in his arms, weeping, and apparently much affected by our departure. Shortly afterward, his large pirogue came alongside with refreshments of all kinds. His women were in the boat and, with them, that same islander who on the day we first landed had come on board the *Etoile*. Ereti took him by the hand and presented him to me, giving me to understand that this man, whose name was Ahu-Toru, wanted to go with us; he begged that I consent."

Bougainville was delighted by this initiative on the part of a Tahitian chief's son. He would be useful to them for the rest of the voyage, since he could serve as an intermediary and sometimes an interpreter with the inhabitants of the other islands; and above all, thanks to him, the commander would be able to complete an investigation that had been much too scant. He was thus later able to revise some of his opinions. For example, it was from Ahu-Toru that he learned that the Tahitians were continu-

ously at war with their neighbors and, when victorious, slaughtered all the men and boys and took the women and girls captive.

Bougainville thought he could make of Ahu-Toru a sort of ambassador, who would return happy and "enriched with useful skills." However, the "writer" of the *Boudeuse,* Louis Antoine de Saint-Germain, was not so optimistic. In his account, he wrote: "This poor wretch will long repent the foolish thing he has done." Saint-Germain's commentaries—unknown to his contemporaries because they were not published until 1921—are extremely useful in that they counterbalance the official enthusiasm. Their bitterness is understandable in the light of the conditions under which he made the voyage. A lawyer, Saint-Germain had just married when he received the king's orders to embark on the *Boudeuse,* where his state of health was none too good. He had to be put ashore, very sick, at the Ile de France in November 1768. Nevertheless, Saint-Germain outlived all his shipmates; he died at the age of ninety-two in 1823.

About the stay in Tahiti, he wrote: "What can we say about this Cythera? Have we seen the inland areas? Does M. Commerson bring back an account of the treasures it may or may not contain as concerns natural history, plants, or minerals? Have we sounded the coast? Do we know a good anchorage there? Of what use will this voyage be to our country?"

Indeed, that was the problem. Cook's voyages, begun the following year, were to be infinitely more profitable; after Bougainville's visit, there would be much talk about what was actually little known.

A strange valet

Hardly had Baret, Commerson's valet, set foot on Tahiti than "all the savages began to pull at him and again and again cry 'Ayenene! Ayenene!' "—which means girl in their language—while making easily understood gestures. "When I came on board the *Etoile*," Bougainville wrote, "Baret tearfully confessed to me that she was a girl."

How had it happened that in a potentially promiscuous situation that had lasted more than a year nobody had noticed? Actually, according to Vivès, there had been some suspicions among the crew, but the officers pretended to be unaware of them. When Baret saw that the truth had been discovered, in order not to compromise Commerson, she told Bougainville that "in Rochefort she had tricked her master by showing up in men's clothing just as he was ready to sail." In truth, Commerson and Jeanne Baret had known each other for two years. The botanist had hired this hardy Burgundian to look after his son. At the time of his departure, Commerson turned the child over to the care of an uncle who was a curé and decided to take this servant with him. As a result, Jeanne Baret may have been the first woman aboard a voyage of circumnavigation.

Once the excitement was over, the naturalist-doctor immediately wrote a letter overflowing with

Leaf, flowers, and fruits of the teak (Tectona grandis). Page from the herbarium of Philibert Commerson, created with samples from the Ile de France. (Laboratoire de Phanérogamie. Muséum d'histoire naturelle, Paris. Photo by Michel Didier © Arch. Photeb.)

enthusiasm to a friend, the astronomer Lalande. It was published in the *Mercure de France* shortly after Bougainville's return and was known to all the leaders of French society well before Bougainville had published his own account. But Commerson was not to accompany the expedition to its end. In November 1768, having asked to make a study of Madagascar, he went there with the famous voyager Sonnerat, the nephew of Poivre, the provincial administrator. He came back exhausted and died of pneumonia on March 13, 1773, on the Ile de France. Eight days later he was elected to the Academy of Sciences. Because of his taste for secrecy and his distrust of his colleagues, his work was left incomplete and unrevised. As for Jeanne Baret, she found on the Ile de France a new protector in the person of a certain Hermans, an ironmaster who had eight hundred blacks in his service.

The English pox or the French pox?

The return of the king's two vessels was not an easy one. A month after leaving Tahiti, Bougainville noted: "Terrible weather. . . . There are no more fresh provisions except for the sick. The wood supply is about to give out, and several officers have pestilential mouths and gums marked by scurvy. As for myself, I can no longer contain my impatience." Two days later, he added: "This isn't living; it is dying a thousand times a day." The fact was that not only scurvy had broken out aboard ship. Twenty men on the *Boudeuse* and twelve on the *Etoile* had come down with venereal disease. Syphilis had been brought to Tahiti by Europeans, but which ones? Obviously the English who had come with Wallis, claimed the French. The resulting argument has never been settled.

After leaving Tahiti, the French, at the beginning of May, traversed the Samoas, which Bougainville called the Navigators because of the large number of pirogues found there. The islanders were not as gentle as the Tahitians; "their features were more savage and it was necessary to be on the alert for the tricks they used for cheating in trading." Ten days later they reached islands they named Aurora, Lepers', and Pentecost. Their inhabitants aimed a hailstorm of stones and shafts at the ships. Bougainville called this group the The Great Cyclades, though he realized that he was dealing with the archipelago in which Queiros had discovered Australia del Espiritu Santo in 1606.

Aboard ship, more and more of the crew sickened, and food supplies began to give out. Saint-Germain wrote: "Yesterday, I shared a rat with the Prince of Nassau: we thought it excellent and would be happy if we could often have more of the same without the others acquiring a taste for them." Their reception was no better in the islands that were named the Louisiade Archipelago in honor of the king, nor did it improve at Choiseul, where the French had to defend themselves against islanders armed with spears. Bougainville then found him-

Land lizard from Antongil Bay. Original watercolor by Philibert Commerson. (Bibliothèque du Muséum d'histoire naturelle, Paris. Photo © Bibl. du Muséum/Photeb.)

self in the Solomon Archipelago discovered by Mendaña in 1568, but he did not recognize it as such. Finally, on July 16, they found an excellent anchorage in an uninhabited bay of New Ireland, Port Praslin. There, buried in the soil, they discovered a lead plaque on which could still be read a few words in English. Bougainville was certain that the plaque had been left by Carteret. They were unable to renew their provisions at Port Praslin. Sailing along the coasts of the island, they encountered nude black men who had woolly hair and pierced ears, but these natives refused to trade. On August 19, the last dog on board was killed and eaten; on the twenty-fourth, the first scurvy victim died.

It was thus with an indescribable joy that in September the navigators reached the Moluccas, a possession of the Dutch—the first Europeans they had encountered in ten months. But at Caieli (Kajeli), on Buru Island, the Resident initially forbade them to anchor, though he eventually yielded and even invited the officers to his table. "More than our words, the spectacle of the avidity with which we ate, convinced him that we had indeed been starving." The French left Buru restored and well provisioned.

From September 28 to October 16, they anchored at Batavia, where Commerson discovered a magnificent plant that he baptized the hortensia. Amazed by the richness of the Dutch Indies, Bougainville was sorry that the French had not yet established a presence in this area, around which the British were already circling. From November 7 to 12, the *Boudeuse* and the *Etoile* remained at the Ile de France. There they left Saint-Germain; Commerson and his servant; the engineer Romainville; the astronomer Véron, who wanted to get to Pondicherry in order to observe the transit of Venus; and Ensign du Bouchage, who was to die a few days later.

At the end of an extremely difficult eleven-month voyage, the *Boudeuse* made its entrance into the port of St. Malo on March 16, 1769. In concluding his journal, the commander noted that in the course of two years and four months, he had lost only seven men. On the *Etoile,* which arrived

a month later, only two men had died. The welcome in Paris was triumphal. Even before his voyage, Bougainville had been popular in the capital. Everybody agreed with Diderot: "He lends himself to the whirlpool of society with as good a grace as he had shown when confronted with the inconstancies of the element on which he had been tossed about. He is amiable and gay—a true Frenchman, balanced on the one side by a treatise on differential and integral calculus, and on the other by a trip around the world."

A Tahitian in Paris

The presence at his side of a flesh and blood Tahitian was the living proof of a success to which it put the final touch. Well received everywhere, even at the Court, adopted by the Duchesse de Choiseul, Ahu-Toru did not have a dull minute during the eleven months he spent in Paris; when he wasn't being the idol of a salon, he would wander around the city alone, never once losing his way. However, the interest aroused by this "savage" declined rather quickly; surprised that he was unable to learn French, people became disenchanted. No longer very young, he was, Commerson had said, "perhaps the ugliest man of his nation." Eventually, some thought had to be given to his return. The kindly Bougainville did things handsomely and reported that it cost him "a third of my wealth." Ahu-Toru was entrusted to a merchant who took him in charge from La Rochelle, where they embarked in March 1770, until they reached the Ile de France. There Ahu-Toru was welcomed by the provincial administrator Poivre. A ship was equipped to take the Tahitian to his own country, but he died of smallpox on the way.

Commerson's letter to Lalande, published in November 1769, caused a sensation. A fervent disciple of Rousseau, Commerson had found in New Cythera a dazzling confirmation of the theses his master had exposed in 1754 in his *Discours sur l'origine de l'inégalité parmi les hommes* (Discourse on the Origin of Inequality among Men). There he had

Small kingfisher from Cape of Good Hope. Original watercolor by P. Sonnerat, about 1780. (Bibliothèque du Muséum d'histoire naturelle, Paris. Photo © Bibl. du Muséum/Photeb.)

discovered "man in his natural state, born essentially good and free of all prejudice, unsuspiciously and unremorsefully following the gentle impulses of an instinct that remained sure because it had not yet degenerated into reason"—which, at the very least, led to the estimable consequence that in Tahiti "neither shame nor modesty exercises their tyranny . . . the act of procreation is a religious act; its preludes are encouraged by the wishes and songs of the assembled people, and the end celebrated by universal applause; every stranger is admitted to participation in these happy mysteries: it is even a duty of hospitality to invite them, and as a consequence the good Utopian continually enjoys either the sensation of his own pleasures or the spectacle of those of others." Needless to say, the younger members of the expedition agreed. For them, the good will of the Tahitian ladies had not been the least of the charms of their stay on Tahiti.

The *Voyage autour du monde par la frégate du roi "La Boudeuse" et la flûte "L'Etoile"* (The Voyage Around the World of the King's Frigate *La Boudeuse* and the Storeship *L'Etoile*) was published in 1771, but Bougainville was considerably more circumspect in it. The book was read, reread, and above all commented on and interminably discussed in the salons. M. de Bougainville, however, was soon bypassed. The following year, Diderot, who was then at the height of his renown, wrote the *Supplément au voyage de Bougainville ou dialogue entre A. et B. sur l'inconvénient d'attacher des idées morales à certaines actions physiques qui n'en comportent pas*

(Supplement to Bougainville's Voyage, or A Dialogue between A. and B. on the Drawback in Attaching Moral Ideas to Certain Physical Actions That Have None), a title which was in itself a complete program. Of course, the *Supplément* was not published during its author's lifetime, but he permitted the circulation of copies that had an enormous *succès de scandale*.

Eager to win popularity, Bougainville had not bothered with scientific data. His book contained little information useful to navigators, no detailed account of the peoples encountered, and even less about the flora and fauna. True enough, this was Commerson's province, but the latter had taken notes only for his personal use and never had the opportunity to edit them. A year after his death, they were sent to Buffon, who used some of them in his *Histoire des oiseaux* (History of Birds); later, Lacépède was to make use of several descriptions of fish, but nobody took the trouble to publish the documents gathered by Commerson. Nevertheless, they were important. Thirty-four cases containing the plants collected had been turned over to Bernard de Jussieu, who said that never had he received so rich a store from one traveler. But Jussieu, who died three years later, did not have the time to make an inventory. His nephew, Antoine Laurent, was to estimate at five thousand the number of species brought back; three thousand of them were new. In addition, there were fifteen hundred drawings done by Commerson with the help of Jossigny, who turned them over to the Jardin du Roi in 1775. In the end, all this remained in the shadows, and the plants were integrated in the general herbarium of the Museum of Natural History. Curiously enough, all that was to remain of Commerson was his *Martyrologue de la botanique* (Martyrology of Botany), published after his death by Lalande, who added his friend's name to the list of the victims of science.

If the naturalist was forgotten in the storm about to break, Louis Antoine de Bougainville withstood and survived it. Appointed squadron leader in 1779, he participated in the American Revolution but was defeated near Martinique by Admiral Hood and fell into disgrace. He was called on again at the beginning of the French Revolution and, in 1792, was promoted to vice admiral. However, because anarchy reigned in the navy, he refused this title and lived in retirement. During the Reign of Terror, he was imprisoned but released after two months, and it was Napoleon who eventually rendered this great sailor the honors that were his due. He named him senator, count, and high officer of the Legion of Honor. When Bougainville died in 1811 at the age of eighty-two, he was given a national funeral at the Panthéon. Married when he was fifty-two, he had had four sons, one of whom, Hyacinthe de Bougainville, was also to sail around the world.

The
three expeditions
of Captain Cook,
1768-1780

Cook's first voyage, 1768–1771

On August 26, 1768, a small three-masted ship left the port of Plymouth for Otaheiti (Tahiti). The Royal Society of London had decided to send astronomers to the South Seas in order to observe the transit of Venus over the sun, which was to take place the following summer. Wallis, having returned in May 1768, had recommended King George Island, which he had just discovered and named, as an observation point. By observing this rare astronomical event—it was not to recur until 1874—it was hoped that the distance between the Earth and the Sun could be determined. For their part, the Russians were preparing an overland scientific expedition charged with observing the same phenomenon from Siberia, where it would be equally visible.

This short and broad three-masted ship had not been built for such a long voyage. She was a coasting vessel meant for the coal trade, but Lieutenant Cook had preferred her to other ships, finding her more spacious, better for getting closer to land, and maneuverable with a smaller crew than other transport vessels would require. The former *Earl of Pembroke,* rechristened the *Endeavour,* was protected against shipworms by a sheathing of treated wood, since the copper sheathing used on the *Dolphin* would have been more difficult to repair in the islands to which the ship was to sail. She had been carefully refitted for her new assignment.

A self-taught sailor

Like his ship, the commander was of very modest origins. Born on October 27, 1728, in a cottage in Marton-in-Cleveland, a secluded Yorkshire village, James Cook was the second of nine children born to a simple agricultural worker. A sullen and obstinate boy, at thirteen he was apprenticed to a grocer in Staithes, a fishing village. At the end of a year, he fled to the neighboring port of Whitby and signed on as a ship's boy on the *Freelove,* a collier belonging to John Walker. As no sailing was done in the winter, Cook spent that season working in the shipyards. Courageous and stubborn, he began to study mathematics with the encouragement of Walker, who had noticed his gifts. All his life, Cook was to retain a profound admiration for the exceptional qualities of the ships built

at Whitby. A sailor at seventeen, James Cook six years later was a mate on board a collier and would probably have continued in this career until his retirement if his life had not taken a completely different turn just when his employer offered him a command.

In July 1755, Great Britain suddenly opened hostilities against France by seizing three hundred commercial ships in different ports. Thus began the Seven Years War—officially declared in May 1756—which united Great Britain and its ally Prussia against France and Austria. Though his duties would have exempted him from military service, Cook immediately joined the Royal Navy. On board the *Eagle,* he was under the orders of Sir Hugh Palliser, then a captain but later an admiral. Palliser soon noticed this modest but energetic man who was studiously acquiring the learning he lacked, teaching himself geography and even astronomy.

In October 1757, Cook was made the deep-sea pilot aboard the *Pembroke,* one of nineteen ships setting out for Canada. Charged with sounding the St. Lawrence, Cook did an admirable job of charting the mouth of this river. In June 1759, he was responsible for several vessels during the nighttime disembarkment at Quebec by General Wolfe, who had come to beseige the French—among whom was Louis Antoine de Bougainville. France's General Montcalm was defeated and mortally wounded on the Plains of Abraham on September 14, 1759. Though Wolfe himself was also killed in the battle, his victory won Quebec and New France for Great Britain.

In 1762, Cook married Elizabeth Batts, a native of Shadwell and the only daughter of a modest provincial family. During seventeen years of marriage, the couple was to be together only for brief intervals; they nevertheless had six children. Having become a hydrographer, Cook followed his patron, Palliser, who in 1763 was named the governor of Newfoundland; and in four years he completed the charting of that island, as well as that of the coast of Labrador.

In 1766, he had written an account of the eclipse of the sun as observed from Newfoundland, and it came to the attention of the Royal Society, which acclaimed its author. Two years later, when the society wanted to organize an astronomical expedition, it initially chose one of its members,

Above: Portrait of Cook in a captain's uniform, painted by Nathaniel Dance Holland in 1776, shortly before Cook's third voyage. (National Maritime Museum, London. Photo © by the museum/Photeb.)

Facing page: Portrait of a New Zealand native. Original wash drawing by Sydney Parkinson, 1770. Parkinson's drawings revealed to the West the amazing facial tattoos of the Maoris. (The British Library, London. Photo © The British Library/Photeb.)

Preceding page: Otoo, king of Tahiti, has his warboats put on a show for Cook, April 26, 1774. Painting by William Hodges. (National Maritime Museum, London. Photo © by the museum/Photeb.)

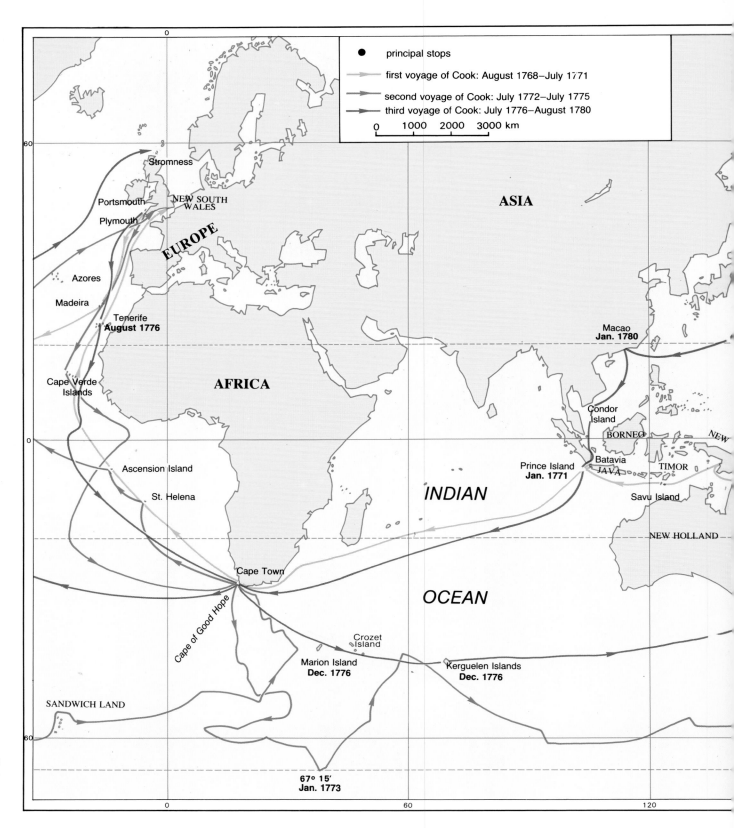

The three expeditions of Captain Cook.
First voyage, 1768–1771.
Second voyage, 1772–1775.
Third Voyage, 1776–1780.

Alexander Dalrymple, to lead it. Though he was not a navy man, Dalrymple demanded that he be made captain of the ship. The Admiralty refused point-blank, and it was then that Palliser recommended his protégé James Cook, who was commissioned lieutenant and given the command.

The Admiralty had made a happy choice; Cook was the man for the job. A Swiss sailor named Zimmermann, who signed on for the third voyage, wrote of him that he was a tall, strong man,

but rather curt. His expression was severe and his temper so hasty that the least contradiction on the part of an officer or another subordinate made him very angry. He was inexorable about rules and regulations—and about punishments for infractions of them. However, he was never unjust; and, above all, he could foresee any danger to his ship and remain calm under the most critical circumstances. He was also greatly concerned with the well-being of his crew. Having himself been a sailor, he under-

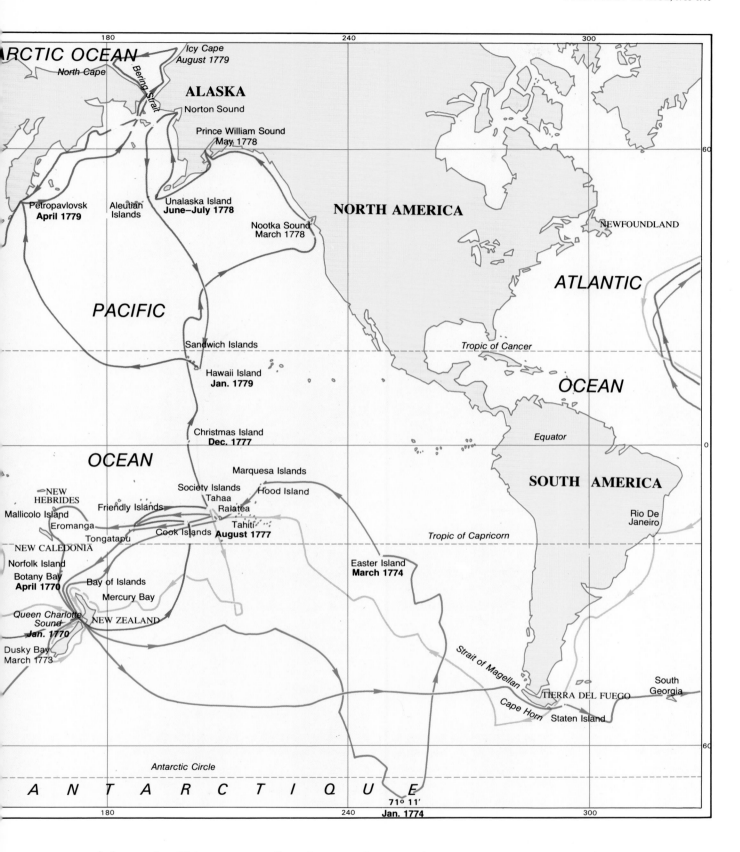

ARCTIC OCEAN

Icy Cape
August 1779

North Cape

Bering Strait

ALASKA

Norton Sound

Prince William Sound
May 1778

Petropavlovsk
April 1779

Aleutian
Islands

Unalaska Island
June–July 1778

Nootka Sound
March 1778

NORTH AMERICA

NEWFOUNDLAND

ATLANTIC

PACIFIC

Sandwich Islands

Tropic of Cancer

OCEAN

Hawaii Island
Jan. 1779

Christmas Island
Dec. 1777

Equator

OCEAN

SOUTH AMERICA

Marquesa Islands

Society Islands
Tahaa
Ralatea

Hood Island

NEW
HEBRIDES

Friendly Islands

Tahiti

Rio De
Janeiro

Mallicolo Island

Eromanga

Cook Islands August 1777

Tropic of Capricorn

Tongatapu

NEW CALEDONIA

Norfolk Island

Botany Bay
April 1770

Bay of Islands

Easter Island
March 1774

Mercury Bay

Queen Charlotte
Sound
Jan. 1770

NEW ZEALAND

Dusky Bay
March 1773

Strait of Magellan

South
Georgia

TIERRA DEL FUEGO

Cape Horn

Staten Island

Antarctic Circle

A N T A R C T I Q U E

71° 11'
Jan. 1774

180

240

300

stood the needs of his men as well as the necessity for the strictest discipline, especially as concerned the cleanliness of the ship.

In his account of his second voyage, he wrote that the crew was on duty one watch out of three, except on special occasions. In this way, the men were less often exposed to the inclemency of the weather than would have been the case if they were on duty one watch out of two, and their clothes were generally dry if they had to change after be-

coming wet; even so, care was taken to expose them to the rain only when absolutely necessary. They were given the means of always keeping their persons, their bedding, and their clothing clean, and to protect themselves against humidity. It was also seen to that the between-decks of the ship was clean and dry. Once or twice a week, it was aerated by fire, and when this was impossible, it was fumigated with gunpowder mixed with vinegar or water.

James Cook was aware of his responsibilities

Cook's Ship and Crew
First Voyage, 1768–1771

The *ENDEAVOUR:* 366-ton bark, 29 meters long;
left from Plymouth, 8/26/1768:
returned to Dover, 5/12/1771:
crew: 94 men, including 12 marines and 11 civilians;
deaths: 38;
deserter: 1.

Commander: James Cook, lieutenant commander.

Lieutenants: Zachary Hicks, 2nd, died at sea in April 1771; John Gore, promoted to 2nd in April 1771.

Midshipmen: Charles Clerke, promoted to junior lieutenant in July 1771; William Harvey; James Magra; Patrick Saunders, deserted at Batavia, 11/25/1770; John Bootie, died during the voyage; Jonathan Monkhouse, died at sea, 2/6/1771.

Master: Molyneux, died at Cape Town, April 1771.

Assistant masters: John Reading, died aboard of drunkenness, 8/28/1769; Richard Pickersgill.

Commanding the soldiers: John Edgecumbe, sergeant.

Surgeon: Monkhouse, died in Batavia, November 1770.

Assistant surgeon: William Perry.

Commander's clerk: May Orton.

Astronomer: Charles Green, died at sea, January 1771,

Naturalists: team directed by Joseph Banks; assistant: Dr. Daniel Solander; scientific secretary: Hermann Spöring, died at sea, January 1771; natural history draftsman: Sydney Parkinson, died at sea, early 1771; landscape painter: Alexander Buchan, died on Tahiti, 4/17/1769.

Passengers: Tupia and his servant, Tayeto, embarked at Tahiti, 7/13/1769, died at Batavia, October 1770.

down to the smallest detail. As a result, everyone on board had the greatest confidence in him. His officers in particular held him in great esteem. Among those who accompanied him on the first voyage, several had already been members of the expeditions of Byron and Wallis. This was true of Second Lieutenant John Gore, Midshipman Charles Clerke, and Master Molyneux.

Nevertheless, there *was* somebody aboard the *Endeavour* who might have challenged the commander's authority, since he had devoted a large part of his fortune to the expenses of the voyage. Joseph Banks, who was later to achieve international fame as a patron of the natural sciences, was not even twenty-five years old at the time. The son of a rich doctor whose heir he had become when he was eighteen, at twenty Banks had embarked to collect plant specimens in Labrador and Newfoundland. When he had been advised to make "the grand tour of Europe" like other rich young men, Banks had replied that any rich young idiot could do that; *his* grand tour would be of the world itself. In Cook's

voyage, he had spotted the opportunity he was waiting for.

His presence on board posed a problem, however. Banks took eight people with him: his assistant, Dr. Daniel Solander, a student of Linnaeus; a scientific secretary, also a Swede, Herman Spöring; a natural history artist, Sydney Parkinson; a landscape painter, Alexander Buchan; and four domestics, two of whom, Richmond and Dalton, were blacks. He also took along two greyhounds. This little team was to suffer most from the hardships of the voyage, and of the nine men, only four returned to England. For the time being, they needed a great deal of room, both for themselves and for the complicated instruments they were bringing along. Banks had his own cabin on the main deck alongside that of the commander. The cohabitation of sailors and scientists might have been mutually irritating, but there was never any conflict between Cook and Banks. Both men became passionately interested in everything they found, and their observations were complementary.

Toward Cape Horn

After sailing for seventeen days, the ship dropped anchor at Madeira from September 14 to 19. The British consul, Cheap, hurried to welcome the new arrivals. While Banks and Solander collected plant specimens in the country, their companions investigated the life-style of the inhabitants with great curiosity.

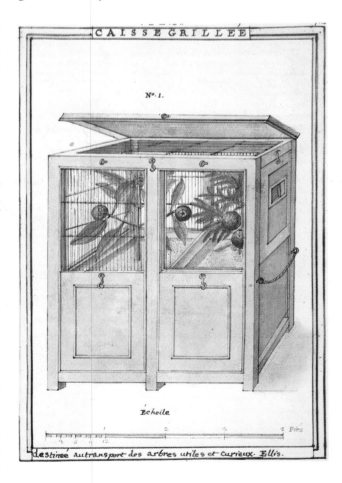

Grilled case for transporting useful and curious trees. Original watercolor by William Ellis, draftsman on the Discovery *(Cook's third voyage). (Service historique de la Marine, Vincennes. Photo by Michel Didier © Photeb.)*

Setting sail again, the *Endeavour*, on October 26, crossed the equator. Banks recorded that, at about dinnertime, a list was brought on which not so much as the name of a ship's boy or a cat or dog was missing. Authorization was asked to gather together all those who had never crossed the equator before. The request was signed by the entire crew.

On November 14, the *Endeavour* reached Rio, where the reception by the Portuguese viceroy was as disagreeable as the one he had given Bougainville two years earlier. He forbade any member of the crew to come ashore, and incidents quickly multiplied. Banks, Solander, and Parkinson managed to evade his surveillance, but they were only able to visit the area surrounding the city. Next, the ship went down the coast. Banks noted in his journal that on Christmas Day all the good Christians—which meant the entire crew—got abominably drunk, and that by nightfall it was hard to find a man who was sober. There was no suffering from either thirst or hunger on board.

When they got to Tahiti, Cook was to note with satisfaction that the crew was in good health, thanks in large part to the sauerkraut, and the "Portable Soup and Malt . . . The Sour Krout the Men at first would not eate untill I put in practice a Method I never once knew to fail with seamen, and this was to have some of it dress'd every Day for the Cabbin Table, and permitted all the Officers without exception to make use of it and left it to the option of the Men either to take as much as they pleased or none at all; but this practice was not continued above a week before I found it necessary to put everyone on board to an Allowance . . ." When the ship reached Tierra del Fuego, however, one man was sick—the painter Buchan, who was suffering from his first epilepsy attack.

In January 1769, they began to sail alongside desolate landscapes over which blew an icy storm wind; they saw seals, penguins, and albatrosses. On January 14, the *Endeavour* entered the Le Maire Strait, which separates Tierra del Fuego from Isla de los Estados (Staten Island). On the sixteenth, they dropped anchor in the Bay of Good Success. There they encountered their first Fuegians, who were so far from being frightened by this arrival that three of them climbed on board. "They are something above Middle size of a dark Copper Colour with long black hair, they paint their bodies with Streakes mostly Red and Black, their clothing consists wholy of a Guanacoes skin or that of a Seal, in the same form as it came from the Animals back . . ." They struck Cook as the most wretched group of human beings to be found on the earth.

To gather plants, Banks decided to ascend a mountain accompanied by Solander, Green, Monkhouse, Buchan, and his four servants. But soon the excursionists were affected by an awful cold. Solander explained learnedly that they absolutely must not stop, because in such a climate anyone who sat down would fall asleep and never awaken. A little farther on, he himself stretched out on the snow and refused to get up despite Banks's

urging; one of the two black servants soon did the same. The others managed to drag these two to a fire, before which all spent the night, each man wondering if he would wake again. At dawn the next day the two blacks were dead.

On January 25, the *Endeavour* saw Cape Horn, but given the unreliability of the maps, Cook could not be sure he had accurately identified it. It took only thirty-three days to get to the Pacific. Finally, on April 4, they spotted land, the first since the *Endeavour* had been in the great ocean. Oval in shape, with a lagoon in the middle, it was Vahitahi, one of the Tuamotus.

Three months in Arcadia

On April 11, Tahiti came into sight. They tacked about for two days in order to reach Matavai Bay on the northern coast, where they anchored. Unlike his predecessors, whose stay had been very brief, Cook was to spend three months at the island—most of it ashore among the natives—while he charted it and made astronomical and meteorological observations. He reported that he had no sooner dropped anchor on April 13 than a large number of inhabitants drew near the ship in their boats, bringing coconuts, which they seemed to esteem highly. Among them was an older man named Ahuhaa (Owhaa), and he recognized a member of the expedition, Lieutenant Gore, who had previously come to the island aboard the *Dolphin* and had been extremely helpful to the natives. "As soon as the Ship was properly secure'd I went on shore accompanied by Mr. Banks and the other gentlemen, with a party of Men under arms. . . . No one of the Natives made the least oppossission at our landing but came to us with all imaginable marks of friendship and submission."

According to Banks, the Tahitians initially seemed afraid; they came creeping forward, getting

Crossing the equator. Engraving by George Cruikshank. Those who cross the equator for the first time are traditionally plunged into a tub during the course of a happy shipboard celebration. On October 26, 1768, the Endeavour *crossed the line. Banks noted that he had to give considerable quantities of brandy to avoid the dunking to which he, his servants, and even his dogs would have had to submit. (National Maritime Museum, London, Photo © by the museum/Photeb.)*

to their knees to offer green boughs in a sign of peace. However, they soon regained confidence and even led the strangers to their plantations. Banks wrote that they walked some four or five miles under breadfruit and coconut trees that were heavy with fruit and provided very agreeable shade. Under the trees were native houses, most of which had no walls. In short, Banks observed, the scene was the best imaginable portrait of an Arcadia in which the English were to be kings.

When they returned to shore the next day, the navigators were led to a chief called Tuburai Tamaide. This extremely hospitable man received them with boiled fish and coconuts, and kept telling them to look to their pockets as a great crowd had gathered about them. "Notwithstanding the care we took Dr. Solander and Dr. Munkhouse [sic] had each of them their pockets pick'd the one of his spy glass and the other of his snuff Box . . ." Since Joseph Banks had shown himself particularly generous, this theft struck him as a veritable betrayal. He stood up threateningly and demanded the immediate return of the stolen objects. Smiles quickly vanished, and a large part of the crowd fled in terror. Tuburai, himself quite upset, immediately sent some men in search of the lost objects and they were quickly restored. Peace was made.

The incident was closed, but there was another the next day that was considerably more serious. Cook had gone ashore with Banks, Solander, and Green in order to choose a spot from which the transit of Venus might be observed. They set up a tent and established boundaries beyond which the Tahitians were not to come. Then, leaving behind a small guard, Cook set off to visit the woods with his companions.

"[W]e had not been gone long from the Tent before the natives again began to gather about it and

one of them more daring than the rest push'd one of the Centinals down, snatched the Musquet out of his hand and made a push at him and then made off and with him all the rest, emmidiatly upon this the officer order'd the party to fire and the Man who took the Musquet was shott dead before he had got far from the Tent but the Musquet was carried quite off."

In describing the incident, Parkinson wrote that a very young man, a midshipman, commanded the troop, and that, when he gave orders to fire, the men responded with unbelievable haste, killing one native and wounding many others. He thought it lamentable for a civilized people to demonstrate such brutality against unarmed and ignorant Indians. This sudden violence had terrified the Tahitians, and it was very difficult for Cook to persuade them to return.

Cook as ethnographer

On April 17, Cook and Green spent the night in a tent on the shore in order to observe an eclipse of Jupiter's first satellite, but clouds kept them from seeing anything. The same day, the painter Alexander Buchan died aboard ship of an internal disorder that had greatly troubled him and was now complicated by an epileptic fit that for forty-eight hours plunged him into a coma from which he never emerged.

As they were wandering about, the astronomer and the surgeon discovered a corpse; it was the man their compatriots had killed. The next day, Cook went to witness his burial, which was rather unusual. Close to the house the man had lived in was a small hut exactly like the houses in which the natives lived. It was completely open at one end, the other end and the two sides being enclosed by a sort of wicker trellis. The corpse lay in this hut on a wooden platform raised about five feet from the ground. The body was covered with a mat above which was spread a white cloth; near it lay a wooden club, one of the weapons they used in war. The head of the corpse was close to the sealed end of the hut, where there were also two coconut shells of the kind used to carry water; at the other end of the hut was a bunch of green leaves and several dried twigs, all of which were bound together and planted in the ground. Nearby was a young banana tree similar to those used as symbols of peace, and alongside lay a stone ax. At the open end of the hut was the trunk of a banana tree set in the soil, and at the top of it was a coconut shell full of fresh water; a small sack containing pieces of roasted breadfruit ready to be eaten was suspended from this stake. Several of these pieces were fresh, others stale. It seemed to Cook that the natives were reluctant to let him and his party draw near the corpse. The natives themselves remained at a distance while the Englishmen examined everything, and they seemed relieved when Cook finally left.

Inhabitants of Tierra del Fuego in their hut. Watercolor by Alexander Buchan, 1768. (The British Library, London. Photo © The British Library/Photeb.)

A "tupapow" bearing the body of a corpse of a Tahitian morai, with the chief mourner in ceremonial dress. Engraving by Robert Benard after S. Parkinson. (Archives Nationales, Fonds Marine, Paris. Photo by Michel Didier © Photeb.)

This description by Cook is the first in his account to show an anthropological awareness, which was the more remarkable for being spontaneous. His concern to understand the mentality and the mores in themselves, without making dubious comparisons, and the sobriety and exactitude of his descriptions—all very rare at the time—make his accounts an unequaled source of information about societies that had not yet been modified by the appearance of white men.

The same exactitude is apparent in his description, made when he was about to leave Tahiti, of the tattooing already mentioned by Wallis. "Both sexes paint their bodys *Tattow* as it is called in their language, this is done by inlaying the Colour of black under their skins in such a manner as to be indelible. Some have ill design'd figures of men birds or dogs, the women generally have this figure Z on ever[y] joint of their fingures and toes, the men have it like wise and both have other defferent figures such as circles crescents etc. which they have on their Arms and legs. In short they are so various in the application of these figures that both the quantity and situation of them seem to depend intirely upon the humour of each individual, yet all agree in having their buttocks cover'd with a deep black, over this most have arches drawn one over a[n] other as high as their short ribs which are near a quarter of an Inch broad; these arches seem to be their great pride as both men and women show them with great pleasure . . ." Cook went on to note that since the operation was extremely painful, expecially the tattooing of the buttocks, it was done only once in a lifetime, and never before the age of twelve or fourteen.

On stopovers at Tahiti during the course of subsequent voyages, Cook would carefully verify and supplement his observations; in general, it was the best possible investigation, given the short time and the inadequate means available to him.

Fort Venus

The small fort that Cook baptized Fort Venus rose little by little. Some forty men worked on it, and the Tahitians had spontaneously joined in to help. About May 1, everything was finished. Inside were some twelve tents, one of which was for Cook and his officers and one for Banks and his team. Until then all had gone well; but on May 2, when they got ready to install the large octant that Green needed to make his observations designed to establish longitude, they became aware that it had disappeared. The alarm was given immediately, and Cook initially decided to take as a hostage a chief named Tutaha, but he soon gave up the idea, since the man was obviously in no way involved in the theft. Thanks to Banks, who maintained the best possible relations with the natives and often served as an intermediary between them and his compatriots, the octant was promptly found, Tuburai having quickly disclosed the identity of the thief. But Zachary Hicks, the first lieutenant guarding the *Endeavour,* spotted a pirogue speeding away and had it followed. Tutaha was found aboard and taken prisoner. When they got back to the ship and Tutaha saw Tuburai, the two men fell weeping into each other's arms. Tutaha was so convinced he was going to be killed that he couldn't be persuaded otherwise until he was reunited with his people, many of whom embraced him in demonstrations of joy.

On April 28, natives from other parts of the

View of Fort Venus, Tahiti. Engraving by S. Middiman from a drawing by S. Parkinson. (Bibliothèque nationale, Paris. Photo by Jeanbor. © Arch. Photeb.)

ety. All in all, he noted, this people seemed to enjoy total freedom, and each individual appeared to be the sole judge of his behavior. Banks's juvenile exuberance made him more positive: He observed that on Tahiti, where love is the principal occupation, the preferred or rather the only luxury of the inhabitants, the bodies and souls of the women are made to perfection!

After so many days of abstinence at sea, how could Cook's sailors have failed to succumb? Before reaching Matavai, the crew had undergone a medical inspection and all were found to be in good health. Two months later, twenty-four sailors and ten marines were stricken with venereal disease. When the *Endeavour* left the island, the number of sick men was more than forty.

Four days before sailing, two soldiers disappeared. They had decided to remain in "Arcadia." After being captured, they explained that they had made the acquaintance of two young women to whom they were greatly attached, and it was for this reason alone that they wanted to remain behind. The manhunt had been a lively affair, since the natives initially refused to participate and joined in only when threatened. Finally, Webb and Gibson were found and each sentenced to two dozen lashes.

The transit of Venus over the solar disk took place on June 3. Even though a severe storm had raged for several days previous, the day was clear and the eclipse could be observed from three different points. But Cook had to remain in Tahiti another month while repairs were made to render the ship seaworthy. The crew, of course, had no objections, and even fewer were heard from Banks and Solander, who were beginning to speak the language fluently. The naturalists profited from this extra delay by completing their research into the flora and fauna; they discovered several very beautiful birds, including a brilliantly colored parakeet that became extinct in 1844. As for the busy Parkinson, he made a number of excellent drawings of vegetation, birds, and tropical fish.

On June 6, Cook noted: "This Day and for some days past we have been inform'd by several of the Natives that about 10 or 15 months ago, Two Ships touched at this Island and stay'd 10 days in a Harbour to the Eastward calle'd *Ohidea,* the Commander's name was *Toottera* so at least they call'd him and that one of the Natives call'd *Orette* Brother to the Chief of Ohidea went away with him." Toottera or Tutiraso was the name that had been given to Bougainville; the chief's brother was Ahu-Turu. But it was not until Cook returned to England that he learned of Bougainville's expedition, for the latter had not returned to France until seven months after Cook himself had left England.

island appeared. Among them was a woman who went to Banks's tent in the fort. Nobody knew who she was until Molyneux, who had sailed on the *Dolphin,* recognized her. She was Oberea, whom Wallis and his men had considered the queen of Tahiti. She had since lost much of her previous authority, but none of her weight. According to one *Dolphin* midshipman, she was the fattest woman he had ever seen. Oberea was about forty years old and, Cook said, very masculine-looking. She was given a royal welcome, which irritated Tutaha, who was then the ruling chief. The queen behaved very provocatively, especially as concerned Banks, who was very successful with the Tahitian women and generally lost no opportunity to profit from such temptations.

Cook's behavior was considerably more reserved. One of his officers wrote that the Tahitian women often made fun of him and treated him as an impotent old man, a reputation he accepted with good humor. It was no doubt necessary for the maintenance of discipline among his men, something he saw to energetically when the crew was ashore. There was great need of such care. Tahitian hospitality, the beauty of these women so welcoming to foreigners, the easy life of this people whom nature had kindly furnished not only with necessities but with superfluities—all conspired to dissipate the British sailors. To prevent this, the commander kept them hard at work every day except Sundays. However, he in no way forbade them to frequent the Tahitian women, and he even went so far as to allow the women to spend nights on board the *Endeavour.*

The fact is that Cook was no puritan. Though his journals demonstrate none of the "philosophic" enthusiasm to be found in the writings of Bougainville and Commerson—who after all spent only thirteen days in Tahiti—he was more amused than shocked by the relaxed mores that would have been considered abominable license in a Christian soci-

The Society Islands

The day of departure dawned. On July 13, between 11 o'clock and noon, the *Endeavour* set sail amid the tears and lamentations of the Tahitians filling the boats surrounding the ship. Thus ended, Cook observed, a stay of just three months, during most of which the visitors had been on good terms with the natives. "For some time before we left this Island several of the natives were daily offering themselves to go away with us, and as it was thought that they must be of use to us in our future discoveries, we resolved to bring away one whose name is *Tupia,* a Chief and a Priest: This man had been with us the most part of the time we had been upon the Island, which gave us an opportunity to know some thing of him: we found him to be a very intelligent person and to know more of the Geography of the Islands situated in these seas, their produce and the religion, laws, and customs of the inhabitants than any one we had met with and was the likeliest person to answer our purpose; for these reasons and at the request of Mr. Banks I received him on board together with a young boy, his servant." The boy was soon a favorite with the sailors, though they were put off by the austere dignity of Tupia; the latter insisted on being respected, and the sailors refused to give way to someone who after all was only a native.

The number of sick men on board decided Cook against leaving these happy islands just yet. On July 16, the ship dropped anchor at Huahine, the king of which came on board accompanied by his wife. As a sign of friendship, he asked Cook to exchange names with him; on his part, the commander gave him a pewter plaque engraved as follows: "His Britannick Majesty's Ship, *Endeavour,* Lieutenant Cook, Commander, 16th July, 1769, Huaheine." On July 21, the *Endeavour* was at Ulietea (Raiatea), where she had to remain a week while a leak was repaired.

Cook formally took possession of the island as well as of its three neighbors—Huahine, Otaha, and Bora-Bora—in the name of King George. Finally, after sailing along the Bora-Bora coast and briefly dropping anchor at Otaha, the ship finally left the archipelago, which Cook baptized the Society Islands in honor of the Royal Society that had been responsible for launching the expedition. On August 13, farther to the south, the island of Oheteroa (Rurutu) was discovered; but the hostility of the inhabitants and the absence of a harbor prevented the English from going ashore.

Toward the unknown continent

Henceforth, the *Endeavour* sailed due south. Cook was about to execute the second half of his mission, as specified in secret instructions that did not become public until 1928: He was to attempt to find the much discussed *Terra Australis Incognita.* However, when, on October 7, after two months at sea, the ship reached a large body of land, it was not unknown; it was New Zealand and had been so named in 1642 by Tasman, who had been unable to explore it. Cook did just that, and at great length, with his usual precision—but not without

difficulty, for the Maoris were by no means like the welcoming Tahitians.

The navigators had scarcely disembarked on the western coast of North Island when the Maoris tried to capture one of their boats. The ship had to open fire, and when one of the attackers fell, the others were dumbstruck, "seemingly quite surprised wondering no doubt what it was that had thus killed their commorade." The morning of the next day, October 10, Cook went ashore and tried to negotiate with the natives, who had gathered in great numbers. Tupia spoke to them in his mother tongue, and it was an agreeable surprise to find that they understood him perfectly. But Tupia warned the English that it would be better to remain on guard because the Maoris did not come as friends— which soon became evident.

Eager to capture the weapons of the invader, in the afternoon of the same day, the Maoris piled into two boats and raced to attack the *Endeavour.* "This obliged us to fire on them and unfortunately

Erythrina indica discovered by J. Banks on Tahiti. Original watercolor by S. Parkinson. (British Museum, Natural History, London. Photo by courtesy of the trustees, British Museum/Photeb.)

Erythrina corallodendrum.

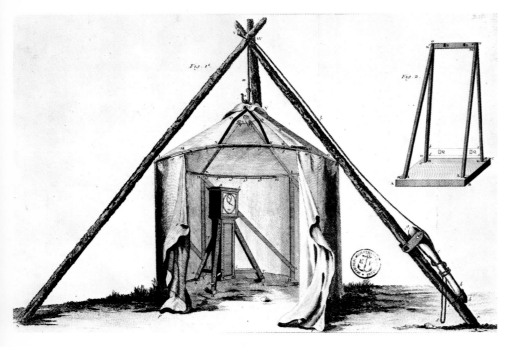

Portable observatory used by Cook on his voyages. Engraving by R. Benard. (Archives Nationales, Fonds Marine, Paris. Photo by Michel Didier © Photeb.)

by warriors who swarmed out in pirogues, but Cook observed that "after they found that our Arms were so much Superior to theirs and that we took no advantage of that superiority and a little time given them to reflect upon it they ever after were our good friends . . ."

Eager to establish an accurate map of the island, Cook sailed along the eastern coast until he arrived at the bay to which he gave the name of the First Lord of the Admirality, Sir Edward Hawke. There the Maoris managed to capture Taiata (Tayeto), Tupia's young servant, and they had to be fired on; two or three were killed, and the boy was able to jump into the water and swim back to the *Endeavour*. Sailing north, on November 3, they reached what they named Mercury Bay, since it was there that Cook decided he would on the ninth observe the transit of Mercury over the sun so that they would have an accurate means of determining the longitude of this country. Cook, Banks, and Solander were here able to visit two villages, which were well fortified and provisioned with all the supplies necessary to withstand a siege. In truth, hostilities between the tribes were continual, and the Maoris were implacable to their enemies—which helped explain their aggressiveness toward these strangers come to their shores.

Sailing still farther north, Cook, on November 19, reached the Bay of Islands. While they were preparing to drop anchor, the Maoris crowded on the shore began a menacing war chant. Tupia tried to calm them, but he could do nothing, and the idea of going ashore had to be given up. The *Endeavour* then rounded the northern end of the island and began to descend the western coast. As the *Endeavour* passed North Cape, another ship was not far off: the *Saint-Jean-Baptiste,* commanded by Surville. The Englishman and the Frenchman missed each other by a day or so and were mutually unaware of each other's presence in these waters.

On January 15, 1770, the *Endeavour* came in sight of a passage toward the southeast that was dubbed Queen Charlotte Sound. Tasman had anchored there but had mistaken it for a bay. The woods resonated with the songs of numerous birds, especially that of the bellbird, which enchanted Joseph Banks. On January 23, he recorded that, while he and Dr. Solander were collecting plant speciments, "The captn went to the top of a hill and in about an hour returnd in high spirits, having seen the Eastern sea and satisfied himself of the existence of a streight communicating with it." Banks immediately called this passage Cook Strait, a name it carries to this day.

New Zealand was therefore made up of two separate islands that the Maoris called Eohei Nomauwe (Island of the North) and Tovai Poenammo (Island of the South). On January 31, Cook claimed the area in the name of King George by planting two stakes on which had been inscribed the name of the ship and the month and year of the landing. Raising a British flag, they drank a bottle of wine and toasted His Majesty.

two or three were killed, one wounded, and three jumped over board, these last we took up and brought on board, where they were clothed and treated with all imaginable kindness . . ." According to Maori traditions, which came to light long after Cook's death, it appears that the natives first took the *Endeavour* for a large bird and then for a floating island, which they were determined to take over by force.

On January 17, 1770, Cook noted: "Soon after we landed we met with two or three of the Natives who not long before must have been regailing themselves upon human flesh, for I got from one of them the bone of the fore arm of a Man or a Woman which was quite fresh and the flesh had been but lately pick'd off which they told us they had eat . . ." Tupia was horrified by this custom and reproached the Maoris, but he aroused no feeling of shame in them.

Cook and his men described the Maoris as "strong rawboned well proportioned . . . of a very dark brown . . ." They were not as plump as the idle and voluptuous islanders of the South Seas, but alert and vigorous, and everything they did was done with skill and unusual dexterity. Their tattoos were particularly unusual. "Many of the old and some of the middle aged men have their faces mark'd or tattow'd with black and some few we have seen who have had their buttocks thighs and other parts of their bodies mark'd but this is less common." The marks on the face were generally spiral-shaped, and engraved and intermingled with a great deal of detail and taste. The work was done with such precision that no difference could be seen between one side and the other of the tattooed faces. As for the women, they injected black coloring under the skin of their lips, and both sexes painted their faces and bodies over a greater or lesser surface with red ocher mixed with fish oil. Every time the *Endeavour* approached a new shore, it was threatened

The *Endeavour* again set sail on February 6, and, for about two months, she followed along the coasts of South Island, charting as she went. Whereas North Island was wooded and watered by numerous streams, Tovai Poenammo seemed arid and little inhabited. Nowhere on Earth, they decided, was there a land more savage and bare than this. From the sea to far inland, nothing could be seen but the summits of rocky mountains, so close to each other that there was no room between them for any valley.

On February 17, Lieutenant Gore thought he saw a distant coast toward the south. Was it finally the *Terra Australis?* Though strongly skeptical, Cook gave orders to sail in this direction, but nothing was found. It was not until a month later, when they had reached the southern end of the island, that the absence of the southern continent became a near certainty. On March 10, Banks himself—who with one of the midshipmen was the only one to believe in its existence—had to note in his journal that they had rounded the point, thus completely destroying the notion of the phantom continent, which had been a product of their imaginations.

Having circumnavigated South Island, the *Endeavour,* on March 27, returned to Queen Charlotte Sound and anchored in Admiralty Bay. They had been journeying for nineteen months, and it was time to start back. Cook could have returned by Cape Horn by sailing much farther south than on the way out, and this route, he observed, would have enabled them to decide the still unsettled question of whether a southern continent existed. That was the itinerary Cook was to follow on his second expedition, but this time it would have meant facing the austral winter, something the *Endeavour*

was no longer in condition to do. At a meeting of the officers, it was decided to return by the East Indies—in other words, to steer west until they reached New Holland. As a result, the east coast of New Holland (Australia) was discovered.

When the *Endeavour* left New Zealand after having circled it, the ship had not only sailed 2,400 miles in little more than six months, but her officers had made a complete and exact chart of its coasts, and Cook had written a very detailed description of the land and its inhabitants, noting that it would not be difficult for foreigners to establish settlements in these areas because the inhabitants were too divided among themselves to unite and resist. Seventy years later, this observation was to lead to the massive immigration of English colonists.

Banks and Solander had not come across any

Maoris in war pirogue shouting defiance at Cook's ship. Wash by S. Parkinson, 1769. (The British Library, London. Photo © The British Library/Photeb.)

Tolago Bay in New Zealand. Drawing attributed to Cook, 1769. (The British Library, London. Photo © The British Library/Photeb.)

Gold-throated bird of paradise brought back to England by J. Banks. Plate from Oiseaux dorés *by Audebert and Vieillot, 1802. (Bibliothèque du Muséum d'histoire naturelle, Paris. Photo © Bibl. du Muséum/Photeb.)*

wild quadrupeds, but they had discovered a great number of completely unknown birds, one of which was the kea, the only carnivorous parrot, and another, Swainson's lorikeet, much smaller and brightly colored. As for the flora, though it wasn't terribly varied, it at least included several interesting species such as the majestic Rimu pine, whose dark reddish wood was much used by the Maoris, and another conifer, the kauri, which formed magnificent forests on North Island. Solander also discovered a beech of an unknown genus which was later named *Nothofagus*—a New Zealand species was dedicated to him—and tetragonia, or New Zealand spinach, seeds of which were planted in Kew Gardens. Three years later, during a stopover in the Bay of Islands at the time of Cook's second voyage, J. R. Foster successfully used tetragonia to nourish the crew, which was short on fresh vegetables and threatened by scurvy. Despite this, the plant for a long time remained unknown outside the botanical gardens; it wasn't until about 1820 that it began to be cultivated as a vegetable, first in Great Britain and later in France.

Botany Bay

On March 31, 1770, the *Endeavour* set sail from Admiralty Bay near Queen Charlotte Sound. The waters were warm, and dolphins jumped "like salmon" around the ship, over which flew big, strong sea birds—wandering albatrosses; Banks shot

down and stuffed some twenty of them. On April 19, they sighted land; it was the east coast of New Holland. On April 28, Cook dropped anchor in a place he called Botany Bay because, during the eight days they stayed there, Banks and Solander discovered hundreds of unknown plants: giant gum trees more than a hundred meters high, which were later called *Eucalyptus obliga;* some *Grevillea Banksii,* which had yellow or red flowers; and several species of acacia or mimosa, *Banksia* with large flowering spikes.

To the north of Botany Bay opened another cove, which Cook baptized Port Jackson but did not visit; it was there that the city of Sydney was established several years later. Australia wasn't an unknown continent, but its coasts had been only partly inspected by the Dutch who had discovered it in the seventeenth century and then by Dampier, the first Englishman to see a kangaroo. Dampier's very brief description was all that was known about the native australians. He had said that the inhabitants of that country were the most wretched people on the face of the earth. They had neither dwellings, clothes, cattle, poultry, or crops. If they hadn't had human features, they could have been taken for animals.

Cook was more indulgent. He said of the inhabitants that they were of medium height and had straight bodies and slender limbs. Their skins were soot-colored, their features pleasant, and their voices soft and harmonious. Both men and women went completely naked, without body covering of any sort. As ornaments they wore necklaces of shells, and their arm bracelets were loops made with interlaced hair and worked like a rope ring; these were worn high on the arm and very tight; belts of a similar sort were also worn. The men had their noses pierced by a bone some three or four inches long and about as thick as a finger. They also had pierced ears in which they wore earrings. Many of them painted their bodies with a kind of white paste.

But even Cook was surprised by the extreme bareness amid which the Australians lived. For weapons they had only pikes and javelins, which he noted were launched by a sling device; their boats were of the most wretched sort and could be used only for crossing a river or fishing along the coast. Nevertheless, Cook concluded as follows: "From what I have seen of the Natives of New Holland, they may appear to be some of the most wretched people upon Earth, but in reality they are far more happier than we Europeans; being wholy unacquainted not only with the superflous but the necessary Conveniences sought after in Europe they are happy in not knowing the use of them. They have very little need of Clothing and this they seem to be full sensible of, for many to whom we gave Cloth, etc. left it carelessly upon the sea beach and in the woods as a thing they had no manner of use for. In short, they seem'd to set no Value upon anything we gave them . . ."

In no way as aggressive as the Maoris, the Australians were a scattered people, inoffensive and fearful. As a result, it was very difficult to make contact with them. Most surprising of all was the fact that they seemed not to notice the presence of the *Endeavour* though it was right before their eyes. The only explanation for this strange behavior was that the sight of the *Endeavour* had no significance for the savages; the event was too strange for them to comprehend it.

On May 6, the *Endeavour* left Botany Bay and sailed north along the coast. In June, she reached an extremely dangerous zone. Off the coast stretched the labyrinth of reefs that have since come to be known as the Great Barrier Reef. Cook described it as a coral wall rising almost perpendicularly above a depthless ocean. When the sea was high, it was always covered by the 7- to 8-foot flood tide, but it emerged when the water was low. The great ocean waves suddenly breaking against this obstacle shattered like mountains of water. Cook navigated in this maze with infinite precautions; nevertheless, on June 11, during the middle of the night, the vessel hit a reef and stuck fast. A rapidly growing leak endangered the *Endeavour* and it took two days of enormous effort to break free. On this occasion, Banks rendered homage to the steadfastness and self-possession of Cook, who galvanized the crew and managed to escape from a seemingly desperate situation. It wasn't until nine days later that the ship was brought to shore on the banks of a river that Cook baptized the Endeavour. Carpenters and smiths immediately went to work, but it was more than a month before the damage was repaired.

When the *Endeavour* was able to set sail at the beginning of August, she faced new dangers: Cook had to navigate through the reefs. On August 16, carried with astonishing rapidity by a swell, the *Endeavour* just managed to escape "being thrown upon this Reef where the Ship must be dashed to pieces in a Moment."

On the inside of the Great Barrier once more, the *Endeavour* henceforth sailed along the coast of New Holland to its extreme northern end. It was at Cape York Peninsula, in a region that had not as yet been visited or seen by any European, that on August 21, 1770, Cook hoisted the flag and in the name of His Majesty King George III took possession of the entire east coast under the name of New South Wales. Two days later, the ship went through Endeavour Strait between the northern end of Australia and an island which Cook named Prince of Wales Island and which separated it from the strait between Australia and New Guinea passed through by Torres in 1606.

Cook wanted to land here but was received by the inhabitants with a hail of javelins. Since the ship was taking on water, he decided, on September 3, to get to Batavia, the Dutch capital of Java, as quickly as possible. This decision was received by the others with relief. On that day, Cook had definitively settled the question of whether New Holland and New Guinea formed a continuous land mass; he could therefore consider his mission accomplished. Not only had he made numerous and

detailed observations, but, by invariably noting them in his log each day, he had avoided the negligence of his predecessors—one of the principal causes for the gross errors that were still to be found in the maps used in his day. In this matter, too, Cook was the first to define and carry out a rigorous method that was to become widespread; once his journal was published, that method became a model that all hastened to follow.

Cook, Banks, and the kangaroos

In June, while the *Endeavour* was being repaired after having narrowly escaped catastrophe, Cook, Banks, and their companions went off to explore the inland area. Passing through woods of giant eucalyptus trees, they came upon termiteria 2 to 3 meters high and, in the trees, a strange gray-furred animal, the size of a big cat and with a prehensile tail. Thinking that it resembled the American opossum, Cook called it the possom; later, naturalists were to classify it as a phalanger. During this same stopover, Banks and Solander discovered and named the "filao," some six species of which they brought back to Great Britain. In the course of Cook's second voyage, Forster was to find "filaos" in New Caledonia; he gave them the Latin name they bear to this day—*Casuarina*—because their long hanging branches that shine in the sun resemble the drooping feathers of the cassowary.

On June 22, the commander sent a party ashore to bag pigeons for the sick men on board. When they returned, the men reported having seen an animal smaller than a greyhound, of slender build,

Rimu pine (Dacrydium cupressinum), *discovered by Solander in New Zealand. Watercolor by S. Parkinson, 1769. (British Museum, Natural History, London. Photo © by courtesy of the trustees, British Museum/Photeb.)*

Botany Bay. Map probably drawn by Cook himself. (The British Library, London. Photo © The British Library/Photeb.)

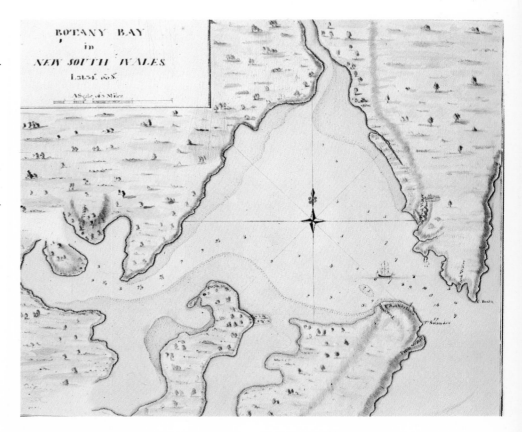

A romanticized impression, done in England many years after the fact, of Governor Phillip landing in Sydney Cove, 1787. In reality, no stone buildings existed at that time. (National Maritime Museum, London. Photo © by the museum/Photeb.)

with fur the color of a mouse, and very fast. It much resembled the quadruped that Solander had spotted in a wood on May 1. Having gone ashore on June 24, Cook was lucky enough to see another one with his own eyes. From July 6 to 8, Banks and four of his companions made a long excursion, and Cook reported that, after walking several miles, they discovered four animals of the same kind, two of which were closely pursued by Bank's greyhound; however, the two animals got away from the dog by leaping over a thick bush that brought the greyhound up short. Finally, on July 14, Lieutenant Gore shot one of these animals, though it was a smaller one; it was a baby that weighed 19 kilos. A little later he managed to bag a bigger one that weighed 42 kilos. Cook reported that "its progression is by hopping or jumping . . . it bears no sort of resemblance to any European Animal I ever saw; it is said to bear much resemblance to the Gerbua [jerboa] excepting in size, the Gerbua being no larger than a common rat." Acting on the best information he could get from the inhabitants, Cook called the strange animal a kangaroo.

Banks brought back a stuffed kangaroo skin and turned it over to the painter Stubbs, who did a portrait of the animal that had been sketched on the site by Parkinson. For a long time it was therefore thought that Cook and Banks were the first Euro-

peans to have seen kangaroos. The truth is, however, that they had been discovered 150 years earlier by the Dutch captain Pelsaert. Having been beached in 1629 near Wallaby Island in the Gulf of Carpenteria to the north of Australia, he found there a female kangaroo of the small species since called the wallaby; in the mother's pouch was a baby clinging to a nipple. But Pelsaert's account went unnoticed and was soon forgotten.

Banks and Solander also brought back an ample collection of hides belonging to animals that were almost as strange and completely unknown, which provided a lot of work for British zoologists. Among these animals were a flying fox, a bandicoot, a dasyure, a wallaby, and a rat kangaroo—all species belonging to the ancient order of marsupials which, in Australia, largely take the place of the placental mammals from which they are distinguished by the ventral pouch in which they shelter and nourish their young. All these species live hidden deep in the woods, and the naturalists had a great deal of difficulty collecting specimens. By contrast, birds were numerous and easily spotted everywhere, especially parrots, parakeets, and cockatoos that formed large, noisy swarms. Banks was lucky enough to be able to bring back to England, alive, a magnificent rainbow lorikeet that had been captured at Botany Bay and tamed by Tupia;

after the latter's death, Banks took care of it.

The Batavia victims

On October 10, at four in the afternoon, the *Endeavour* dropped anchor in the Dutch port of Batavia and found there the civilized world with which it had lost contact for two years. The news from Europe aroused lively interest: The American colonists were refusing to pay taxes, and even in Great Britain public opinion was unsettled. Cook learned that Carteret's *Swallow,* considered lost when the *Endeavour* had sailed, had gotten back to Spithead in March 1769, and that the Tutiraso of whom Cook had heard talk in Tahiti was none other than Bougainville.

They had to remain in Batavia for two and a half months while the damage to the ship was being repaired. This long stay during the rainy season had fatal consequences. The scurvy victims were cured, but the unhealthiness of the climate brought about an epidemic of dysentery, and it was somewhat as a "hospital ship" that the *Endeavour* left Java on December 26, 1770.

In Batavia, they had lost only seven men, including the Tahitian Tupia and his young servant Tayeto. During the course of the two-and-a-half-month voyage from Batavia to the Cape, as the result of weather that was constantly hot and heavy and of "unhealthy air," the disease continued to spread; it got so bad that any man who was stricken considered himself dead. For some time, there were only twelve sailors healthy enough to be available for duty. Only fifty-six of the ninety-four men who had originally sailed with Cook returned to their native land; of the thirty-eight deaths, thirty were due to dysentery and malaria during the final weeks of the voyage.

The *Endeavor* remained at the Cape of Good Hope for a month so that the sick men might recover. The ship left with the India fleet, but as she was slower, she was soon outdistanced. After a three-day stopover at St. Helena, on July 10, they finally spotted England on the horizon. On the twelfth, they were in Dover, and on July 17, 1771, Cook disembarked to go to London.

A triumphal welcome

The scientists were the special beneficiaries of their compatriots' enthusiasm, since Banks had had connections before his departure, whereas Cook was unknown. Banks and Solander were given an audience with King George III, and Oxford University gave them *honoris causa* doctoral degrees. As for the Royal Society, it was overjoyed; not only had the transit of Venus been successfully observed, but the naturalists had brought back with them more than a thousand species of dried plants in their herbaria and seed collections, five hundred fish preserved in alcohol, five hundred bird skins, several hundred mineral samples, and innumerable insects. The documentation was illustrated by thirteen hundred accurately detailed drawings executed by the unlucky Parkinson. Banks and Solander had collected weapons, clothing, jewels and ornaments, musical instruments, and fishermen's nets—in other words, ethnological material that was complemented by notes on the first linguistic rudiments of languages until then unknown.

Having become heroes, Banks and Solander were for a long time the focus of society dinners. Even the goat that had furnished the milk for the coffee drunk by these gentlemen and had circumnavigated the globe twice in five years—it had previously been on Byron's expedition—was not overlooked: the illustrious Dr. Samuel Johnson dedicated a Latin distich to it.

Though more modestly than Banks, Lieutenant James Cook also triumphed. For more than an hour, he too was received by the king, and the Admiralty expressed its gratification at his successful completion of the mission assigned him. Cook's geographical and meteorological observations, as well as his reflections on the appointments of a ship traveling to the tropics, were obviously very useful. He had explored the all-but-unknown New Zealand, discovered the east coast of New Holland, and filled in with many islands the blank spaces on maps of the Pacific. Having found no current moving south, he had concluded that Dalrymple's famous southern continent did not exist; but he had brought back no irrefutable proof. Under the circumstances, it was difficult to give up an idea that had been popular for some two hundred years. He would have to set out again, and upon his return Cook had already decided to do so.

He was already far off when the account of his first voyage was published in 1773. It was not

First painting of a kangaroo, done by George Stubbs for J. Banks from a stuffed animal brought back by the latter and sketches done on the site by S. Parkinson. This painting was shown at the Royal Academy in 1772. (Parham Park, Pulborough. Photo from the collection of the Hon. Clive and Mrs. Gibson/Photeb.)

written by Cook himself, as it was thought that the style of an almost illiterate sailor would not suit the general public. Dr. John Hawkesworth, a well-known literary man, was given the job of reworking Cook's journal before publication. Having obtained access to the notes taken by Banks and Solander, Hawkesworth integrated them into Cook's text. Though he did a respectable job with the task assigned him, Cook's descriptions lost not only their sobriety but the impartiality, the absence of prejudice, that gave them their value. Hawkesworth was unable to restrain the impulse to add his personal viewpoints, which were sometimes very different from Cook's. Like Bougainville and Commerson, Hawkesworth believed in the "noble savage," and the details Banks had furnished on Tahitian life only corroborated this belief. Despite this—or perhaps because of it—the publication was enormously successful. It was reprinted twice in 1773 and the following year, and published first in French and then in German and Italian.

However, there was no lack of critics in Great Britain. The flowery and somewhat rapturous descriptions that were the work of Hawkesworth—not of Cook or even Banks—aroused some skepticism, but it was especially the exaltation of this pagan and sensuous paradise that seemed an attack not only on Christianity but on the very idea of progress. Public opinion in Great Britain did not respond to the myth of the "noble savage" in the same way that public opinion had in pre-Revolutionary France.

Cook himself was somewhat embarrassed by this opposition when he later learned of it; he had not been able to check Hawkesworth's text before it was published, and he promised himself to be more careful in the future. In the introduction to his second voyage, he wrote that he left the account of this expedition in the hands of friends who had been kind enough to accept the responsibility and correct the proofs in his absence—he had already left on his third voyage. He added that they were obliging enough to believe that it would be better to tell the story in his own terms rather than in those of somebody else, as the purpose of his book was not only to amuse but to teach; it was therefore felt that the fidelity and absence of deviations from the text would compensate for the lack of ornaments.

Cook's second voyage, 1772–1775

Cook had spent only fourteen months on land when he again left Plymouth, on July 11, 1772, for a voyage whose program he had sketched in the conclusion of the manuscript account of his first journey. According to him, the most expeditious way to make new discoveries was to head directly south toward the Antarctic Ocean in search of the alleged southern continent. The second voyage was therefore to follow a direction opposite to that of the first.

Experience had shown that the *Endeavour* was the best type of ship with which to undertake such expeditions, but unfortunately, she was no longer available; in addition, Cook had become aware of the imprudence of leaving with a single vessel. With the concurrence of the Earl of Sandwich, First Lord of the Admiralty, he chose two ships of the same kind, both built at Whitby by the same firm that had been responsible for the *Endeavour*. The larger of these vessels was called the *Resolution,* and, having been appointed commander, Cook took over the captaincy; command of the *Adventure* was given to Tobias Furneaux, who had been a lieutenant on board the *Dolphin* at the time of the Wallis expedition. Each of these two ships carried on board the framework of a small twenty-ton vessel that could be assembled to transport the crew in case the ship was lost. They also carried cannon, ammunition, and some marines. Another condition for success was the quality of the supplies, and Cook and the navy administration paid particular attention to that concern. The ships carried malt, sauerkraut, salted cabbage, bouillon tablets, mustard, carrot preserves, and concentrated grape and beer must. There had been occasion to observe the energetic action of some of these items against scurvy, and others were brought along to be tested—particularly the carrot marmalade and concentrated beer.

As for Joseph Banks, he was only too ready. He had already assembled a team that was twice as large as the one taken on the first voyage: it included fifteen people, one of whom was the celebrated painter Zoffany; two others were French horn players. Work was begun on the deck structures he considered necessary, but when an attempt was made to sail the ship on the Thames, it became apparent that the prow of the *Resolution* was overloaded and the ship in danger of capsizing. Banks was therefore asked to make do with the space

A serval. Original watercolor by J. R. Forster done at the Cape of Good Hope in 1772. (British Museum, Natural History, London. Photo © by courtesy of the trustees, British Museum/Photeb.)

originally allowed, but he obstinately refused to modify his team. He protested to the Admiralty and finally gave up the idea of going along. But his passion for exploring had by no means been extinguished. Accompanied by Solander, he left on July 12, 1772—the day after Cook's departure—with his own expedition headed for the Hebrides and Iceland; he had enticed into his service John Gore, whom he had known as a lieutenant aboard the *Endeavour*.

Cook had to find another naturalist. He chose Johann Rheinold Forster, a German who lived in London and who had just translated the account of Bougainville's voyages. He was the very opposite of Banks. A man of mature years, pedantic, fastidious, and prudish, Forster proved contentious and managed to argue with just about everyone. On the other hand, his son, Johann Georg, was loved by all. A young man, not yet eighteen, he was lively, curious, passionate about natural history, and, in addition, an excellent draftsman. The scientific team also included two astronomers: on the *Resolution,* William Wales, a careful, capable, and educated scientist; on the *Adventure,* William Bayly. They were both supplied with the best available instruments, in particular with the chronometer invented by John Harrison. By means of this instrument, it would be possible to establish the ship's distance to the east or west of the prime meridian more exactly than

Cook's Ships and Crews
Second Voyage, 1772–1775

The *RESOLUTION:* 462-ton bark with 12 cannons; left from Plymouth, 7/11/1772; returned to Spithead, 7/30/1775; crew: 112 sailors and 5 civilians; deaths: 4.

Commander: James Cook, commander.

Lieutenants: Robert Palliser Cooper, Charles Clerke, Richard Pickersgill.

Midshipmen: James Colnett; William Harvey; Charles Plymouth; Thomas Willis; James Burney, promoted 2nd lieutenant on the *Adventure,* November 1772; George Vancouver.

Surgeon: James Patton.

Assistant Surgeon: William Anderson.

Astronomer: William Wales.

Naturalists: Johann Reinhold Forster: Johann Georg Forster; Anders Sparrman, came on board at Cape Town, 9/19/1772, disembarked at Cape Town, 3/23/1775.

Painter: William Hodges.

Passengers: Francis Masson, botanist, disembarked at Cape Town in November 1772; Odiddy, from Bora Bora, came on board in September 1773, disembarked at Raiatea, May 1774.

The *ADVENTURE:* 336-ton bark with 10 cannon; left from Plymouth, 7/11/1772; returned to Spithead, 7/14/1774; crew: 81 men, including 13 marines; deaths: 17, including 10 men eaten by the Maoris in New Zealand.

Commander: Tobias Furneaux, commander.

Lieutenants: Joseph Shank, put ashore sick at Cape Town, 11/19/1772; 2nd Arthur Kempe, promoted to 1st lieutenant, November 1772; James Burney, promoted to 2nd lieutenant, November 1772.

Midshipmen: Thomas Woodhouse, killed by the Maoris, 12/17/1773; Love Constable; Richard Hergert; George Moorey; Samuel Kemp, died at sea, 9/9/1772; Henry Lightfoot; John Lambrecht.

Master: Peter Fannin.

Assistant Master: John Rowe, killed by the Maoris, 12/17/1773.

Commanding the Marines: John Edgecumbe, promoted 2nd lieutenant.

Surgeon: Thomas Andrews.

Astronomer: William Bayly.

Passenger: Omai, from Raiatea, came on board, September 1773.

A bubalis from the Cape of Good Hope. Drawing by A. Sparrman illustrating his Voyage round the World, 1783. *(Bibliothèque du Muséum d'histoire naturelle, Paris. Photo © Bibl. du Muséum/Photeb.)*

previously. This miraculous timepiece that Cook called "our trustworthy guide" is still running today at the National Maritime Museum in Greenwich.

Some of the men from the first voyage had volunteered: Charles Clerke, now second lieutenant, and Richard Pickersgill, now third lieutenant—both on board the *Resolution.* Among those who did not leave again was a boy who had, at the age of twelve, signed on as Master Molyneux's servant. When Isaac George Manley died sixty-nine years later, having in the interval become an admiral, he was the last survivor of the crew that had left with Cook on his first voyage.

Among the new crew members were young James Burney, who was also to participate in the third voyage and who later achieved fame with his *Chronological History of the Voyages and Discoveries in the South Sea or Pacific Ocean* before ending his days as a rear admiral; and a fifteen-year-old boy, George Vancouver, who was also to become famous. William Hodges, who had already gained a fine reputation as a painter of theatrical scenery and landscapes, was chosen to make the voyage, and he brought back splendid pictures that were both documentary in nature and of a pre-Romantic dramatic intensity.

Toward the south

Having set sail from Plymouth, they immediately drove for Madeira; then Cook, fearing to run low on water, made a supplementary four-day stopover (August 10–14) at the Cape Verde Islands. Two and a half months later, when they made their following stop at Cape Town, the contrast struck the navigators. Cook noted that they had come from a rather fine country, completely neglected by its idle and oppressed inhabitants; here they saw a clean and well-built city in the middle of a desert, surrounded by intersecting black and terrifying mountains—and it was a picture of happy industry.

During the three weeks spent at Cape Town, Forster met a Swedish naturalist, Anders Sparrman, who had been a student of Linnaeus's. Thanks to him, Forster was able to make a relatively detailed investigation of the region's extraordinarily rich flora and fauna and to give Buffon, with whom he corresponded, some previously unpublished data on the still relatively unknown antelopes that he had seen either in nature or in the Cape Town zoo. Afterward, he never stopped taking notes—especially on seals—destined for the French naturalist, who in his *Histoire naturelle* expressed his gratitude to him. The excursions with Sparrman were so profitable that Forster wanted to continue this collaboration; he easily got Cook to agree to take the Swede along. Sparrman was returned to Cape Town two and a half years later on the homeward voyage and went back to his investigations there before publishing his memoirs in 1783.

At Cape Town, Cook learned that two ships commanded by Yves Joseph de Kerguelen-Trémarec had just discovered, far south in the Indian Ocean, the island that was to bear the name of this Breton sailor.

Marion du Fresne had stopped in New Zealand. French navigators were beginning to plow through the Pacific and might forestall Cook's discoveries. He had to move quickly. Besides, Admiralty instructions specified that after leaving Cape Town the *Resolution* and the *Adventure* were to continue south and try to find Cape Circumcision, which Captain Bouvet said he had discovered at 54° S and which, it was thought, might be part of the much sought-after southern continent. Twice, Cook set out to look for it without success.

The two ships left Cape Town on November 23, 1772, and sped south. Cook left in time to profit from the southern summer, which lasts only four months. The cold had become so intense that the men received a double ration of alcohol and supplementary heavy flannel clothing. The worst problem, Cook wrote, was that the ice so clung to the tackle, the sails, and the pulleys that they couldn't be worked without a great deal of effort. The sailors, however, stubbornly overcame these difficulties, and they put up with the cold better than he would have expected.

On December 10, the *Resolution* and the *Adventure* penetrated a fantastic world in which they were to sail for three months amid great dangers. Milky fogs would suddenly rise from shining icebergs that could provoke disaster by abruptly reversing direction. On January 17, 1773, the *Resolution* and the *Adventure* crossed the Antarctic Circle: It was the first time that any ship had done so. But the next day, having reached 67° 15′ and being faced with an endless ice floe, Cook made a half turn and sailed toward warmer waters. The weather was clement, but, on February 8, the fog became so intense that it was impossible to see from one end of

The crew of the Resolution *encounters the first "islands of ice" in January 1773. Engraving by Robert Benard from a drawing by Hodges. (Archives Nationales, Paris. Photo by Michel Didier © Photeb.)*

the ship to the other. The two ships lost sight of each other, but Cook had provided for this eventuality: Furneaux was to rejoin him in Queen Charlotte Sound in New Zealand. Nevertheless, the situation became ever more critical for both of the separated ships. Cook profited from the fact that the southern summer was not yet over to explore these regions until March 17; then, crowding on sail, he headed toward New Zealand.

It was sighted on March 25, 1773. He had sailed 3,600 miles in almost four months without once seeing land. Cook decided not to head immediately toward Queen Charlotte Sound but to stop in the first convenient bay he came across so that his men might have some rest. The *Resolution* dropped anchor in Dusky Bay on the southwest coast of South Island. After so long a trip in the high southern latitudes, he noted, it might be expected that many of his men would be down with scurvy; actually, only one sailor was seriously afflicted.

An observatory, some tents, and a forge for making necessary repairs were immediately set up on the shore. The navigators had great difficulty entering into contact with the natives, who were few in number and avoided them; but, finally, a chief and his daughter were persuaded to come on board and presents were exchanged. Exploration of the inland areas proved most difficult, for the island was bristling with incredibly tall mountains, their crags bare and arid. The coast was covered with "thick woods" dominated by tall and powerful Rimu pines. The naturalists discovered many birds, some of which—the New Zealand plover, a thrush called piopio, corvidae, bush wrens, the kokako or wattle crow, and several species of parakeets—all particularly interesting because so many would become extinct in the next 100 years. On the other hand, there seemed to be an absence of quadrupeds. Though exposed to continuous rain, the crew regained health and strength thanks to the fresh food collected on the commander's orders.

At the time, Cook was unaware that Marion du Fresne's two ships had visited New Zealand a year earlier. He was not to learn of this voyage until he encountered Julien-Marie Crozet, Marion's second in command, at Cape Town in March 1775. Crozet had written a very detailed description of New Zealand and the life of the Maoris, but it was not published until much later; along with Cook's observations, it constitutes the principal source of information about eighteenth-century Maori culture.

The two Forsters and Sparrman considerably enriched the first inventory of New Zealand flora and fauna that had been prepared by Banks and Solander. J. R. Forster compiled long lists of the plants native to these islands and described several species of unknown animals such as the Australian sea lion; and Sparrman discovered such birds as the New Zealand parakeet, the spotted cormorant, and a species of flightless rail, called wekas.

On May 11, the *Resolution* left Dusky Bay, following the coast in order to rejoin Furneaux in Queen Charlotte Sound, where the *Adventure* had already been for six weeks. It had been three months since the ships were separated. Unable to find his leader, Furneaux had anchored in the bay—it took the name of his ship—on the coast of Van Diemen's Land (Tasmania). After an attempt to learn if that island was separated from New Holland, he concluded that there was no passage but only a deep bay. This was an error that was not rectified until the discovery of Bass Strait in 1798.

The two ships left New Zealand on June 7 in order to explore the unknown parts of the sea between New Zealand and Cape Horn. If no land was discovered, they would go on to Tahiti and from there return to New Zealand. Should the ships become separated again, two rendezvous were established: the first was in Tahiti before August 20, the second in Queen Charlotte Sound before November 20. However, though health conditions aboard the *Resolution* were good, the same was not true on the *Adventure*. The cook was dead, and twenty of the best sailors were stricken with scurvy and dysentery. This was because Furneaux, unlike Cook, had not taken the precaution of making his crew eat fresh vegetables. On the way, they came across only the small islands already discovered by Bougainville in the Dangerous Archipelago (Tumamotus), but obviously found no trace of the southern continent.

Tahiti revisited

On the morning of August 16, the *Resolution* and the *Adventure* entered Oaiti-Pika Bay, near the southeast end of Tahiti. A light breeze carried a delicious perfume from the land and made the surface of the water undulate, wrote Forster, who was seeing the island for the first time. It was not until several days later, when the ships dropped anchor in Matavai Bay, that they came into familiar surroundings and learned that events since Cook's first stay four years earlier had considerably altered the

situation. A war had broken out between the two peninsulas—Big Tahiti and Little Tahiti—and they now formed two distinct kingdoms whose names Cook gave as Opoureonu and Tearrabou. In the course of the fighting, several chiefs whom Cook had known, including Taburai, had been killed. As for Oberea, the former queen, she now lived in poverty, and it was her nephew, a young man named Otoo, who ruled in the larger peninsula.

No sooner had Cook arrived than he was taken to him and tried to win his friendship with presents. At Matavai, as had been true in Otaheiti, everybody asked for the absent officers, especially Banks, who was still popular; on the other hand, news of Tupia's death was met with indifference. The pigs and poultry with which the island had formerly been overflowing had become very rare as a result of the war, and consequently Cook did not want to extend his stay beyond the time necessary to allow those men suffering from scurvy to recover. A previously unknown sickness was rampant in the island; "it effected the head, Throat, and Stomach and at last kills them." This disease had been transmitted by the sailors of a European ship initially believed by Cook to have been French; he later learned that she was Spanish and had come from America: the *Aguila,* commanded by Domingo de Boenéchea, who had visited Tahiti in 1772 in the interval between Cook's first and second voyage and attempted to annex to the Spanish empire not only Tahiti but also Easter Island.

Cook himself, a good and clearsighted man, was perfectly aware of the progressive deterioration that must follow contacts between Europeans and natives. He even wrote in his journal: "We de-

bauch their morals already too prone to vice and we introduce among them wants and perhaps diseases which they never before knew and which serve only to disturb that happy tranquility they and their fore Fathers had enjoyed. If any one denies the truth of this assertion let him tell me what the Natives of the whole extent of America have gained by the commerce they had had with Europeans.''

The sick men recovered. The two Forsters had with great amazement covered a large part of the island and discovered several birds not listed by Banks and Solander—among them a swallow, a curlew, a small parrot, and the fly catcher—as well as several interesting plants, including a beautiful tree, *Barringtonia speciosa*. Meanwhile, Cook had continued his research into Tahitian beliefs and customs by visiting a morai, where human beings were occasionally sacrificed. (He was assured that the latter were always "bad men.")

The two ships raised anchor for Huahine and the other Society Islands, where they planned to take on supplies. At Huahine, on September 3, old King Oree welcomed his friend Cook with tears of joy. Cook recorded that before leaving the island, Captain Furneaux agreed to accept on board his ship a young man called Omai, from Raiatea. He noted that he was surprised to see Furneaux encumber himself with this man, who did not seem to him to be a well-selected sample of the inhabitants of those happy islands, having the advantages neither of birth nor of acquired rank and being unremarkable in features, height, or color. But Cook was later to acknowledge his error: Omai showed a remarkable facility in understanding, a lively intelligence, and an honest disposition. Cook himself took on board a Tahitian named Odiddy.

The Friendly Islands

On September 17, leaving the Society archipelago, the *Resolution* and the *Adventure* headed west. On the twenty-third, they discovered an apparently deserted island that they named Hervey Island. On October 2, they landed on Middleburg Island (Eua), where the welcome of the inhabitants was enthusiastic. They seemed as eager to give presents as to receive them; Many completely nude men and women swam out to the ships, and those who couldn't get close tossed entire bundles of goods at the English. While an enormous crowd shouted joyful exclamations, Chief Tioony came on board and presents were exchanged. On October 4, the ships anchored before a larger island—Amsterdam Island (Tongatapu)—and one of the chiefs, a man called Otago (Hatago), gave Cook a detailed tour.

Several of these islands had been discovered by the Dutch at the beginning of the seventeenth century, but the mores of their inhabitants were unknown. Cook therefore made careful notes about the natives: copper-colored, well built, and regular-featured, they were active, alert, and lively. The

men were tattooed from mid-thigh to just above their haunches. There was one peculiar fact about most of them, both men and women: they had lost one or two of their pinkies. Cook could not discover the reason for this mutilation.

Barringtonia speciosa, *tree discovered in Tahiti by J. R. Forster. Original watercolor by Forster. (British Museum, Natural History, London. Photo by courtesy of the trustees, British Museum/Photeb.)*

Return to New Zealand

Leaving Tongatapu on October 7, the two ships kept heading west, and at five o'clock on the morning of the twenty-first, the northern tip of New Zealand's North Island came into sight. As soon as weather permitted, two chiefs in a boat drew near and came on board with little urging. They were given presents, including nails, which pleased them

Tongatapu landscape (Friendly Islands). Watercolor by William Hodges, 1773. (Rex Nan Kivell Collection, National Library of Australia, Canberra. Photo © National Library of Australia/Photeb.)

so much that they grabbed for them with an avidity that made it clear they could have been given nothing more precious. But Cook was particularly eager to give them some animals and some useful seeds. To the one who seemed to have the highest rank he presented two boars, two sows, four hens, and two roosters. The man promised not to slaughter them and Cook drew comfort from the idea that if he kept his word the island would soon be well stocked.

As they were going down the coast on the way to Queen Charlotte Sound, a violent storm broke out and the *Adventure* was once more separated from the *Resolution*. After searching in vain, Furneaux decided to return to Great Britain alone; it was not until seventeen months later that Cook had word of him. The *Adventure* had not been able to reach Queen Charlotte Sound until November 30. There Furneaux had found, in a corked and sealed bottle, a letter from Captain Cook informing him of his arrival on the third and his departure on the twenty-fourth.

On December 17, Furneaux wrote, he sent the large cutter and its crew—under the orders of Mr. Row, poop deck officer—to collect edible plants and return that very evening, as he intended to sail the next morning. When the boat did not return that evening or the next morning, Furneaux was very uneasy and sent out the launch with Second Lieutenant Burney, a crew, and ten marines to look for it. On his return, Burney reported his macabre discovery. After finding the remains of the cutter and several shoes, and then an arm that, thanks to its tattoo, was identified as belonging to a sailor, Burney and his men suddenly came upon so terrible a spectacle of carnage and barbarism that it could not be contemplated without horror: The heads, hearts, and lungs of several of the ship's company lay on the sand, and a short distance off, dogs were devouring their entrails. Ten men, two of whom were officers, had perished in this massacre. Shocked by

the disaster, Furneaux decided to leave New Zealand immediately and return to Great Britain by the shortest route. Three months later, on March 17, 1774, he put into Cape Town; and on July 14, 1774, he dropped anchor at Spithead, almost a year before the *Resolution* returned.

Cook himself did not linger in Queen Charlotte Sound. He noted with resignation that several of the animals he had given the Maoris had already been eaten and that the rest had scattered. Relations with the inhabitants remained ambiguous; they stole whatever they could and the English had to remain on their guard. It was also obvious that they were cannibals.

In sight of the Antarctic continent

Once repaired, the *Resolution* left New Zealand on November 25 and, now alone, began its second cruise toward the extreme south; this time, however, it went toward the west to see if the hypothetical southern continent was to be found in these regions. On December 12, the ship was surrounded by icebergs, several of which were almost a hundred meters high. Because of snow and sleet, "our ropes were like wires, Sails like board or plates of Metal, and the Shivers froze fast in the blocks so that it required our utmost effort to get a Top-sail down and up; the cold so intense as hardly to be endured; the whole Sea in a manner covered with ice, a hard gale and a thick fog."

Forster, who was suffering from a severe attack of rheumatism, noted that the overall spectacle looked like the debris of a world that had flown apart, or the description of Hell imagined by poets— a notion that was even more overwhelming because of the curses and maledictions to be heard everywhere. Cook himself was pale and could no longer eat. Nevertheless, he remained inflexibly determined to carry out his mission. Confiding in no one, he seemed to be sailing without a plan. Suddenly he gave orders to head for warmer latitudes; a breath of hope swept through the ship and it was rumored that they were going to head home—but several weeks later, Cook again headed south. Forster recorded that a dark and gloomy expression spread over everyone's face, and an oppressive silence reigned everywhere. At least the naturalists had the compensation of being able to study the almost unknown fauna. Among the sea birds that abounded in the area, they sighted the snow petrel and the giant fulmar, the snow prion and the Antarctic prion, the emperor penguin and the king penguin—which completed the observations previously made in New Zealand on the small blue penguin and the rock hopper.

On January 30, 1774, the *Resolution,* having gone far beyond the Antarctic Circle, reached the highest latitude it had ever attained: 71° 11' S. The ship then found itself before a field of ice that seemed to extend into infinity. Cook wrote that he would not say it was impossible to go farther south "but

I will assert that the bare attempting of it would be a very dangerous enterprise and what I believe no man in my situation would have thought of."

Easter Island

On February 6, he decided to return to the tropics in order to spend the southern summer there. Cook was completely convinced that there was no southern continent to be discovered in this ocean. No doubt, he admitted, he might have reached the Cape of Good Hope in April and thus put an end to his explorations, but that would have meant assuming that the southern Pacific had been so completely explored that there was nothing left to discover. He therefore decided to continue, but not without having consulted his men. The officers were in complete agreement, and even the sailors were so far from wishing to put an end to the voyage that they rejoiced at the prospect of prolonging it a year and of soon profiting from the advantages of a milder climate.

Cook's men had absolute confidence in him and grew more and more devoted. This became obvious a little later, when, at the end of February, he fell sick with a "bilious colic" that forced him to remain in bed and turn the command over to his second, Lieutenant Robert Palliser Cooper. There

being no fresh meat aboard, Forster himself, who had previously had many quarrels with Cook, sacrificed his favorite dog so that the commander might get well. And when Cook recovered fifteen days later, assistant gunner John Marra wrote that joy replaced consternation on the faces of all, from the highest officer to the lowly ship's boy.

On March 11, the *Resolution* sighted the first land encountered since leaving New Zealand four months earlier. It was Easter Island, which Jacob Roggeveen had discovered but which neither Byron, nor Wallis and Carteret, nor Bougainville had been able to rediscover. (Two years earlier, Boenéchea's *Aguila* had anchored there before going to Tahiti, and traces of his stay were now found.) Two days later, Cook and several of his officers disembarked on a sandy beach on which were assembled several hundred natives, many of whom had been so impatient to greet them that they had swum out to the launches. The Easter Islanders were welcoming, but also larcenous: Cook reports that the English found it difficult to hold on to their hats and that it was almost impossible to conserve the contents of their pockets, even when those items had just been sold to them.

The island was barren and rocky, and the scant population—Cook set it at six or seven hundred inhabitants—lived off small fields of potatoes, banana trees, and sugar cane, as well as some poultry. The

Chinstrap penguin, species discovered by J. R. Forster. Original watercolor by Forster. (British Museum, Natural History, London. Photo by courtesy of the trustees, British Museum/Photeb.)

Giant Easter Island statues. Painting by William Hodges. (National Maritime Museum, London. Photo © by the museum/Arch. Photeb.)

English were able to put in some supplies, but, since the island lacked fresh water, the *Resolution* stayed only three days. Cook immediately noticed that the Easter Islanders shared their origin with the peoples of the most western islands—Odiddy understood their language—and decided that the Polynesian race was extremely widespread. Needless to say, he tried to discover the enigma behind the colossal statues erected on platforms. His feeling was that they were not idols but the tombs of tribes or families, and on one of the terraces he did indeed see "a human Skeleton lying in the foundation of one just covered with stones." In his opinion, the present inhabitants of the island—who totally lacked mechanical aids—were not the ones who had raised these amazing statues and then topped them with large cylindrical stones.

Heading north, the *Resolution* next encountered the Marquesas, discovered in 1595 by Mendaña and never since seen; Cook fixed their exact position and discovered, in addition to the four islands mentioned by the Spanish navigator, a fifth, which he named Hood Island (present-day Fatuhiva). There too the language resembled that of the Tahitians. Trading with the inhabitants was lively, but the Marquesans were also inclined to theft, and one of them was killed by a marine while he was running off with an iron gangway lamp. The *Resolution* stayed in the Marquesas only four days (April 7–11), and, after having discovered four small islands to which Cook gave the name of the man who had promoted his career, Sir Hugh Palliser, the ship dropped anchor in Matavai Bay in Tahiti—where Wales, the astronomer, wanted to set up his observatory so that he might check the chronometer in relation to observed longitude.

Sailors and Tahitians celebrate the feast of St. George

The situation in Tahiti had once more evolved. Only a few months of peace had been necessary for the natural luxuriance of the island to set everything to rights. As a result, the population was happy and the *Resolution*'s crew received every possible sign of friendship. In the early morning, the Tahitian women would leave the ship wearing the sailors' shirts, and they would return in grass skirts that evening to ask for others. On April 23, the crew was celebrating the Feast of St. George, so the young women invaded the *Resolution* and each got a shirt—many without even having to dance. The sailors, Forster wrote, combined the pleasures of Venus with the orgies of that festival, and the excesses committed that night were unbelievable.

On April 24, young King Otoo came to make a formal visit to the captain, and the two men exchanged gifts. Two days later, Otoo put on a naval spectacle that amazed all the men. There were "160 large double Canoes, very well equip'd, Man'd and Arm'd. . . . The Chief and all those on the Fighting Stages were dressed in their War habits, that is

in a vast quantity of Cloth, Turbands, breast Plates and Helmmets. . . . Vessels were decorated with Flags, Streamers, etc. so that the whole made a grand and Noble appeerence such as was never seen before in this Sea. . . . Besides these Vesels of War there were 170 sail of Smaller double Canoes. . . . In these 303 Canoes I judge there were no less than 7,760 Men, a number which appears incredible, especially as we were told that they all belonged to the districts of Attahourou and Ahopatea . . ."

On May 13, the evening before their departure, Odiddy, the young Tahitian who had embarked with Cook, failed to appear, and a party was sent to look for him. He came back on board, but Cook noticed that he preferred to remain among his people and therefore set him down on Raiatea several days later; the young man took his leave in tears, for he was very attached to his former companions but feared that if he went to Great Britain he would never be able to return.

Somebody else wanted to remain in Tahiti, but this was a member of the crew, the assistant gunner James Marra, an Irishman who had sailed in the service of the Dutch. On May 14, just as the *Resolution* was leaving Matavai Bay, Marra jumped overboard. A boat was immediately sent in pursuit, and it was then noticed that a Tahitian boat was waiting for him, as he had made sure of help from the islanders. Once Marra was recaptured, Cook had no choice but to put him in irons—though he demonstrated great indulgence toward him by keeping him there only overnight. If Marra had asked for his consent, Cook noted, he might very well have obtained it.

From this return to Tahiti, J. R. Forster brought back, in addition to numerous natural history curiosities, a study of comparative anthropology that he completed during the rest of the voyage and that made him a pioneer in this new discipline. In it, he distinguished two large human groups: the Polynesians—light-skinned, with delicate and well-proportioned bodies—who inhabited the Society Islands, New Zealand, and Easter Island; and the Melanesians—darker-skinned, woolyhaired, squatter, and more primitive—who were found in the New Hebrides and in New Caledonia. Forster also described differences within the Polynesian group itself: the insouciant Tahitians; the more belligerent Maoris, who nevertheless had a more advanced art; and the Marquesans, to whom he gave the prize for physical beauty.

One of the more interesting accounts of Tahiti came from Wales, the expedition's astronomer, who protested against Bougainville's exaggerated impressions. Insofar as he was concerned, the Tahitian women were far from deserving their reputation. He even cast a critical eye on the dances themselves. "The wriggling of their hips, especially as set off with such a quantity of furbelows, is too ludicrous to be pleasing and the distortion of their mouths is really disagreeable." Such judgments indicated the beginning of a change; Wales was no longer enchanted by the amazement of the

Odiddy, the young Tahitian taken aboard the Resolution *by Cook. Pastel by W. Hodges. (National Library of Australia, Canberra. Photo © National Library of Australia/Photeb.)*

discovery, and he simply described what he saw.

Before leaving the Society archipelago, the *Resolution* stopped for a week at Huahine—in order to visit their friends, Cook noted—and then for twelve days in Raiatea. On this island, the Forsters caught two specimens of a parakeet breed, the Raiatea kakariki. Later Anderson, the naturalist on Cook's third voyage, was to find no trace of this bird and it is probably extinct since it has not been seen since. On June 6, the English took their "final leave of these happy isles."

Cook set sail toward the west in the direction of Eua and Tongatapu, already visited the previous year. On the way, the *Resolution* discovered two new bodies of land—the island to which Cook gave the name of one of the Lords of the Admiralty, Palmerston, and then another which he took possession of and called Savage Island (Niue) because of its bushy aspect and the hostility of its inhabitants. In the archipelago that Cook had baptized the Friendly Islands (because he felt that a durable friendship seemed to reign among the occupants and because their courtesy to strangers gave them the right to this) Cook dropped anchor (June 27) at Rotterdam Island (Namuka or Anamooka).

The Melanesians of the New Hebrides

Setting out to sea again on July 2, Cook discovered a new island that was the home of innumerable tortoises and was thus baptized Tortoise Island. His goal was the archipelago discovered by Queiros in 1605 and visited by Bougainville, who had called it the Great Cyclades. The *Resolution* dropped anchor at Mallicolo (Malekula), where some four to five hundred inhabitants were assembled on the shore to watch the disembarkment. Though armed with spears and shafts as well as clubs and pikestaves, they made no resistance. The Englishmen noted that this people, who did not speak the same language as the Tahitians, did not belong to the Polynesian group but to a race of men that resembled the monkey. Cook wrote that they were "the most Ugly and ill-proportioned of any I ever saw . . ." He felt that their deformity was increased by a belt they wore about the waist and which they so tightened about the belly that their bodies somewhat resembled enormous ants.

The impression that he was dealing with a population of different origin was intensified when he visited other islands; indeed, the Mallicolo (Malekula) inhabitant is a mixture of Polynesian and Melanesian, whereas those of the southern islands (Erromanga and Tana) belong to a pure Melanesian type. However, if the New Hebridians were ugly, they were also perfectly honest and loyal. They showed themselves hospitable, polite, and obliging, at least at Mallicolo (Malekula); but when, on August 5, Cook and his men wanted to set foot on Erromanga, they were received by "clubs, Darts . . . and Arrows." After discharging their rifles, the

Passiflora aurantia (New Caledonia). Original watercolor by Forster. (British Museum, Natural History, London. Photo by courtesy of the trustees, British Museum/Photeb.)

Europeans thought it more prudent to reembark.

On Tana, at the extreme south of the archipelago—where a volcano "made a terrible noise, throwing up Prodigeous columns of Smak and fire at every iruption, at one time great stones were seen high in the air"—the navigators made their longest stay (August 6–11), and Cook gave a detailed description of it; meanwhile, the naturalists collected numerous plants that they had never seen before and brought together a large collection of birds. When Cook left the archipelago, which he called the New Hebrides, he had fixed its position and drawn up the first more or less complete map of these numerous islands to which he had given individual names.

Moving south toward New Zealand, after sailing for three days, he discovered, on September 5, a large and unknown body of land; it was Balahiha off the north coast of New Caledonia, where the Melanesian population welcomed the visitors with perfect courtesy. Unfortunately, it soon became apparent that they could not reprovision there. Aided by Lieutenant Clerke, Wales set up his instruments on land so that he could observe an eclipse of the sun by means of a Hadley quadrant, which was used for the first time.

Again setting out to sea, Cook followed the coast of New Caledonia, but he had no time to explore the western coast. Despite the brevity of his stay on shore, he set down some observations about the Kanakas—among other things, about their dwellings, with which he was particularly struck. To the south of New Caledonia, he discovered a small island remarkable for its high conifers, which were so crowded together that from a distance they looked like basalt columns. The species belonged to the genus *Araucaria*, then unknown. These *Araucaria columnaris*, which measured as high as 70 meters, looked like giant pines, and Cook therefore called the place the Isle of Pines. Some distance away, there was another island, where the two Forsters found so much to do that it was decided to call it Botany Island. After sailing on for some ten days, they came in sight of a third uninhabited land body midway between New Caledonia and New Zealand, and Cook baptized it Norfolk Island. J. R. Forster found there a new araucaria that was even taller than those they had just seen. On Lord Howe Island, minute and desolate, the naturalists discovered another very beautiful palm, *Howea foresteriana*. These species were particularly precious, since neither of them existed anywhere else.

On October 18, 1774, the *Resolution* was once again anchored in Queen Charlotte Sound in New Zealand, where Cook intended to "refresh my people and put the Ship in a condition to Cross this great Ocean in a high latitude once more." The fact was that, though they were about to return by way of Cape Horn, he planned to take advantage of this last part of the voyage to make a third attempt to settle the question of the southern continent. Some Maoris encountered by the navigators told them that a ship had been wrecked in the sound and that there had been a battle in which the natives had won the upper hand, killed the crew with their "patu-patus and eaten them"; the informants took care to specify that they themselves had taken no part in the affair. The rumor worried the commander, who questioned his informants, but they contradicted themselves and denied everything they had said previously. Cook came to the conclusion that there had been a misunderstanding and that the victims had been enemies who lived on the island.

On November 11, Cook once more sailed south and then east, but he had given up all hope of finding other land in this ocean and decided to steer directly for the western entrance of the Strait of Magellan, with the idea of following the coast off the southern part of Tierra del Fuego. When the coast of South America came into sight on December 17 after a very rapid forty-four-day crossing, Cook noted with relief: "I have now done with the southern Pacific Ocean . . . and flatter myself that no one will think that I have left it unexplored . . ."

Several days later, the *Resolution* anchored in the channel a little to the west of Cape Horn and called it Christmas Channel because they had gotten there on December 24 and worthily celebrated that holiday. The naturalists completed their collections and their observations on the flora and fauna they had been the first to account for. They discovered two more varieties of penguin—the Papuan penguin and the Magellan penguin—bringing to eight the number of species they reported. Their game bag included three more albatrosses, the white sheathbill, and the arctic tern, as well as a raptor native to South America, Forster's caracara. They were also able to describe several species of seals and cetaceans that lived in those waters. All in all, the Forsters and Sparrman had created a survey of previously unknown fauna that was remarkable for the time. They had even made several important acquisitions in the vegetable kingdom, including the *Nothofagus*, or antarctic beech; the *Embothrium*, or fire tree; and, finally, the bush that since the sixteenth century furnished "Winter bark" but was still not known, *Drimys winteri*.

On January 17, to the east of Cape Horn, they discovered a vast icy land; it was savage and horrible, and not so much as a tree was to be seen, but Cook nevertheless named it South Georgia in honor of the king. Farther to the east stretched other icy coasts that were named South Thule and Sandwich Land. The penguins were so numerous that they seemed to form a crust on the rock. But still no southern continent. This time, January 27, Cook felt able to write: "I think I may now venture to assert that the extensive Coast laid down in Mr. Dalrymple's Chart of the Ocean between Africa and America and the Gulph of St. Sebastian does not exist. . . . It is however true that the greatest part of this Southern Continent (supposing there is one) must lay within the Polar Circle where the Sea is so pestered with ice that the land is thereby inaccessible. The risk one runs in exploaring a Coast in these unknown and Icy Seas is so very great that I can be bold to say that no man will ever venture farther than I have done and that the lands which may lie to the South will never be explored. Thick fogs, snow storms, Intense cold and every other thing that can render Navigation dangerous one has to encounter, and these difficulties are greatly heightened by the inexpressible horrid aspect of the Country, a Country doomed by Nature never once to feel the warmth of the Sun's rays, but to lie for ever buried under everlasting snow and ice."

On March 23, the men of the *Resolution* rejoined civilization at Cape Town, where Sparrman took his leave. On May 16, they were at St. Helena. After two stopovers, at Ascension Island and the Azores, they saw the coast of the mother country on July 29. The next day, the *Resolution* dropped anchor at Spithead, having gone 70,000 miles in three years and eighteen days, and having lost four men, only one of whom died of disease—and that not scurvy.

Cook returns and departs again

"It was a glorious voyage!" exclaimed Solander in a letter to Banks as soon as he learned of Cook's arrival. The latter had indeed carried out his mission more successfully than had been hoped for, having reached lower latitudes than any other navigator before him and reconnoitered almost all the archipelagos of the southern hemisphere. He was bringing back precise information about these unknown lands and peoples, and he was also bringing back a ship crammed with strange objects: a mummified head; three living Tahitian dogs; maps destined for King George and charting his new possessions in the Pacific; cases full of bird skins, dried plants, and other natural history specimens intended for Banks; numerous drawings by Hodges; and, finally, a considerable mass of scientific observations of all kinds.

Those of the naturalists were of primary importance. Whereas Banks and Solander were basically botanists, Sparrman and J. R. Forster had a wide knowledge of animals and especially of birds. In this domain, the species they discovered were considerably more numerous than those described by the naturalists on the first voyage, even in areas the former had prospected. There was but one shadow on the picture—the constantly growing disagreement between Cook and Johann Reinhold Forster. Cook complained of the naturalist's behavior to the Earl of Sandwich, the First Lord of the Admiralty, and had him forbidden to publish anything about the voyage since they had not been able to reach an agreement. Only Forster's son, young Johann Georg, was authorized to publish his account, which met with great success; the following year Johann Georg took advantage of that suc-

cess to publish the *Observations* which complemented his account and which were written by his father, who had left England shortly after his return.

James Cook was received in London with the highest honors. He had an audience with the king and was elected a member of the Royal Society. It seemed that, at forty-seven, he had the right to a well-deserved rest; the Lords of the Admiralty therefore promoted him to the rank of ship's captain and appointed him to the post of fourth captain at the Greenwich Hospital for disabled sailors. It was a well-paid honorary post, but, as Cook wrote to his old Whitby employer, to whom he had remained faithful: "A few months ago the whole Southern Hemisphere was hardly big enough for me, and now I am going to be confined to the limits of Greenwich Hospital, which are far too small for an active mind like mine. I must confess it is a fine retreat and a pretty income but, whether I can bring myself to like ease and retirement time will show."

Time gave its answer immediately. Cook never even had a chance to establish himself at his new home. Though he had definitely destroyed the centuries-old hypothesis of a southern continent, an equally important problem remained. Was there or was there not a passage joining the Pacific to the Atlantic in the north of the American continent? Such a passage would considerably shorten the voyage between Europe and the Far East, and international commerce would benefit greatly. It was thought that if such a passage existed it would be between Hudson Bay or Baffin Island and a point situated somewhere north of California on the west coast. Contemporaries of Queen Elizabeth had already gone in search of it, but, like Drake, they had

Above: Branch of the Araucaria excelsa *discovered by Forster on Norfolk Island, 1774. Original watercolor from Genus Pinus by A. B. Lambert, 1837. (British Museum, Natural History, London. Photo by courtesy of the trustees, British Museum/Photeb.)*

Left: View of the Isle of Pines showing the Araucaria columnaris. *Engraving by R. Benard after a drawing by W. Hodges. (Archives Nationales, Fonds Marine, Paris. Photo by Michel Didier © Photeb.)*

been unsuccessful. Since then, many other navigators—including the British captains Smith, Moore, and Mulgrave—had vainly explored the arctic coasts of America. David Nelson, who was to accompany Cook on his third voyage, had taken part in one of those expeditions to the North Atlantic.

In 1775, the question was to become newly important. Samuel Hearne of the Hudson's Bay Company—the first to venture so far into the territory situated to the northwest of Hudson Bay—had decided that there probably was no Northwest Passage. Following his report, Parliament had offered a large reward to the first captain who would complete the voyage by sea. In addition, Omai had to be brought back to Tahiti. With these two goals in mind, the Admiralty decided to fit out a new expedition, but since the Earl of Sandwich dared not suggest that the man who seemed born for the job take over its leadership so soon after his return, Cook proposed himself. On February 9, 1776,

having again received the command of the *Resolution,* he hoisted his pennant and began to enlist sailors.

During this time, Omai was the darling of London society. On his return to Great Britain in July 1774, Captain Furneaux had turned him over to Banks, who spoke Tahitian and asked nothing more than to show off the first native from the South Seas. Having furnished Omai with a frogged coat and a sword, and having taught him a few words of English, Banks took him everywhere. The Tahitian was granted an audience by George III, dined at the Duke of Gloucester's, went to the theater to see Garrick, visited the House of Lords, and had his portrait done by fashionable painters. Thanks to the generosity of his London friends, Omai returned to his country loaded with gifts that were to dazzle the Tahitians: a complete wardrobe, a portable organ, a panoply of arms, and an entire battery of kitchen equipment.

Costume of the "Enchantress" Oberea, queen of Tahiti, for the pantomime Omai, or a Trip Around the World *evoking Cook's second and third expeditions and given at the Covent Garden Royal Theatre in 1785. Watercolor by P. J. de Loutherbourg. (National Library of Australia, Canberra. Photo © National Library of Australia/Photeb.)*

Cook's third voyage, 1776–1780

In February 1776, seven months after his return, Captain Cook was actively preparing to leave again. He resumed his position on the *Resolution,* but since the *Adventure* was being used elsewhere, a ship of the same type was acquired; another product of the Whitby shipyards, the *Diligence,* was renamed the *Discovery.* Charles Clerke, second lieutenant aboard the *Resolution* during the second voyage, was to be her commander. On board the *Resolution,* First Lieutenant John Gore had taken part in the first voyage, and several other members of the crew had previously accompanied Cook: Lieutenant James Burney, Midshipmen William Harvey and George Vancouver, Surgeon William Anderson, and William Bayly, the astronomer.

Like the preceding expeditions, this one was prepared with careful foresight. The Earl of Sandwich and Sir Hugh Palliser had seen to this and came in person to inspect the installations. The Board of Longitude provided the ships with all the necessary scientific instruments and gave Cook the Harrison-Kendall chronometer, which had already worked miracles. On the other hand, no professional naturalist had been signed on. The inconvenient installations demanded by Banks, and Forster's bad temper, had undoubtedly been discouraging experiences for Cook; he therefore turned the vacant post over to the surgeon, Anderson, who was personally interested in the natural sciences and had learned much from the Forsters, whose assistant he had volunteered to be. In addition, Midshipman David Nelson was a botanist and had even worked at Kew Gardens under Banks's direction. A painter, John Webber, was taken along to do the landscapes, while the natural history drawings were to be the responsibility of William Ellis, the assistant surgeon of the *Discovery.*

The king himself had ordered the navigators to take along and turn over to the native populations such useful animals as a bull, two cows and their calves, and several sheep; this supply of livestock was to be supplemented at Cape Town. In addition, the ships carried a supply of cereal grains and other edible plants. Finally, they took on an assortment of useful tools for distribution, completing the sampling brought along by Omai—who was leaving London, Cook noted, with a mixture of regret and satisfaction. When they spoke together of England and all those who during his stay had

The famous chronometer by John Harrison carried by Cook for the first time during his second voyage. (National Maritime Museum, London. Photo by the museum/Photeb.)

honored him with their friendship, the sensitive Omai burst into tears; but as soon as the conversation turned to his native island, his eyes would shine with joy.

Cook's instructions traced the approximate itinerary of the voyage. The *Resolution* and the *Discovery* were to descend to the southern part of the Indian Ocean "in search of some islands said to have been lately seen by the French, in the latitude of 48° 0′ South, and about the meridian of Mauritius." These were a small group of isolated islands visited by Marion du Fresne and Crozet in 1772 and called the Austral Islands. Cook had gotten information about them from Crozet himself when the two sailors had met at Cape Town in 1775.

Cook was next to reconnoiter the island that Kerguelen had taken possession of, also in 1772. From there, after having once more visited the Polynesian islands, he was to go to the northern Pacific to explore the northwest coast of North America between Drake's New Albion (northern California) and the region explored in 1728 and 1741 by the Danish navigator Vitus Bering while in Russian service. Bering had established that, contrary to contemporary belief, there was no junction

Cook's Ships and Crews
Third Voyage, 1776–1780

The *RESOLUTION*: 462-ton bark with 12 cannon; left from Plymouth, 7/12/1776 returned to Stromness, 8/23/1780 crew: 117 men, including 12 marines; losses: 10.

Commander: James Cook, captain; after Cook's death (February 1779), Charles Clerke; after Clerke's death (August 1779), John Gore.

Lieutenants: 1st, John Gore, then J. King, then J. Burney; 2nd, James King, made 1st lieutenant (February 1779), then commander of the *Discovery* (August 1779); 3rd, John Williamson, made 2nd lieutenant (August 1779); the vacant lieutenancy was given to Midshipman Harvey.

Midshipmen: William Harvey, Richard Hergert, James Trevenan, James Ward, William Midd (or Medd), John Hatley, John Watts, John Shuttleworth.

Master: William Bligh.

Commanding the marines: Lieutenant Molesworth Philipps.

Surgeon and naturalist: William Anderson, died 8/3/1779, replaced by Law, surgeon of the *Discovery*.

Assistant surgeons: 1st, David Samwell, transferred to the *Discovery* (August 1779); 2nd, then 1st, Robert Davies.

Astronomer: Joseph Billings.

Painter: John Webber.

Passenger: Omai.

The *DISCOVERY*: 295-ton bark; left from Plymouth, 7/12/1776; returned to Stromness, 8/23/1780; crew: 75 men; losses: 0.

Commander: Charles Clerke, commander of the expedition after the death of Cook (February 1779); John Gore after the death of Clerke (August 1779); James King.

Lieutenants: 1st, James Burney, after the death of Clerke, 1st lieutenant on board the *Resolution;* 2nd, John Rickman, then 1st lieutenant (August 1779).

Midshipmen: Edward Riou, named lieutenant on the *Discovery,* then on the *Resolution;* George Vancouver; Alexander Mouat; David Nelson; John Henry Martin.

Master: Thomas Edgar.

Surgeon: John Law, made surgeon on the *Resolution* (August 1779), replaced on the *Discovery* by David Samwell.

Assistant surgeon and natural history draftsman: William Ellis.

Astronomer: William Bayly.

Kerguelen cabbage, antiscorbutic plant. Original watercolor by John Webber. (British Museum, Natural History, London. Photo by courtesy of the trustees, British Museum/Photeb.)

between northern America and northern Asia; he had revealed that between the two continents was the strait that now bears his name, and he had discovered the Aleutian Islands and part of Alaska. Cook was to determine if these lands constituted an archipelago or were the continuation of the North American coasts. The goal of this voyage was thus completely different from that of the previous ones; after having explored the Antarctic, this time Cook was to head toward the great unknown North.

Political circumstances in 1776 were clearly unfavorable to such an undertaking. A few days before Cook's departure, on July 4, England's American colonies rebelled against the mother country and proclaimed their independence. War would surely break out, and France would probably side with the Americans. Cook's expedition must not suffer because of this, so the French and the Americans decided that Cook would be treated as the commander of a neutral power. These arrangements were to remain secret, and Cook's fellow voyagers were not to hear of them until three years later.

Sailing from Plymouth on July 12, 1776, the *Resolution* and the *Discovery* made their first stop at Santa Cruz de Tenerife (August 1–4). There, Cook encountered the Chevalier de Borda, a French navigator and mathematician who was charged with determining the exact position of the Canary Islands, and Borda gave him whatever information he had about Kerguelen's discovery. On October 28, they arrived at Cape Town, which they left on November 30. In December, the ships reached the Austral Islands. Cook named the largest of them for Prince Edward, Duke of Kent, the future father of Queen Victoria; the four others were given the names of their discoverers, Marion and Crozet. On December 24, the ships anchored at the island discovered by Kerguelen, and Cook realized that he was dealing not with a single island but with an archipelago. A six-day halt was made in a convenient anchorage that was baptized Christmas Harbour. Though wood was lacking, they were at least able to put in an ample supply of fresh meat, for the area abounded in sea calves as well as penguins and sea birds; they also harvested some kerguelen cabbage, which was later to save the crew from scurvy.

On December 30, the navigators started east. A thick fog now surrounded the ships, and they blindly sailed some 300 leagues before dropping anchor on January 26, 1777, in Adventure Bay in Tasmania. There they provisioned themselves with water, wood, and fodder for the animals—several of which had already died—intended for the Tahitians. Furneaux had landed there in 1773 after the *Adventure* had been separated from the *Resolution,* but it was Cook's first visit. He therefore made careful notes of observations made by himself or his officers following their contacts with the natives. The latter, who showed no fear, "were quite naked & wore no ornaments . . . most of them had their faces anointed with red ointment and some had their faces painted with the same composition." The conditions under which they lived were wretched; they didn't even fish, and they seemed not to have any boats. Their habitations were only little shelters made of sticks.

The stopover in Adventure Bay lasted only four days. On January 30, Cook set sail for New Zealand, which he reached on February 11. The following day, the two ships anchored in Queen Charlotte Sound. They were immediately surrounded by boats, but their occupants, who had recognized the navigators, seemed fearful: they were convinced that Cook had returned to avenge the death of the men from the *Adventure.* This time the British remained on their guard and left New Zealand after February 23.

A month later, between the Friendly Islands and the Society Islands, Cook discovered new lands that were to be known as the Cook Islands. The first island was called Mangaia; on the second, Atiu, a group made up of Lieutenants Gore and Burney, the surgeon Anderson, and Omai went ashore and were received by inhabitants who held green branches in their hands and who greeted the British by rubbing noses with them. Gore reported that the islanders often had them undress so that they could examine their skins, and when they had done this to their satisfaction, a murmur of approbation could be heard. This scene—frequently repeated during the course of these first contacts between Europeans and Oceanics—had a significance that the seamen were unaware of: For these dark-skinned peoples, white skins indicated the ghosts of dead ancestors.

A third island visited by Gore and Anderson was found to be uninhabited, but when they reached Hervey Island—first discovered in 1773 and believed to be uninhabited—they were met by savage-looking islanders armed with long pikes. Omai was able to communicate with them and managed to overawe them by relating that the English in their own country had ships bigger than the island, and that there were weapons on them (he meant the English cannon) that were large enough to hold several people in their interiors; a single shot from them would be enough to pulverize the entire island. To explain the power of gunpowder, he took a small amount from the cartridges he had in his pocket and set it off by means of a brand he took from a fire over which dinner was cooking. The immediate explosion, the noisy echo, and the mixture of flame and smoke amazed the assembled islanders: they no longer doubted the terrible power of English weapons, and they believed everything Omai had told them.

Since unfavorable winds had delayed the ships, it was now too late to sail, as had been planned, to the northern coasts of America. This part of the expedition would have to be postponed until the following year. Before going to Tahiti, Cook therefore decided to head for the Friendly Islands, where he was sure to find an abundance of everything he needed. But before they got there, they came across a group of nine or ten small coral islands—the Palmerstons—and since scientists could not at all agree as to their origin, Cook studied their structure.

Celebrations on the Friendly Islands

On May 1, 1777, Cook was at Anamooka, in the very place he had landed three years earlier. Greeted with joy by the natives, he set up his observatories and was received by Tobou, the island chief. A few days later, on May 6, Chief Finau—who had immediately been informed of the arrival of the ships—came to the island. He was said to be the king of the entire archipelago, and all the natives bowed at his feet, whose soles they had to touch first with their palms and then with the backs of their hands. Finau so appreciated the society of the English, Cook noted, that he dined aboard ship almost every day.

Despite this hearty welcome, there was nevertheless a theft. The chiefs advised Cook to put the guilty party to death. Cook, of course, refused; but some means had to be found to punish him, and the natives seemed insensitive to the pain and the disgrace that accompanied corporal punishment. Charles Clerke finally found a treatment that seemed more or less effective: He put thieves into the hands of a barber, who shaved their heads—which not only made them look ridiculous in the eyes of their compatriots, but prevented them from renewing their thievery by making it possible for the English to keep them at a distance.

On May 18, Finau talked Cook into letting him take him to another island, Ha'apai, to the north of Anamooka. There a great feast had been prepared for him by Chief Earoupa. "I had not sat long before about a hundred people came laden with Yams, Bread fruit, Plantains, Cocoanuts and Sugar Cane." These items were laid in two piles on which were also placed pigs, chickens, and turtles. Then began a spectacle of unusual sportive combats. But what amazed Cook most was "a couple of lusty wenches, who without the least ceremony fell to boxing, and with as much art as the men." When the entertainments were over, the chief told Cook that the pyramid of provisions on the right was a present for Omai, and the one on the left, about two-thirds of the total, was for him. There was so much that it filled four boats, and Cook could not help but be struck by Finau's munificence, which "far exceeded any present I had ever before received from an Indian Prince." The celebration lasted several days

Ranina crab found from coasts of Japan to those of Africa. Original watercolor by William Ellis. (British Museum, Natural History, London. Photo by courtesy of the trustees, British Museum/Photeb.)

Natche *celebrating the majority of the king of Tongatapu, July 8, 1777. Engraving by R. Benard from a drawing by John Webber. (Archives Nationales, Fonds Marine, Paris. Photo by Michel Didier © Photeb.)*

and ended with a demonstration that quite impressed the Polynesians: a fireworks display, which amazed them beyond all measure and left the advantage with the English.

On June 10, the two ships dropped anchor at Tongatapu, whose king, Paulaho, in turn organized entertainments and overwhelmed Cook with presents. Then Paulaho invited Cook to go to another island, Mua, to attend a *natche*—a rite celebrating the majority of his son. It began by the preparation of *kava,* a sort of spice that the inhabitants grew to make into a brew. Cook was neither allowed to drink it nor to participate in the mysterious ceremony, which was considered as taking place under the eyes of a Supreme Being. He had to be content with observing it from a distance.

From July 12 to 17, he anchored before Eua, the last stop in the Friendly Islands. For three months, Cook and his men had been feted from island to island; for these happy natives, everything was a reason for celebration. Bayly, the astronomer, and Lieutenant King had been able to observe an eclipse of the sun thanks to their astronomical telescope, while Clerke made use of a reflecting telescope. Cook had devoted himself to a more detailed ethnographic investigation; for example, he had discovered the meaning of the missing fingers. It turned out that the operation was performed on those who suffered from a serious illness and thought themselves in danger of dying. They believed that the god would accept their little finger as a sacrifice sufficient to bring about the restoration of their health.

At the Friendly Islands, Cook heard the word *taboo* for the first time. On June 10, he recorded in his journal that during a walk he had come across a half dozen women eating together. He observed that two of them were being fed by the others. When he asked why, the women replied, "Tabumati." (*Mati* means "killed" in Polynesian.) Inquiring still further, Cook discovered that two months earlier one of the women had washed the corpse of a chief and that because of this she could touch no

food for five months. The other woman had performed the same office for the corpse of someone of lesser rank, and the same abstention was imposed on her, but for a shorter period. Before leaving the islands, Cook was able to discover that the word *taboo* had an extended meaning—for example, human sacrifices were called *tangata tabu.* The word *taboo* was also used to indicate something that it was forbidden to eat or to make use of. Cook was told that if a chief entered the home of one of his subjects, that house was henceforth *taboo* and could no longer be used by its owner. As a result, wherever the king went, he found houses intended solely for his use.

The passage in which Cook relates this information is a good example of the rigor with which he carried out his investigations. He never stopped asking questions until he understood the significance of customs, and he scrupulously set down the exact expressions of his informants, lest he distort what they said.

Omai's return

On August 13, 1777, the *Resolution* and the *Discovery* were back in Tahiti, where the welcome was just as warm. Once there, Cook felt it necessary to inform his men of his projects and tell them that the voyage would have to last a year longer than planned if they wanted to win the reward offered by Parliament to those of His Majesty's subjects who were the first to discover a link between the Atlantic and the Pacific in the northern hemisphere. On this occasion, Cook once again had the satisfaction of seeing that the crew did not even take time to examine his proposal but immediately and unanimously approved it without any objections.

Upon his arrival, Cook had learned that in the interval between his two voyages the Spanish had twice come to Tahiti. The situation on the island had changed once again. King Otoo had just declared war on the inhabitants of Eimeo Island

(Mooréa) and hoped that his English ally, who was invited to the council of war, would take part in the fighting. Cook refused, but, despite his repugnance, he attended the human sacrifice that served as a prelude to military operations and was designed to assure divine good will.

"The unhappy sufferer seemed to be a Middle aged man, and as we were told a *Tou tou* but I never understood he had done any crime so as to merit death; it is however certain that they make choice of such for these sacrifices, or else common low fellows who stroll about from place to place . . . Those who fall a sacrifice to this barbarous custom are never apprised of their fate till the Moment that puts an end to their existence. Whenever any of the Great chiefs thinks a human Sacrifice necessary on any particular occasion, he pitches upon the Victim, sends some of his trusty Servants who fall upon him and kill him; The King is then acquainted with it, whose presence at the Ceremony, as I was told, is absolutely necessary."

The rite was called *poure eri,* or chief's prayer, and the victim *tabu-tabu,* or consecrated man. Cook further observed that the *morai* where the sacrifice took place was undoubtedly a site for religious celebrations, sacrifices, and burials. The high chiefs of the entire island were buried there, and it was reserved for their families and some few of the island leaders. Only in size did it differ from other such sites. It was constructed principally of piled stones forming an oblong about 14 or 15 feet high, narrowing at the top. On each side was a square of flat land covered with pebbles under which the bones of the chiefs were buried. Cook was particularly struck by a pile of stones on which were set the skulls of human victims, who were dug up several months after their burial. Above these skulls were a great number of pieces of sacred wood, which sometimes served as the home of the divinity, and it was there too that, during the ceremony, the bundle that was thought to contain the god *Ouro* was placed, a feature which made it not unlike the altar of other peoples.

Despite the objective understanding that Cook strove for, he could not hide his indignation at a custom that caused the Tahitians no shame since it was pleasing to their god, who delighted in it; as they saw it, the god came to nourish himself on sacrifices and in return granted them what they prayed for. In any case, the custom was widespread in all the islands, and Cook had proof that human sacrifices took place in the Friendly Islands. Even in Tahiti, there was still a vestige of the cannibalism about which the Tahitians professed such horror. After the human sacrifice, the priest set aside the left eye of the victim, presented it to the king, and asked him to open his mouth; however, the eye was immediately withdrawn. This was called "eating the man." As for the crews of the two ships, they were horrified by these barbaric customs, and their feelings of friendship toward the Tahitians were considerably shaken.

Cook continued his tour of the archipelago, anchoring successively at Eimeo, from September 30 to October 10; at Huahine, from October 11 to November 2; at Uliatea, from November 3 to December 7; and, finally, at Bora-Bora, on December 8. After the livestock intended for the islanders was turned over to them, a last task remained: to resettle Omai at Huahine. They built him a small house

Cook attends a human sacrifice on Tahiti, September 1, 1777. Original watercolor by John Webber. (The British Library, London, Photo © The British Library/Photeb.)

surrounded by a garden, and on November 2 Omai took his leave of Cook with tears that he was unable to restrain.

At Uliatea, several sailors unable to resist the charms of these islands deserted, and several chiefs were taken as hostages to force the return of the guilty men. The *Resolution* and the *Discovery* then left the archipelago on December 8 and headed north.

The discovery of the Sandwich Islands

On December 25, they were on a small deserted island that they called Christmas Island, and, on December 30, Cook, Bayly, and King were able to observe an eclipse of the sun there. On January 20, the navigators reached land that was not marked on any map: it was Atoui (Kauai), the first of the Hawaiian Islands. Four others—he recorded their names as Wouahoo (Oahu), Eneeheeou (Niihau), Orrehoua (Lehau), and Otaoora (Tahura or Kaula)—the westernmost of the archipelago, were reconnoitered; but Cook did not see the group's largest island, Hawaii, which is farther east. It is almost certain that he was the true discoverer of the islands to which he gave the name of the Earl of Sandwich, First Lord of the Admiralty, even though a legend, probably of a later date, holds that they had been reconnoitered as early as 1555 by an Italian, Juan Gaetano, a companion of the Spaniard Ruy Lopez de Villalobos. Cook himself noted that, if the Spanish had discovered these islands in former days, they would no doubt have profited from their excellent position and used Atoui or one of the other islands as a stopping place for vessels that sailed annually from Acapulco to Manila.

The *Resolution* and the *Discovery* made only a twelve-day stopover, staying first at Atoui and then at Eneeheeou. The English were greatly astonished to find that the Hawaiians spoke a language quite similar to that of the Tahitians and were therefore Polynesians. Cook wondered, "How shall we account for this Nation spreading itself so far over this Vast ocean? We find them from New Zealand to the South, to these islands to the North and from Easter Island to the [New] Hebrides—an extent of 60° of latitude or twelve hundred leagues north and south and 83° of longitude or sixteen hundred and sixty leagues east and west, how much farther is not known . . ." However, what he had learned from this voyage and the previous one was that, if the race was not the most numerous on the Earth, it was certainly the one spread over the greatest area. He was therefore the first to pose a problem that preoccupies scientists to this very day: the migrations of the Polynesians.

Of medium height and sturdy build, the Hawaiians were remarkable neither for their beauty nor for their vivacity. An "open, candid, active people," they maintained "extremely friendly" relations with the navigators. As always, there were

Sandwich Islands woman. Engraving by C. L. Desrais and J. M. Mixelle illustrating the Encyclopédie des Voyages by J. Grasset de Saint-Sauveur, 1788. (Bibliothèque nationale, Paris. Photo © Bibl. nat./Arch. Photeb.)

Masked man of the Sandwich Islands. Engraving by R. Benard (1785) from a drawing by J. Webber. (Bibliothèque nationale, Paris. Photo © Bibl. nat./Arch. Photeb.)

several thefts, but what struck Cook in Hawaii was the attitude of the inhabitants toward the things they saw aboard ship. "I never saw Indians so much astonished at entering a ship before. . . . Their eyes were continually flying from object to object, the wildness of their looks and actions fully express'd their surprise and astonishment at the several new objects before them and evinced that they had never been aboard of a [European] ship before." Cook thought it only right that they felt deeply their own inferiority. Very likely, as became obvious a year later, the Hawaiians looked upon their invaders as supernatural beings. Despite this, the travelers were given to understand that they would have been eaten if they had been killed on the coast.

The Nootka Indians

Having left the Sandwich Islands on February 2, 1778, the *Resolution* and the *Discovery* discovered the northwest coast of Canada on March 6; hugging the shore, they made many observations and tried to draw up a map. Though bad weather kept them from sighting the Strait of Juan de Fuca between Vancouver Island and the continent, the two ships, on March 29, entered Nootka Sound, which separates the small island of the same name from the large island of Vancouver.

Immediately, thirty-two canoes came alongside the ships. One of these pirogues drew attention because it was painted to represent the eyes and beak of an enormous bird; the man who was in it was no less remarkable and seemed to be a chief. There were a great number of feathers on his head,

he was covered with unusual paint marks, and in his hand was a sculpted wooden bird the size of a pigeon, which he shook to make a rattling sound while he harangued the English in a loud voice accompanied by expressive gestures.

It was soon obvious that the Nootka Indians were also cannibals, for they offered the newcomers human skulls and hands which were not completely bare of the flesh they had eaten. "Their face is rather broad and flat, with highish Cheek bones and plump cheeks. Their mouth is little and round, the nose neither flat nor prominent; their eyes are black, little and devoid of sparkling fire." They were usually beardless. Even though the bodies of the women were colored with red paint, they often made use of a black, bright red, or white coating which, when put over their faces gave them a terrifying and repulsive aspect.

More surprising still were the ceremonial clothes worn by the Indians; the hides of bears or wolves trimmed with long fringes of fur or of animal hair woven into various designs. On these occasions, the most common head covering was made of several wicker strands or bands of bark rolled around the head and decorated with various kinds of large feathers. Their faces were painted with a variety of colors that were not the same on top as on bottom, with the brush strokes simulating recent gashes; alternately, careful and varied designs that gave the impression of relief work were traced on their grease-smeared faces. Thus accoutered, the natives presented a really savage and grotesque appearance, which became even more so when they raised what struck Cook as monstrous ornaments. These consisted of an infinite variety of wooden full or half masks that were placed over the face or on the forehead and on the top of the head. Some of these looked like human faces garnished with hair, beards, and eyebrows; others were like birds' heads, particularly eagles, and many were like the heads of land or sea animals. In general, these figures were larger than life; they were painted and often strewn with bits of foliaceous mica that made them sparkle and that increased the impression of enormous deformity. Not content with these results, the Indians would attach to various places on their heads similarly painted large pieces of sculpted wood that seemed like the prows of canoes; they stuck out like protruberances. The Indians were so fond of these disguises that Cook saw one of them use as a mask an iron kettle he had been given.

Comparable to these masks were the large sculpted figures to be found in the houses, in which an indescribable stench and disorder reigned because the natives, who lived mostly on fish—principally sardines—would gut them on the floors. The sculptures were human faces cut into the trunks of trees 4 or 5 feet high and erected either singly or in pairs in the highest part of the room; arms and hands were cut into the sides and painted various colors, so that the effect was truly monstrous. These figures were called *klumma* (totems). "This made some of our gentlemen think they were their gods, but I

am not altogether of that opinion, at least if they were they hild them very cheap, for with small matters of iron or brass, I could have purchased all the gods of the place, for I did not see one that was not offered me, and two or three of the very smallest sort I got."

After the stopover at Nootka, the *Resolution* and the *Discovery* continued north along the Alaskan coast, a region frequented by many Russian trappers who were collecting furs. From May 12 to 18, the two ships reconnoitered Prince William Sound. The Indians there were slightly different from those of Nootka, their physiognomies generally suggesting to Cook considerably more vivacity, candor, and good nature. When it rained, these Indians would cover their tunics with a second item of clothing—this one waterproof—that was skillfully made of the intestines of a whale or some other large animal, and so ingeniously prepared that it looked to Cook like the work of European goldbeaters.

But the most bizarre and disagreeable manner of embellishing themselves, adopted by some of both sexes, was to split the lower lip, cutting it across the width of the mouth a little below the fleshy part. Done even to children at the breast, the cut was often more than 2 inches long. "It was so large as to admit the tongue, which I have seen them thrust through." This is evidently what happened the first time one of Cook's men saw a native with this incision. He called out in astonishment that he had seen a man with two mouths, and the fact is that one might easily have believed it. The natives would fix in this false mouth a flat and narrow ornament carved into what seemed like little teeth that descended toward the thicker part of the lip; a projection sustained these teeth at each end, and all that could be seen between the lips of the slit was the toothed part.

Sailing in a fog of ever-increasing density, the two ships followed the coast and found themselves

Nootka wooden mask representing a bird's head. (British Museum, Natural History, London. Photo by courtesy of the trustees, British Museum/Photeb.)

69

descending southeast; it was then that Cook noticed that the continent extended much farther to the west than the maps indicated. This made the existence of a passage even more improbable, since the distance between the northwest coast and Hudson Bay or Baffin Bay was much greater than had been believed. Cook then sailed first along the Alaskan peninsula, which did indeed thrust toward the south, and then along the string of Aleutian Islands that extended toward the west. The sea abounded in fish, and the sailors caught salmon and plaice; one weighed 254 pounds.

After a stopover (June 27–July 2) in one of these islands, Unalaska, they entered the sea, and then the Bering Strait. There, on a clear day, they could see simultaneously the shores of Asia and of America. On August 3, the last honors were paid to the *Resolution* surgeon, William Anderson, dead of the tuberculosis that had been undermining his health for more than twelve months. The draftsman Ellis was henceforth entrusted with the natural history research. From that point of view, however, Cook's third voyage was much less fruitful than the two others, which had benefited from the presence of great scientists on board.

Nevertheless, Anderson should be credited with some interesting observations—among others, those concerning the penguin—and with the discovery of new species of birds in Alaska, the Aleutians, and particularly the Sandwich Islands, whose special bird population, then intact but soon to decline seriously, he was the first to describe. Thanks to Anderson, ornithologists gained knowledge of an entire family of birds native to this archipelago—the drepanididae, which succumbed, one after the other, to the environmental changes following the arrival of the white man in these islands.

Shortly thereafter, Cook stopped at the northern end of the Asiatic coast. The Chukchi, the Siberian population inhabiting this peninsula, were observed with a great deal of interest. They seemed fearful and suspicious, and it was difficult to get them to trade. Far from resembling the American Indians, they had long faces and were well built and robust. During the summer, they lived in primitive huts covered with the skins of sea animals, but, in winter, they withdrew to half-buried habitations.

The passage does not exist

On August 18, 1778, the *Resolution* reached 70° 44' of latitude, the northernmost point attained by Captain Cook. The weather was gloomy and visibility very bad. During a clear interval, a bright light was glimpsed, similar to what the reflection of ice might produce. By midday, surrounded by floating blocks of ice, the ship found herself confronting a high translucid wall that seemed higher still to the north. If there was a passage between the two oceans, for the moment at least, it was impassable.

Since the *Resolution* was taking on water dangerously, Cook decided not to linger in the region but to go directly south and return to the Sandwich Islands. They could winter there and return the following year to look for the northwest passage, which they might have approached too late in the year. Eager not to let any opportunity slip, Cook followed the Alaskan coast south, discovered Norton Sound, and visited the Aleutians, where he met the Russians who were involved in fur trading. Fi-

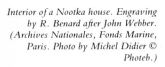

Interior of a Nootka house. Engraving by R. Benard after John Webber. (Archives Nationales, Fonds Marine, Paris. Photo by Michel Didier © Photeb.)

nally, on October 26, 1778, the two ships got under way for the Sandwich Islands.

Upon his arrival, the captain realized that he had incompletely reconnoitered the archipelago several months earlier. To the south he discovered two new islands, Maui, and then the largest of all, Hawaii. He spent several days sailing around the latter, and, on January 17, he anchored on the western coast off Karakakooa (Kealakekua) Bay, which Bligh had gone to reconnoiter the day before. Remaining out to sea, the *Resolution* and the *Discovery* were surrounded by some one thousand pirogues filled with natives bringing pigs and other island products.

Having come without arms, the Hawaiians seemed disposed to be most friendly. As Cook saw it, they were acting under the impulse of curiosity and the desire to trade. He therefore let them come on board. There were so many of them that it was expected some would inevitably take advantage of the disorder to steal—which is what happened. Cook thought it best to profit from the occasion to demonstrate the use of firearms to the islanders, but the Hawaiians seemed more surprised than frightened. When the two ships entered the bay, crowds of Hawaiians came running from everywhere. Here Captain Cook's manuscript ends. The official journal of the end of the voyage was written by James King, then second lieutenant aboard the *Resolution;* but events soon took so dramatic and unforeseen a turn that several members of the crew, including a simple sailor, immediately set down what they had seen.

The fervent homage of an entire nation

They all testified to the delirious native enthusiasm of which Cook was the special focus. A priest of high rank, Koah, soon appeared on the *Resolution*. "Being led into the cabin," King records, "he approached Captain Cook with great veneration, and threw over his shoulders a piece of red cloth, which he had brought along with him. Then stepping a few paces back, he made an offering of a small pig, which he held in his hand, whilst he pronounced a discourse that lasted for a considerable time. This ceremony . . . appeared to us, from many circumstances, to be a sort of religious adoration. . . . In the evening, Captain Cook, attended by Mr. Bayly and myself, accompanied him on shore. We landed at the beach, and were received by four men, who carried wands tipt with dog's hair, and marched before us, pronouncing with a loud voice a short sentence, in which we could only distinguish the word *Orono*. The crowd, which had been collected on the shore, retired at our approach; and not a person was to be seen . . ."

Without having quite understood what was happening to him, the son of the Marton-in-Cleveland farmer had become a god. He was *taboo,* and, on pain of death, one had to prostrate oneself be-

fore him with lowered eyes. As soon as the leading chief of the archipelago, King Terreeoboo, arrived on January 25, 1779, the natives proceeded to the enthronement of Orono (sometimes called Lorono or Lono), the god of peace and prosperity.

Neither Cook nor any of his men could understand the exact significance of this apotheosis. Later, historians were to doubt that the Hawaiians had really taken Cook for a god, and only a relatively recent study of Polynesian institutions makes it possible for us to understand just what happened in 1779. The arrival of these two enormous and powerful ships—the first of their kind to be seen by the Hawaiians—loaded with unheard-of riches and incomprehensible objects, manned by men who were white from head to foot, struck them as the sudden appearance of something from another world. The bay in which Cook had landed was

Vestiaria coccinea male and female, species native to the Hawaiian Islands. Original watercolor by William Ellis. (British Museum, Natural History, London. Photo © by courtesy of the trustees, British Museum/Photeb.)

Ku-Kaili-Moku, god of war of the Sandwich Islands. This amazing piece was probably brought back by the crew of the Resolution *in 1780. (Musée de l'Homme, Paris. Photo by D. Destable © coll. Musée de l'Homme/Photeb.)*

called "the path of the god" who was thought to have sprung from it. There could be no doubt—he had come back among men.

As it happened, less then a month after this triumphal arrival, Cook was killed. What had occurred in the interval? On February 4, after solemn farewells, the *Resolution* and the *Discovery* left Karakakooa Bay, but once out to sea they were hit by a storm in which the foremast was seriously damaged. On the seventh, the ships returned.

"Upon coming to anchor," wrote King, "we were surprised to find . . . a solitary bay . . . Terreeoboo was absent, and had left the bay under the *taboo.*" Incidents between Cook's men and the natives, trivial to start with, multiplied and grew more serious. Cook's men started to carry their weapons, and both sides were in fear of each other. It was to lead to disaster. Following a confrontation, one of the chiefs seemed upset and asked if Lorono would kill him. He had to be reassured. Cook himself was uneasy. Until then, he had behaved with his usual magnanimity, making a great effort to understand; but on the evening of February 13, exasperated, he said to King: "I am afraid that these people will oblige me to use some violent measures; for they must not be left to imagine that they have gained an advantage over us."

The tragedy

At dawn on February 14, it was noticed that a cutter moored to a buoy had been stolen. Cook took immediate action. He decided to use a means that had previously been successful: to keep the leading chief on board until the stolen object had been returned. Initially, the operation proceeded without difficulty. Cook was received at the village with the usual marks of respect. The inhabitants prostrated themselves before him and brought little pigs as offerings. As for old King Terreeoboo, he immediately agreed to follow Cook, accompanied by his two sons. The atmosphere was nevertheless tense. There were crowds everywhere, and some believed that their king was going to be mistreated. To prevent any escape, armed English longboats barred the bay. The little troop was advancing toward the longboat and the pinnace brought by Cook when the latter, "finding that the alarm had spread too generally, and that it was vain to think any longer of getting him [the king] off without bloodshed, at last gave up the point . . .

"Though the enterprize, which had carried Captain Cook on shore, had now failed, and was abandoned, yet his person did not appear to have been in the least danger, till an accident happened, which gave a fatal turn to the affair. The boats which had been stationed across the bay, having fired at some canoes that were attempting to get out, unfortunately had killed a Chief of the first rank. The news of his death arrived at the village where Captain Cook was, just as he had left the king, and was walking slowly toward the shore. The ferment it

occasioned was very conspicuous; the women and children were immediately sent off; and the men put on their war-mats, and armed themselves with spears and stones. One of the natives, having in his hands a stone, and a long iron spike (which they call a *pahooa*) came up to the captain, flourishing his weapon, by way of defiance. . . . The Captain desired him to desist; but the man persisting in his insolence, he was at length provoked to fire a load of small-shot. The man having his mat on, which the shots were not able to penetrate, this had no other effect than to irritate and encourage them. Several stones were thrown at the marines; and one of the *Erees* [chiefs] attempted to stab Mr. Phillips with his *pahooa;* but failed in the attempt and received from him a blow with the butt end of his musket. Captain Cook now fired his second barrel, loaded with ball, and killed one of the foremost of the natives. A general attack with stones immediately followed, which was answered by a discharge of musketry from the marines, and the people in the boats. The islanders, contrary to the expectations of everyone, stood the fire with great firmness; and before the marines had time to reload, they broke in upon them with dreadful shouts and yells. What followed was a scene of the utmost horror and confusion.

"Four of the marines were cut off amongst the rocks in their retreat, and fell a sacrifice to the fury of the enemy; three more were dangerously wounded; and the Lieutenant, who had received a stab between the shoulders with a *pahooa,* having fortunately reserved his fire, shot the man who had wounded him just as he was going to repeat his blow. Our unfortunate Commander, the last time he was seen distinctly, was standing at the water's edge, and calling out to the boats to cease firing, and to pull in. If it be true, as some of those who were present have imagined, that the marines and boat-men had fired without his orders, and that he was desirous of preventing any further bloodshed, it is not improbable that his humanity, on this occasion, proved fatal to him. For it was remarked that whilst he faced the natives, none of them had offered him any violence, but that having turned about, to give his orders to the boats, he was stabbed in the back, and fell with his face into the water. On seeing him fall, the islanders set up a great shout, and his body was immediately dragged on shore, and surrounded by the enemy, who snatching the dagger out of each other's hands, shewed a savage eagerness to have a share in his destruction."

On board they could not believe that Cook had been killed. James Trevenan, midshipman on the *Resolution,* probably reflected the general feeling when he wrote that because he and others were so accustomed to see in Cook their good genius, their trustworthy leader, and a sort of superior being, he could not bring himself to believe—did not dare believe—that Cook could have fallen into the hands of those Indians over whose spirit and body he had exercised a never-disputed domination. Paradoxically, the Hawaiians themselves continued to believe Cook a god—and therefore immortal.

Before the scene of the tragedy could be left, there was a mission to be fulfilled: to see to the return of Cook's body. This took a long time and was not achieved without difficulty. It was known that he had been hacked to pieces and carried inland, and the English even wondered if he had been eaten. Little by little, in small packages carried in procession by the priests and the chiefs eager to reestablish peace, Cook's bones were returned. "Nothing now remained, but to perform the last offices to our great and unfortunate commander. Eappo [a chief] was dismissed with orders to *taboo* all the bay; and, in the afternoon, the bones having been put into a coffin, and the service read over them, they were committed to the deep with the usual military honours."

Thirty years later, some of Cook's bones that had not been returned were still the object of religious worship on the island. Wrapped in a woven basket, they were solemnly carried by the priests of Lorono during the annual Makahiki rite of fertility and confirmation of the reigning chief. In 1820, with the arrival of the first American missionaries, the Makahiki festival was forbidden; at the same time, all taboos were abolished, and parts of the temples of the former religion destroyed. In 1825, Lord Byron, cousin of the poet and commander of the *Blonde*, anchored in Karakakooa Bay. The English went through a sort of ceremony in which they gathered fragments of the rock near which the crime had been committed. In 1846, the rock had completely disappeared, taken as relics by the European crews who came to pray on the site. For the natives Hawaii still remained the island of Lorono, the island of the god Cook.

This prodigious man had in a different way become immortal in his own country. Initially, it was very difficult to admit that the invincible man had finally succumbed; however, his death in action, in the midst of the magnificent tropics, on an island he had just discovered—a death that came when he had almost completed his task—somehow seemed worthy of him. Painters and poets celebrated the glories of the dead man. Engravings showed Cook raised to Heaven by Genius and Fame, or by Neptune himself. In London, there was a pantomime called *Omai, or A Trip Around the World,* and, in Paris, *La mort du capitaine Cook* was so successful that it was later given in London.

A sad return

On February 22, 1779, two days after Cook's remains had been consigned to the sea, the *Resolution* and the *Discovery* finally left their Hawaiian anchorage. The leader of the expedition was henceforth Charles Clerke, who took command of the *Resolution,* while John Gore, who had been first lieutenant aboard the same ship, replaced Clerke on the *Discovery*. The ships headed for Kamchatka. On April 29, they entered the Russian port of Petro-

pavlovsk, which they found considerably inferior to the worst English fishing village, but whose inhabitants were extremely hospitable. From there, a detachment was sent to the governor of the province who resided in Bol'sheretsk. He was soon to return to St. Petersburg and agreed to take the news of Cook's death back to Europe.

The expedition then went north in order to see if it would be possible to reach the Northwest Passage earlier in the season. Clerke traversed the Bering Strait at the end of June and then went northeast along the coast until Icy Cape, but he could not get through, anymore than Cook had been able to the year before. In his log, he recorded that if Cook had still been alive, he would have recognized the impossibility of a northeast or northwest passage between the Pacific and the Atlantic. As for King, he wrote: "We were all heartily sick of a navigation full of danger, and in which the utmost perseverance had not been repaid with the smallest probability of success."

His health undermined by tuberculosis, Clerke died at sea on August 22, 1779. Lieutenant Gore took over the expedition on the *Resolution,* and King became the commander of the *Discovery*. They had to stop at Petropavlovsk to repair the damage done to the ships by floating blocks of ice. The ships then went down the coast of Japan without stopping and reached Macao in December 1779. Only then was it learned that Great Britain was at war not only with its North American colonies, which had declared their independence, but with France and Spain as well.

The death of Cook. Painting by J. Zoffany done according to details supplied by the survivors. (National Maritime Museum, London. Photo © by the museum/Photeb.)

Feathered helmet brought back by the crew of the Resolution *in 1780 and shown in the painting by Zoffany. (British Museum, Natural History, London. Photo by courtesy of the trustees, British Museum/Photeb.)*

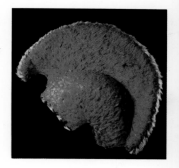

Finally, on January 12, 1780, they set sail for Great Britain by the fastest route. Gore stopped only on the coast of Cochin China, traversed Sunda Strait, and arrived in Cape Town on April 13. The expedition dropped anchor on August 22 at Stromness on the British coast. It had lasted four years and two months, without the two ships ever losing sight of each other. During the course of the voyage, King wrote, the *Resolution* lost only five men to sickness, and three of them had been in a precarious state of health when they left England. The *Discovery* had not lost a man. The strict observance of the rules established by Captain Cook could justly be considered the principal reason—along with the protection of Divine Providence—for this brilliant success.

The harbor of Petropavlovsk in Kamchatka. Engraving by R. Benard, after John Webber. (Archives Nationales, Fonds Marine, Paris. Photo by Michel Didier © Photeb.)

M. de La Pérouse:
his voyage,
his disappearance,
and the
search for him,
1785-1794

Voyage of La Pérouse, 1785–1788

The French were able to read the story of Cook's first voyage as early as 1772. They awaited impatiently the account of the second, which appeared in 1778, and even more feverishly that of the third, which told of Cook's death and was rushed off the presses in 1782. One of the most enthusiastic readers was Louis XVI, and, beginning with the king, every Frenchman felt that his country ought to try to equal these exploits.

After Bougainville's semi-success, two expeditions had set sail for the Pacific. The first, commanded by a captain of the moribund French India Company, Jean François Marie de Surville, left from India on the *Saint-Jean-Baptiste* in order to seek a "very rich island," the existence of which was presumed from badly interpreted data. Nevertheless, in October 1769, Surville did discover an island, which he baptized Terre des Arsacids; it belonged, however, to the Solomon Archipelago reconnoitered by Mendaña in 1568. He then went to New Zealand, without running into Cook, who was in the area. From all points of view, this voyage was catastrophic. Of the 173 men who set out, seventy-nine died—almost all of scurvy—and there were twenty-eight deserters.

In October 1771, Marion du Fresne left the Ile de France on the storeship *Mascarin,* accompanied by the *Marquis de Castries,* in order to bring Bougainville's Ahu-Toru back to his native island. The Tahitian having died at Madagascar, du Fresne decided to continue his voyage. He discovered the Marion and Crozet Islands, touched Tasmania, and then anchored in the Bay of Islands in New Zealand, where he was massacred by the Maoris on June 12, 1772. When the two ships returned to the Ile de France in April and May 1773, they had lost a large part of their crews to scurvy, and this voyage had no useful results either.

These expeditions were undertakings based on private initiative, but this was not true of the two led by Yves Joseph de Kerguelen de Trémarec. Sailing from the Ile de France with the *Fortune* and the *Gros-Ventre,* this captain found in the south of the Indian Ocean an island he was able to reconnoiter only imprecisely, and which he called Austral France. When he returned, he claimed to have finally discovered the "Southern Continent" on which one could "form establishments situated so as to command the routes to Asia and America."

A second expedition was fitted out with the vessel *Rolland* and the frigate *Oiseau,* manned by seven hundred officers and men. It left on March 26, 1773, and ended disastrously. Kerguelen had been unaware that "Austral France" was only an island—as Cook was to discover—and that it was all but useless. He was brought to trial and sentenced to twenty years in prison, but he was released four years later in 1778. Fitted out at great cost, Kerguelen's second voyage was to have been the French reply to Cook's successes. The failure of this navigator, who was not only an uninspired braggart but ultimately dishonest, was felt all the more strongly.

In 1783, the Treaty of Versailles, which recognized American independence, also allowed France to compensate in some measure for the territorial losses she had suffered twenty years earlier following the Treaty of Paris. No attempt was made to retake Canada or to increase French trading posts in India, but France did recover Louisiana, Senegal, and several islands in the Antilles. Above all, on the high seas she was henceforth able to rival Great Britain, which had been weakened by the war.

Acting on the king's orders, Claret de Fleurieu, a renowned scientist and the Director General of Ports and Arsenals, immediately outlined a plan for a long expedition. To lead it, Fleurieu recommended an energetic, popular, and unpretentious seaman: Jean-François Galaup de La Pérouse. Having joined the navy when he was fifteen, the latter had achieved fame when, in August 1782, he led the

Sceptre, the Astrée, and the Engageante in a bold raid against Hudson Bay posts that the English had considered inaccessible. Following this exploit, La Pérouse had finally obtained his family's consent to his marriage to Louise-Eléonore Broudou, a young Ile de France Creole of modest origins whom he had wished to marry for the past seven years; he was then forty-two.

La Pérouse's Ships and Crews

Portrait of Jean-François de Galaup, Comte de La Pérouse, attributed to J.-B. Greuze. (Musée Toulouse-Lautrec, Albi. Photo © the museum/Photeb.)

La *BOUSSOLE:* 500-ton storeship; left Brest, 8/1/1785; crew: 114 officers and men.

Commander: F. de Galaup, comte de La Pérouse, captain, made squadron chief, 11/2/1786.

Lieutenants: d'Escures, died at Port des Français, 7/13/1786; de Clonard, made captain, 11/2/1786.

Ensigns: Boutin, made lieutenant commander, 5/1/1786, made major, 4/14/1787; de Pierrevert, died in Port des Français, 7/13/1786; Colinet, frigate lieutenant, made lieutentant commander 5/1/1786.

Gardes de la marine: Mel de Saint-Céran, put ashore sick in Manila, 4/16/1787; de Montarnal, died at Port des Français, 7/13/1786; de Roux d'Arbaud, *volontaire,* made lieutenant commander, 4/14/1786; Frédéric Broudou, *volontaire,* made frigate lieutenant, 8/1/1786.

First pilot: Lemaître, died in Port des Français, 7/13/1786.

Surgeon: Rollin.

Chief Engineer: Monneron, captain in the Engineers.

Surveyor: Bernizet, assistant to Monneron.

Astronomer: J. Lepaute d'Agelet.

Physicist, mineralogist, and meteorologist: Lamanon, died in Manua Islands, 12/11/1787.

Chaplain, physicist, and mineralogist: Abbé Mongès.

Draftsman of figures and landscapes: Duché de Vancy.

Draftsman for botany: Prévost the younger.

Gardener-botanist: Jean Nicolas Collignon.

L'*ASTROLABE:* 500-ton storeship; left from Brest, 8/1/1785.

Commander: P. A. Fleuriot de Langle, captain, died at Manua Islands, 12/11/1787.

Lieutenant: de Monti, made captain.

Ensigns: de Vaujuas, made lieutenant commander; Daigremont, died in Manila, March 1787; La Borde Marchainville, supernumerary ensign, died in Port des Français, 7/13/1786; Blondela, frigate lieutenant and draftsman.

Gardes de la marine: La Borde de Boutervilliers, made lieutenant commander, 5/1/1786, died at Port des Français, 7/13/1786; Law de Lauriston, made lieutenant commander, 5/1/1786; Raxi de Flassan, supernumerary, made lieutenant commander, 5/1/1786, died in Port des Français, 7/13/1786.

Surgeon: Lavaux.

Assistant surgeon: Guillou.

Interpreter: Barthélemy de Lesseps, disembarked at Petropavlovsk, September 1787.

Chaplain: Father Receveur, naturalist, "responsible for gastropods," died in Port Jackson.

Botanist: La Martinière.

Naturalist: Dufresne, disembarked at Macao, January 1787.

Astronomer: Louis Monge, put ashore sick in Tenerife, 7/29/1785.

Draftsman for botany: Prévost, *oncle.*

The *Boussole* and the *Astrolabe*, 1785–1788

The vessels turned over to La Pérouse were two approximately 500-ton storeships, nailed and double-keeled—the *Portefaix* and the *Autruche*—which were reclassified as frigates and renamed the *Boussole* and the *Astrolabe*. La Pérouse entrusted the command of the latter to his friend Fleuriot de Langle, who had commanded the *Astrée* in the 1782 raid and had the following year been named president of the Royal Naval Academy. An Academy of Sciences memorandum listed some points that it judged "most important for the voyage undertaken"; these dealt with geometry, astronomy, physics, chemistry, mineralogy, anatomy, zoology, and botany. The team recruited to carry out this extensive program included a member and correspondent of the Academy of Sciences; the astronomer Lepaute d'Agelet and the geologist Lamanon; a mathematics professor from the Ecole Militaire, Louis Monge; several naturalists, and a gardener recommended by Buffon. Even the two chaplains—Father Receveur, a Franciscan friar, and Abbé Mongès, a canon at Sainte-Geneviève—were scientists. In addition, there were three draftsmen, two of whom were skilled in natural history; and an interpreter, Barthélemy de Lesseps, the French vice consul at Kronstadt. Chief Engineer Monneron, who had also taken part in the Hudson Bay escapade, was sent to London, where he met Sir Joseph Banks, who gave him two dip needles previously used by Cook.

Aboard the ships were highly perfected instruments that formed a veritable "portable observatory"; in addition, the holds were crammed with items thought likely to appeal to "natives." The selection ranged from two thousand hatchets and two thousand combs, to a million assorted pins and fifty-two plumed dragoons' helmets. The king himself had written personal instructions: "The sieur de La Pérouse, on all occasions, will treat the different peoples visited during the course of his voyage with much gentleness and humanity. He will zealously and interestedly employ all means capable of improving their condition by procuring for their countries useful European vegetables, fruits, and trees, which he will teach them to plant and cultivate . . ."

The expedition was also to concern itself with France's political and commercial interests. The loss of "New France" had put most of the fur-trading posts into the hands of the English Hudson's Bay Company, but the independent trappers had set up a new company, called the North West Company, that was partly sponsored by French capital. On this same northwest coast of America, La Pérouse was to examine the extent and condition of the Spanish possessions, and when he reached the Aleutians, he was to look into the Russian establishments and their maritime relations with the mother country. It was obviously a large order—too large, La Pérouse thought.

The *Boussole* and the *Astrolabe* left Brest on August 1, 1785, and made the usual stops at Madeira, Tenerife, and Santa Caterina Island in Brazil. On April 1, 1786, they reached Cape Horn, whose unusually calm waters led La Pérouse to conclude that their bad reputation had been exaggerated. On February 23, the ships entered the roads of Talcahuano near the Chilean city of Concepción, where the navigators were feted by the Spanish governor,

Chilean vine called quilboqui *by the inhabitants. Original watercolor by Prévost, oncle, draftsman on the* Astrolabe. *(Service historique de la Marine, Vincennes. Photo by Michel Didier © Photeb.)*

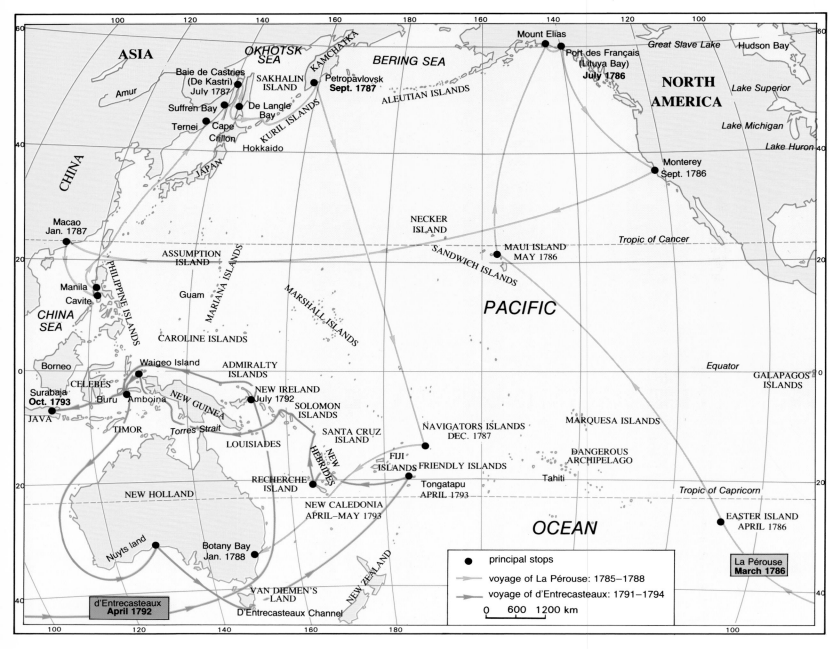

Voyage, disappearance, and search for M. de La Pérouse. Voyage of La Pérouse, 1785–1788. Voyage of d'Entrecasteaux, 1791–1794.

Ambrosio O'Higgins—whose son, Bernardo, was twenty-five years later to become the liberator of Chile.

Following his instructions, La Pérouse began his investigation by describing the Spanish administration in Chile. Noting that its power hardly extended beyond the principal cities, the rest of the country being inhabited by indomitable Indians, he emphasized the fact that the Spanish colonial system prevented all economic and commercial development, and also encouraged idleness, credulity, and superstition. This testimony confirmed the severe judgments of Abbé Raynal's *Histoire philosophique et politique des Deux Indes* (Philosophic and Political History of the Two Indies), the third edition of which (1781) La Pérouse had read; it included an accusatory but talented contribution by Diderot.

At Easter Island, where La Pérouse spent only a few hours on April 9, he was given a better reception than Cook had received, probably because he brought goats, lambs, and pigs. The natives who came to greet the navigators "numbered at least 800, and among them there were 150 women (they had been hidden at the time of Cook's stay). The features of many of these women were agreeable; they offered their favors to all those willing to make them some present. The natives encouraged us to accept, and several of them gave a demonstration of the pleasures these women could provide; they were not separated from the spectators by more than a simple covering of local cloth . . ." However, all these "provocations" were simply meant to distract the attention of the sailors, who could then be more easily robbed.

La Pérouse was next supposed to set sail for Tahiti, but summer was approaching, and it was the best season in which to explore the northwest coast of America. He therefore decided to turn north. Only one day (May 29) was spent at Maui, one of the Sandwich Islands.

"The most terrible misfortune . . ."

On June 23, the fog that had hindered navigation lifted, and the French could see "the masses of snow covering" Mount St. Elias. They had reached the coast of Alaska, where, after some investigation, they found a safe anchorage in a deep channel. There, on a little island, they were able to set up a camp sheltered from the Indians. La Pérouse named this site Port des Français—present-day Lituya Bay.

A horde of savages soon put in an appearance. They were "barbarous and coarse . . . always quarreling among themselves, indifferent to their children, true tyrants over their women . . . as terrible as the country they inhabited." Come to trade fish and furs for iron, they "spent their nights looking for a favorable moment to rob us." A local chief went so far as to offer to sell the French the island on which they were camped, and though La Pérouse had no illusions about the value of the transaction, he accepted the offer. Exploring the arm of the sea, he hoped to find some kind of passage, but the fiords were closed by glaciers and sheer rock faces, and "in a few hours we returned on board, having completed our trip into the interior of America."

On July 13, the first tragedy of the voyage took place. The barge and two longboats went to take soundings in the mouth of the bay; the longboats got too close to the current of the channel—turbulent with the tide—and were thrown against the reefs. It was impossible to come to their aid, and six officers and fifteen sailors died. After remaining in the area for several days in the hope that the men might be cast up on the shore, the French weighed anchor on July 30.

On September 14, the *Boussole* and the *Astrolabe* entered Monterey Bay. La Pérouse was supposed to examine Spain's California settlements, about which practically nothing was known. Since 1770, they had been considerably developed thanks to the missions of the Franciscans—"spiritually and temporally superior" to the Indians. The latter were subjected to "seven hours of work a day, two hours of prayer and four or five hours on Sundays and holidays. . . . Corporal punishments were inflicted on Indians of both sexes who missed exercises of piety. . . . From the moment a neophyte was baptized, it was as though he had pronounced eternal vows; if he fled back to his parents . . . he was thrice summoned to return; if he refused, the missionaries called on the authority of the governor, who sent soldiers to tear him from the bosom of his family and return him to the missions, where he was sentenced to a quantity of lashes . . ."

The naturalists, who had carefully examined the Alaskan flora and fauna, made interesting collections in Monterey. Seeds of Monterey pine were shipped back to the Museum of Natural History by Jean Nicolas Collignon. In addition, several species of birds were discovered, including the beautiful California partridge.

Blackbird from Port des Français (Lituya Bay). Original drawing by J. R. Prévost the younger, draftsman on the Boussole. (Service historique de la Marine, Vincennes. Photo by Michel Didier © Photeb.)

On September 24, the ships left to cross the Pacific. There they discovered a tiny rocky islet that they called Necker Island, and they touched on Asuncion in the Marianas. On January 2, 1787, the navigators reached Macao, where they sold the furs acquired in Port des Français and divided the profits among the crews. But the finest skins were sent to France for the queen, taken there by Dufresne, the *Astrolabe* naturalist, who also carried with him the logs and maps that had been made up to that time. In March, at Cavite in Manila Bay, the *Castries* sent by Bruni d'Entrecasteaux, then commanding the French India Naval Station, brought crew reinforcements to compensate for the losses suffered. La Pérouse and his companions left to visit the environs of Manila and were enchanted. The naturalists procured some Luzon Bleeding Hearts, beautiful doves native to the Philippines.

Leaving Manila on Easter Monday, 1787, La Pérouse undertook the exploration of the sea bounding the coasts of Northern Asia, "where no European ship had penetrated until we came." Sailing between Formosa and the Ryukyus, he found Quelquepart Island (Cheju), situated at the strait separating Korea from Japan and known only from the wreck there of a Dutch ship in 1635. The coasts were shown only on a map made by French Jesuits who lived in China but had never visited them. La Pérouse was the first navigator to verify the data. However, these lands were "inhabited by peoples savage to foreigners, and we did not think of visiting them. On the other hand, we knew that the Tartars were very hospitable. . . . We were burning with impatience to visit this land. . . . It was the only portion of the globe that had escaped the attention of the indefatigable Captain Cook."

Moving north, the frigates anchored in the Baie de Ternay (Ternei) on June 27 and in Suffren Bay on July 4, but they found no one. Consequently, La Pérouse dropped anchor at Sakhalin Island, in a

California partridge, male and female. Watercolor by J. R. Prévost the younger. (Service historique de la Marine, Vincennes. Photo by Michel Didier © Photeb.)

bay that was given Fleuriot de Langle's name. There the natives put in an appearance. "They beached their little boats on the sand and came to sit among our sailors with an air of assurance that spoke in their favor. . . . We finally managed to make them understand that we wanted them to draw their country and that of the Manchus. Then one of the old men got up and with the end of his pipe traced the Tartary coast, to the west, running more or less from north to south. On the east, opposite, and in the same direction he drew his island [Sakhalin]. . . . To the south of this island he had drawn another [Yeso, present-day Hokkaido], leaving room for a strait indicating that there was a route for our ships." Sailing to the west of Sakhalin in the channel that separated that island from the Tartary coast, the frigates would be able to emerge on the north in the Okhotsk Sea. But the native informants had underestimated the draft of the ships, and this was to lead to trouble for La Pérouse.

The French were enchanted by this friendly people. "Since leaving France, we had not encountered others who so excited our interest and admiration. . . . It went against our preconceived ideas to find among a hunting and fishing people, who neither cultivated the earth nor raised domestic animals, manners which were in general more gentle and grave—and who perhaps had greater intelligence—than that to be found in any European nation."

The sea having become heavy, the ships returned to the shelter of the Tartary coast, but farther north; on July 28, they anchored in the bay which was given the name of the Minister of the Navy, Maréchal de Castries (De Kastri). The inhabitants were Tartars, who called themselves Orochis. As generous as they were honest, they were nevertheless "filthy and stank disgustingly"; they avidly ate raw the salmon that they fished for with extraordinary skill.

Unable to proceed farther north, which pre-

vented him from verifying his belief that Sakhalin was an island, La Pérouse had to turn south and look for a passage that would allow him to regain the open sea. Finally, having reached a cape that he called Crillon (Mys Krilon), at the end of Sakhalin, he discovered a channel—since then known as La Pérouse Strait—that separated Yeso (Hokkaido) from Oku-Yeso (Sakhalin). In the Baie de Crillon, the navigators made the acquaintance of a new tribe. "Their beards descended to their chests, and their arms, necks, and backs were covered by hair." These were the Ainus. Finally, the ships traversed the Kuriles through a channel since called Boussole Strait. As they went, they reconnoitered the islands discovered in 1643 by Holland's Martin de Vries.

On September 6, 1787, the expedition anchored at Petropavlovsk, the only city on Kamchatka. They stayed there twenty-four days, resting and enjoying the continual celebrations offered by the Russians. The Kamchatkan women dancers surprised the French. "Their exhaustion after these exercises is such that they drip perspiration and remain stretched on the ground without strength enough to rise. The abundant exhalations that emanate from their bodies perfume the room with a smell of oil and fish which our European noses are too little accustomed to to appreciate properly."

At Petropavlovsk, the navigators found letters from Paris. La Pérouse was promoted to the rank of squadron commander and Clonard was made a captain—events that were properly feted with more celebrations offered by Lieutenant Kaborov, the Russian governor. The new instructions received by La Pérouse modified his itinerary. The French government had gotten wind of a settlement of colonists in New South Wales, and La Pérouse was instructed to investigate this. Before leaving, he charged young Barthélemy de Lesseps with the responsibility of taking to France the expedition's documents and journals. His voyage across a deserted and icy Siberia and a half-civilized Russian empire was epic, but on October 17, 1788, he arrived safely at Versailles, where the king in person deigned to interview him.

"I shall have only misfortunes to tell you"

Thus began a letter La Pérouse addressed to his friend Fleurieu. In it, he related the disaster that had overtaken them at Navigators Islands (Samoa). However, when they first anchored at Manua (Tutuila) on December 9, 1787, the French saw this island with as romantic an eye as Bougainville had seen Tahiti. "These islanders . . . are no doubt the happiest people in the world; surrounded by their women and children, they spend the days in innocence and tranquility." But it was soon noticed that "the bodies of these Indians are covered with scars that show that they are often at war or engaged in private combat." La Pérouse observed that "the all but savage man who lives in anarchy is wickeder than the most ferocious animals." He was, in fact, in complete disagreement with the *philosophes:* "They write their books by the fireside and I have been voyaging for thirty years"; this man "who is portrayed to us as so good because he is very close to nature," was in fact "barbarous, wicked, and sly."

La Pérouse was soon to have a clear demonstration that the "noble savage" was only an illusion. Since the Tutuilans had proven themselves great scoundrels and bold thieves, he was eager to leave this disappointing island. He decided to sail the day after his arrival, but de Langle wanted to renew the water supply. No sooner had he filled his barrels than the natives, whose number had increased to a thousand, suddenly attacked. Of the sixty-one men present, twelve were massacred, twenty others wounded. Greatly shocked by this new catastrophe, the crew also began to suffer from scurvy, and one man died. In addition, several of those who had been wounded failed to recover; one of them, Father Receveur, was to die in Australia.

The French were therefore relieved to reach Botany Bay on January 26, 1788. La Pérouse arrived just as Captain Philip was secretly transferring the small settlement of colonists—and especially the convicts—from Botany Bay to Port Jackson; nevertheless, the British welcomed him courteously. Unfortunately, given the circumstances, they were unable to offer him either supplies or munitions. The journals of the voyage from Kamchatka to New Holland were embarked on a British vessel and eventually arrived at their destination.

On February 25, La Pérouse wrote to Paris that he was preparing to carry out "absolutely everything enjoined upon me by my instructions": the reconnaisance of New Caledonia, the Santa Cruz Islands, the Solomon Islands, and the Louisiades. In September and October, he "would visit the Gulf of Carpentaria and the entire western coast of New Holland as far as Van Diemen's Land, but in such a manner as would make it possible to sail north early enough to arrive at the Ile de France by December 1788." On March 10, 1788, the *Boussole* and the *Astrolabe* sailed out of Botany Bay and headed for the Friendly Islands. They were never to be seen again. The expedition's only survivors were those who had disembarked at the stopovers. One of them, Barthélemy de Lesseps, was to live long enough to identify the few vestiges found forty years later.

Massacre of Fleuriot de Langle, Lamanon, and ten men in what is now called Massacre Bay at Tutuila in the eastern Samoas, December 11, 1787. Lithograph after N. Ozanne, from the Atlas of the Voyage de La Pérouse. *(Musée de la Marine, Paris. Photo © the museum/Photeb.)*

Searching for La Pérouse: d'Entrecasteaux's voyage, 1791–1794

The last news of La Pérouse dated back to February 25, 1788. The *Boussole* and the *Astrolabe* were due to reach the Ile de France toward the end of the year. After July 1789, it became obvious that the expedition had run into unforeseen difficulties. A silence that seemed to bode no good worried both the authorities and the public, despite a rapid succession of events that absorbed the attention of all; the Bastille was taken on July 14, and, in October, under pressure from the mob, the king had to take up residence in the Tuileries.

The fact that scientists had been part of the expedition excited particular interest. In a burst of patriotic eloquence, the Society of Natural History exclaimed in an appeal addressed to the National

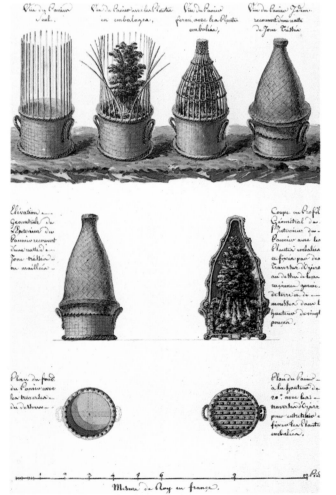

The use of baskets to transport plants. This type of basket and the case on the following page were used by botanists after the La Pérouse expedition. Anonymous watercolor. (Archives Nationales, Fonds Marine, Paris. Photo by Michel Didier © Photeb.)

Assembly on January 22, 1791: "May they return to our shores even if they were to die of joy in embracing this free land." The Constituent Assembly announced that immediate measures would be taken. Actually, it had been anticipated by Fleurieu, the Minister of the Navy, who had already submitted to the king several memoranda indicating the routes that might be searched. The Assembly decreed that a sum of 600,000 livres would be available for a searching expedition; an additional 100,000 livres were allotted for the scientific work with which that expedition would also be charged.

The command was given to d'Entrecasteaux, who had recently been promoted to division chief and who was familiar with the regions to be visited. Fifty-four in 1791, he had long since distinguished himself by his boldness and his talents as a navigator. The mission he was entrusted with was not easy; he was to look for traces of La Pérouse amid the hundreds of islands in the southwest Pacific. No less difficult was the problem of the state of indiscipline—if not anarchy—in which the navy found itself in those troubled times. The officers had difficulty exercising their authority and could at any moment be denounced as aristocrats. Nevertheless, Fleurieu prepared for this voyage as admirably as he had done for La Pérouse's. D'Entrecasteaux's instructions were to inspect the coasts of New Holland "as though it were being done for the first time," go to Van Diemen's Land, from there to the Friendly Islands, and then to New Caledonia. He would next follow the route that La Pérouse must have taken—the New Hebrides, the Solomons, the Louisiades, and the northeast coast of New Guinea. The commander did not have to conform to this program exactly, but could act as circumstances permitted. The only iron-bound condition was that the voyage not last more than three years.

Two ships were outfitted. Named frigates for the occasion, the *Truite* and the *Durance,* rechristened the *Recherche* and the *Espérance,* were actually only 500-ton storeships. D'Entrecasteaux had no sooner left than he became aware that they handled badly. The *Recherche* was commanded by d'Entrecasteaux, seconded by Hesmivy d'Auribeau; the *Espérance,* slower and heavier, was placed under the command of Huon de Kermadec, who had sailed the China coasts with d'Entrecasteaux when he had commanded the *Résolution.* The third in command

D'Entrecasteaux's Ships and Crews

Total manpower: 219 men.
Deaths: 89, most following the stay in Java.

La *RECHERCHE*: 500-ton storeship;
left from Brest, 9/29/1791;
crew: 113 officers and men.

Commander: A. R. J. de Bruni, Chevalier d'Entrecasteaux, rear admiral, died at sea, 7/20/1793.

Second: A. Hesmivy d'Auribeau, died in Semarang (Java).

Lieutenants: Chevalier de Rossel, Crétin, La Fresnaye de Saint-Aignan, Singler de Welle.

Elèves and **volontaires:** du Mérite, *volontaire,* made ensign; Achard de Bonvouloir, *élève* made ensign; de Longuerue, *élève* made ensign; Forestier, made *volontaire;*

Henri de Lambert, made *volontaire;* Hippolyte Deslacs, made *volontaire.*

Chief hydrographer: C. F. Beautemps-Beaupré.

Astronomer: Abbé Bertrand, died in Cape Town, January 1792.

Naturalists: J. J. Houtou de La Billardière; Louis Ventenat, "serving as chaplain"; Deschamps, assistant naturalist.

Draftsman: Piron.

Gardener-botanist: Lahaie.

Surgeon: Renard.

Assistant Surgeon: H. Boideliot.

L'ESPÉRANCE: 500-ton storeship;
left from Brest, 9/29/1791;
crew: 106 officers and men.

Commander: J. M. Huon de Kermadec, captain, died at Balade, 5/6/1793.

Lieutenants: Denis de Trobriand, La Seinie, La Grandière, Luzançay, La Motte du Portail, Le Grand.

Ensign: J. B. P. Willaumez, elder.

Elèves and **volontaires:** Leignel, *volontaire,* made ensign; P. R. Jurien de la Gravière, *volontaire,* made ensign;

Boynes, *élève,* made ensign; Filtz, made *volontaire.*

Hydrographer: Jouvency.

Astronomer: Dom Pierson, "serving as chaplain."

Naturalists: Claude Riche; Blavier, disembarked at Cape Town, January 1792.

Draftsman: Ely, left sick at Cape Town, January 1792.

Surgeon: Joanet.

Assistant surgeon: Gauffre.

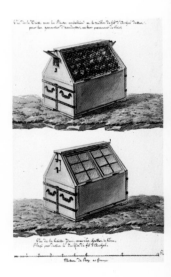

Case containing plants protected by a netting of brass wire; the same case closed by a glass frame. Anonymous watercolor. (Archives Nationales, Fonds Marine, Paris. Photo by Michel Didier © Photeb.)

aboard the *Recherche* was also of noble birth; at the age of twenty, Chevalier de Rossel had served in India under the orders of d'Entrecasteaux, who had after that taken him under his wing. Responsible for the astronomical work, he was to bring back important observations on terrestrial magnetism and end his days as a rear admiral. Two other young officers later rose to the rank of vice admiral; Jean-Baptiste Philibert Willaumez, son of a simple gunner and at the time an ensign, and the *volontaire* Pierre Roch Jurien de la Gravière, who was only nineteen years old.

Since the reform of the navy in 1786—which, like the reform of the army, had strengthened the opposition between officers of noble birth and commoners—there were on the one hand the *élèves,* young men belonging to the nobility and obliged to furnish proof of the fact, and the *volontaires,* commoners whose recruitment was nevertheless selective. They could rise no higher than the rank of second lieutenant—and even then only with exceptional service records. The Revolution could not allow such privilege to remain unchallenged, and an egalitarian reform was under way. Afterward there would only be *aspirants,* young men of fifteen to twenty who were learning their profession, and then *enseignes,* who had the lowest rank in the hierarchy of officers and who could come from the merchant marine. (Previously, the separation between the two navies had been watertight.) When the *Recherche* and the *Espérance* left France, however, this reform had not yet been carried out. The young men who accompanied d'Entrecasteaux were aware of the changes to come; some awaited the end of inequalities with impatience, others insisted on having them respected. This was naturally a source of friction that was to poison relations during the course of the voyage.

The claims of the *volontaires* were supported by the scientists of the expedition, most of whom were advocates of the new ideas. The most determined and ardent of these men was the botanist and doctor Houtou de La Billardière, who was in the course of events to become a leader of the disaffected. With him on the *Recherche* was the naturalist Louis Ventenat, who "served as a chaplain," since he belonged to the Order of the Génovéfains. On the *Espérance,* the naturalist was Claude Riche, who, like La Billardière, was a doctor. A consumptive who had been advised to sign on for "a change of

Eucalyptus (Eucalyptus globulus) discovered by La Billardière in Tasmania. Plate by P. J. Redouté for the Atlas of Voyage à la recherche de La Pérouse *(1799). (Bibliothèque nationale, Paris. Photo by Michel Didier © Photeb.)*

shortage of water. "It is impossible, unless you experience it . . . to imagine how painful it is to spend a part of the day under the sun's burning rays and be reduced to three-quarters of a bottle of water (sometimes foul) every twenty-four hours," wrote the anonymous author of a *Recherche* journal. The two ships spent eighty-four days on the African coasts and did not reach Cape Town until January 17, 1792.

There, d'Entrecasteaux received a message that was to modify his plans. A French frigate had left for him dispatches affirming that an English captain had seen, off the Admiralty Islands, canoes filled with natives wearing French uniforms. This Englishman was a Captain Hunter, who, though he was at Cape Town when d'Entrecasteaux arrived, made no effort to get in touch with him. The information was therefore suspect.

D'Entrecasteaux nevertheless considered it his duty to look into it, and instead of heading for New Holland, he decided to go to the Admiralty group by way of the Moluccas. He had to make haste if he wanted to pass through the Sunda Strait no later than the end of March, before the southeast monsoon made navigation impossible. On departing from Cape Town, he had to leave behind the naturalist Blavier; the draftsman Ely, who was sick; and Abbé Bertrand, the *Recherche* astronomer, who had suffered a fall in climbing Table Mountain and who was to die shortly after his compatriots left.

Exploration of Tasmania

The slow progress of the ships soon forced d'Entrecasteaux to modify his plans once more. Twenty-one days after leaving Cape Town, the ships were still at 35° of south latitude and 46° 20′ of longitude and had to fight against a heavy sea and violent winds. Food supplies were in a pitiful condition. "Maggots from the biscuits spread through our food, jumping and wriggling like those ordinarily found in cheese," wrote La Billardière. Finally, d'Entrecasteaux decided to head for Van Diemen's Land as quickly as possible.

On April 21, the *Recherche* and the *Espérance* reached the Tasmanian coast, but instead of finding themselves, as had been expected, at the entrance to Adventure Bay—discovered by Tobias Furneaux in 1773—they were in a still-uncharted bay which they baptized Recherche. Two boats were sent to sound it, and the officers discovered the entrance to an unknown channel separating two islands from Tasmania. The first was called Bruni (Bruny Island)—the patronymic of the rear admiral, who had given the channel the name of his estate (Entrecasteaux). It was on the second of these islands that Adventure Bay opened; it therefore did not belong to Van Diemen's Land as Furneaux had thought. As a matter of fact, the Tasmanian coast was much more indented than had been believed, and it had several "bays of great depth that were all equally protected against the winds." A month was

air," he was to die on his return. The naturalists were assisted by a botanical gardener from the King's Garden, who was to be responsible for living plants. The staff of the scientists also included Chief Hydrographer Beautemps-Beaupré, who, though only twenty-five, had already acquired a reputation by drawing up the maps of the Baltic; those he made during the d'Entrecasteaux expedition were to be very useful to future navigators.

First indications

When, on September 29, 1791, the *Recherche* and the *Espérance* sailed from Brest, the course of the Revolution had accelerated considerably and taken a fatal path. On June 22, the king and his family had fled and been arrested at Varennes; henceforth, they were for all purposes prisoners, and emigration was at its height. The Constituent Assembly had completed its work and held its last session the day after the expedition left. It was to be replaced in October by the much less moderate Legislative Assembly, which declared the *émigrés* "suspect of plotting against the nation."

Once at sea, d'Entrecasteaux opened his sealed orders. They promoted him to the rank of rear admiral, and Huon de Kermadec, previously a vice chief of naval staff, was made a captain. Navigation between the Canary Islands and the Cape took longer than had been foreseen, and there was a spent charting its coves. It was this map that later attracted the attention of the British to the settlement possibilities offered by the southeast coast, where they were to establish the island's capital, Hobart Town.

The look of the country was impressive. Profiting from d'Entrecasteaux's notes, Rossel, who wrote the official account of the voyage, observed: "At every step, side by side with the beauties of Nature abandoned to herself, one sees signs of her decrepitude; trees of great height and proportionate diameter, with no branches along the trunks but crowned with an evergreen foliage; some seem as old as the world; intertwined and dense to the point of impenetrability, they serve as supports for other trees of similar dimensions but crumbling with age and fertilizing the soil with their rotting remains . . ." Greatly excited by this untouched environment, La Billardière, Riche, and Ventenat left to explore it. On May 6, La Billardière discovered the blue eucalyptus (*Eucalyptus globulus*), a species that was much easier to naturalize than the one brought back by Banks. In 1804, he planted some seeds in the Empress Josephine's Malmaison garden; fifty years later, this eucalyptus was flourishing on the Côte d'Azur. He also identified two new species belonging to the same genus: the white eucalyptus (*Eucalyptus viminalis*) and a veritable giant, *Eucalyptus amygdalina*, that can grow as high as 150 meters. The botanists found many other species of plant life, including some wonderfully flowering bushes. Among the animals discovered were a little kangaroo with a soft thick coat, the La Billardière thylogale. The naturalists also brought on board birds, rock specimens, and numerous mollusks, but since the latter were edible, the scientists could not collect them as quickly as the sailors, who were overjoyed by this unforeseen addition to their austere diet. D'Entrecasteaux had to give orders that all catches were first to be submitted to the scientists.

The navigators would have liked to establish contact with the natives, described in 1772 by Marion du Fresne as leading a primitive existence hardly better than that of the animals around them. But as soon as the Tasmanians were spotted, they disappeared into the impenetrable brush. It was only toward the end of the stay that it was possible to offer them some gifts from a distance. This gesture was not wasted; when the French returned to Tasmania the following year, the natives were less fearful.

On May 28, the *Recherche* and the *Espérance* left these shores. Southwest winds carried them to New Caledonia, discovered by Cook during his second voyage. D'Entrecasteaux sailed along the western coast, which Cook had not seen. It was bordered by reefs, and he could not land. At the end of June, the rear admiral turned northeast, the direction of the Solomon Archipelago. At Buka Island, natives drew near the ships. Remembering the bad reputation they had been given by earlier navigators, d'Entrecasteaux behaved cautiously. However, their

features did not seem at all fierce, and their faces lit up when "M. de Saint-Aignan played a rather lively tune on his violin. The sound of this instrument, new to them, struck them as very pleasant, and they laughed and jumped on the seats of their canoes. In exchange for the violin they offered not only the bow asked of them but some clubs they had not previously displayed."

On July 17, the two ships docked at Carteret Harbour in New Ireland. A week was spent there amid diluvian rainfalls while they took on necessary supplies of water and wood. Unfortunately, the wood turned out to be infested with insects, *Blatta germanica*, a species that multiplied and "caused us extreme discomfort. Not content with our biscuits, they attacked clothing, paper, etc.—they liked everything."

The Admiralty Archipelago

Finally, on July 26, 1792, the first of the Admiralty Islands hove into view. But, as d'Entrecasteaux noted: "Given the great number of islands forming this archipelago, only luck could help us run into the one that was mentioned by the two French captains."

Relying on the account of Carteret, who had discovered the archipelago in 1767, the French were expecting hostility from the natives, whom he had described as fierce, but "the inhabitants called to us loudly and made all sorts of friendly gestures." To the French, their faces had a "look of goodness." The longboats approached the coast but were unable to land as the reefs were too numerous. Nevertheless, some trading was done in an atmo-

"As soon as the women had finished dancing, several men stood up, all holding small clubs . . . which they moved about in time to the music . . . making various movements with their feet." Drawing by Piron done at Tongatapu in March 1793. (Archives Nationales, Fonds Marine, Paris. Photo by Michel Didier © Photeb.)

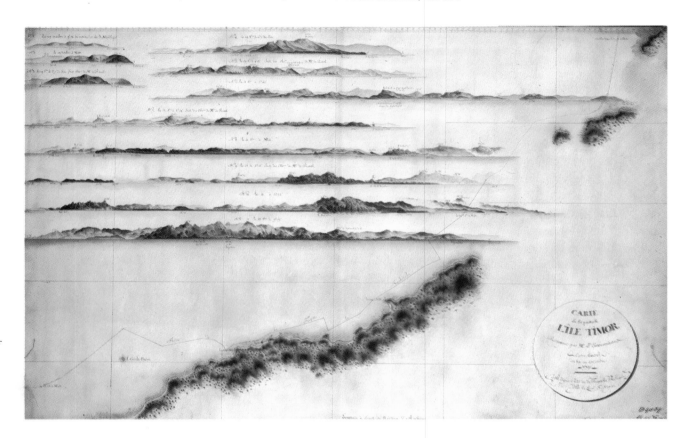

Map of the portion of the island of Timor reconnoitered by d'Entrecasteaux from October 19 to 23, 1792. Drawn by Lieutenant Saint-Aignan. (Archives Nationales, Fonds Marine, Paris. Photo by Michel Didier © Photeb.)

sphere of great calm. There was no trace, however, of the uniforms Hunter claimed to have seen. The islanders were naked, except for a shell over their sex, some belts, and shell bracelets and necklaces. Could those light-colored ornaments on their dark skins have created the illusion of European uniforms? the French wondered.

Scurvy broke out aboard ship, and the only thing to do was to head for some Dutch settlement, where they could regain their health before returning to Van Diemen's Land. On September 6, the *Recherche* and the *Espérance* dropped anchor at Amboina. It was their first sight of other Europeans since leaving Cape Town. In the interval, the relations of revolutionary France with the other European nations had deteriorated considerably. War had been declared in April; since then, French troops had invaded Belgium as far as the Dutch border, and the king of France had been deposed and imprisoned with his family in the tower of the Temple. The navigators did not learn this news, but the Dutch authorities were now more reserved. Nevertheless, the governor of Amboina allowed the French to reprovision, which they did so amply that the "ships were everywhere encumbered" with pigs and fowl.

Amboina was an important trading post of the Dutch East India Company, which managed the clove and nutmeg plantations and severely oppressed the natives. Since they were to remain more than a month, the navigators lived on shore. The naturalists were lodged together and were able to make several expeditions that furthered their investigations. They found new plants, birds, and several curious reptiles, including the Indies varan,

which reached a growth of 1.5 meters. Louis Ventenat fell so dangerously ill, La Billardière wrote that "we were unable to leave him for four days running. . . . His distorted features suggested that he was lost, but soon abundant perspiring relieved him and after a few days of convalescence he was up and about." Presumably, he had had a violent attack of malaria. In December, when they were off the coast of New Holland, Ventenat fell overboard into a shark-infested sea; he was pulled up just in time.

On October 13, the *Recherche* and the *Espérance* left Amboina. On the nineteenth, Timor was in sight; and, on the twenty-fifth, Savu. The two vessels were then carried toward the west in the Indian Ocean until November 23, when, thanks to a west wind, they were able to change direction and reach Cape Leeuwin, on the west coast of New Holland. Several days later, a violent wind surprised the two ships and pushed them into a labyrinth of islands from which they tried to disengage. The *Espérance,* being in danger, however, decided to continue and soon found a sheltered bay. They called it Esperance Bay; the islands were baptized the Recherche Archipelago.

On December 14, Huon de Kermadec sent a boat on shore, and La Billardière and Riche penetrated an unknown region in which they hoped to make important discoveries; they were soon separated, and Riche did not return to the boat. The *Espérance* waited a day and a half, and then Huon decided to lift anchor as no fresh water had been found, and it was in short supply. La Billardière protested and got a new delay, but it was not until fifty-four hours later that the unfortunate naturalist reappeared—haggard and famished, for he had found nothing to eat during all this time. But there had been a compensation. "I ran into three kangaroos of a giant species . . . after having run some fifty paces they sat on their bottoms and faced me."

The ships again set sail on December 17 and d'Entrecasteaux began to carefully explore Nuyts Land. But, "on all sides it offered only a land that was sandy and arid, and at very different latitudes conserved the same aspect and the same barrenness." The lack of water was reaching crisis proportions. On January 3, 1793, therefore, d'Entrecasteaux had to give orders to head for Van Diemen's Land. It was still not known that a strait separated Australia from Tasmania. In passing through the region, d'Entrecasteaux suspected as much, but was unable to verify it. Several years later, the English discovered Bass Strait—no doubt with the aid of documents from the French expedition.

The naturalists had discovered a kind of ashy-colored goose, whose apple-green beak and pink feet gave it a very strange look. They also captured a varicolored, extremely long-tailed parakeet that lived not in trees but on the ground, along which it raced at high speed. La Billardière identified two beautiful bushes with white or bright red flowers, which he baptized *Mazentoxeron*—these are the *Correa* of our gardens—and two new *Banksia, repens* and *nivea;* finally, there were two bushes that bore edible fruit and that were later named *Billardiera* by Robert Brown.

On January 21, 1793, the expedition reached Recherche Bay on the Tasmanian coast. On that very day, the head of Louis XVI fell in Paris. During this second visit, which lasted a month, the reassured Tasmanians came to the navigators of their own volition. "Three of our sleeping boatmen were surprised upon awaking to find a considerable number of the inhabitants of this country only a short distance from them. They came forward confidently and gave proofs of their natural goodness by indicating that they had not wanted to awaken the sleepers. No longer doubting their pacific disposition, our three men began to dance with them. In emulation, all the sailors stripped themselves of whatever they had to give it to the natives." The

Native graves on Maria Island on the coast of Van Diemen's Land. Drawing by C. A. Lesueur. (Bibliothèque du Muséum d'histoire naturelle, Paris. Photo © Bibl. du Muséum/Photeb.)

A Tasmanian. Drawing by Piron during the d'Entrecasteaux expedition. (Musée de l'Homme, Paris. Photo by Ponsard from the museum collection.)

French felt a real affection for these Tasmanians, who were so wretched and yet not thieves. Perhaps their fate might have been a happier one if France and not Great Britain had settled the country. There is a symbolic coincidence in the fact that it was on Bruny Island, which bears the name of its former benefactor, that the last Tasmanians took refuge before disappearing.

On February 27, the *Recherche* and the *Espérance* definitively left Adventure Bay to head for New Zealand. Without even stopping, the French made some exchanges with the Maoris, who came out to them in their canoes. D'Entrecasteaux was in a hurry to reach Tongatapu, for it was there that La Pérouse must have stopped after leaving Botany Bay. As soon as the ships had anchored off the northern coast of the island, natives swarmed out to greet the navigators in a veritable carnival atmosphere. They were not only turbulent—invading the ships from which it was impossible to dislodge them—but thieving and predatory. In a fortnight, the French bought four hundred pigs and five hundred fowls, to say nothing of yams, bananas, and coconuts. They also took away three hundred breadfruit trees. But no information was obtained about the missing navigators.

D'Entrecasteaux next headed for New Caledonia, where he dropped anchor in Balade Bay from April 21 to May 9, 1793. Forster had portrayed the New Caledonians as gentle and peaceful, but the French saw that they were fierce and cannibalistic. "One of them having in his hand a freshly roasted bone and eating away at a morsel of flesh still attached there, came up to Citizen Piron and urged him to join in his meal." Thinking that it was an animal bone, Piron was going to accept, but he showed the bone to La Billardière, who "recognized it as belonging to the pelvis of a fourteen- or fifteen-year-old child. . . . The various awkward signs by which we tried to make them confess that they ate humans caused a great misunderstanding. . . . They thought . . . that we too were cannibals and feeling that their last moment had come began to weep." On May 6, Huon de Kermadec, who had been sick since they left Tasmania, died.

The expedition arrived in sight of the Santa Cruz Islands on May 19. To the southeast, they discovered land that was not shown on any map. No anchorage was found, and the inhabitants tried to attack the ships. This discovery was baptized Ile de la Recherche. It was actually Vanikoro, where La Pérouse had been shipwrecked. But d'Entrecasteaux went off to seek for traces of him in the Solomons in May and June, and then in the Louisiades. Weary and overwhelmed by tropical rains, the crew was exhausted.

A lamentable end

Finally, on July 9, the search was abandoned and d'Entrecasteaux decided to head for Java. He himself was suffering from scurvy aggravated by dysentery. D'Auribeau urgently pressed the admiral to head for the closest port and see to his health, but d'Entrecasteaux stubbornly refused until July 19, when he realized that this was his only hope for survival. But it was too late: "In the night of July 19–20, M. d'Entrecasteaux's suffering became intense and caused him such agitation that an unsettling of the mind that presaged delirium was noticed . . ." The doctors "agreed that the only way to relieve his extreme suffering was to give him a bath. But no sooner was he plunged into the water than his condition became desperate. Terrible convulsions began and he lost consciousness . . . at half past seven in the evening, he breathed his last."

Since the winds were weak and inconstant, the ships made little progress. In the early days of August, the expedition reached the western end of New Guinea; from August 15 to 27, it sojourned at Waigeo Island. There were more than sixty cases of scurvy. When they left, d'Auribeau, who had been sick since the death of his chief, grew worse, and, on the twenty-eighth, he lost consciousness.

It was henceforth Rossel who was to determine the route to be followed. The most prudent solution would have been to reach Surabaja as quickly as possible so that the crew might rest, but Rossel feared that d'Auribeau would never survive the trip. He therefore headed for Buru, and, on September 3, the ships anchored before Caieli. The Dutch Resident received the French most hospitably, and old natives came to see them to speak of the earlier visit by Bougainville. When the ships left Buru twelve days later, many of the scurvy victims had recovered. They reached Butung on October 8. With the scurvy now more or less under control, d'Auribeau was able to take command again; but then dysentery broke out and afflicted more than fifty men, six of whom died.

It was therefore with great relief that the French arrived at Surabaja on October 19. Initially reluctant, the Dutch finally agreed to receive the expedition but demanded that the frigates' cannon be surrendered before the expedition entered the roads, which it did on the twenty-seventh. "A letter brought us the news that France and Holland were at war. We learned that the king had been decapitated by a faction that had seized power and that France was torn by a civil war . . ." Rossel classed himself among the adversaries of the Revolution, but, unlike d'Auribeau, he was a moderate. Henceforth, the crew was divided into two opposing factions, the revolutionaries being led by the impetuous La Billardière, the sworn enemy of the authoritarian d'Auribeau. The Dutch did not make matters easier. Initially, the sick men were allowed to come ashore, but after ten days they were ordered to return to the ships; a little later, the sailors were free to come and go.

Eventually, the men were more or less left to their own devices. D'Auribeau sold what remained of the cargo, but it brought in very little; his financial resources exhausted, he had to borrow from the Dutch. The departure for the Ile de France seemed

Malaspina and Bustamente measuring gravity by means of the pendulum at the Islas Malvinas (Falkland Islands) during their voyage of circumnavigation, 1789–1794. (Museo naval, Madrid. Photo by Oroñoz © Photeb.)

more and more problematical. In fact, d'Auribeau was in no hurry to return to France, where, if the news they had received was true, he ran the risk of being guillotined. But the situation could not drag on, and it was necessary to come to some decision. On February 20, 1794, the commander decided to throw in his lot with the *émigrés*. He urged his officers and men to wear the white cockade, but most of them refused. Fearing he might lose control of the situation, d'Auribeau asked the Dutch for help. On the night of February 20–21, seven officers and naturalists who disapproved of the steps taken by the commander were placed under arrest, and La Billardière's natural history collections were confiscated. However, the latter had had time to remove eleven breadfruit trees, which he entrusted to the gardener Lahaie with orders to plant them on the Ile de France. On February 21, d'Auribeau flew the royalist flag and had it saluted by salvos of cannon-fire.

The situation of the republicans was precarious—henceforth, they were prisoners of the Dutch—but that of the royalists was no less dangerous, since they were unwilling to head for French territory. On February 25, the seven men under arrest were taken to Semarang, a city situated between Surabaja and Batavia. Riche and Le Grand wanted to go to Batavia in order to embark for France as soon as possible; authorized to do so on May 6, they left for the Ile de France two months later on the corvette *Nathalie,* which had come in a vain attempt to have the ships restored to France. Accompanied by Lahaie, Riche did not reach France until three years later, in 1797. Sick, he went to Mont-Doré, where he died on September 5, 1797.

Lahaie, who had planted nine of his eleven breadfruit trees on the Ile de France, brought two back to Paris, along with an important collection of living plants and a large herbarium, which were accepted by the Museum of Natural History, where the gardener once more took up his work. He died in Versailles in 1819 or 1820.

A second group composed of Willaumez, Leignel, and Ventenat left Semarang for Batavia on May 18. They were able to embark for the Ile de France, but Ventenat died there on August 8, 1794. La Billardière and Piron were the only ones at Semarang when d'Auribeau came to negotiate with the Dutch. He confiscated from La Billardière the manuscript of his observations, and was accused by the naturalist of trying to sell the ships to the Dutch. The situation of the royalists had worsened. The French armies everywhere were defeating their adversaries; the cause of the *émigrés* seemed lost; and the Terror ruled in France. D'Auribeau died on August 23, 1794. According to Jurien de la Gravière, it was rumored that he had been poisoned; others said that he had succumbed to dysentery and despair. The fact remains that he died at the very moment in which revolutionary delegates came from the Ile de France to ask for the head of the "traitor" d'Auribeau.

Finally, on March 30, 1795, La Billardière left Batavia for the Ile de France, where he arrived on May 4. He left again aboard the *Minerve,* commanded by Leignel, and reached Batz Island on March 13, 1796. Shortly afterward, he was in Paris and had the French government ask for the natural history collections that had been sent to Great Britain. Sir Joseph Banks intervened strongly in his favor, and they were restored. Setting to work immediately, La Billardière, in 1799, published his *Relation du voyage à la recherche de La Pérouse* (Account of the Voyage in Search of La Pérouse) along with a beautiful album in which Piron's drawings showed the most important discoveries made by the naturalists; some of those drawings had been reworked and improved by P. J. Redouté, who was later to become famous. This "republican" work preceded by nine years the official account by Rossel. The latter, bringing with him the results of the expedition as well as the maps made by Beautemps-Beaupré, had embarked at Batavia aboard a Dutch ship, but it was seized by an English frigate and Rossel taken to England. He was not freed until the Peace of Amiens in 1802. Meanwhile, the British Admiralty had had the maps copied, which allowed the English to study the conclusions of the French. When Flinders's expedition was being prepared, he was able to take advantage of information not available to his French rival, Baudin, who had left for Australia in 1800.

In the interval between the departure of La Pérouse and the return of the survivors of the d'Entrecasteaux expedition, two other important

expeditions had set out. The Spanish navigators Malaspina and Bustamente, reviving the traditions of their country, left Cadiz, (July 30, 1789) aboard the *Descubierta* and the *Atrevida;* they visited the northwest coast of America, traversed the Pacific as far as Macao, and came back by way of Peru. But on his return to Spain in 1794, Malaspina, denounced for his liberal ideas, was imprisoned; the scientific results of his voyage remained buried in Spanish archives until 1885.

On April 1, 1791, an expedition commanded by George Vancouver, who had accompanied Cook on his second and third voyages, sailed from Falmouth. The *Discovery* and the *Chatham* were under orders to complete Cook's reconnaisance of the western coast of America. There, Vancouver explored the large island that was later to bear his name. At the Sandwich Islands, he became a friend of King Kamehameha, who declared himself an ally of Great Britain. Vancouver returned in September 1795. His companion, the Scottish botanist Archibald Menzies, had made some very interesting discoveries, especially the California sequoia and the Chile pine.

Araucaria imbricata discovered in Chile by Archibald Menzies, botanist of the Vancouver expedition. Original watercolor from Genus Pinus by A. B. Lambert, 1837. (British Museum, Natural History, London. Photo by courtesy of the trustees, British Museum/Photeb.)

The French
and English
in New Holland,
1800-1805

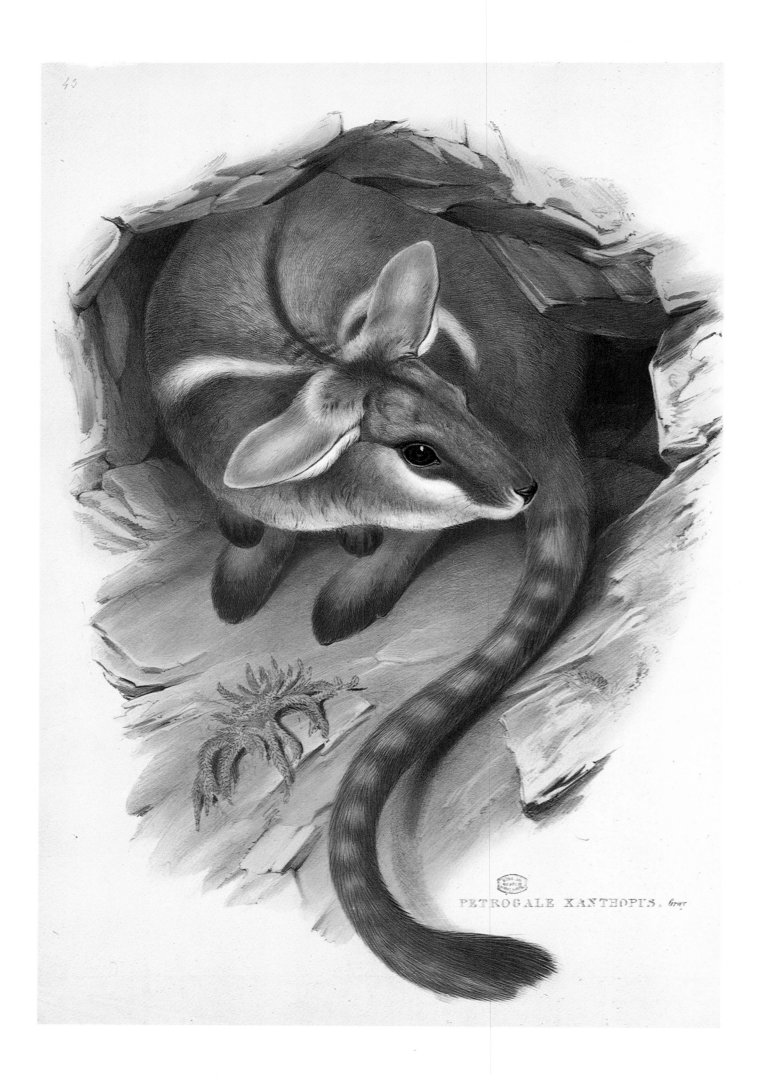

PETROGALE XANTHOPUS. Gray

The deadly mission of Captain Baudin, 1800–1804

At the end of the eighteenth century, Great Britain had lost most of her overseas possessions in America. Henceforth she was to turn her attention toward the Orient, searching for new outlets necessary for her budding industry.

After having strengthened their hold on Bengal, the British, spurred on by Richard Colley Wellesley, conquered the principal Indian States one after the other. The wars following the French Revolution gave them the opportunity to extend their nascent colonial empire. In 1795—taking as a pretext the proclamation of the Batavian Republic, which was allied to revolutionary France—Great Britain seized the Dutch colony at the Cape of Good Hope, a stopping-off place on the way to the Far East. That same year, Mungo Park, a bold explorer financed by the African Association—whose treasurer was none other than Sir Joseph Banks—penetrated to the interior of black Africa; he was to reach the Niger. In 1791, the British had created the Sierra Leone Society and, in 1792, founded Freetown; but following the exploration of Australia's eastern coast by Cook, they were established most solidly in New Holland (Australia). The first colony, New South Wales, was founded in 1788. The successful in-depth exploration of the south of Van Diemen's Land (Tasmania) under d'Entrecasteaux should have made it possible for the French to establish themselves on that island and thus to control the Indian Ocean route followed by English ships on their way to Port Jackson—in other words, to pose a threat to New South Wales. Unfortunately for France, the Revolutionary upheavals had put an abrupt halt to all exploration, and the English had not wasted any time. In 1800, a new expedition was being prepared in London, and the French government was aware of this.

As soon as internal order was reestablished, France's First Consul hastened to organize a maritime voyage designed to establish a footing on the still-unexplored coasts of New Holland in competition with Great Britain, with whom France was still at war. Nevertheless, the mission entrusted to Baudin in 1800 did not have—at least ostensibly—any political goal. He himself seemed to regret this when, in 1802, he wrote from Port Jackson to the Minister of the Navy: "The English fear that it is our intention to establish ourselves along the

D'Entrecasteaux Channel—on the south of Van Diemen's Land. . . . I am convinced that fearing to have us for neighbors, they are going to occupy this section of Van Diemen's Land in an attempt to establish their proprietary rights in no uncertain terms. If this is so, it will truly be a loss to France, since a base on Van Diemen's Land cannot but be greatly advantageous."

Initially alarmed but quickly reassured, the British decided that they would not only tolerate but, if necessary, come to the aid of the French expedition. Officially, after all, it was only a question of a scientific mission; and Bonaparte, who three years earlier had associated the sciences with the Egyptian expedition, wanted to give this voyage every chance to be a brilliant success. Nicolas Baudin, who was promoted to captain, was appointed the leader; he had already undertaken—for the for-

Baudin's Ships and Crews

Le *GÉOGRAPHE:* 350-ton corvette;
left from Le Havre, 10/19/1800
returned to Lorient, 3/25/1804

Commander of the expedition: Nicolas Baudin, captain, died on the Ile de France, 9/16/1803; Pierre Milius took over command 9/28/1803 and brought the *Géographe* back to France.

Lieutenants: Le Bas de Sainte-Croix, frigate captain, second in command, put ashore sick at Timor, 11/2/1801; Pierre Guillaume Gicquel, lieutenant commander, left sick at the Ile de France, 4/25/1801; François André Baudin, lieutenant commander, left sick on the Ile de France, 4/25/1801.

Ensigns: Henri de Freycinet, made lieutenant commander, 10/20/1801; Jean Antoine Capmartin, left sick on the Ile de France, 4/25/1801; Francois Michel Ronsard, naval engineer, 10/20/1801.

Midshipmen, 1st Class: Bonnefoi de Montbazin, ensign, 10/20/1801; Peureux de Mélay, left sick on the Ile de France, 4/25/1801; Pierre Antoine Morin, left sick on the Ile de France, 4/25/1801; Désiré Breton, transferred to the *Naturaliste* at Timor, 10/29/1801.

Midshipman, 2nd class: Hyacinthe de Bougainville, midshipmen 1st class, Timor, 10/20/1801, transferred to the *Naturaliste* at Port Jackson, 11/3/1801; Charles Baudin (from the Ardennes); Jacques Philippe Montgery, left sick on the Ile de France, 4/25/1801; Jean-Marie Marrouard, assistant helmsman, made midshipman 1st class at Timor, 10/20/1801, transferred to the *Naturaliste* at Port Jackson, 11/3/1802.

Doctors: Lharidon de Créménec, surgeon; Hubert Jules Taillefer, assistant surgeon, transferred to the *Naturaliste* at Port Jackson, 11/3/1802.

Surveyor: Charles Pierre Boullanger.

Astronomer: Frédéric Bissy, left sick on the Ile de France, 4/25/1801.

Botanist: Leschenault de la Tour, left sick on Timor, 6/2/1803.

Zoologists: René Maugé, died on Maria Island (Tasmania), 2/21/1802; Francois Péron; Stanislas Levillain, died at sea, 12/29/1801.

Mineralogist: Louis Depuch, died on the Ile de France, February 1803.

Painters and draftsmen: Charles Alexandre Lesueur; Nicolas Martin Petit; Jacques Milbert, left sick on the Ile de France, 4/25/1801; Louis Lebrun, left sick on the Ile de France, 4/25/1801.

Gardeners: Anselme Riedlé, died on Timor, 10/21/1801; Antoine Sautier, died at sea, 11/15/1801; Antoine Guichenot.

Le *NATURALISTE:* 350-ton transport vessel;
left from Le Havre, 10/19/1800;
returned to Le Havre, 6/7/1803.

Commander: Emmanuel Hamelin, frigate captain.

Lieutenants: Bertrand Bonie, lieutenant commander, left sick on the Ile de France, 4/25/1801; Pierre Milius, lieutenant commander, made frigate captain at Timor, 10/20/1801.

Ensigns: Louis de Freycinet, lieutenant commander at Timor, 10/20/1801, commander of the *Casuarina,* 9/23/1802; Jacques de Saint-Cricq, lieutenant commander at Timor, 10/20/1801; Francois Hérisson; Furcy Picquet, disembarked at Timor, 8/26/1801.

Midshipmen, 1st class: Joseph Ransonnet, ensign at Timor, 10/20/1801; Charles Moreau, ensign at Timor, 10/20/1801; Julien Billard, left sick on the Ile de France, 4/25/1801; Étienne Giraud, left sick on the Ile de France, 4/25/1801; Victor Couture; Joseph Brue, embarked at the Ile de France 4/21/1801.

Midshipmen, 2nd class: Mengin Duvaldailly; André Bottaud, left sick on the Ile de France, 4/25/1801; Brèvedent de Bocage, assistant helmsman, made midshipman, 2nd class, at Timor, 10/20/1803, transferred to the *Casuarina,* 9/23/1802, ensign, 10/26/1803.

Doctor: Jérôme Bellefin, surgeon.

Pharmacist: Francois Collas.

Astronomer: Pierre Francois Bernier, died at sea, 6/6/1803.

Surveyor: Pierre Faure, disembarked on the Ile de France, 4/25/1801.

Botanists: André Michaux, disembarked on the Ile de France, 4/25/1801; Jacques Delisse, left sick on the Ile de France, 4/25/1801.

Zoologists: Bory de Saint-Vincent, left sick on the Ile de France, 4/25/1801; Désiré Dumont, left sick on the Ile de France, 4/25/1801.

Mineralogist: Charles Bailly.

Painter: Michel Garnier, left sick on the Ile de France, 4/25/1801.

Gardeners: Francois Cagnet, left sick on the Ile de France, 4/25/1801; Merlot, disembarked on the Ile de France, 4/25/1801.

Le *CASUARINA:* 30-ton schooner;
commissioned at Port Jackson, 9/23/1802;
decommissioned at the Ile de France, 8/29/1803.

Commander: Louis de Freycinet.

Lieutenant: Brèvedent du Bocage, then Joseph Ransonnet.

A Bedji native (New Holland). Pastel and charcoal by Nicolas Petit, painter of the Baudin expedition. (Muséum d'histoire naturelle, Le Havre. Photo © the museum/Photeb.)

mer Jardin du Roi, which in 1793 became the Museum of Natural History—two botanical voyages to the Far East and the South Seas; in 1796–1798, a third voyage, to the Antilles on the *Belle Angélique,* so increased the holdings of the Museum that A. L. de Jussieu declared: "Never before had such large collections of such well-chosen vegetation in full growth been brought back to Europe."

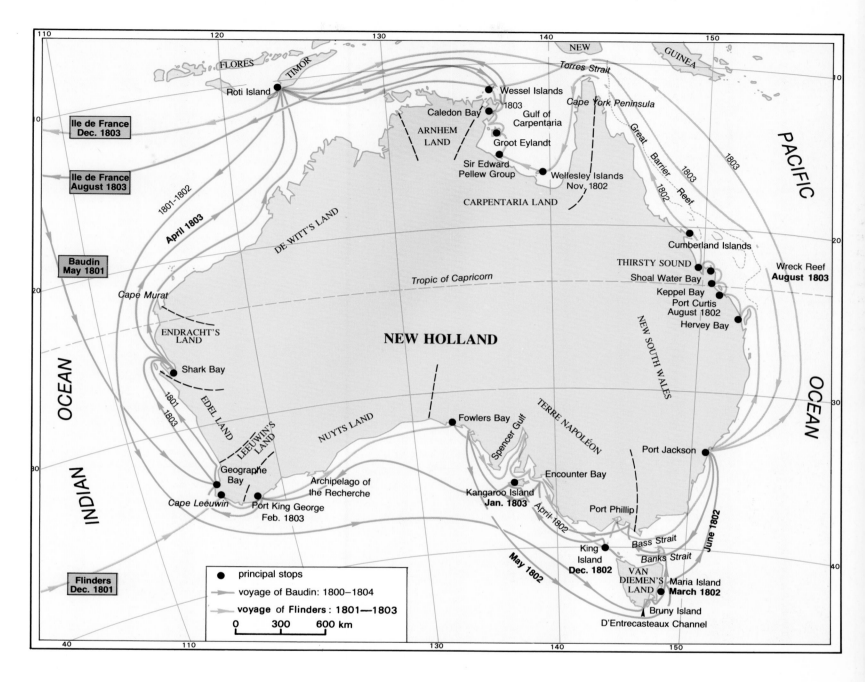

NEW GUINEA

Torres Strait

Wessel Islands
1803
Caledon Bay · Gulf of Carpentaria
ARNHEM LAND · Groot Eylandt
Cape York Peninsula

Sir Edward Pellew Group · Wellesley Islands **Nov. 1802**

CARPENTARIA LAND

Great Barrier Reef

FLORES

TIMOR

Roti Island

Ile de France **Dec. 1803**

Ile de France **August 1803**

1801-1802

April 1803

Baudin May 1801

DE-WITT'S LAND

Tropic of Capricorn

Cumberland Islands

THIRSTY SOUND
Shoal Water Bay
Keppel Bay
Port Curtis **August 1802**
Hervey Bay

Wreck Reef **August 1803**

NEW HOLLAND

NEW SOUTH WALES

Cape Murat

ENDRACHT'S LAND

Shark Bay

EDEL LAND

1801 *1803*

LEEUWIN'S LAND

Geographe Bay

Cape Leeuwin · Port King George **Feb. 1803**

NUYTS LAND

Archipelago of the Recherche

Fowlers Bay

Spencer Gulf

TERRE NAPOLÉON

Encounter Bay

Port Jackson

Kangaroo Island **Jan. 1803**

April 1802

Port Phillip

May 1802

King Island **Dec. 1802**

Bass Strait

Banks Strait

June 1802

VAN DIEMEN'S LAND

Maria Island **March 1802**

Bruny Island

D'Entrecasteaux Channel

Flinders Dec. 1801

PACIFIC OCEAN

INDIAN OCEAN

- principal stops
→ voyage of Baudin: 1800–1804
→ voyage of Flinders: 1801—1803

0   300   600 km

Shortly thereafter, Baudin had conceived a bold project. He planned not only to reconnoiter the still-unknown southern coast of New Holland, but to make a vast circuit across the Pacific—where it was hoped new islands would be discovered—and even as far as the South American seaboard. Convened by Bonaparte, the commission of the Institute of France (on which served, along with Bougainville—who, though he was seventy-one, had for a time hoped to lead the expedition himself—the zoologists Etienne de Lacépède and Georges Cuvier and the botanist Jussieu) reduced this overambitious program and limited it to New Holland. "The goal proposed by the Government is to make a detailed exploration of the coasts of the southwest, the west, the northwest, and the north of New Holland, some of which are still unknown and others imperfectly known. . . . By uniting the work that will be done in this region with that of the English navigators, we will gain knowledge of the entire seaboard of this great southern body of land." There was still some question as to whether this fifth continent was split in two near the middle, with a large strait perhaps uniting the deep bend charted on the southern coast with the Gulf of Carpentaria noted in the north.

Twenty-four scientists on board

At the instigation of the Institute, the First Consul personally appointed the most impressive scientific team that had ever been assembled for a maritime voyage. It included astronomers, geographers, mineralogists, botanists, and zoologists, as well as gardeners and draftsmen; they were equipped with every necessary instrument, made by the best specialists. Among the scientists were four men who had accompanied Baudin on his last expedition: the astronomer Bertnier, the zoologist Maugé, the as-

French and English in New Holland, 1800–1805.
Voyage of Nicolas Baudin, 1800–1804.
Voyage of Matthew Flinders, 1801–1803.

97

Portrait of a Bara-Uru native (Van Diemen's Land). Watercolor by N. Petit, 1802. (Muséum d'histoire naturelle, Le Havre. Photo © the museum/Photeb.)

sistant naturalist Levillain, and the gardener Riedlé. None would see France again.

As a precaution, there were two or even three representatives of each discipline. Baudin was worried. "There seemed too much to cover, and I made several objections to this—but to no effect." For the most part, those chosen were enthusiastic and inquisitive young men, and though they were remarkable for the extent of their learning, they were little able to accept shipboard discipline and quickly found themselves in conflict with a hard and authoritarian commander. Twenty-four set out and only six returned; and even two of the latter died soon afterward of the hardships they had endured. Of the eighteen others, five died during the voyage and thirteen were put ashore at ports of call, most of them sick.

In Le Havre, two ships had been fitted out for the expedition: the *Géographe,* a 350-ton corvette armed with thirty cannon, and the *Naturaliste,* a large and sturdy storeship. Baudin took command of the *Géographe;* that of the *Naturaliste* was given at his request to frigate captain (commander) Emmanuel Hamelin, hero of the struggle against the British navy. The officers were chosen from among the elite. Of special note were the Freycinet brothers, Henri and Louis Claude, ensigns; the former was twenty-three, the latter twenty-one, and both were to play significant roles during the voyage. The midshipmen included a young man of seventeen, Hyacinthe de Bougainville, the eldest son of the celebrated navigator. By a curious coincidence, there were on board the *Géographe* three Baudins who were not related: the commander of the expedition; the ship's lieutenant, François André Baudin, who was put ashore sick at the Ile de France (Mauritius) in 1801; and a sixteen-year-old second-class midshipman, Charles Baudin, whose father had represented the Ardennes at the Convention and who fifty years later was one of the last naval officers to bear the title of admiral.

On orders from the "august leader who presided over the destiny of France," everything had

been done to assure the good health of the crew; the holds were crammed with carefully chosen provisions and fresh stores, and distillation apparatus was to be found aboard each vessel. Complete sanitary instructions had been especially drawn up by a leading naval medical officer, M. Keraudren. The expedition was provided with passports issued by all the European governments and could draw unlimited funds from accounts opened with major European banking establishments in Africa and Asia. Success seemed so assured that a medal had already been struck by the Mint.

Saluted by a military fanfare and by artillery salvos, the *Géographe* and the *Naturaliste* left Le Havre on October 19, 1800. But they were scarcely out of the port when they were stopped by a British frigate, the *Proselyte,* which checked to see that they had been given safe conducts by His Britannic Majesty—a useless but symbolic gesture meant to emphasize that, though Bonaparte dominated the continent, Great Britain remained mistress of the seas.

From the first to the thirteenth of November, the two ships dropped anchor at their first port of call, Santa Cruz de Tenerife. Well received by the Canary notables, the young naturalists went to work with a will. The painter Milbert wrote: "We saw coming toward us through these charming wilds the good M. Riedlé, the head gardener of our expedition; he was weighed down by his ample harvest, which he set down nearby, displaying its glorious richness." A little later, the zoologist Stanislas Levillain appeared: "His hat, completely covered with insects pinned to it, gave him a comic aspect; his specimen case was similarly well furnished."

But these enchanting landscapes were juxtaposed with the sordid. Wandering around the environs of Santa Cruz, the voyagers, Milbert wrote, arrived at "one of those places of repulsive aridity, surrounded by crumbling rocks the color of sulfur and charred by a devouring sun. On coming upon this place of horror, one wonders if it could possibly be inhabited. Yes: It serves as a shelter for several wretched families, and especially for prostitutes, who have made it, far from the city, the scene of their debauchery. It is in these awful lairs that the soldiers of the garrison and the sailors of the port come to carry out their disgusting orgies. . . ."

After turning over their harvests for the museum to a Spanish ship that was returning to Cadiz, the naturalists reembarked.

Discontentments and desertions

It took 145 days, almost five months of navigation, to reach the Ile de France. Baudin had not taken the usual ocean route but had followed the African coast, where the ships were immobilized by equatorial calms. Food supplies were giving out, and the civilians were beginning to be discouraged. Milbert noted: "Surrounded on all sides by a fluid that seems like a vast lake of oil reflecting the color of an overcast gray sky that reaches to the edge of the horizon, we are drawn from our gloomy reveries only by the ocean surge that sluggishly raises the ship and makes it turn every which way without making it possible to give it any direction."

A further mishap occurred at the Ile de France, which was finally reached on March 15, 1801; the third ship that was to join the expedition failed to appear. The commander having quarreled with the local administrator who was to procure food supplies, the stock of provisions taken on board turned out to be insufficient. At this point there was a massive desertion; forty men refused to continue the voyage. There were even several officers among them, including two of the three lieutenants from the *Géographe* and one of the two lieutenants aboard the *Naturaliste*. A significant part of the scientific team also went ashore, some of them really sick but others simply unable to put up any longer with Baudin's authoritarian behavior. The astronomer Frédéric Bissy, the botanists André Michaux and Jacques Delisle, the zoologists Bory de Saint-Vincent and Désiré Dumont, and the painters Jacques Milbert and Louis Lebrun remained on the Ile de France.

These men turned out to be foresighted. The *Géographe* and the *Naturaliste* had scarcely left the Ile de France, setting sail for New Holland, before the commander announced that the bread ration would be cut in half, the wine ration replaced by a single goblet of cheap alcohol, and biscuits and cured provisions served in lieu of fresh meat. The threat of scurvy already hovered over the crew, and in addition, the delay encountered on the African coast made it necessary to modify the itinerary. Instead of putting in at the relatively hospitable Van Diemen's Land, they were to go directly to the barren and dangerous coasts of western and northern New Holland.

It was now necessary to move quickly to outstrip Captain Matthew Flinders, who, charged with a similar mission, must already have left England; they would probably soon cross his path in the region. On June 1, 1801, the *Géographe* and the *Naturaliste* reached the coast of Leeuwin's Land at the extreme southwest of Australia and dropped anchor in what was called Geographe Bay. A detachment was sent ashore but was unable to make contact with the natives, who fled as soon as anyone came near them. A few days later, they were finally able to get close to one of them— a pregnant woman who had been unable to flee with the others. "She was horribly ugly and disgusting."

Until August, the two ships sailed north, going around the continent and successively touching at the different points that had been noted by seventeenth-century Dutch navigators but had not yet been explored. Each ship did this on its own, because they were soon separated by bad weather and were not to join up again until three months later at Timor.

The *Géographe* skirted Endracht's Land and came to the vast Shark Bay, where they found an

NOUVELLE-HOLLANDE: Île Bernier.

extraordinary abundance of whales; the absence of water points, however, made it impossible to foresee an eventual fishing installation. The naturalists were amazed at the wealth of marine fauna, which contrasted with the rarity of land animals. Despite this scarcity, twenty-four kangaroos were taken on board; but, with the exception of one that lived until the ship reached Timor, they all soon died. On July 6, at Bernier Island, while he was examining the strange red-headed marine serpents that bred in these warm waters, the intrepid Péron was thrown against the rocks by waves; bloody and covered with wounds, he had to be rescued by a boat.

Then the *Géographe* followed the coast along the north to which the name of Witt's Land had been given. The English explorer William Dampier had been there a century before, and no other navigator since. The rediscovery was nevertheless extremely disappointing. "None of the land that we have explored up to Geographe Bay seems to offer resources to navigators. The soil is sandy and in many places lacks vegetation." Along the way, the Frenchmen noted and named islands, capes, and gulfs. In the *Atlas hydrographique du voyage* (Hydrographic Atlas of the Voyage) that was published in 1812, they were given names that were later to disappear: Cape Murat, Champagny Archipelago, Arcole Islands . . .

The first deaths

By August, the crew had become so exhausted that Baudin, despite his obstinacy, had to put in at hospitable Timor, near the north coast of Australia. The *Géographe* dropped anchor in the bay of Kupang on August 22, 1801, and the commander immediately visited the Dutch governor to arrange for the hospitalization of the scurvy cases.

Striped bandicoot, species discovered on Bernier Island off the coast of New Holland. Engraving by Choubard from a drawing by C. A. Lesueur. (Bibliothèque du Muséum d'histoire naturelle, Paris. Photo © Bibl. du Muséum/Photeb.)

The governor kindly put three buildings at his disposal—one of which was to be used as a hospital—and overwhelmed the navigators with gifts.

As for the young scientists, after so many privations and sufferings, they profited from the exquisite hospitality of the Malays. According to custom, Péron received a proposal to exchange names with his new friend, a local kinglet, and he tells us of his difficulty: He could not bring himself to call the king Péron, whereas the Malays would never address him as other than Lord Amadima.

The naturalists were excited by the celebrations given for them. "Soon the dances began to the sound of several simple instruments that were particular to these regions and accompanied the singing of the dancers. . . . We admired the energy with which these islanders expressed the nature of each of their dances; the women, especially, gracefully modified the tunes that indicated the change of dance figures intended to evoke or express various passions. This spirited and animated tableau became even more so in the warlike pantomimes to which the regional costumes infinitely lent themselves. The sable darkness surrounding us endowed the spectacle with something fierce, especially after a sad and muffled song that was very much like a howl."

But sickness was rampant. Though by September 15 most of the scurvy cases had been all but cured, a new plague, dysentery, forced eighteen men to take to their beds. They were cared for with admirable devotion by the surgeon of the *Géographe*, Lharidon, who paid from his own pocket for the necessary medicines, going so far as to leave some of his clothes as a pledge. But his treatment was of no avail against this disease, and "those who were gravely ill inevitably died."

Among those stricken was Captain Le Bas de Sainte-Croix, Baudin's second in command, who had to be left at Timor while still sick; the mineralogist Depuch; the zoologist Maugé; and the gardener Riedlé. The last-named, having refused to stop

gathering specimens—he had brought together a large collection of dried plants and seeds that were sent from Timor to France—paid for his imprudence with his life. Following upon the death of several sailors, he died on October 21 and was buried next to another victim of duty, David Nelson, the botanist of Captain Bligh's voyage, who had died of fever at Kupang on June 20, 1789. Baudin himself was stricken by a pernicious "ataxic" fever that was so violent that for several hours he was thought dead. However, he recovered, which was not true for the gardener Sautier and the naturalist Levillain; they died at sea after the departure from Timor.

On September 21, the *Naturaliste,* having in the interval explored the banks of the Swan River, rejoined the *Géographe*. Luckily, there were only two cases of scurvy aboard. Shortly afterward, a new incident again caused an outburst of general indignation against the leader of the expedition.

Ensign Picquet, a good seaman but an impertinent troublemaker, was informed by letter that he was to quit the *Géographe* and, if possible, take up his place aboard the *Naturaliste*. "Having received this letter," Baudin wrote, "he came storming into my cabin, foaming with rage, and began thus: 'Damn it, sir, I find it very strange that you should write to me in this way . . .' " Picquet was interned in the Timor fort for six weeks, but the entire staff of senior officers openly declared their sympathy for him; every day, an officer or a naturalist came to share his captivity. Baudin did not allow himself to be impressed and managed to have the Dutch authorities transfer the prisoner to Batavia and "plunged into those deadly cells of the city's fortress," Péron wrote. He added that, despite objections from the commander, Picquet was soon freed by the Dutch and, upon his return to France, was made a lieutenant. "That should give some idea of his crimes!"

Lovable savages

On November 13, 1801, the *Géographe* and the *Naturaliste* left Timor for Van Diemen's Land, reaching the D'Entrecasteaux Channel, south of the island, on January 13, 1802, after two months of difficult sailing during which men died almost every day. There was a shortage of water, and since Baudin refused to increase the rations, some of the thirsty men ended by drinking their urine. There were still twenty-five sick men on board the *Géographe* and eighteen on the *Naturaliste;* nevertheless, from January to March, the exploration of Tasmania and the islands along the southeast coast was carried out. For the first time, the young naturalists penetrated to the heart of the vast rain forest, which they described in terms worthy of the writer Bernadin de Saint-Pierre, in whose works they were steeped.

"A mysterious shadow, an extreme coolness, and a penetrating humidity reign there all the time;

Malay horseman from the island of Timor. Engraving by the Frères Lambert from a drawing by N. Petit, extract from the historical Atlas of the Voyage aux terres australes. (Bibliothèque du Muséum d'histoire naturelle, Paris. Photo © Bibl. du Muséum/Photeb.)

trees fall into decay, and from them spring vigorous sprouts; the old trunks, now decomposed by the joint action of time and humidity, are covered with mosses and parasitic lichens; their interiors harbor cold reptiles and legions of insects, and they choke all the forest paths, criss-crossing in a thousand different directions; on all sides, like so many protective boundaries, they prevent one from going forward and multiply obstacles and dangers in the traveler's way; often they give way beneath his weight and drag him down with their debris. . . . To this tableau of disorder and devastation, to these scenes of death and destruction, nature opposes, almost by way of complaisance, everything that is most impressive in its creative powers. Everywhere on the ground one sees these beautiful *Mimosas,* these superb *Metrosideros,* these *Correa* till recently unknown in our country and yet already the pride of our wooded areas. From the shores of the ocean to the summit of the highest interior mountains, we could see powerful *Eucalyptus*—those giant trees of the southern forest, many of which are no less than 160 to 180 feet high and 25 to 30 and 36 feet in circumference. *Banksia* of different varieties, *Protea, Embothrium,* and *Leptospermes* grow like charming borders at the edge of the forest. Elsewhere there are *Casuarina,* so remarkable for their foliage, so precious for the solidity and the rich marbling of their wood. . . . Surrounded by so many unknown things, the intelligence is amazed and can only admire this inconceivable fecundity of nature, which has furnished to so many different climates products so special to them, and always so rich and so beautiful."

In conformity with their mission, the navigators tried to win the good will of the natives. The younger members of the expedition, of whom Péron in his *Voyage* is the spokesman, initially conceived a most romantic image of this savage population. Péron recounts in the following terms the first contacts made with a Tasmanian family:

"The young daughter seemed more and more remarkable for the gentleness of her physiognomy and the expression of her glances, both affectionate and intelligent. Like her parents, Uré-Uré was completely nude and seemed totally unaware that this absolute nudity might have been considered immodest or indecent. . . . M. Freycinet, who was seated alongside her, seemed to be the particular object of her teasing. . . . He took Uré-Uré by the arm; the old man fell to my lot; M. Lesueur gave his hand to the young man; M. Brue, our midshipman, led the child. . . . This sweet confidence the inhabitants show in us, these affectionate demonstrations of good will of which we are the constant object, the sincerity of their behavior, the candor of their manners, the touching innocence of their caresses, all seem to join in developing in us feelings of the most tender interest. The general union of the different members of the family, this kind of patriarchal life of which we have been witnesses, has moved us greatly; it was with inexpressible pleasure that I saw come to life those brilliant descrip-

tions of happiness and simplicity in the primitive state whose seductive charm I had so often savored in my reading."

But soon, having studied these charming savage women more closely, the young men noticed that "almost all were covered with scars, sad fruits of ill treatment by their fierce spouses." A little later, the spouses put in an appearance. Initially intimidated, they soon grew bolder, and eventually demanded everything the Frenchmen were wearing. "One of the big gold rings," wrote Péron, "that I wore in my ears attracted the attention of a savage, who without saying anything, slipped behind me, quietly put his finger in the ring, and pulled with such force that he would surely have torn my ear off if the loop had not opened." And this despite the fact that to charm the Tasmanians the French

Metrosideros glauca, *Australian bush brought back by the Baudin expedition and planted in the Malmaison gardens. Plate by Redouté for* Description des plantes rares cultivées à Malmaison et à Navarre, *1813. (Bibliothèque du Muséum d'histoire naturelle, Paris. Photo © Bibl. du Muséum/Photeb.)*

Acacia linifolia (mimosa), Australian species brought back by the Baudin expedition and cultivated at Malmaison. Plate by Redouté. (Bibliothèque du Muséum d'histoire naturelle, Paris. Photo © Bibl. du Muséum/Photeb.)

had sung the "Marseillaise"! The disillusionment was complete. "I must frankly declare that all their actions were of a faithlessness and ferocity that revolted both me and my comrades. . . . We decided that it would be best not to appear before these people without sufficient means to control their ill will or to fight off their attacks."

Scurvy

On February 21, 1802, at Maria Island, the zoologist Maugé died. As he breathed his last, he told Baudin: "I die because I was too attached to you and ignored the advice of my friends, but as a compensation for the sacrifice I made you, at least remember me. . . ." Responsible for the death of his faithful collaborator, Baudin was this time unable to hide his emotion. "Then," wrote Péron, "all the areas below deck filled with sick men reverberated with their cries of grief: Never was a more heartrending sight offered to the imagination." In his journal, Baudin noted: "I had only four men, including the officer of the watch, capable of remaining on deck." Dr. Taillefer added: "Everything combined to overwhelm our patients: Having for nourishment nothing but rotting meat, biscuits gnawed at by worms and weevils, a very small ration of stagnant and putrid water; finding themselves deprived of efficacious medicines, crammed into a small ship that was the plaything

of the wind and the sea, and still far from any port, they grew sicker every day."

Stubborn and inflexible, Baudin nevertheless continued his rigorous exploring. On March 6, the two ships sailed along the east coast of Tasmania toward the Banks Strait. In the course of this reconnaissance, the topographer Boullanger, having left in a boat with six men aboard to make some readings, failed to return to the ship. On board, the officers and the scientists called together by Baudin unanimously decided to return south "in order to carefully search the bay which he had been seen to enter." But all their efforts were in vain, and it was decided that Boullanger had been lost at sea. In the meantime, the *Géographe* had not waited for the *Naturaliste,* which had lingered behind. Once more the two ships had lost contact. They were not to join up again—and then only by chance—until Sydney, three months later. Obsessed by the performance of duty, Baudin noted at the time: "Despite myself I had to give up finishing the complete reconnaisance of the east coast of Van Diemen's Land, but the fault is entirely that of the officers."

Shortly after having left the *Géographe,* the *Naturaliste* met up with a British brig that had taken Boullanger and the six sailors on board. While they were being searched for in the south, their boat had drifted out to sea and gone as far north as the Bass Strait.

By the end of March, the *Géographe* reached the low, sandy, and reef-strewn southeast coast of

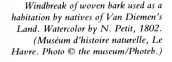

Windbreak of woven bark used as a habitation by natives of Van Diemen's Land. Watercolor by N. Petit, 1802. (Muséum d'histoire naturelle, Le Havre. Photo © the museum/Photeb.)

New Holland, and the area was baptized Terre Napoléon. The point was to lay claim to these still partially unexplored shores, and it was decided that there was no better way than to deck them out in names borrowed from the family of the First Consul, members of the government, and the Institute. Almost nobody was overlooked. Tallyrand Bay extended from Cape Richelieu to Cape Marengo, the site of present-day Melbourne. Bonaparte Gulf and Josephine Gulf, which contained Hortense Bay and Caroline Bay, were united by Lacépède Strait and separated by the Cambacérès Peninsula, at the end of which was Cape Berthier. In 1816, when Freycinet published the "Navigation and Geography" section of his *Voyage aux terres australes* (Journey to the Southern Lands), he felt he had to apologize for having conserved "a nomenclature now objectionable to the political and moral situation of France and Europe"; but the names had already been made familiar by the publication in 1807 of Péron's first volume.

While at work one day "we spotted a ship. . . . Everybody was sure it was the *Naturaliste,* but later they noted with some surprise that the ship was flying a white flag." Shortly afterward, "the British flag and pennant was substituted for it." It was Matthew Flinders; though he had left on the *Investigator* nine months after Baudin's departure, he had followed the Australian coast in the opposite direction, from west to east, and had already discovered a large island—Kangaroo Island—and two deep gulfs that Baudin was not to reconnoiter until later. The meeting between the two captains on April 8, 1802, was most cordial. They spoke of their reciprocal undertakings, and, the next day, Flinders was even obliging enough to come to the *Géographe* and give his rival a copy of a map he had made.

Baudin nevertheless kept sailing toward Nuyts' Land to the west, passing over the route Flinders had already covered. The situation on board had not improved; more than half the sailors were incapable of duty, and there had again been several deaths. It was only when wood and water gave out that the commander consented to change direction. On May 20, the *Géographe* was once again in Adventure Bay on the Tasmanian coast, where she took on provisions. The men were exhausted. Scurvy continued to decimate the crew. As for the surviving scientists, their condition was precarious. "Most of them complained loudly that I wanted to make them die at sea by not putting in to a place where they could obtain some relief. . . . As I did not see things the way these gentlemen did, I continued to keep to the sea rather than be obliged to turn back a fourth time." Finally, Baudin agreed to head for Port Jackson.

A prosperous colony

The port was sighted on June 20, but the crew was in such bad shape that they could not execute the maneuvers necessary to bring the ship in. Seeing

their dilemma, the English sent out a sloop with a pilot and sailors. It was then that Baudin learned that the *Naturaliste,* her supplies exhausted, had dropped anchor at Sydney for twenty days and then set out to look for the *Géographe,* having determined to head for the Ile de France if she did not succeed. He also learned that France and England had signed the preliminaries for the Treaty of Amiens. The French were therefore well received.

Governor King, Baudin wrote, "overwhelmed us with kindness and provided the means to cure our sick." It was not a moment too soon. "At this point," wrote Péron, "almost all our scurvy victims were so sick that in another few days half of them must inevitably have died; two perished the day after we dropped anchor, but with the exception of these unfortunates, all the others regained their health with a speed that bordered on the miraculous; not one died, and a few days were sufficient to return to health men who had been on the edge of the grave."

Delivered from these preoccupations, the French, with King's kindly aid, were finally able to visit the land. Since its establishment fourteen years earlier, the future Sydney had grown impressively. "Europeans whom events at sea or particular reasons bring to Port Jackson," Baudin observed during his stay, "cannot help but be surprised at the

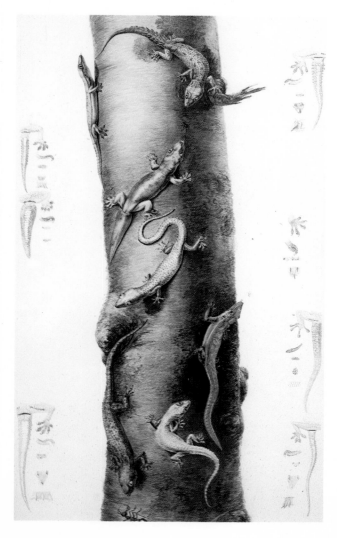

Gecko lizards (New Holland). Watercolor on vellum by C. A. Lesueur. (Muséum d'histoire naturelle, Le Havre. Photo © the museum/Photeb.)

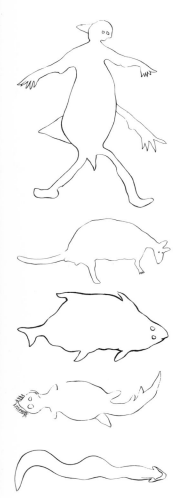

Drawings done by Australian aboriginals and collected on the scene by Petit. From top to bottom: the god of the Blue Mountains, kangaroo, fish, bearded dogfish, moray. (Bibliothèque du Muséum d'histoire naturelle, Paris. Photo © Bibl. du Muséum/Photeb.)

state of ease and prosperity to which this colony has risen since the time of its establishment. Its population, land clearings, and crops have increased by a third in four years."

"The population of the colony," Péron noted, "amazed us. Settled there were frightful brigands who had long been the terror of the government. Most of them, obliged to interest themselves in the maintenance of law and justice, had reentered the ranks of honest citizens. The same revolutionary change had taken place among the women. . . . Wretched prostitutes are today intelligent and hardworking mothers of families."

As for the aboriginals, chased from their lands, they had withdrawn to the arid interior of the country, surviving with difficulty by hunting frogs, lizards, snakes, and even spiders, which "are part of their disgusting meals." They were already suffering from the famines that were to decimate a people pushed little by little toward the desert center of Australia by the progressive penetration of the British.

But at the time, nobody cared—not even the French, who were dazzled both by the harbor installations, which in a few years had made the roadstead of Port Jackson one of the most beautiful ports in the world, and by the work of the colonists, which had already metamorphosed the countryside. They had planted the first grapevines, and fruit trees from Europe grew alongside the eucalyptus, casuarina, and metrosidero. There were even a few Frenchmen among the farmers: an émigré, Baron de La Clampe, who had never heard of Bonaparte and who, with the aid of twelve convicts, looked after plantations of cotton and coffee; a thief and counterfeiter; the former deportee Larra, who, having married a female convict brought here for "infamous behavior," had reordered his life and received the French "with an elegance and even a luxury that one would never have thought possible on these shores."

Thanks to Governor King—who, according to Baudin, made the stay "useful to science by contributing to the increase of our collections"—the naturalists accumulated specimens, particularly in Botany Bay, endowed with some of the most luxuriant flora in the world. During the course of this stay, Lesueur—who, since the disappearance of most of the scientists, had become Péron's collaborator—assembled on his own two hundred birds and sixty-eight quadrupeds that he killed and preserved. With meticulous care, he made several hundred drawings or paintings of landscapes and city views—and especially of animals and vegetation of all sorts—while Nicolas Martin Petit drew portraits of the natives that were remarkable for both their vigor and exactitude.

Finally, in August, to Baudin's great surprise, the *Naturaliste* appeared in the bay of Port Jackson, to which it had been obliged to return by contrary winds. In October, after several months of rest, the crews were not yet completely well. Baudin therefore ordered Captain Hamelin to return to France

with those who were still sick. The *Naturaliste* was also to carry back more than 150 cases of natural history specimens as well as of growing shrubs, some sixty living animals, and innumerable items of ethnological interest.

Baudin took advantage of the opportunity to rid himself of those *Géographe* officers "who had the misfortune to arouse [his] particular dislike." Among these were Midshipman Hyacinthe de Bougainville and Dr. Taillefer, whom Baudin himself had only recently praised for his devotion and who was on his return to France named Surgeon-major of the Navy of the Imperial Guard. The *Naturaliste* reached Le Havre without incident on June 7, 1803, nearly a year before the return of the *Géographe*.

The Géographe *continues alone*

On November 18, 1802, the two ships left Port Jackson together; they were not to separate finally until December 10 in the Bass Strait. At Port Jackson, a small 30-ton schooner, the *Casuarina,* was acquired and was to accompany the *Géographe* as far as the Ile de France. Her command was turned over to Louis Claude de Freycinet. From December 1802 to July 1803, Baudin continued taking bearings on the Australian coast, but this time he was closely watched over by the English; having witnessed the comings and goings of the *Géographe,* they now feared the creation of a rival settlement by the French. The latter were exploring Hunter Island and King Island, off the southern coast, over which the British flag already waved.

Ever since he had become the only zoologist on board—the four others having either been put ashore or died en route—François Péron had exerted himself so that the expedition might not suffer from his failings. When it was a question of his work, he confronted the worst dangers and committed a number of imprudences that were eventually to destroy his health. At King Island, where he had gone ashore with his companions, a sudden squall drove off the *Géographe,* which disappeared. For twelve days, it was not seen again. Péron remained calm. Taking advantage of the occasion, he collected 180 kinds of mollusks and zoophytes, and studied the habits of elephant seals, whose existence was already threatened. Finally, the naturalists were aided by natives "who lived off cassowaries and kangaroos captured by dogs they had trained to hunt, and off wombats they had domesticated." Péron took advantage of this hospitality to take measurements of these natives—to calculate, as he had done elsewhere, the strength of their hands and their backs by means of a manometer recently invented by Régnier. He noted at the time: "These men are tall, slim, and very agile; they have long hair, short noses that are thick and reinforced at the root, sunken eyes, large mouths, protruding lips, and very beautiful and very white teeth."

Finally they came to Kangaroo Island, which had already been discovered and named by Flinders. Baudin nevertheless claimed to be the first to have sailed around it and rebaptized it Borda Island, a name which was replaced in the *Atlas du Voyage* by that of the Minister of the Navy, Decrès—which was to lead to justified complaints by Flinders.

At King Island, they managed to capture three black emus, a kind of Australian ostrich belonging to a variety particular to this island; two of them were to reach France alive. In January–February 1803, when the French returned to Terre Napoléon and continued their prospecting, they captured twenty-seven small kangaroos—Eugene Island wallabies—all of which were put on board alive.

At this time, Baudin wrote to the minister: "An eight-month stay at sea since our departure from Port Jackson enabled me to completely determine all that belongs to the south and southwest coast of New Holland—the two gulfs on which the work had been incomplete are finished, as well as the southern and western part of the great Kangaroo Island."

The *Géographe* next sailed along Nuyts' Land, following the western and then the northern coast. Baudin recorded at the time: "The exploration of this coast would require a ten-year stay." On board, there were fresh outbreaks of sickness and exhaustion. As a result, Baudin was obliged to put into Timor from May 6 to June 3. Péron and Lesueur profited from the occasion to hunt crocodiles, to the great amazement of the population, which was very afraid of them. They managed to bring a completely preserved skin back to the museum. At Timor, they were obliged to put the botanist Leschenault de la Tour ashore, as he was too sick to go on; a few days after they left (June 6), the astronomer Pierre François Bernier, twenty-three, died at sea.

The ships were reprovisioned at Kupang, but there were now so many living animals and plants aboard that the water supply could not last longer than ninety-five days. As it would take forty days to reach the Ile de France, there was scarcely any time left to spend on the Australian coasts; Baudin had to be content with a rapid reconnoitering of the vast Carpentaria Gulf and a portion of the unexplored shore of Witt's Land.

During an expedition on shore, the naturalists got lost. Ensign Montbazin, who was sent to look for them, was able to find them, but he was late in getting back to the ship. According to Péron, Baudin accused him of "behaving criminally in not having abandoned all three (these were the captain's words)"; Montbazin was condemned to pay a fine for every cannon shot that had called him back to the ship.

The sea was heavy, the number of sick men increasing; soon there was not crew enough to man the ship. On July 7, sick himself and sorely depressed, Baudin had to give up. They set sail for the Ile de France.

The *Géographe* arrived there on August 8, 1803; the *Casuarina* arrived on the fifteenth and was im-

mediately decommissioned. Baudin had the pleasure of learning that the *Naturaliste*, which had stopped there in February, had, after several encounters with the English navy, managed to reach France safely with all its collections. But the commander was himself worn out after three years of incessant effort. He died on the Ile de France on September 16, 1803, the last victim of the voyage. On September 23, frigate captain Pierre Milius took command of the *Géographe*, which left the Ile de France on December 15 and, after dropping anchor at the Cape of Good Hope (January 3–24, 1804), entered the Lorient roads on March 25, 1804, after three years and five and a half months of absence.

Black emu couple and its young. Captured on King Island, these birds were brought back to France. Engraving by the Frères Lambert, from a drawing by C. A. Lesueur. (Bibliothèque du Muséum d'histoire naturelle, Paris. Photo © Bibl. du Muséum/Photeb.)

Australian black swan. Plate by John Gould from Birds of Australia. *(Bibliothèque du Muséum d'histoire naturelle, Paris. Photo © Bibl. du Muséum/Photeb.)*

Two men save the situation

The next day began the unloading of a "mass of cases of minerals, dried plants, and shells; of quadrupeds and stuffed or dissected birds; of seventy large cases filled with growing plants, including more than two hundred varieties of useful ones; of about six hundred kinds of seeds contained in several thousand little bags; and finally of about one hundred living animals of rare or completely unknown species." Among these animals, of particular notice were a black panther that lived in the museum zoo; kangaroos of many varieties, and other marsupials; astonishing birds such as the Baudin cockatoo, black and spotted with white; and, especially, the two emus from King Island, which were immediately installed in the Malmaison park amid the animal and vegetable curiosities with which the future Empress Josephine liked to surround herself. The last of the black emus died in 1822. With it vanished a species that in the interval had been completely exterminated in its original habitat.

As soon as he arrived in Paris, François Péron set to work classifying the collections and preparing a catalog that he turned over to the museum. His task completed, he went to Cérilly in the Allier to be with his mother and sisters. He had been greatly weakened by the long fatigue of the journey and was sapped by tuberculosis contracted during those years of deprivation. But, in 1805, having been told that a rumor was being spread that the expedition had been a failure, Péron immediately returned to Paris and asked for an audience with Decrès, the Minister of the Navy.

Before him and before the venerable Fleurieu,

whom Bonaparte had made a counselor of state and a senator, the young naturalist made so convincing an exposition that he turned the situation around. Sent by Decrès to Minister of the Interior Champagny, Péron was entrusted by the latter with the responsibility of co-authoring, with his friend Lesueur, an official account of the voyage; an Institute commission presided over by Cuvier, permanent secretary of the Academy of Sciences, was ordered to examine the collections, to which were added the fifteen hundred drawings and paintings made on the spot and from living models by Lesueur.

On June 9, 1806, during a session of the Academy of Sciences attended by several survivors of the expedition, Cuvier had the following to say: "More than 100,000 samples of animals both great and small make up the collection, which has already furnished information about several important genera; a great many more are still to be examined, and according to the report of the professors of the Museum the number of new species is more than 2,500 . . . as a result, Messieurs Péron and Lesueur have made known more new animals than have all the other naturalist travelers in recent times."

Cuvier added what was at least as important: "The descriptions of M. Péron, following a uniform plan including all the details of the exterior organization of these animals, establishing their natures in a definitive manner and making known their habits and the use that can be made of them, will survive all revolutions of systems and methods." In fact, the zoological investigations of Péron and Lesueur were so complete that they survived as a reference for naturalists at least until British scientists were able to penetrate the interior of the continent.

And Cuvier had mentioned only the zoological results of the missions. Hundreds of living specimens of vegetation were added to the collections of the Jardin des Plantes (Botanical Gardens) and especially to the two experimental gardens—one at Malmaison and the other at the Château de Navarre in the Eure—in which Josephine had a strong interest.

These new species were there cared for by Bonpland, the botanist who had several years earlier accompanied Humboldt to South America and who, until 1814, was the steward of the empress's gardens. In 1812, Bonpland published *Description des plantes rares de Navarre et de la Malmaison* (Description of the Rare Plants of Navarre and Malmaison) with sixty-four magnificent color plates by Redouté. In this work are illustrated the Australian species that had been brought back by the Baudin expedition and had prospered and flourished in France. Among the metrosideros and the acacias or mimosas, particular attention was paid to several shoots of eucalyptus, seeds of which were planted in 1813 in the Toulon botanical garden, where the species adapted itself very well. Fifty years later, systematically planted eucalyptus invaded the Côte d'Azur and then Corsica and Algeria.

"Kangaroo Dance." Charcoal drawing done in New Holland by C. A. Lesueur. (Muséum d'histoire naturelle, Le Havre. Photo © the museum/Photeb.)

Péron was unanimously elected a member of the Institute. Suddenly famous, he was invited everywhere and surrounded by attentive audiences, to whom he spoke only of the positive aspects of the voyage. Still, he refused with dignity the honorable and lucrative post the government wanted to give him. "I would fill it conscientiously and have no time left to myself." Contenting himself with the modest pension awarded him, he settled with Lesueur in a small apartment near the museum so that he could write *Voyage aux terres australes sur le "Géographe" et le "Naturaliste"* (Voyage to the Southern Lands on the *Géographe* and the *Natural-*

iste), the first volume of which appeared in 1807.

His health deteriorated day by day, and he left for Nice in the company of his faithful Lesueur; but he was unable to keep himself from working on his collections of mollusks and ocean fish, even in bad weather. Growing worse, he returned to Paris and then to Cérilly. He spoke of his coming death with a surprising tranquility and serenity. Becoming perceptibly weaker, François Péron died on December 14, 1810, at the age of thirty-five. He left unfinished the *Voyage,* which Louis Claude de Frecinet undertook to complete between 1811 and 1816.

Eucalyptus diversifolia; *species brought back by the Baudin expedition; flowered in 1813 at Malmaison. Plate by Redouté. (Bibliothèque du Muséum d'histoire naturelle, Paris. Photo © Bibl. du Muséum/Photeb.)*

Captain Flinders's shipwrecks, 1801–1803

In 1795, Captain Hunter had been appointed governor of New South Wales. On the *Reliance,* which was bringing him to Port Jackson, he had become friends with the ship's surgeon, George Bass, as well as with a twenty-one-year-old midshipman named Matthew Flinders. Four years earlier, Flinders had accompanied Captain Bligh to Polynesia to transport breadfruit trees from the Society Islands to the Antilles. That mission, which had failed two years earlier because of the *Bounty* mutiny, met with complete success this time; three hundred trees were planted in Jamaica.

Shortly after his arrival in Sydney, Hunter had begun the exploration of the surrounding bays. "He took me with him," wrote Flinders, whose passion for exploration made him grateful for the opportunity to be part of a duty tour that offered the widest scope for his favorite projects. In 1796–1797, he visited with Bass the southeast coast of the fifth continent. The maps made by d'Entrecasteaux's officers and confiscated by the British led to the supposition that there was a channel separating Van Diemen's Land and New Holland. On December 5, 1797, George Bass, on board a whale boat manned by six men and provided with supplies for six weeks, left from Port Jackson to check this. He was able to confirm that there was indeed in the east a channel in which there were merely a few islands,

but, his supplies having given out, he was unable to take readings to the west. Soon after, Bass set out again, accompanied by Flinders, and he discovered that this channel also opened on the west through another strait which he called Hunter. Then Flinders sailed around Van Diemen's Land, on which a French installation would have constituted a grave threat to the New South Wales colony.

Having returned to England in 1800, Matthew Flinders turned to the only person capable of helping him—Joseph Banks. Since 1790, when in the company of Cook he had discovered New South Wales, Sir Joseph had maintained an interest in this possession, to which, from 1779 on, he had suggested that convicts be shipped. President of the Royal Society and the royal adviser for Kew Gardens (the Royal Botanic Gardens), he had become the promoter of all distant scientific expeditions. It was he who had proposed the transporting of breadfruit trees to the Antilles, where they would provide food for black slaves; and it was he who, having founded the African Association, had dispatched Mungo Park to Gambia in 1795. Banks was establishing a network of Kew Gardens botanist-collectors everywhere in the world, and, in 1799, one of these, George Caley, had left for New South Wales.

Sir Joseph therefore showed the liveliest inter-

Flinders's Ship and Crew

The *INVESTIGATOR:* 334-ton sloop, previously called the *Xenophon,* armed with 6 carronades of 12, 2 of 18, 2 cannon of 6, and 2 pierriers; left from Spithead, 7/18/1801; remained at Sydney, 6/9/1803; returned to England in October 1805; crew: 88 men, including officers and scientists; deaths: 19; disembarked: 24; left sick: 15.	**Surgeon:** Hugh Bell.
	Assistant surgeon: Robert Purdie.
	Naturalist: Robert Brown.
	Painter of natural history: Ferdinand Bauer.
	Landscape painter: William Westall.
Commander: Matthew Flinders, frigate captain.	**Astronomer:** John Crosley.
Lieutenants: Robert Fowler, Samuel W. Flinders.	**Mineralogist:** John Allen.
Master: John Thistle, died at Cape Catastrophe, February 1802.	**Gardener and assistant botanist:** Peter Good, died at Port Jackson, 6/11/1803.

est in Flinders's proposal that an expedition be set up to explore the greatest possible extent of New Holland's unknown coasts. This would widen the field of scientific prospecting, and Banks even had in mind a naturalist for the expedition. He had an extraordinary gift for spotting vocations, which his natural generosity helped to develop. In 1798, he had made the acquaintance of a certain Robert Brown, who at the time was only an assistant surgeon in a Scotch regiment; Banks had immediately seen that he was potentially a great scientist and had taken him under his wing. He already knew an excellent artist of natural history, the painter Ferdinand Lucas Bauer, whom Dr. Sibthorp, an Oxford botany professor, had discovered in Vienna. Bauer had accompanied Sibthorp on his voyage to Greece and to the Levant, and in less than two years he had painted a thousand watercolors of plants and 363 of animals. The former served to illustrate Sibthorp's *Flora graeca,* "the most beautiful Flora of all times"— an extremely costly work which was to begin appearing in 1806.

It remained to win over the Lords of the Admiralty, and Banks undertook to do so. He immediately saw that they were eager to be convinced. The Baudin expedition had just left, so it was important to act quickly. Appointed frigate captain, Flinders was given the command of the *Xenophon,* which was rebaptized the *Investigator* and equipped with light arms. Banks saw to it that a cabin was reserved for storing the plants and appointed a Kew Gardens gardener, Peter Good, to look after them. A hothouse was constructed on the deck. Even though France was officially at war with England, the First Consul granted the expedition a passport in exchange for the one that the English had given Baudin.

Brown and Bauer had been joined by the mineralogist John Allen, the astronomer John Crosley, and a nineteen-year-old painter, William Westall, who was given the responsibility for landscapes and figures. The crew comprised eighty-eight sailors and several marines. The fifteen-year-old cabin boy, John Franklin, was one day to become a famous explorer himself.

On July 18, 1801, the *Investigator* left Spithead. She made only brief supply stops at Madeira and then at the Cape, and, on December 6, reached Cape Leeuwin on the extreme west of New Holland. The *Géographe* and the *Naturaliste,* having completed their first visit to western Australia, were now en route to Van Diemen's Land and were not to return to the Australian coast until March 1802, exploring the southern shore from east to west while Flinders was sailing in the opposite direction. On December 10, the *Investigator* dropped anchor in King George Sound, of which Vancouver had taken possession in 1791, and remained there until January 3, 1802.

On December 14, Brown and several officers came across the first inhabitants, who, though surprised, seemed unafraid and "made signs to our gentlemen to return whence they came." Two

View of Port Lincoln (Australia). Oil painting by William Westall, painter for the Flinders expedition. (National Maritime Museum, London. Photo © by the museum/Photeb.)

weeks later, having become more at ease with the strangers, many of the natives had camped near the English tents, but they remained completely uninterested in the exchanges proposed by the English. They were extremely jealous of their women, whom they imagined the English had hidden aboard ship. Flinders noted that they were lively and vehement, and could not speak to one another without shouting. To put on an impressive show, Flinders had the marines drill before them. The red coats and white crossed belts pleased the aboriginals greatly, "having some resemblance to their own manner of ornamenting themselves." The drums excited them, but when they heard the fife they seemed amazed and listened silently for a long time.

Brown was overwhelmed by the incredible floral richness he came across day after day. In three weeks, he gathered five hundred specimens, almost all of them new. Since he had no guide available, he had to do a detailed on-the-spot study of the structure of the plants before drying them and then grouping them in improvised genera. At the following stop, in the Archipelago of the Recherche, he found about a hundred new species, several of which—the nepenthes—were insectivorous.

The fauna was also almost unknown, and the naturalists sent on board kangaroos and emus, as well as a collection of snakes, lizards, and fish. They were beginning to wonder if there were enough scientists on hand to complete the task, but the ship's officers pitched in and helped.

In the Archipelago of the Recherche, they put in to Fowler's Bay on St. Francis Island, where they found an abundance of ashy petrels, black-and-white cormorants, and small blue penguins. They also picked up a hare-sized kangaroo which they had seen hunted down by an all-white eagle, a species of goshawk. Burning winds swept over the land, where the temperature reached almost 39° Centigrade; on board ship it never went above 20°. The

Site of Port Jackson in 1802. Watercolor by William Westall. (Mitchell Library, Sydney, State Library of New South Wales. Photo by courtesy of the Mitchell Library/Photeb.)

vegetation was scorched, and it became difficult to move about.

The first incident

After a curve, the coast began to descend toward the southeast. On February 11, they came across a handful of islands they called the Investigator Group, the principal island being given the name Flinders. These bodies of land were only dried marshes, and it was difficult to find wood. On February 21, the coast veered northwest, and they spotted an island. "There were seals upon the beach, and further on, numberless traces of the kanguroo [sic]. Signs of extinguished fire existed everywhere. . . . " Though the island was covered with woods, it seemed to lack water points, so the captain sent a longboat ashore to investigate. It was never heard from again, and all searching proved vain. Flinders gave to the new island the name of the man in charge of the launch. He had known John Thistle since 1794, and, in 1797, Thistle had been one of the six men with Bass on the whaleboat, later sailing around Tasmania with Flinders. This terrible loss caused great consternation, and present-day maps of Australia have preserved the memory with Cape Catastrophe.

Having climbed a high granite mass, Flinders saw that the gulf extended far behind the coast and formed a vast port; it was named Port Lincoln. Though the site was terribly sterile, there were signs of recent human habitation. Some distance away, a spring was found, and several natives, who did not come near, were glimpsed. When the *Investigator* left

Port Lincoln, Flinders became aware that he was in a vast bay, which he forthwith named Spencer Gulf in honor of the First Lord of the Admiralty. On taking his bearings, he saw that he had penetrated about 148 miles into the interior. He was surrounded by an immense wooden plain overlooked by a chain of reddish clay mountains. One of these heights became Mount Brown.

Still sailing east, not far from Port Lincoln, the *Investigator* came upon a large island covered with forests and crossed by waterways with enchanting banks. Even before they had come close, the sailors had spotted moving gray masses—giant kangaroos measuring more than 1.4 meters high. Once on shore, Flinders and his officers went hunting, for the crew had had no fresh meat in several months. Since these animals did not know man, the island being uninhabited, Flinders alone bagged ten, and the rest of the group thirty-one; the smallest weighed 35 kilos, and the largest, 60. To the north of Kangaroo Island, there was a second gulf surrounded by arid landscapes, Gulf St. Vincent. In between the latter and Spencer Gulf was a peninsula "bearing some resemblance to a very ill-shaped leg and foot"—present-day Yorke Peninsula. The ship next decended toward Kangaroo Island, where a supply of wood was put in while Brown and Bauer collected plant specimens and captured magnificent shiny black cockatoos.

The *Investigator* was following along the dune-bordered lower coast opposite King Island and beyond Cape Jervis when, on April 6, 1802, at nine in the morning, the lookout announced that a white rock lay ahead.

As they drew closer, they became aware that

it was a ship under sail and that the crew was taking up battle stations. "She showed a French ensign . . . I hove to, and learned . . . it was the French national ship *Le Géographe,* under the command of Captain Nicolas Baudin. . . . As I understood no French, Mr. Brown, the naturalist, went with me in the boat . . . I requested Captain Baudin to show me his passport from the Admiralty; and when it was found and I had perused it, offered mine from the French marine minister, but he put it back without inspection." In his account of the expedition, which did not appear until 1814, Flinders complained that Péron, who had published his own account in 1807, did not mention Flinders's discoveries but attributed them to the French.

On April 21, Flinders disembarked on the northeastern coast of King Island situated between Australia and Tasmania. It was covered with such a dense undergrowth that the naturalists had to hack their way through. They gathered a harvest of plants richer than anything they had previously collected elsewhere and found small kangaroos of an unknown variety—the wallabies of King and Flinders Islands—as well as wombats and some marsupials similar to very small bears.

The *Investigator* next entered Bass Strait. At daybreak, a large flock of gannets was seen, followed by more fulginous petrels than had ever been seen before. It looked like a ribbon at least 300 meters wide. The birds flew in as compact a group as the movements of their wings would permit, and for a good hour and a half this ribbon of petrels moved past without interruption at a speed hardly less than that of a pigeon. Flinders estimated that the total number of these birds—belonging in fact to a species that the navigator had just discovered, the short-tailed shearwater—was more than 150 million, a figure that seems fantastic but is completely probable.

On May 9, the *Investigator* reached Port Jackson and found the *Naturaliste* anchored there. Flinders informed Hamelin that Baudin intended to come to Port Jackson as soon as the weather permitted. On June 4, he and his officers went to pay their respects to His Excellency the Governor and to the naval officer in charge. In honor of His Majesty, a splendid dinner was offered to the settlement.

At that time, the governor of New South Wales was Philip Gidley King. He offered Flinders, for use along with the *Investigator,* a 60-ton brig, the *Lady Nelson,* which, in December 1801, under the command of Lieutenant Grant, had been the first ship to go through Bass Strait from end to end. Under the command of Lieutenant Murray, the *Lady Nelson* set out again with a crew composed mainly of convicts, some of whom also shipped out on the *Investigator* to compensate for the losses she had suffered. In addition, King gave Flinders two aboriginals, Bongaree and Nabaree, who were to serve as interpreters to the tribes encountered. Several cases containing natural history collections were dis-

patched to London, but the naturalists set out in the governor's gardens the living plants they were to pick up on their return.

On July 22, the two ships started north. On August 1, they reached Hervey Bay and, on the seventeenth, Keppel Bay. There Flinders discovered and named seventy small islands. The coast was flat, covered with mangrove swamps; farther inland were salt marshes and then rocky hills. Brown found eucalyptus and cycas, one of which was a new species, *Cycas angulata;* and Allen collected minerals. The region was all but uninhabited, though they encountered several aboriginals, "black and naked"; these showed little interest in the presents offered them, but they set the naturalists back on the path from which they had strayed. They did not understand a word said to them by Bongaree.

Beyond Keppel Bay, navigation became dangerous. At varying distances from the coast, the Great Barrier Reef—some of it submerged and some breaking through the surface of the water and separated by channels—extended for hundreds of miles. At Port Bowen, no inhabitants were seen, but traces of fire were found; the waters were alive with fish, but the soil was barren.

The *Investigator* then dropped anchor in several unknown bays and, on September 28, discovered a group of islands which, though uninhabited, were visited by fishermen who probably came in search of tortoises. Here the naturalists caught several large fruit-eating bats. In this region the *Lady Nelson* struck a reef and lost her keel. She could no longer follow along, and Flinders sent her back to Port Jackson. The *Investigator* then had to sail some 500 miles inside the Great Barrier Reef before finding a channel that would permit her to regain the open sea. During this time, Flinders made some important observations about the formation of coral reefs, the nature of which he was among the first to understand; he recognized that the skeletons of madrepores transformed themselves into rock at the very spot in which they have grown, while the upper branches continue their growth and create new elements on the base thus raised.

Arriving at the extremity of Cape York Peninsula, which points toward New Guinea, the ship, having with some difficulty passed through the shoals of Torres Strait, reached the Murray Islands on October 29. Some fifty Australians in three boats sailed out to the *Investigator*. Flinders described them as chocolate-colored men of medium height, lively, muscular, and apparently intelligent. They offered coconuts, bamboos filled with water, bows and arrows. The natives were much taken with the hatchets and iron they were given in exchange, but they refused to come on board, and Flinders, on the alert since the disappearance of the launch, warned his men to be on their guard.

The ship then followed along the flat sandy coasts of the Gulf of Carpentaria. Having sailed up the Coen River, the naturalists found large white cockatoos with yellow crests, cuckoo-pheasants, pelicans, pigeons, sea gulls, and all kinds of wad-

Cephalotus follicularis, insectivorous plant from the Australian marshes. Watercolor by Ferdinand Bauer. (British Museum, Natural History, London. Photo by courtesy of the trustees, British Museum/Photeb.)

ers; many of these species were unknown. Some sailors investigated "huts" seen on the shore; they turned out to be very tall termite mounds. A little farther on, the sailors saw some natives, but the latter immediately fled. Reaching the southern part of the gulf, the coast of which grew progressively lower, Flinders hoped to find a passage that would make it possible to penetrate the interior, since at the time it was thought that the continent might be divided in two; but as they continued, the coast veered toward the northwest. Just as the maps indicated, the gulf was sealed.

Damaged during her passage through the Great Barrier Reef, the *Investigator* was in sore need of repairs, and she was careened at Sweers Island. Her hull was split, and the carpenters said she could go no farther. Flinders wondered if he would have to return to his point of departure, but to go from where he was to Port Jackson presented enormous difficulties. These considerations, joined to his desire to finish his reconnaisance of the Gulf of Carpentaria, made him decide to proceed during the season of the northwest monsoon.

From November 1802 to March 1803, the *Investigator* continued the exploration of the west coast of the gulf, Flinders coming successively upon two groups of islands, which he named in honor of Sir Edward Pellew and of Wellesley, before reaching Cape Wessel at the northwestern extreme of the gulf. At the Wellesley Islands, the naturalists found a new species of marine tortoise, very similar to the green tortoise. In the Pellew Group, Brown discovered two varieties of pigeon, a duck, an owl, two bushes of the *Santalum* genus, and, above all, a robust palm tree, *Livistona australis,* of the kind now planted along the Côte d'Azur.

On January 21, 1803, as a result of a misunderstanding, the aboriginals attacked the crew of a dinghy that had gone ashore; a noncommissioned officer, disobeying his orders, commanded his men to open fire. One native was killed. The corpse was brought back so that it might be examined and drawings made of it.

Relations with the natives they encountered remained ambiguous. Naturalists on a plant-gathering expedition one day found themselves surrounded by apparently friendly aboriginals who accompanied them, but two men got on either side of Brown, and, while one seized his arm, the other grabbed his musket. Unable to catch him, Flinders took as hostage a young man named Wonga and turned him over to the care of Bongaree. His tears of despair touched the hearts of the sailors, and on his promising that he would bring back the stolen musket, Flinders let him go. He was never again seen. Having noticed that the aboriginals were circumcised, Flinders wondered if this practice had not been taken from the Malay Moslems; in point of fact, it was indigenous.

Arnhem Bay proved to be particularly rich in both animal and vegetable species; the naturalists collected eucalyptus, casuarina, and sandalwood, and they captured kangaroos, oyster catchers, black cockatoos, and white cockatoos. Some of the birds were previously unknown—for example, the Australian saurus crane, which grew to a height of 1 meter, and the Torres Strait pigeons, which were almost completely white and came and went in large flocks.

On March 31, the *Investigator* anchored in Kupang Bay, Timor, where she took on a supply of rice, sugar, palm syrup, and arrack—as well as several domesticated buffalo, or carabao, in order to have a supply of fresh meat. Thus equipped, the ship headed toward Port Jackson, but the two-month voyage was a difficult one. The crew was exhausted, and dysentery broke out; seventeen men were sick, and three died at sea.

After the disembarkation at Port Jackson on June 9, four more died—including the gardener, Peter Good—and Flinders was not able to leave until August 10. The *Investigator* being in no condition to take to the sea, Governor King placed three small ships belonging to the British East India Company—the *Porpoise,* the *Cato,* and the *Bridgewater*—at his disposal. The command of the *Porpoise* was given to First Lieutenant Fowler, and Flinders went aboard as a passenger along with the other officers and twenty-two men; the rest of the crew were on the other two ships. Nine men who refused to return were left at Sydney. The naturalists also remained behind. Brown, Bauer, and Allen were to remain there until Flinders returned with a new ship on which they could continue their work.

Grevillea banksii, bush brought back from Australia in 1805 by Robert Brown. Watercolor by F. Bauer. (British Museum, Natural History, London. Photo by courtesy of the trustees, British Museum/Photeb.)

"Wreck Reef Bank," the coral reef on which, in August 1803, Flinders's ships were wrecked. Oil painting by W. Westall. (National Maritime Museum, London. Photo © by the museum/Photeb.)

If, at the end of eighteen months, he had still not come back, they were to return to England on their own.

Seven days after the three ships had sailed, on August 17, off the Great Barrier Reef, the *Porpoise,* carried by the wind, ran aground on a coral reef. Shortly thereafter, the *Cato* in her turn hit a reef and was destroyed. The *Porpoise,* still intact, was pushed farther forward on the reef, and the crew disembarked on a sand bank with the supplies. As for the *Bridgewater,* she had disappeared. The captain, Flinders wrote, had left them to their fate, heading for Batavia without having made the least effort to come to their aid. The *Bridgewater,* after putting in to Bombay, was to be lost at sea on the return trip to Europe.

The bank on which Flinders and the others had taken refuge consisted of sand and bits of coral deposited by the waves on a portion of the reef. They erected a topgallant yard on the bank and flew a blue flag upside down. It was decided that one officer would leave on a cutter and try to reach Port Jackson in order to bring help. The *Porpoise's* provisions were sufficient for three months.

On August 26, christened the *Hope* and commanded by Flinders himself, the cutter left Wreck Reef Bank. On September 8, at Sydney, King, who was at dinner with his family, was so amazed by the entrance of an exhausted and unshaven Flinders, who he thought was sailing toward England, that an involuntary tear ran down his cheek. He immediately placed the *Cumberland,* a very small 29-ton schooner, at the disposition of the unfortunate navigator. Two other ships, the *Rolla* and the *Fran-*

cis, were to escort her in order to pick up the shipwrecked men for whom there would be no room on the *Cumberland.*

The three ships reached Wreck Reef Bank on October 7 and were received with joy. Only a few of the sailors could take ship with Flinders on the *Cumberland,* which put into the Wessel Islands on October 29 and reached Timor on November 10. On the fourteenth, she set sail for England, but Flinders's misfortunes were by no means over. The ship sailed badly, and she was soon so damaged that there was no possibility of going around the Cape of Good Hope.

On December 6, Flinders decided to head for the Ile de France. He was unaware that the Treaty of Amiens had already been broken and that France and Great Britain were once more at war; he was to learn this only on disembarking at Port Louis on December 17. Immediately taken to the governor, he was led into a room where two officers sat behind a table. One of them, a small, spare man laced into his uniform, was Captain-General Decaen, who stared at him and, without so much as a greeting, demanded his passport. Decaen merely glanced at it before brusquely asking how it was that Flinders had come to the Ile de France with a small schooner when his passport had been issued for the *Investigator.* When the Englishman tried to explain, he was interrupted sharply by Decaen, who insisted that Flinders was obviously not telling the truth since the governor of New South Wales would hardly have sent him to lead an expedition on so small a craft. Suspected of espionage, Flinders was immediately placed under arrest. All his papers were confis-

113

Captain Flinders on his return to London after six years of captivity on the Ile de France. (National Maritime Museum, London. Photo © by the museum/Photeb.)

the Flinders wombat, and, later, the koala bear. The plant collection increased, especially the orchids, and Brown made some important observations on their reproductive organs, the functioning of which was not known.

Still expecting Flinders's return, the botanist next went to Tasmania, which had just been declared an English colony. He spent ten months there and made numerous discoveries, notably that of the Tasmanian wolf, or thylacine. During this time, Bauer had left to prospect the flora of Norfolk Island. In 1805, the three naturalists were once more at Port Jackson, from which they embarked with their collections on the *Investigator,* once again seaworthy. They made a long stopover at the Cape, where Brown collected proteas—bushes with giant flowers that grew only in South Africa—as well as several other such decorative varieties as the silver money tree and the lion's tail, which brought the number of species with which they returned to thirty-nine hundred; seventeen hundred of these were new.

The naturalists returned to London with several living animals, including a bare-nostriled wombat that survived for two years in the home of the surgeon Cliff, where it amazed scientists and enchanted children. Thanks to his discoveries, Brown was able to establish the first comprehensive survey of Australian flora, which was later added to but not modified; on the other hand, Brown and Bauer were able only to complete the zoological investigation of Péron and Lesueur, especially in the regions the latter had not visited.

It took Brown five years to study and classify his plants; he had to create fourteen new genera. In 1810, his *Prodromus Florae Novae Hollandiae* was published, followed by an atlas owing to the talent of Ferdinand Bauer. To accomplish this enormous task, Brown had at his disposition the herbarium brought back from New Holland by Sir Joseph Banks, among whose enormous collections at Soho Square he henceforth lived. In 1823, after the death of Banks, he inherited this material and turned the collections over to the British Museum. He nevertheless did not leave the Soho Square house, where he continued Banks's work until his own death in 1858, when he was eighty-five. Bauer went back to his own country in 1814, where he lived in Hietzing—very close to the imperial gardens of Schoenbrunn—and where he continued to paint plants until his death in 1826.

cated, Decaen claiming that he was convinced Flinders had completely distorted the mission for which he had obtained from the First Consul a passport signed by the Minister of the Navy and dated the fourth of Prairial in the year 9. That passport in no way permitted him to put into the Ile de France to note the prevailing winds, the port, and the present state of the colony, and so forth; and by his actions he had violated the neutrality under which he had indirectly been permitted to approach the island.

For the next six and a half years, Flinders was to be the victim of an arbitrary captivity and treated as a criminal by Decaen, who refused even to answer his letters. The intervention of many important people, French as well as British, carried no weight with the irascible general. The insistence of Banks even provoked the accusation that he was trying to maintain an espionage network under the guise of literary correspondence. It was not until Decaen was recalled to France to command the Catalonian army that Flinders was finally authorized to return to England. He arrived there on October 24, 1810, a broken man; but he immediately began to write his account of this voyage full of incident. He died on July 19, 1814—the very day, according to some, that his book was published; other say that he was still correcting the proofs at the time.

The naturalists continue

After Flinders left, Brown, Bauer, and Allen continued their research in the region of Sydney. They captured several new animals, among them a charming little beast that resembled a bear cub and fed only on eucalyptus leaves. It was initially called

114

The Russians in the Pacific, 1803-1829

From Kamchatka to the Marquesas: Krusenstern's Voyage, 1803–1806

The principal preoccupation of Peter the Great had been to draw Russia from its secular isolation and make it into a modern power. Open to the outside world, it would be endowed with an army and especially a navy, corresponding to the role he wanted to see his country henceforth play. As early as 1696, he had wrested Azov from the Turks, and it served as an opening on the Black Sea. Having declared war on Sweden in order to gain access to the Baltic, he succeeded in establishing himself at the mouth of the Neva, where St. Petersburg was founded. In 1716, the tsar dispatched from Okhotsk, on the Siberian coast, a vessel that was to assure the first maritime liaison with the Kamchatka peninsula, discovered twenty years earlier, and to explore the Kuriles. In 1725, Peter I, who was to die that same year, decided to launch a great expedition charged with verifying if Siberia and North America were or were not separated by the sea, and if there was a passage near the pole linking the Atlantic and the Pacific. Commanded by Vitus Bering, the expedition did not leave until 1728; it fixed the position of the strait that separates Asia from America. On a second voyage, in 1740–1741, during which he was to die, Bering and his lieutenant, Aleksey Ilyich Chirkov, discovered Alaska and the Aleutian Islands. After 1739, two Russian ships landed at several points on the Japanese littoral; in 1743, Khmitevskoi reconnoitered the coast of Siberia from Okhotsk to the Kamchatka peninsula.

Afterward, Russian merchants organized voyages designed to bring back from the American northwest furs that they sold at substantial profits to the Chinese, who were particularly partial to sea otter skins. This commerce, initially unregulated, led to the loss of many ships and, eventually, to a rapid depredation of the fauna; it was finally regularized by the rich merchant Chelikov, who, with some difficulty, managed to unite all those who participated in this commerce in a "Russian-American Company" which established trading posts protected by small forts in almost all the Aleutian Islands. Nevertheless, things remained difficult. The completely isolated settlements could not exist without food and equipment sent overland from Russia and then shipped from Okhotsk to the Aleutians by sea. Two years passed before the collected furs were sold, as they first had to be shipped to Okhotsk; it took western sailors only a third of

this time to obtain furs on the American coast and sell them in Macao.

Adam Ivan (Johann) von Krusenstern understood this problem. Having served in the British navy, he had had the opportunity to sail aboard a merchant ship to India and China, where he spent several months in Canton. During his voyages, Krusenstern had become convinced that Russia had to be linked to her American colonies by sailing across the Pacific and rounding Cape Horn, and especially that the fur trade had to be carried out from the colonies directly to Canton. He wrote the Russian Minister of Trade, Saimonov, a memorandum showing how the obstacles to such trade could be overcome. He received no reply. But, in 1801, Alexander I ascended the throne, and he soon turned his attention to these questions, which had been neglected by his father. The following year, Krusenstern sent the new Minister of the Navy, Mord-

vinov, a second memorandum that was strongly supported by the Minister of Trade, Count Romanzof, a great patron of the sciences. The emperor named Krusenstern captain and asked him to carry out his plans himself.

Krusenstern had not foreseen this possibility. In fact, recently married and "awaiting the joy of being a father," he had even planned to leave the service and devote himself to his family. However, on August 7, 1802, he was "named the commander of two ships destined for the northwest coast of America." These ships were still to be found, since the Russian navy had no vessels capable of undertaking such a voyage. Krusenstern chose as his second in command a Captain Lisiansky, who had served with him in the British navy and been to America and the Indies, and sent him first to Hamburg in the company of the shipbuilder Kasumov and then to London, where he bought two vessels, one of 450 tons and the other of 370 tons. They were christened the *Nadezhda* (Hope) and the *Neva*. In London, Lisiansky had also obtained anti-scorbutics and a variety of medicines. During this time, Krusenstern had turned to the German universities in order to recruit scientists for the expedition, for in this matter Russia was still—and would long remain—dependent on Germany. The men selected were the astronomer J. K. Horner, from Zurich, and a Leipzig doctor, W. G. Tilesius von Tilenau, who was also a naturalist and a draftsman. A Göttingen naturalist, G. H. von Landsdorff, tardily asked to be taken along and caught up with the ships at Copenhagen, where he was accepted on board; he was to quit the expedition at Kamchatka. The German poet August von Kotzebue, who had official duties in St. Petersburg, persuaded Krusenstern to take along two of his sons who were navy cadets: Otto and Moritz, then fifteen and fourteen years old, respectively.

While he was preparing the expedition, Krusenstern was charged with a second responsibility: He was to transport to Japan an ambassadorial mission directed by N. P. Resanov, the son-in-law of Chelikov and a chamberlain of the emperor's. As imperial plenipotentiary, Rezanov was to renew with the Nipponese empire relations originally established by a first mission in 1792, which had obtained permission for an unarmed Russian vessel to go to Nagasaki. In addition, five Japanese who had been shipwrecked in the Aleutians in 1796 were to be returned to their country. "It is difficult," Krusenstern wrote, "to imagine nastier men. They were dirty, lazy, always in a bad temper, and highly malicious."

Arriving in Kronstadt from London on June 5, 1803, the *Nadezhda* and the *Neva* set sail on August 7 and reached Copenhagen on the eighteenth, but it was a month before they were able to leave, because some of the salted foods that had been loaded had to be replaced. There was only a one-day stopover at Falmouth on the English coast before the *Nadezhda* and the *Neva* set sail for Tenerife, where they anchored from October 18 to 27.

Brazilian horned frog discovered by Tilesius, naturalist of the Krusenstern expedition. (Bibliothèque nationale, Paris. Photo by Jeanbor © Photeb.)

Krusenstern's Ships and Crews

The *NADEZHDA:* 450-ton English vessel; left from Kronstadt, 8/7/1803; returned to Kronstadt, 8/19/1806; crew: 85 men.

Commander: Adam Ivan (Johann) von Krusenstern, captain-lieutenant (captain).

Lieutenants: 1st, Chevalier Macary Ratmanov; 2nd, Fedor de Romberg; 3rd, Pierre Golovatchev; 4th, Hermann von Loewenstern; 5th, Baron von Bellingshausen.

First doctor: Dr. Carl Espenberg.

Surgeon: Johann Sydham.

Naturalists: Dr. Tilesius von Tilenau, Baron G. H. von Langsdorff.

Astronomer: J. K. Horner.

Cadets: Otto von Kotzebue, Moritz von Kotzebue.

Russian embassy to Japan: Resanov, chamberlain to the emperor, ambassador; Hermann de Friderici, chief of staff; Count Fedor Tolstoi, lieutenant of the guards; Dr. Brinkin, medical doctor and botanist; Etienne Kurlandtzov, Academy painter.

The *NEVA:* 370-ton English vessel; left from Kronstadt, 8/7/1803; returned to Kronstadt, 8/4/1806; crew: 54 men.

Commander: Yuri Lisiansky, captain.

Lieutenants: 1st, Pavel Arbusov; 2nd, Povalichkin; 3rd, Fedor Kovedaev; 4th, Vasili Berg.

Doctor: Dr. Labaud.

The sailors strolled through the streets of Santa Cruz, a city, Krusenstern wrote, "in which one encounters more disgusting objects than anywhere else in the world: all that is to be seen are ragged and disgustingly diseased beggars of both sexes and all ages, prostitutes, drunken sailors, and shameless thieves." The Russian officers were hospitably received by the governor, the Marquis de la Casa Cahigal. Krusenstern proudly noted: "The strange ideas that are current about Russia and Russians in distant lands contributed more than a little to the surprise of our hosts when they saw that these Hyperboreans lost nothing when compared with the cleverest peoples of southern Europe."

In a month, the ships reached the Brazilian coast. At sea, Langsdorff made microscope studies of the marine animalcules that in some places made the sea phosphorescent. Tilesius also did research on the marine microfauna; during the voyage, he began studying diphyes—animals native to warm seas—which floated by means of two swimming

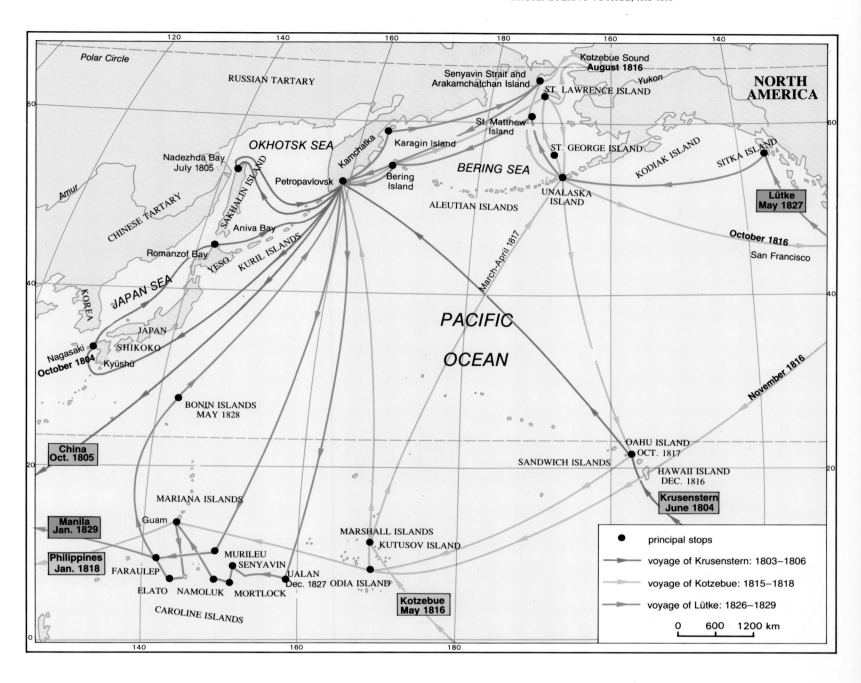

The Russians in the Pacific,
1803–1829.
Voyage of Krusenstern,
1803–1806.
Voyage of Kotzebue, 1815–1818.
Voyage of Lütke, 1826–1829.

bells. The scientists who worked on shipboard during these very long voyages were fortunate in this regard; they had available an abundant and constantly renewed supply of material, and were thus able to make considerable progress in a field that science had only just begun to study.

In Brazil, Krusenstern chose as the site of his stopover Santa Catarina Island, south of Rio, and thus was able to avoid the port "in which foreigners, especially if they arrive aboard merchant vessels, are subjected to all sorts of humiliating formalities." Since the *Neva* was in need of repairs, he remained at Santa Catarina five weeks, and an observatory was set up in Fort Santa Cruz. Delays having accumulated since the departure from Kronstadt, Krusenstern was afraid that at this time of year he would run into storms at Cape Horn. "We were assailed by cold, fog, and contrary winds. . . . Extremely violent blasts of wind accompanied by hail and snow followed one another cease-

lessly." The Cape was rounded on March 3. Luckily, there were no sick men aboard the two ships, which, on March 24, were separated sooner than had been foreseen. According to plan, if this happened, they were to rendezvous at the Marquesas, toward which the *Nadezhada,* having given up the idea of visiting Easter Island, immediately set sail.

Deserters and Marquesans

As they were about to anchor at Nuka Hiva on May 7, 1804, the Russians were surprised to see a European approach in a canoe flying a white flag. It was an Englishman named Roberts, who, like the natives, was naked and wore only a belt around his waist. Roberts had been set down in the Marquesas by the crew of a merchant vessel for having refused to participate in a plot against the captain. For two years, he had lived on Santa Cristina Island and, for

119

Distinguished inhabitant of Nuka Hiva, armed and tattooed. Engraving from Voyage autour du monde sur la Nadjedjeda et la Neva, *1813. (Bibliothèque nationale, Paris. Photo by Jeanbor © Photeb.)*

Tattoo artist's model from the Marquesas. Piece of wood covered with painted bark; probably from a temple. (Musée de l'Homme, Paris. Photo from the collection of the museum.)

a few bits of iron, the men would offer little girls of ten and twelve. One girl who was not even eight offered herself "without the least shame."

The most beautiful tattoos in the world

The Russians were charmed by these people. According to Krusenstern, the Marquesans were the handsomest men he had seen, but he reproached them for their indifference and apathy. He noticed with astonishment that in its natural state their skin was white; only the tattoos and the oil with which they coated themselves made it appear blackish. All seemed in excellent health. The women had harmonious features, but they were small, short, and walked awkwardly.

On the very first day, the king of Nuka Hiva, Tapeya Kettenovie, had come on board. He was "tattooed everywhere, even on his head, several areas of which had been expressly shaved for this purpose." He returned the next morning accompanied by his family. They were astounded by the mirrors in the commander's cabin and "examined the backs of them for some explanation of the marvelous effect." Afterward, every time Tapeya entered Krusenstern's cabin, he would rush to the standing mirror and remain looking at himself, "often for hours."

Krusenstern took advantage of this opportunity to examine the extraordinary Marquesan tattoos. "When they reached the age of manhood, the Nuka Hivans tattoo their entire bodies with a perfection achieved nowhere else. It is a true painting made up of different elements . . . ordinarily they choose black, which gradually changes into a dark blue." However, only the king, his father, and the high priest were tattooed from head to foot; the lower in the social scale an individual was, the fewer his tattoos, and some had none at all. These paintings were done by true professional artists, one of whom established himself on board and tattooed most of the Russian sailors.

On shore, the Nuka Hivans surrounded the seamen, but politely and respectfully. Nevertheless, the two Europeans living on the island described them as being depraved, barbarous, and cannibalistic. Krusenstern wrote that this contrasting judgment was explained by the fact that the islanders believed the navigators were spirits. "Foreign ships fall from the skies, and they believed that thunder could be explained by the cannonades exchanged by the ships in the clouds, where they sailed with the greatest of ease. That is why these islanders are so afraid of our cannon."

A serious incident disturbed the stay in this apparent paradise. A rumor having spread that the king was being detained on board the *Nadezhda,* the inhabitants ran for their arms. The misunderstanding was cleared up, but it was evident that the king himself had provoked it at the instigation of the

the past seven, at Nuka Hiva, where he had married a relative of the island's king. He informed them that there was also on the island a French deserter, a mortal enemy of his whom he warned the Russians against.

On these distant islands, it was already possible to encounter isolated Europeans who were more or less voluntarily living among the natives. They had adopted the local life-style and were most often well treated. They were escaped English convicts or deserters, or sometimes adventurers of every nationality who had deliberately chosen to live in exile. In the decades that followed, there were more and more of them. In 1842, an American sailor was to desert at Nuka Hiva and live for several months with a tribe of cannibals. His name was Herman Melville, and he gave an account of his adventures in two books, *Typee* and *Omoo.*

The Nuka Hivans welcomed the Russians, and the barter began. "At the sight of a piece of iron, they demonstrated a childish joy expressed in bursts of laughter. With an air of triumph, they showed this treasure to their less fortunate companions." Women, eager to seduce the sailors, "swam around the ship for more than five hours," Krusenstern having forbidden them to come aboard. "At nightfall, these poor creatures asked so piteously to be taken on board that I could no longer refuse"—but two days later the commander had to reinstate his interdiction. As he saw it, the women did not come of their own free will but in deference to their fathers or their brutal and tyrannical husbands. To obtain

Frenchman, Joseph Cabri, whom the Russians were later to make an ally and take to Kamchatka. From there, Cabri managed to return to France; in Paris (1817) he displayed himself as a "savage" in a circus at the Saint-Germain fair.

Thanks to Roberts, Krusenstern was able to visit a morai, access to which was usually forbidden to foreigners. Each family had its own. Only the men attended funeral rites; a pig would be beheaded and offered to the gods, then its flesh would be eaten by those present. (Pigs were generally eaten only under these circumstances.) The dead man's body would then be rubbed with coconut oil to preserve it from putrefaction, after which it would become as hard as a rock. At the end of twelve months, the corpse was cut to pieces in a new ceremony and the bones placed in the morai.

On May 11 the *Neva* reached Nuka Hiva, and the two ships sailed at the end of the month for the Sandwich Islands, where Krusenstern planned to reprovision the expedition. But the Hawaians had become exigent and would exchange pigs only for pieces of cloth. Though they struck the Russians as being considerably less handsome than the Marquesans, they seemed "very superior as to intelligence and industry." Unable to get the provisions he wanted, Krusenstern decided to head for Kamchatka immediately. Lisiansky chose to remain in the Sandwich Islands for some time before going to Kodiak Island near the American coast.

It took the *Nadezhda* thirty-five days, but, on July 15, she reached Petropavlovsk in Avacha Bay. Count Romanzof had asked that they look for a land that the Spaniards believed was rich in gold and silver and which was to be found to the east of Japan. Neither the Dutchman De Vries in 1643 nor La Pérouse in 1787 had been able to find it. Krusenstern was convinced that this island did not exist. At Petropavlovsk, Langsdorff left the expedition and went overland to return to Europe by way of Siberia. The entire cargo having been turned over to the Russian colonists, a considerable supply of food was loaded onto the *Nadezhda,* which had been refitted. In the waters of Avacha Bay, which had not as yet been prospected, Tilesius discovered many new species of fish such as the Pacific cod and the blenny; polyparia, for which he created the genus *Krusensternia;* and holothurians, of which he made an anatomical study.

Krusenstern hoped to reach Nagasaki on Kyūshū Island, the southernmost island of the Japanese archipelago, before the northeast monsoon; but rain and fog kept him in Kamchatka until September 6. At sea, the weather was constantly bad, and a storm off the Kuriles caused the ship to spring a leak. Nevertheless, Krusenstern carefully charted the Japanese coasts, but he did not find the four islands that figured on La Pérouse's itinerary. Clearing Cape Van Diemen to the south of Kyūshū, he noted that it was incorrectly marked on earlier maps. The good weather had returned, and from a distance one could admire the mountainous landscapes topped by high peaks and also get indica-

tions of the "industry of Japan, the richness of whose cultivations is unequalled."

Japanese suspicion

In October 1804, the *Nadezhda* entered the vast bay of Nagasaki, the only port open to European ships. Following widespread conversions made in the sixteenth century by St. Francis Xavier and his companions—conversions that had resulted in violent persecution—the Nipponese empire had closed in on itself. The Dutch had been permitted to found a small permanent settlement, relegated to the artificial islet of Deshima in the Nagasaki roads; but they were carefully watched and subjected to innumerable vexations. Their trading post, however, was the only channel for relations between Japan and Europe.

The arrival of a Russian ship brought about a new wave of severity. "From the first to the last moment of our stay . . . we have been prisoners aboard our ship. . . . We are not only forbidden to go on shore, but even to take a longboat any distance from the ship . . ." If the Japanese consented to repair the *Nadezhda* at their expense, it was because they hoped to see her leave that much faster. No sooner had the ship arrived than some magistrates, or *banios,* had come on board. They inquired after the route taken by the ship, pointed out where she was to anchor, and confiscated all powder and weapons, including the hunting rifles of the officers. Only the soldiers in the ambassador's guard remained armed, at the express request of the latter, who finally obtained permission to live on shore; however, by a typically Japanese paradox, the prince of Fisen insisted on sending his own boat for him. "She was enormously large and magnificent—her length being 120 feet—and the sides shone with the most dazzling lacquer; matting and precious rugs covered all the planks . . ."

The house placed at the ambassador's disposition was behind a great door with two locks—one on the outside and the other inside—the keys to which were retained by two Japanese officers. Re-

Drawings of tattoos on inhabitants of Nuka Hiva. Voyage Around the World *by G. H. Langsdorff, 1812. Engraving by J. C. Bock. (Bibliothèque du Muséum d'histoire naturelle, Paris. Photo © Bibl. du Muséum/Photeb.)*

Artificial islet of Deshima in the Nagasaki roads, site of the Dutch trading post—the only authorized European establishment in Japan. Anonymous watercolor. (Musée de la Marine, Paris. Photo by Michel Didier © Photeb.)

121

Krusenstern visits a morai isolated in the Nuka Hiva mountains in May 1804. (Bibliothèque nationale, Paris. Photo by Jeanbor © Photeb.)

Ainu men from the northern coast of Yeso. The one smoking the pipe is dressed in sealskins. (Bibliothèque nationale, Paris. Photo by Jeanbor © Photeb.)

sanov was not permitted to go to Edo, the imperial residence. After a five-month wait, on April 3, 1805, an official brought a response to his request: The emperor refused to receive him and returned all his gifts, for he had no intention of sending any himself. Henceforth, all Russian ships were forbidden in Japanese ports. In the end, as a result of this embassy, the Russians lost even the "privilege they had of entering Nagasaki."

After having obtained the necessary provisions, there was nothing for the commander to do but quit the port. For the return to Kamchatka, Krusenstern chose the longest route so that he might explore the western coast of the Nipponese archipelago—the coast facing China—from south to north right up to the large island, Saghalien (Sakhalin), discovered by La Pérouse. Along the way he gave Russian names to the newly discovered capes and bays. Having passed Tsugaru Strait, the *Nadezhda* reconnoitered the coasts of Yeso (Hokkaido), whose name in Japanese means "land of the barbarians." Its savage aspect contrasted with that of intensely cultivated Japan proper.

The Ainus and the Tartars

Having dropped anchor at the northern part of the island in Soya Bay, which was given Romanzof's name, the Russians entered into contact with the indigenous non-Japanese population. "The inhabitants of Yeso call themselves Ainus; they also live in the southern part of Sakhalin. . . . They are dark-skinned, almost black, and have thick and bushy beards and black hair. . . . Their women are ugly. . . . The principal characteristic [of the Ainus]

is kindness. . . . They brought us fish without asking anything in return . . ." Though relations between the navigators and the peaceful Ainus were excellent, the Japanese who controlled the ports of Yeso demanded that the Russians leave immediately. Once the La Pérouse Strait had been crossed, they anchored in Aniva Bay at the southern end of Sakhalin; but the Japanese were settled there too, and Ambassador Resanov was in a hurry to reach Kamchatka. After having reconnoitered the gulf, which he called Patience and which is La Pérouse's De Langle Bay, Krusenstern therefore cut east toward the Kuriles, which he traversed.

On June 6, the *Nadezhda* was back in Petropavlovsk. The unfruitful mission embarked several weeks later on the *Maria* and returned to St. Petersburg in October. Krusenstern now had only to attend to the affairs of the Russian-American Company, and he made a detailed on-site investigation of its functioning. The status of its sailors and employees was extremely precarious. Having come there in hopes of making their fortunes, they were stagnating under extremely primitive conditions in this frozen land, and they were subjected to cruel and tyrannical leaders. Exhausted by sickness, by insufficient and irregularly available food, and by bad treatment, few of them saw their homes again. The fate of the colonists established on the American coast was no more enviable.

On July 9, Krusenstern left to complete the exploration of Sakhalin. This time he followed its northern coast in search of the channel which, according to La Pérouse, separated this island from the Asiatic continent; he failed to find it. The crops that could be seen on the island "suggested a population more civilized than the Ainus." The Russians were greeted by the Tartars with "sweeping gestures and embraces," but their greed was in painful contrast with the friendly disinterest of the Ainus, whom they had driven from this part of the island. Krusenstern did not continue his exploration to the coasts of Tartary because he was fearful of confrontation with the armed ships the Chinese maintained in their ports.

Back in Petropavlovsk on August 29, he sent to St. Petersburg a courier carrying a résumé of his voyage, as well as maps, drawings, and natural history collections so that this material might not be lost in case of shipwreck. On September 9 he set out for China, where he was to join up with the *Neva*. The *Nadezhda* reached Macao on November 20, the *Neva* on December 3. The two ships had been separated for eighteen months.

In the meantime, Lisiansky had visited the company's settlements on Kodiak and Sitka Islands to the south of the Alaskan peninsula. He had brought with him a large cargo that was to be exchanged for Chinese goods. But at Canton the sale of the furs was hindered by the bad will of the authorities, and it took interminable negotiations to bring it off. The Russians were not able to leave Canton until February 6, 1806—twenty-four hours before orders for the seizure of the two vessels arrived from the Peking court. The ships traversed Sunda Strait in March, and after a four-day stay at St. Helena and another stop at Copenhagen, were back in Kronstadt in August 1806.

In three years and twelve days of navigation in all but unknown seas, Krusenstern had not lost a single man and he had brought his crew back in good health. The Russian navy had demonstrated that it was capable of competing with its powerful British and French partners, and drew legitimate pride from this. True, it had still been necessary to turn to Great Britain to procure the ships capable of making so long a voyage, but the following expeditions left in Russian-built ships.

As for the immediate goal he had set himself, Krusenstern had met it by creating a maritime link between Russia proper, Kamchatka, and the Russian colonies in North America; and between the latter and the Chinese market. Upon his return, Krusenstern made a report severely critical of the

Russian-American Company's administration—a criticism to which he returned in his *Journey Around the World* published in 1810–1814; it led to the elimination of some abuses and considerably improved the situation of those dependent on the company. As for Lisiansky, he published an account of the journey of the *Neva*, which had in great part been different from that of the *Nadezhda*.

The naturalists had brought back a harvest of precious information about the flora and fauna of the countries visited, and they made a new contribution to the study of life in the then largely unknown seas. The results were contained in three works published by Tilesius and Langsdorff.

After having completed the account of his voyage, Krusenstern left again in 1815 to explore the Bering Strait and seek out the Northwest Passage. He later published important hydrographic studies, including the excellent *Atlas of the Pacific Ocean*. Promoted in 1826 to rear admiral and director of the Naval Academy, he was a member of the scientific committee of the Ministry of the Navy and was thus able to help prepare the great expeditions that followed. In 1829, he was made a vice admiral, and, in 1841, an admiral.

Breadfruit. Lithograph by Langlumé, from a drawing by L. Choris at the Ratak Islands. (Bibliothèque nationale, Paris. Photo © Bibl. nat./Photeb.)

The poet Chamisso goes around the world: Kotzebue's voyages 1815–1826

The Russians had to wait until the end of the Napoleonic Wars before being able to organize another voyage around the world. Though a private individual took the initiative for this voyage, he was a man who was as rich as he was powerful. Nicholas Petrovitch Romanzof, who had been Minister of Trade when Krusenstern left, had, in 1807, become Minister of Foreign Affairs and then Grand Chancellor. Strongly interested in the arts and sciences, he willingly played the role of Maecenas. In 1815, Romanzof gave Krusenstern the responsibility for preparing a new expedition that would be charged with reconnoitering several Pacific islands and with once more exploring the northwest coast of America south of the Bering Strait to see if a passage to Baffin Bay could finally be found.

Krusenstern had a small brig built, christened it the *Rurik,* and turned its command over to the man who at fifteen had been his clerk aboard the *Nadezhda*—Otto von Kotzebue, who for this purpose was made lieutenant commander. A young Estonian doctor, J. F. Eschscholtz, and the botanist C. F. von Ledebour were designated as naturalists, but Ledebour had to resign for reasons of health. The poet Chamisso—who had, a year earlier, been made famous by the publication of one of the masterpieces of German Romatic literature, *The Marvelous History of Peter Schlemihl*—offered to replace him.

Born in 1781 at the Château de Boncourt in Champagne, Louis Charles Adelaide de Chamisso, who afterward chose the German name Adelbert von Chamisso, had while still young immigrated to Prussia with his family. In 1812, he registered at the University of Berlin, where he studied botany, anatomy, and zoology. "In my childhood," he was to write, "Cook had raised the curtain hiding a world that was still as seductive as a fairy tale." As an adult, Chamisso had decided to find that world.

Come from Abo (Turku), Finland, where she had been equipped, the *Rurik* left Kronstadt on July 30, 1815. On August 9, she was in Copenhagen, where Chamisso came on board in the company of Lieutenant Morten Wormskjöld, who, on his return from a voyage to Greenland and Kamchatka, had asked permission to assist him as a volunteer naturalist.

From the beginning, the poet was struck by the limited space to which he would have to accommodate himself for the next three years. "The cabin is about twelve feet square. . . . On either side were two bunks, two wall cupboards installed for sleeping purposes. . . . My bunk and the three drawers underneath are the only space on this ship that belongs to me. . . . In the cabin, four men sleep, six men live, and seven men eat. . . . Between meals, the painter and his drawing board take up two sides of the table, and the third side belongs to the officers. . . . If anybody wants to write or in any way make use of the table, he has to wait to take it over for a few fleeting moments that are parsimoniously counted and avariciously employed; as for me, I cannot work this way." To this confinement was soon added seasickness, "against which I ceaselessly struggle, but in vain"—all of which made "this phase of the voyage a time of difficult apprenticeship" for the unfortunate poet. Soon Chamisso was at odds with the captain, who constantly "complained about the natural history collections piling up" on the deck or between-decks; with the second lieutenant, who was "sickly and irritable"; and even with the sailors, who expressed enormous contempt for his research and unhesitatingly threw his harvests overboard. Though Eschscholtz became his friend, his relations with the painter Choris and particularly with Wormskjöld

South Seas jellyfish drawn by A. von Chamisso. Lithograph by L. Choris and Langlumé. (Bibliothèque nationale, Paris. Photo © Bibl. nat./Photeb.)

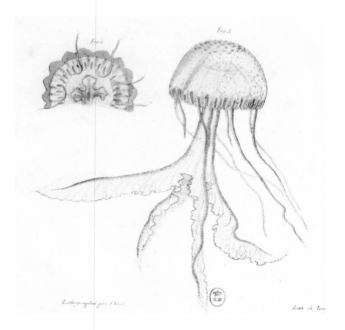

Kotzebue's Ship and Crew

The *RURIK,* very small 2-masted brig, 180 tons and 8 small cannon;
left from Kronstadt, 7/30/1815;
returned to St. Petersburg, 8/3/1818;
crew: 32 men;
deaths: 1 (of tuberculosis).

Commander: Otto von Kotzebue, lieutenant commander.

Lieutenants: 1st, Gleb Simonovitch Chichmarev; 2nd, Ivan Jacovlevitch Sakharin, left sick in Petropavlovsk, July 1816.

Doctor and naturalist: Dr. Johann Friedrich Eschscholtz.

Naturalist: Adelbert von Chamisso.

Assistant naturalist: Lieutenant Morten Wormskjöld, left the expedition at Petropavlovsk, July 1816.

Painter: Louis Choris.

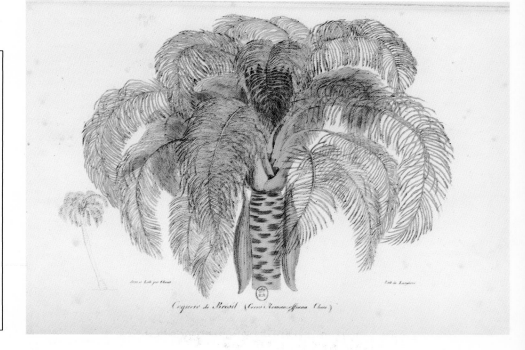

Cocos romanzoffiana, Brazilian palm discovered by Chamisso. Lithograph by L. Choris and Langlumé from a drawing by Choris. (Bibliothèque nationale, Paris. Photo © Bibl. nat./Photeb.)

were badly strained. Wormskjöld got along with no one and very soon made known his intention to disembark. He was to quit the *Rurik* at Petropavlovsk in June 1816.

The first stages were the same as had been followed by Krusenstern twelve years earlier. After stopping at Plymouth from September 7 to 25, the *Rurik* anchored at Santa Cruz de Tenerife and reached Santa Catarina Island on the Brazilian coast on December 10, 1815. On board, when not on duty the men amused themselves as best they could. Every Sunday there was a concert. "A chorus formed by the sailors had band instruments available, and our Bengali cook played the violin." Chamisso and Eschscholtz devoted themselves to observations of marine animals that were fished for from the deck with the help of a cloth net attached to a pole. The two naturalists made an important discovery about mollusks known as salps: "The same species has two very different basic forms according to the alternation of generations." They also studied jellyfish and found several new species, the acalephae—about which Eschscholtz was later to publish a basic study—being of particular interest.

Chamisso was less and less sorry about having joined the expedition, and the sight of the natural splendors of Brazil completely restored his enthusiasm. Here "the animal world is in harmony with the vegetable world. The creeper form of the vegetation corresponds to the climbing grip of the birds and the corkscrew tail of the mammals, found even in beasts of prey. . . . In the insect world, richness and splendor reign, and the butterfly rivals the humming bird. . . . When night falls on this green world, the animal world shines around its fires. The air, the thicket, and the earth are filled with flashes and illuminate the sea." Here, "all is new for science." Indeed, Chamisso discovered many new plants, among them an extremely beautiful palm tree with feathery foliage which he baptized *Cocos romanzoffiana.*

The *Rurik* left Santa Catarina carrying young chattering toucans and a capuchin monkey. She followed a very different route from the one taken by Krusenstern; Cape Horn was rounded amid storms, and, ascending the coast of Chile, the ship reached Talcahuano in Concepción Bay on February 13, 1816. On the way, the naturalists observed whales and dolphins, and collected the gigantic austral algae that were characteristic of the region. The arrival of the *Rurik* initially provoked both surprise and fear, for its flag was unknown, but the Russians were nevertheless well received by the Spaniards, who gave balls and banquets in their honor.

On March 8, the *Rurik* left Concepción Bay. On that date, Chamisso noted: "The voyage of discovery . . . begins here." Until his arrival in Avacha Bay on June 19, Kotzebue sailed through vast ocean spaces that had scarcely been entered since the heroic times of Le Maire and Schouten. On March 28, at Easter Island, the poet finally touched on the unknown. Thus was realized "the first great promise of this voyage."

"A large number of people awaited us peacefully, noisily, and impatiently on the shore, demonstrating their childlike joy by agitated movements on the beach." However, an atmosphere of suspicion and menace seemed to reign over the island, and it was not to be explained until much later. In 1805, the American schooner *Nancy* had come to the island in search of laborers; despite energetic resistance by the Easter Islanders, the Americans seized twelve men and ten women and kept them chained for three days, freeing them only when land was out of sight. The men immediately jumped overboard and perished, and the women had to be forcibly restrained from following suit. Since then, the

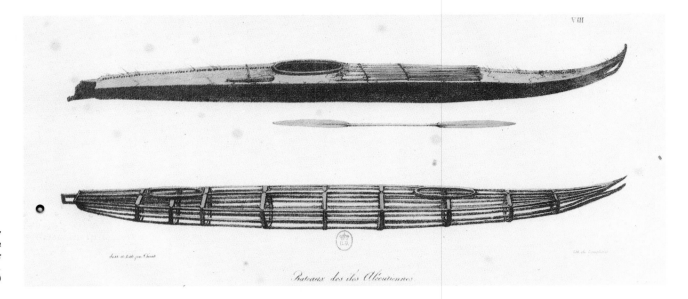

islanders had been on the defensive.

The Russians spent only a few hours on Easter Island before leaving in search of new lands. The first to be found may have been Schouten's Isle of Dogs and was therefore called Doubtful Island, but the following one was certainly unknown. Kotzebue decided to disembark there. "Despite the strong surf, we managed to land by means of a raft. One by one, the sailors got on the raft and let themselves be towed along a rope, profiting from a high wave to cross the reef and reach the shore." Though there were traces of human habitation, they met no one; it seemed the natives from neighboring islands would come to fish there. Chamisso quickly completed his natural history inventory as there was little flora and only a few land and sea birds, a small

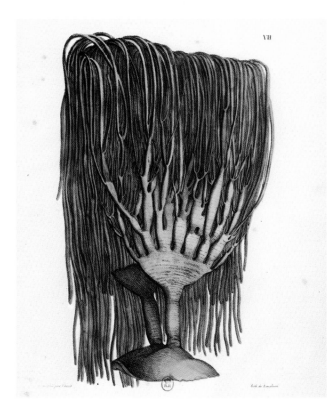

lizard, and some butterflies. The first discovery was dedicated to Romanzof, the sponsor of the expedition, and saluted with cannon and a double ration for the crew, it being the Russian Easter. Krusenstern's name and that of the *Rurik* were given to two small coral groups sighted near the Palliser Islands discovered by Cook.

On April 30, the Penrhyns—other low-lying islands linked by reefs and enclosing a lagoon—came into view. The natives, "vigorous, well built, but somewhat frightening as they were covered not with tattoos but with chest and back scarifactions, the most recent of which were bloody," soon became so numerous that they were made to keep their pirogues on one side of the ship, since the crew was unable to defend itself against three hundred savages hungry for nails and pieces of iron. Several days later, the *Rurik* was east of the Marshall and Gilbert Islands. There Kotzebue discovered two new islands, dubbed Kutusov and Suvarov.

On June 19, the *Rurik* entered the vast Avacha Bay. It was the first time that Chamisso—who had never been to Russia and was only beginning to learn the language—"put foot on Russian soil." He was all the more surprised to find himself in the home of an American, who had somehow ended up in this small town of Petropavlovsk, before a "cunningly painted portrait on glass of Madame Récamier, the amiable friend of Madame de Staël, in whose home I had long enjoyed her friendly commerce."

The month-long stopover in the capital of Kamchatka was devoted to various excursions and above all to almost daily parties, sometimes on shore and offered to the navigators by their compatriots, sometimes shipboard returns of hospitality. Lieutenant Chichmarev's birthday was celebrated there "with an unbridled joy, especially among the sailors, as he was loved by all." Second Lieutenant Sakharin, who was sick, had to leave the expedition, and Wormskjöld finally disembarked, after having often threatened to do so.

It was only then that Kotzebue unveiled his navigation plan, though only in part. During the summer of 1816, they had to content themselves with reconnoitering a safe anchorage on the American coast and preparing for a second summer cruise, which would be devoted to a detailed exploration with the help of employees of the Russian-American Company and the assistance of Aleuts in their bidars. "To these peoples the one-seat bidar is what the horse is to a Cossack. This skiff is a long and narrow swim bladder made of sealskin and ending in a tapering point. Everything is stretched over a light wooden framework. In the middle there is a circular opening; the man sits in it with outstretched legs, his trunk sticking up from the opening. . . . His light paddle in hand, his weapons before him, maintaining his balance like a horseman, he speeds over the mobile surface like an arrow."

Between two cruises, in the winter of 1816–1817, the *Rurik* descended to the tropical islands for several months. On July 17, she left Petropavlovsk. Three days later, a high, rocky, and snow-covered land that "looked terribly sad" came into view; it was Bering Island, where the unfortunate explorer had died and been buried. On the twenty-seventh, they reached St. Lawrence Island at the entrance to the Bering Strait. Initially fearful, the islanders were soon loudly asking the sailors for tobacco. "Having learned that I was their leader," Kotzebue wrote, "they came in turn to embrace me by rubbing their noses against mine and ending their compliments by spitting into their hands, which they then passed over my face." The ship next entered the channel in which on his third voyage Cook had explored three islands; Kotzebue discovered several others.

To the north of Bering Strait, the Russians found a great arm of the sea on the American coast; they thought they had finally discovered the Northwest Passage, but they soon saw that it was an illusion: The gulf to which it led was Cook's Goodhope Bay. The sound was given Kotzebue's name. In this vast gulf, the *Rurik* anchored in the shelter of Chamisso Island in little Eschscholtz Bay. The officers left to explore the island. "We had climbed these slopes," Kotzebue records under the date August 8, 1816, "without noticing that we were walking on a veritable iceberg. Dr. Eschscholtz found a part of a talus that had melted and to his great surprise noticed that the interior of the mountain was made of pure ice." In one of these gashes, the naturalist found the teeth and tusks of a mammoth. The inhabitants, who seemed never to have seen a European, watched the ship in astonishment from the coast. Once established in their on-shore camp, the Russians were convinced they were surrounded by "Americans." In the middle of the night, Kotzebue decided to break camp. Of this decision, he wrote: "I saw no other way to escape death." However, as Chamisso notes, these men "were not hostile but simply curious."

The *Rurik* next followed the Asiatic coast "in order to get to know the people who inhabit it and to compare them with the Americans." They were the Chukchi, an independent Eskimo tribe. "They recognize Russian sovereignty only to the extent that they pay tribute where they trade with the Russians to mutual advantage. . . . They welcomed us on shore as official hosts—amiably, but with a solemnity that deprived us of all spontaneity."

The goal of the first cruise having been achieved, the *Rurik* set sail toward the south, stopping once more in St. Lawrence Bay. On leaving (August 29), she was struck by a violent storm and did not reach Unalaska Island in the Aleutians until September 7. Kotzebue was received there by the

View of icy slopes of Chamisso Island, where Eschscholtz discovered the tusks of a mammoth in August 1816. Lithograph by L. Choris and Langlumé from a drawing by Choris. (Bibliothèque nationale, Paris. Photo © Bibl. nat./Photeb.)

The hula dance celebration of the Hawaiians. Lithograph by Choris and Langlumé from a drawing by Choris. (Bibliothèque nationale, Paris. Photo © Bibl. nat./Photeb.)

agent of the Russian-American Company and told him of his needs for the second summer cruise. Leaving the port of Unalaska on September 14, the ship went to the California missions, where the crew was to have a few weeks of rest before heading for the South Seas.

"On October 2, at four in the afternoon, we made our entry into the port of San Francisco." The Russians were received there by an officer of the *Présidio,* the Spanish military authority that was responsible for several missions, each mission being directed by two Franciscans who had contracted to spend ten years there. The Feast of St. Francis, which took place the next day, gave the Russians "the opportunity to observe the activities of the missionaries. . . . The pious Franciscans who maintained the New California missions are not educated in any of the arts and crafts that they practice here, that they are supposed to teach; they speak none of the languages spoken by the people to whom they have been sent." The results they achieved were damning. "The death rate of the Indians in the missions rises terrifyingly. Their race is in the process of becoming extinct." Kotzebue and Chamisso wondered why the Spanish bothered to occupy California at great expense and then let the country go to ruin and become depopulated. The only reason that the governor of the province could give them was "the pious intention of propagating the faith of Christ." Chamisso noted: "Well then, here's another good work begun backward and badly carried out." Great Britain and the United States constantly encroached upon the Spanish settlements, and the Russians were doing the same.

During their stay in California, the naturalists had collected and described the sea lion, or California-eared seal, and a great many birds, including a "humming bird with dazzling plumage." Eschscholtz identified as many as three species of salamander. Though the season was hardly favorable, Chamisso made several interesting discoveries, including the *Eschscholtzia californica,* beautiful papaveraceae with bright yellow flowers, and *Ceanothus thyrsiflorus,* a fine shrub with pale blue flowers. Fresh provisions having been loaded on and the crew being in good health, the *Rurik* left the roads of San Francisco on November 1 to head for the Sandwich Islands.

She reached the Sandwich Isles on November 28. Guided by John Elliot de Castro, a half-English, half-Portuguese surgeon who had become the king's personal doctor, the Russians were presented to Kamehameha I, who had united the archipelago into a single kingdom. "An armed crowd stood on the shore. We landed before the house of the old king, who was seated on a magnificent terrace, surrounded by his wives and wearing his people's national costume, the red *maro* [which goes around the loins] and the black *tapa* [an ample fiber mantle with magnificent folds]."

Kamehameha and his subjects were somewhat alarmed by this unexpected landing. Two years earlier, the crew of a Russian-American Company ship had profaned a morai and raised the Russian flag: "With the help of some Europeans, bloodshed was avoided and the arrogant foreigners murmuring threats of war were forced to re-embark." Had the *Rurik* come to carry out reprisals? Kotzebue dispelled these fears, and the welcome was very cordial. Chamisso records: "We were introduced to the queens, tall, strong women who were still almost beautiful. . . . In a straw hut, they were all stretched out together on a floor softly covered with delicate mats. We had to take our places among them. The looks directed at me by the neighboring queen made me, a novice, almost uneasy. On following Eschscholtz, who had already slipped out of the house, I learned from him that his queen had expressed herself even more directly."

Chamisso, "eager to attend the mysteries of Hawaiian religious rites," appealed to an island friend he had made and was invited by the latter "with no hesitation . . . Compared to the joy with which [the sacred gestures] are made, the pleasures of one of our masked balls have all the allure of a burial. The religious ceremonies take up only a few hours. . . . The intervals are filled with the most joyous conversations and goods meals are had. . . ." Chamisso was disappointed, but if he had been so readily admitted to the ceremonies, wasn't it just because they no longer had their earlier initiatory character? On the other hand, he was enraptured by the hula, the Hawaiian festival dance. "In the well-balanced rhythm of the dance, the human figure is shown to magnificent advantage, and as the movement becomes lighter and freer, it offers the spectacle of the beautiful stances to be found in nature. We seem to be watching the metamorphoses of antique statuary; only the feet carry the dancer. He enteres quietly. His body unfolds, his arms, all his muscles, stir, and his face becomes animated. . . . These festivals make the Hawaiians drunk with joy."

On December 14, the *Rurik* left the Sandwich Islands and once more turned in the direction of the Marshalls, visited the year before. There the Russians discovered several new islands: New Year Island (Miadi), the Romanzof Archipelago (Wotje), the large island of Otdia, the Kasen Group (Maloelap), and the Ternei Group (Aur). These islands formed two more or less parallel lines, and the chain visited by the Russians was the Ratak; the other, which "consists of nine groups," was the Ralik. "The weakness of the Ratak inhabitants eliminated any suspicion about them; their gentleness and generosity made them trust the foreigners who dominated them with all their power; we became friends without reservations."

Kadu

At Ratak, Chamisso met Kadu, "one of the most beautiful natures that I have met in all my life, one of the men I have loved most." Volunteering to serve as an intermediary with the islanders, Kadu was soon so attached to the Russians that he could not leave them. A friend was also made of an Otdia inhabitant, "who distinguished himself from the others by his wit and intelligence. . . . Lagediack understood that we intended to introduce useful but still unknown plant species to these islands for the

Crested auklet from the Bering Sea. Lithograph by L. Choris and Langlumé. (Bibliothèque nationale, Paris. Photo © Bibl. nat./Photeb.)

good of his people." Thanks to him, the Russians were able to set up an island garden in which they sowed peas, corn, and other edible plants. Chamisso finally gave way to rapture. "Nowhere else is the sky more beautiful, the temperature more equable, than on these low islands. The sea and the wind balance one another, and the brief passing showers maintain the forest in its luxuriant green splendor." Until March 18, when they returned to the Kutusov (Utirik) and Suvarov (Taka) groups discovered the previous year, the *Rurik* sailed from island to island before regretfully leaving these enchanting places behind and returning toward the Bering Strait, which had to be reached in time. "April 13 was a terrible day on which my best hopes were destroyed," Kotzebue wrote. The *Rurik* was hit by an extremely violent storm during which several men—including the commander—were injured.

On April 24, the Russians arrived safe and sound at Unalaska. Kadu was stupefied by the snow-covered mountains, whose existence he had never even suspected. The equipment asked for by Kotzebue was almost ready, and it was assembled in haste. On June 29, the *Rurik* departed with fifteen Aleuts and some bidars aboard. The naturalists had had time to assemble a detailed inventory of the little-known flora and fauna of the Aleutians. They had made a considerable collection that included northern sea birds and raptors, some small carnivores and rodents, and the cranium of a whale that had been cut apart by the Aleuts. All these things were carefully wrapped and placed in large nailed and tar-sealed cases, which were under Kotzebue's personal protection.

The *Rurik* was about to enter the Bering Strait when suddenly the commander decided to go no farther. On July 12, he wrote: "At twelve midnight, just as we were preparing to anchor at the northern promontory, to our great horror we noticed an ice floe that stretched to the northeast as far as the eye could see. . . . The cold air hit my weak chest so strongly that I could not breathe and suffered an angina attack in which I kept fainting and spitting up blood. I realized that my condition was more dangerous than I had previously admitted. . . . I sent word to command headquarters that my health forced me to return to Unalaska." This lapse on Kotzebue's part was severely criticized by his men, who greeted his decision with "silent and downcast faces." Chamisso strongly regretted that the commander had not at least discussed the question with the staff. Nevertheless, on the ship's return, Count Romanzof simply accepted Kotzebue's report.

On July 12, 1817, therefore, the expedition was virtually over. But there was still the return to be considered, in other words to "unwind backward what had been accomplished until now," as Chamisso put it with wry irritation. On July 22, the *Rurik* left Unalaska, anchored at Oahu in the Sandwich Islands from October 1 to 14, and headed for the Marshalls, where several new islands were discovered.

At Otdia, the navigators were received with demonstrations of great joy. Kadu, enriched by the experiences of the last few months, "proved himself indefatigable and brimming with activity. . . . He was still firmly resolved to remain with us." Later, "his very gay humor gave way to a peaceful gravity" and he announced that he would "remain at Otdia to look after the animals and plants, which

would not otherwise be cared for. . . . Before the assembled inhabitants of Otdia, Kadu was proclaimed our representative. . . . Having already come to Ratak three times, we solemnly promised that we would return after a while to visit him and ask for an accounting."

Kotzebue was indeed to return to Otdia, but not until seven years later. The islanders gave him an enthusiastic welcome. "Several waded out up to their waists to be the first to greet us. . . . Four of my old friends lifted me from the launch and carried me to the shore, where Lagediack awaited me with open arms and joyfully pressed me to his heart." But "of all that we had brought to Ratak, Monsieur von Kotzebue saw only a cat, which had gone feral, and a yam root." Kadu was gone; he was at Aur with King Lamari, and "thanks to his care the animals and plants that the king had transplanted there had, it would appear, multiplied considerably." "Lagediack secretly urged Kotzebue to seize power at Ratak and offered to help him do so. As the ship was about to set sail, he brought his friend a last gift: young coconut trees that he wanted to be planted in Russia, since he had heard there were none there."

Leaving the Marshalls on November 5, 1817, Kotzebue decided to stop at Guam in the Marianas. "This green and scented island seemed a garden of delights," wrote Chamisso; however, "it was only a desert. . . . The missionaries from Rome had raised their cross there; 44,000 human beings had been sacrificed to it, and their survivors, mixed with the Tagals who had been brought from Luzon, had become a small silent nation, sad and subjugated. . . ."

At Guam, Chamisso learned about trepang—smoked holothurians that are the basis of a lucrative trade with China, where they are considered a delicacy. The naturalist made a collection of these echinoderms for the zoological museum in Berlin. On January 17, 1818, the *Rurik* anchored at Cavite in Manila Bay. Chamisso had time to make a one-week excursion, climbing the slopes of the Taal and collecting numerous insects, including the phasma, which looks like a living leaf.

The *Rurik* left Cavite on January 29 at the same time as the *Eglantine* out of Bordeaux, a merchant ship on board which was Dussumier, one of the best animal collectors of the Museum of Natural History in Paris. The Russians had aboard several monkeys, of which at least one belonged to an unknown species; however, almost all died, except for a pair of a species common in Luzon. They "animated our rigging as they had their native forest," arriving safely in St. Petersburg. On March 31, 1818, the *Rurik* entered Table Bay, at the Cape, where it met up with Freycinet's *Uranie*. From June 16 to 30, the navigators stopped at Portsmouth, and this gave Chamisso time to go to London, where he met several famous scientists: the venerable Sir Joseph Banks, then seventy-five; Captain James Burney, who had also been a companion of Cook's; Sir Robert Brown, who had traveled with Flinders;

Landscape of the Ratak Islands (Marshall Archipelago). Drawing and lithograph by Choris. "The appearance of this unusual archipelago is very pleasant. The islanders raise their huts in the shade of breadfruit trees. Large ferns and other plants native to equinoctial regions cover the ground . . ." (Bibliothèque nationale, Paris. Photo © Bibl. nat/Photeb.)

and finally Baron Cuvier, who was passing through.

On August 3, 1818, the *Rurik* dropped anchor in front of the home of Count Romanzof in St. Petersburg. The voyage had lasted three years, and there had not been a single death.

Kotzebue's second voyage, 1823–1826

After his return to Berlin, Chamisso remained there and was named first the conservator of the Botanical Gardens and then the Royal Horticulturalist. (He also married, and fathered seven children.) His reputation as a poet continued to grow, especially when, in 1829, he published the poem *Salas y Gomez,* written on board the *Rurik,* and, the following year, *Woman's Love and Life,* which was set to music by Robert Schumann. It was this fame that led him to return to and publish—but not until 1835—his *Voyage Journal.* Previously, with his notes entitled "Remarks and Ideas," he had collaborated on Kotzebue's *Riese um die Welt* (Journey Around the World), published in Weimar in 1821.

Promoted, on his return, to captain-lieutenant of the Marine Guards, Otto von Kotzebue was to circumnavigate the globe once more (1823–1826), this time on the *Predpriyatiye* (Enterprise). His voyage that took him to Tuamotus, Tahiti, the Navigators Islands (Samoa), the Marshalls—where he stayed in Ratak from April to May of 1824—and finally to Kamchatka and the northwest coast of America. Initially conceived as a scientific expedition, this voyage took on a political slant when Kotzebue's extremely unfavorable report on the Protestant missions in the Pacific islands caused a sensation.

A nineteen-year-old doctor, H. F. E. Lenz, who was later to become famous, joined the expedition. Dr. Eschscholtz once again accompanied Kotzebue. He discovered a certain number of species new to science: several birds, including the

limicolae, the Patagonian seed snipe, and some reptiles, such as the pustular hydrosaurus native to the South Seas. Of particular interest was his discovery of many marine invertebrates: jellyfish and Alaskan mollusks. On his return from his second voyage, Eschscholtz began to publish his discoveries in a *Zoological Atlas,* the last volumes of which appeared posthumously. He died of exhaustion at the age of thirty-eight in 1831.

The painter Choris did not live even that long. In 1819, he went to Paris, where he remained for eight years and learned lithography so as to be able to reproduce his drawings himself. They were published from 1823 to 1826 in his *Voyage pittoresque autour du monde, 1815–1818* (Picturesque Journey Around the World 1815–1818). In 1827, he went to Mexico, where he was killed in an ambush the following year; he was thirty-three.

St. Helena, "a rock lost in the ocean." Access to it was forbidden the Rurik on April 24, 1818, by Sir Hudson Lowe, Napoleon's jailer. Lithograph after Choris. (Bibliothèque National, Paris. Photo © Bibl. nat/Arch. Photeb.)

131

The first exploration
of the Antarctic:
Bellingshausen, 1819–1821

In the interval between Kotzebue's voyages, there had been several other Russian expeditions. In 1817, even before the *Rurik* had returned, Captain Vasily Mikhailovich Golovnin—who, in 1813, had been captured at the Kuriles on the *Diana* by the Japanese and been their prisoner for two years—had sailed on the *Kamchatka* to visit the northwest coast of America. He was assisted by two young officers: Fyodor Petrovich Lütke and Baron Ferdinand Petrovich von Wrangel. When he returned in 1819, Golovnin had determined the position of several islands in the Bering Sea.

Of considerably more geographical importance was the first official attempt to explore the Antarctic by Fabian Bellingshausen.

He commanded the *Vostok* (East), which, on July 3, 1819, left Kronstadt accompanied by the *Mirny* (Peaceful), commanded by Mikhail Petrovich Lazarev. In January 1820, the navigators crossed the Antarctic Circle; two weeks later, at 67° S latitude, they saw land through the fog. It was assuredly the Antarctic Continent, which they were therefore the first to see. In the spring, Bellingshausen headed north, explored the Tuamotus, anchored at Tahiti, sailed through the Fiji Islands, then went to Port Jackson and Tasmania before moving south in November to take advantage of the austral summer.

During his stopovers and while on the seas, Bellingshausen worked as a naturalist. He was the first to observe the southern migration of whales at the beginning of the austral summer. In Van Diemen's Land, he noticed that, like the Tasmanians themselves, the island fauna were in the process of becoming extinct. The Macquarie Islands near the Antarctic Circle had been ravaged by seal hunters.

Reaching the waters near Antarctica in December 1820, Bellingshausen discovered at 69° S latitude and 91° W longitude the island he called Peter I, and then a body of land to which he gave the name of the reigning tsar, Alexander I. It was in fact a large island, but an impenetrable ice floe prevented the ships from going farther. On December 15, 1820, Bellingshausen captured the first emperor penguin, a giant bird measuring 1.15 meters high and weighing 30 kilos. The navigators then explored the South Shetland Islands, South Georgia, and Sandwich Land, discovered by Cook. At the Shetlands, the Russians witnessed the fierce battles fought among the sealers. Three of the eighteen ships present were sunk, and nobody seemed concerned about the number of dead. One of the captains declared that he had killed sixty thousand seals in a single season. Sickened by these massacres, Bellingshausen was sure that all the animals in this region were doomed to imminent extinction.

On his return in 1821, Bellingshausen brought back scientific data of all kinds. Though he had found only two islands in the Antarctic, he had completed Cook's long tour by skirting the South Pole in the opposite direction; he had also discovered some twenty islands in the Tuamotus and as many in the Fijis. In addition, he had assembled a rich collection of birds. Many died in the cold, but as soon as the weather permitted, the survivors were placed on a sunny deck and began to sing; some were even still alive when the ship reached Russia. A magnificent cockatoo died of indigestion after having devoured a stuffed kookaburra (a giant Australian kingfisher), and a parrot profiting from its refound liberty flew to the top of the *Vostok*'s main mast. When a sailor was sent up to retrieve it, the frightened bird flew to the bow, where luckily it accepted a perch that was extended to it.

Bellingshausen, his biographer concluded, was one of the last of the maritime explorers in the grand style established by Cook. Thanks to his account of the voyage, we have a last glimpse of the Antarctic Ocean before it was thoroughly invaded, and of the tropical islands before they became a world of adventurers, convicts, and persecuted natives decimated by alcohol and venereal diseases brought by the white man—before their beaches became tinged with blood, before all the disasters foreseen by Cook.

While Kotzebue was finishing his second expedition, Baron Wrangle had sailed on the *Krotky* (Easy Going) for a two-year cruise (1825–1827) which enabled him to demonstrate the nonexistence of Pacific islands some European navigators had claimed to discover. In 1827, the *Krotky* left again, this time under the command of Captain Haghemeister, and sailed the ocean between Australia and Kamchatka, making a special stop in the Tuamotus.

The naturalists of the *Senyavin,* 1826–1829

The *Predpriartie* of Kotzebue's second voyage returned to Kronstadt on July 10, 1826. On September 1, a newly built ship, the *Senyavin,* "which held the sea excellently but did not have speed," left the same port. It was commanded by Lütke, aide-de-camp to Tsar Nicholas I, who had mounted the throne the year before and now promoted Lütke to captain-lieutenant for the expedition. On board was a scientific team composed of Dr. Karl Heinrich Mertens, a naturalist; "deputy-professor" Alexander Postels, serving as mineralogist and draftsman; and Baron Kittlitz, a retired Prussian captain and an eminent ornithologist.

Mertens, who had just turned thirty, was the son of the famous botanist Francis Karl Mertens. He had twice been to Paris to study at the Museum of Natural History and had established relations with Jussieu, Lamarck, and Humboldt; he had also visited Sir Joseph Banks and Robert Brown in London, and in Germany had met with Johann Reinhold Forster. These connections had given him a taste for distant voyages, and he had wanted to sign on as botanist for the Bellingshausen expedition; but his father had insisted that he first finish his studies. In Russia, Mertens worked as a doctor and watched for the first chance to sail off. It was offered him by Krusenstern, who had the Academy of Sciences name him the *Senyavin* naturalist.

The ship left in the company of the *Möller*—commanded by a Captain Staniukovich—which accompanied her as far as Valparaiso and then left for Tahiti, sailed to Kamchatka, and, in August 1827, visited the Aleutians. Afterward, the *Möller* stopped for several months in Honolulu in the Sandwich Islands. In April 1828, Staniukovich was back in Kamchatka, from where he left to explore the northern coast of the Alaskan peninsula.

The two ships made their first stop at Tenerife in November 1826. They were in Rio in January 1827, and then, going around Cape Horn, reached Concepción in Chile on March 16 and Valparaiso on the twenty-sixth. To give the *Senyavin* crew a rest after a seven-month voyage, Lütke remained ashore until April 15. Since the effective liberation of Chile by General San Martin in 1817 and the opening of the country's ports to ships of all nations, Valparaiso—which had previously been a simple, almost wretched village—had become the most important commercial center of the South Pacific. Its population had increased enormously.

Kaloches in their hut. Smoked fish are suspended from the beams. Lithograph from a drawing by A. Postels, extracted from the Voyage of the Senyavin. *(Bibliothèque nationale, Paris. Photo © Bibl. nat./Photeb.)*

"The streets were filled with people rushing here and there on foot and on horseback; the multitudinous shops are crammed with all sorts of goods from Europe." It was Lent and the upper classes lived in strictest seclusion, but the crowd continuously amused itself. "The cafes are always full and there is music, singing, and dancing everywhere."

Mertens began a collection of plants and most especially of algae, specimens of which were drawn by Postels as soon as they were gathered. He himself saw to the mineralogical samples, while Kittlitz established an inventory of Chilean birds. He discovered several little-known species, the most remarkable of which was the tapaculo—"cover your bottom"—with its constantly moving tail and recognizable "shrill and throbbing notes that follow one another and become lower and lower."

From Valparaiso, the Russians went up the western coast of America until Sitka Island, not far from the Alaskan peninsula. The shoreline looked savage: "Two steep mountains covered with virgin forest from the foot to the summit. . . . All was quiet and wild. . . . A navigator sailing off the coasts could see the Russian flag floating over the fortress."

New Archangel

They had reached Novo-Arkangelsk, a fort

133

Lütke's Ship and Crew

Novo-Arkangelsk, a settlement of the Russian-American Company on Sitka Island. Lithograph from a drawing by von Kittlitz for Voyage of the Senyavin. *(Bibliothèque nationale, Paris. Photo © Bibl. nat./Photeb.)*

> The *SENYAVIN:* bark with an 86-foot keel, carrying 16 carronades, like the *Möller,* constructed in the Okhta shipyards especially for the expedition, launched May 1825; left from Kronstadt, September 1, 1826, with the corvette *Möller,* Captain Staniukovitch; the 2 ships separated at Valparaiso in March 1827 and joined up again at Kamchatka in June 1828;
> returned with the *Möller* to Kronstadt, 9/6/1829;
> crew: 11 officers and 51 men;
> deaths: 1, in an accident.
>
> **Commander:** Captain-lieutenant Fedor Petrovitch Lütke.
>
> **Lieutenants:** Zavalichine, Abolechev.
>
> **Ensigns:** Ratmanov, Mayet, Butakov, Glazenapp.
>
> **Midshipman:** Pavel von Krusenstern (son of the admiral).
>
> **Surgeon and naturalist:** Dr. Karl Heinrich Mertens.
>
> **Mineralogist and draftsman:** Alexander Postels.
>
> **Ornithologist:** Baron von Kittlitz.

established in the bay of Sitka by the Russian-American Company. The local population of Kaloches had burned it down in 1804 when the *Neva,* commanded by Lisiansky, was at Sitka, but with Lisiansky's aid, Governor Baranov had vanquished the Kaloches and reconstructed the fort. Novo-Arkangelsk then had eight hundred inhabitants—three hundred Russians, four hundred Aleuts, and some halfbreeds fathered by the Russians on Aleut women. The colony was linked to the mother country by ships that sailed from Okhotsk in Siberia only once a year.

Thanks to Krusenstern's report, the status of the company's employees had improved significantly; they received regular salaries and had the right to free lodging. The governors were now navy officers. Novo-Arkangelsk was of extreme importance, since all the Russian settlements in America and even in the Kuriles on the Asian coast depended on it. Nevertheless, the fort had almost been abandoned because of the persistent hostility of the natives.

The Aleuts of Unalaska, where the *Senyavin* remained from August 21 to 30, were, on the contrary, already "Christians and showed a great disposition to become civilized. . . . Good, sturdy, and skillful, they made the sea their true element." Next going north to the Bering Sea, Lütke made brief stopovers at the islands of St. George and St. Paul, both of which were covered with moss and entirely deforested.

Farther to the north, the *Senyavin* visited the island Cook had spotted in 1778 and named Gore Island, unaware that it had previously been discovered by the Russian navigator Sindt and named St. Matthew. Lütke was the first to make a detailed reconnaissance of it. Next he sailed along the Asiatic coast, and having on the way visited Bering Island—then inhabited by 110 people of Russian,

Aleut, and mixed descent—he arrived at Petropavlovsk on September 25. There preparations were made for the winter cruise, which was to be in the tropics. At Kamchatka, the naturalists assembled collections of rocks, algae, birds, and marine animals.

"Not having had until now a tropical station for experiments with the invariable pendulum, I resolved to stop at Ualan Island [Kausaie or Strong's Island]." In 1824, this island had been visited by Duperrey, and it was in the same harbor that the *Senyavin* dropped anchor on December 4, 1828. Until April 1829, the Russian expedition was to remain in the Carolines, which it sailed through in every direction, discovering numerous islands, which were explored and named.

Ualan, the first stop, was mountainous and covered with an all-but-impenetrable forest. Some eight hundred inhabitants lived along the shore. They were of medium height, well built, and extraordinarily agile; their brown skin, covered with coconut oil, was tattooed, but without great skill. They went nude, wearing only a belt woven of banana-tree bark. Content with breadfruit, bananas, and fish, they led an idle life, especially their chiefs, the most powerful of whom owned all the land and lived apart. "A chief spends his life eating, sleeping, and sitting around in circles and talking." The people of Ualan had neither weapons nor musical instruments. They knew nothing of war, and their only distraction was dancing, in which the women were not allowed to join. Gentle and peaceful, they received the navigators hospitably. The naturalists were always accompanied on their expeditions by natives, who would climb the trees for them and be helpful in many ways. Mertens found strange insects and collected many ferns; Kittlitz discovered several unknown birds, among them the Caroline rail, small and black, of which he captured two that are now in the Leningrad Museum and considered very precious, for no more have ever been found. Numerous fish were also taken from the reefs, including a magnificent surgeon fish with orange jaws—a drawing of which was made by Postels before it was preserved in alcohol—crustaceans, and mollusks, which were painted by Mertens.

On January 3, 1828, the *Senyavin* left to make a tour of the archipelago. To the northwest of Ualan, the navigators found a previously uncharted large high body of land surrounded by small groups of islets and bordered by reefs. Its inhabitants called it Ponape, which the Russians transcribed as Puynipet. "Soon boats with sails began to appear. From a distance, the Puynipets began to sing at the top of their voices, to dance, and to gesticulate with their heads and hands," but once on board, they shouted and jumped about, brandishing their spears menacingly, "their boldness and importunity increasing from moment to moment." Seeing that he could not land without risk, after having cruised about for a week Lütke left this group of islands, which he called the Senyavin Islands. In January, he also discovered Ngatik (Palau), previously named Los Valientes by the Spaniard Lazeano, who had discovered the archipelago in 1636; and then the Mortlocks, reconnoitered in 1796 by the Englishman Wilson. Like the Ualanders, the inhabitants of these islands were "hospitable, good, reserved, and pleasant mannered. . . . We learned that the group of islands was called Lukunor." To the northeast were the Truk Islands, named Hogoleu Islands by Duperrey, who had visited them in 1824, and the Namonuito group.

Leaving the Carolines, Lütke sailed toward the Marianas and was well received by the governor of Guam, Don José Medinilla, who a year earlier had been so helpful with the sick men on Dumont d'Urville's *Astrolabe;* Lütke remained on this island from February 26 to March 19. An observatory was set up on shore, the ship was put back into shape, and the crew was able to rest. "It was still not time for us to go north," wrote Lütke. "Therefore, on leaving Guam we returned to the Carolines to continue its exploration." The *Senyavin* then visited Namorik, Elato, and Namoliaour, and finally, thanks to indications from the inhabitants of these islands, Olimario and the Farauleps.

On April 9, the Russians left the tropics to head north, arriving on May 1 at the Bonin Islands off the Japanese island of Kyūshū, where they stayed until the fifteenth. The *Senyavin* dropped anchor at Port Lloyd on Peel Island, where there were only two inhabitants, survivors of the British whaler *Williams,* which had been shipwrecked there three years earlier. Another ship, the *Timor,* had come to look for survivors, but the two men—the Prussian Wittrien and the Norwegian Petersen—had decided

to remain where they were. "A house of ship's planking and an entranceway covered with cloth . . . was the residence of our hosts. A table, two hammocks, a trunk, some muskets, a Bible, several fishing implements, and two engravings formed the furnishings of this solitary human habitation in the Bonin Islands." With some disappointment, Lütke then learned that Great Britain's Captain Frederick William Beechey had visited and reconnoitered these islands a year earlier. He had offered to take Wittrien and Petersen with him, but, thinking that another ship would come for them, they had refused. However, weary of waiting and no longer able to bear the solitude, they asked Lütke to repatriate them, and he agreed. Kittlitz had captured two unknown birds—the bush warbler and the Bonin hawfinch, a rare species that was to disappear after 1857.

The Chukchi

Having returned to Petropavlovsk on June 9, the *Senyavin* left again on the twenty-sixth to visit the Asian coast north of Kamchatka. First following along this peninsula, Lütke, having rounded Cape Kronotski, saw Klyuchevskaya Sopka, a gigantic volcano; then he reached Karaginskiy Island. Only the Russian navigator Sindt had seen this part of the coast. The land, once inhabited by the Koryaks, about whom Lütke had been ordered to obtain information, was now deserted.

Moving farther north, he next went along the coast and the islands explored by the Bering expedition in 1740–1741, and he discovered the channel that separates the continent from Arakamchechen Island; it was named Senyavin Strait. After visiting what Bering had called Holy Cross Island, a small group was sent along the Anadry River. They were then in the land of the Chukchi, who inhabited the northern end of the Asiatic continent near the Ber-

Departure of an excursion on Ualan Island (the Carolines). Lithograph from a drawing by von Kittlitz. (Bibliothèque nationale, Paris. Photo © Bibl. nat./Photeb.)

Cascades surrounded by mangroves on Peel Island (Bonin Archipelago). Lithograph by Sabatier from a drawing by A. Postels. (Bibliothèque nationale, Paris. Photo © Bibl. nat./Photeb.)

13–30, 1829), the *Senyavin* was put into shape and reprovisioned. On February 13, she dropped anchor on the coast of Sumatra at the entrance to Sunda Strait. On April 14, she was at the Cape and, on April 30, at St. Helena. After a brief stopover on the English coast, the ship reached Kronstadt on September 16, 1829, having been on the seas for three years. "The *Senyavin* had the joy of being visited by His Majesty the Emperor and that same day she entered the port of Kronstadt and struck her colors."

The geographic and hydrographic results of the voyage were remarkable, but even more so, perhaps, were those of the naturalists. Though they brought back only a small number of mammals, including some rare species of bats and a seal, Kittlitz alone had collected, prepared, and painted three hundred species of birds, of which there were 750 samples. Mertens had done the same for 150 species of crustaceans and seven hundred species of insects, whereas Postels painted 245 of the three hundred types of fish caught and twenty-three of the one hundred amphibians collected. The fish were afterward identified by Cuvier during a visit Kittlitz and Postels made to Paris. Postels, who had been responsible for mineralogical research, brought back 330 specimens. In addition, Mertens had collected more than four thousand plants, including twenty-five hundred phanerogams, and his collection of algae was the largest ever made. During the voyage, thirteen hundred drawings were made, seven hundred by Postels, 350 by Mertens, and 250 by Kittlitz. No other expedition had ever brought back so generous and so expertly executed a pictorial record.

Because of this success, Lütke was named a correspondent of the Academy of Sciences in Paris and a member of the one in St. Petersburg, of which he was to become a president in 1864. Before his departure, Lütke had published *Four Voyages in the Polar Seas from 1821 to 1824;* soon after his return, he left again on the *Senyavin* for a new cruise of the coasts of Iceland and only afterward published his *Voyage Around the World by the Corvette Senyavin,* along with an atlas reproducing some of the drawings by Postels and Kittlitz.

On his second voyage, Lütke had taken Mertens with him, though the latter had been in bad health during the first expedition. He nevertheless behaved fearlessly and refused to listen to prudent counsel. A "nervous fever" having broken out on board, Mertens devotedly tended the sick. On his return to St. Petersburg, he joyously greeted the woman he had married the year before, but his wife and his brother thought he looked so ill that they persuaded him to take to his bed that very day. Thirteen days later, on September 17, 1830, he died at the age of thirty-four.

ing Strait. They proved extremely hospitable, especially after receiving a gift of tobacco, of which they were passionately fond. According to Lütke, the Chukchi were divided into two groups, one of which was the Namollo, settled along the river banks. In the winter, they lived in huts of wood and, in the summer, in huts made of seal skin; their principal foods were walrus and seal. The Russians stayed with them and only met members of the other group, the "reindeer Chukchi," when the latter visited the Namollo. The reindeer raisers were nomads who lived in tents all year round; they would trade tanned reindeer skins for iron utensils offered by Russian trappers.

Returning to Petropavlovsk on October 5, 1828, the *Senyavin* stayed there for five weeks and then returned toward the Carolines before starting back to Europe. Until December, Lütke worked on completing his exploration by visiting the western islands of this vast archipelago. At Manila (January

The great
French scientific
voyages under the
Restoration and the
July monarchy,
1817-1829

Freycinet
and the naturalists of the *Uranie*,
1817–1820

The survivors of the Baudin expedition had returned in March 1804; before the end of the year, First Consul Bonaparte became the Emperor Napoleon. While he was busy on the continent with a series of wars, the British were establishing a blockade of western Europe's coasts, and they obtained a mastery of the seas that made all new expeditions impossible. Nevertheless, Russia had launched the Krusenstern expedition, and Kotzebue was getting under way from Kronstadt in 1815.

That same year, after the brief episode of the One Hundred Days, Louis XVIII recovered his throne. Peace reigned in France, but it was a France humiliated by the treaties of 1815. It was vital to make the French flag once more float over the distant seas. Taking advantage of the troubles of the Revolution and the empire, the British had seized Tasmania in 1803, the Dutch colony at the Cape in 1810, and, finally, the Ile de France and the Seychelles in the Indian Ocean, leaving France only Réunion, which they considered valueless and which, in 1815, was once again called Bourbon Island.

It was during this same period that the great movement to explore the far-off continents began again, a movement that had been interrupted by the revolutionary wars. The Prussian Alexander von Humboldt and the French botanist Aimé Bonpland were back in Paris in August 1805 from a five-year voyage to South America. In 1806, the French Academy of Sciences paid them formal homage. Henceforth, the monumental *Voyage aux régions équinoxiales du Noveau Monde* (Voyage to the Equinoctial Regions of the New World), the publication which Humboldt, now living in Paris, supervised from 1814 to 1825, was to serve as a model to their successors. In 1816, to mark the marriage of Brazil's future emperor, Pedro d'Alcantara, to an Austrian archduchess, a great expedition was fitted out to explore Brazil's unknown territories. The British naturalists were beginning to take stock of the enormous riches of the Australian continent, and Captain King, with the assistance of the botanist Allan Cunningham, was methodically charting its coasts. In 1816, Captain John Ross sailed to North America to look for the much-discussed Northwest Passage that Cook had been unable to find.

In August 1816, while the allied armies were still occupying French soil, the Minister of the Navy received a plan for a voyage around the world; its author was Louis de Freycinet. He had just finished the last volume of Baudin's Voyage, and this publication had put him in touch with all the great scientists of the time—Pierre-Simon Laplace, Georges Cuvier, and François Arago. After having emphasized the continuing uncertainty about the form of the earth, Freycinet gave his opinion about how the problem could be solved. "All these doubts can be resolved by observations with the invariable pendulum. The precision of this ingenious instrument is such that it would not be necessary to remain at a stop for more than twelve days. There is, therefore, no reason why these measurements could not be multiplied; and by suitably choosing the spots, we could obtain a multitude of elements that would lead to the solution of one of the most important problems in physical astronomy. . . . But the expedition given the responsibility for this research could also concern itself with other things: the intensity of magnetic forces, the inclination and declination of the magnetic needle . . . The atmospheric refractions in the torrid zone, the variations in weight at different latitudes, the hourly and daily temperature of water and air, the barometer reading, and the periodic variations so little observed in the southern hemisphere, the tides, the currents, the winds, and other atmospheric phenomena. Observations about natural history and the mores of the savage peoples visited could be added as secondary goals. . . ."

Such a project could not help but interest the government, which, in order to raise French prestige, was getting ready to resume great maritime expeditions. On March 1, 1817, the frigate *Cybèle*, commanded by Captain Kergariou, left Brest for Asia, where she was to visit the French missionaries who had long been established in Cochin China.

Given the responsibility for leading the expedition for which he had established the program, Freycinet decided to take with him two rising young men—Charles Hector Jacquinot, twenty, and Louis Isidore Duperrey, who had already distinguished himself as a hydrographer during a survey of the Tuscany coast in 1809. The ship's journal keeper, who also served as a draftsman, was Jacques Arago, the young brother of the celebrated astronomer.

Facing page: Inhabitants of Port Dorey (New Guinea). Original wash drawing by L. F. Lejeune. Voyage de la Coquille. *(Service historique de la Marine, Vincennes. Photo by Michel Didier © Photeb.)*

Preceding page: Inauguration of the monument raised to La Pérouse at Vanikoro, March 14, 1828. Watercolor by L. A. Sainson (Rex Nan Kivell Collection, National Library of Australia, Canberra, Photo © National Library of Australia/Photeb.)

It remained only to recruit the expedition's naturalists. After his voyage on the *Géographe,* Freycinet had come to the conclusion that the presence on board of civilians foreign to the rigors of sea life was to be avoided at any price. He knew that there were competent naturalists among the navy surgeons. In consultation with the navy's medical service, he selected Dr. Quoy as surgeon and zoologist, with Joseph Paul Gaimard as his assistant; the pharmacist Gaudichaud-Beaupré was put in charge of botany. Born in 1790, Jean René Constant Quoy, a young navy surgeon at Rochefort, had studied in that city under Gaspard Vivès, who, fifty years earlier, had sailed around the world with Bougainville. Dr. Quoy and his companions were unknown to Freycinet when, nine months before the departure, they came to Paris to study at the Museum of Natural History under Cuvier, Lamarck, and a young naval officer who was also an excellent botanist and entomologist, Dumont d'Urville. Freycinet and Quoy soon became the fast friends they were to remain all their lives. The surgeon brought onto the *Uranie* an excellent microscope, a thousand white glass bottles, and three large barrels of alcohol. He had taught himself drawing so as to be able to reproduce whatever could not be preserved, such as the soft parts of mollusks. Cuvier thought highly of the watercolors he did in the course of the voyage.

The ship chosen for the expedition was a twenty-gun, 350-ton corvette called the *Ciotat.* It was renamed the *Uranie* in honor of the muse of astronomy and geometry, and reoutfitted for its new mission. It was decided to inaugurate the use of iron bins to hold drinking water, something that had long been done in Great Britain. Two machines for distilling sea water were loaded on board, and there was a considerable provision of canned food prepared according to a method perfected by Nicolas Appert.

Reception of Captain and Madame de Freycinet at Dili on November 17, 1818, by the governor of the Portuguese settlements on Timor. Lithograph from an anonymous watercolor. (Musée de la Marine, Paris. Photo by Michel Didier © Photeb.)

Freycinet's Ship and Crew

L'*URANIE:* 350-ton corvette with 20 cannons, previously called *La Ciotat;*
left from Toulon, 9/17/1817;
crew: 126 men;
deaths: 7.

Commander: Louis Claude Desaulses de Freycinet, frigate captain, made captain 12/30/1820.

Lieutenants: Le Blanc, lieutenant commander, disembarked the day before the ship left Toulon; J. F. Lamarch, lieutenant commander; J. J. Labiche, lieutenant commander, died at sea, 1/9/1819.

Ensign: L. I. Duperrey, lieutenant junior grade, responsible for the hydrographic work; C. L. Théodore Laborde, lieutenant junior grade, died at sea, 11/23/1818.

Clerk: Gabert.

Elèves: Th. Fabré; N. F. Guérin; L. Railliard; Auguste Bérard; Ch. L. Prat-Bernon, died at sea, 10/7/1817; J. Alphonse Pellion; P. J. R. Ferrant; J. E. Dubaut.

Chaplain: Abbé F. L. de Quelen de la Villeglée.

Surgeon and zoologist: Dr. Jean René Constant Quoy.

Assistant surgeon and zoologist: Joseph Paul Gaimard.

Pharmacist and botanist: Charles Gaudichaud-Beaupré.

Draftsmen: Jacques E. V. Arago; Adrien Aimé Taunay, embarked at Rio, December 1818.

The clandestine passenger

When the *Uranie* left Toulon on September 17, 1817, she took with her Rose Pinon, Freycinet's wife, who had come on board dressed in men's clothes. Intelligent, courageous, and determined, as soon as the voyage had been announced she had made it clear that she had no intention of being separated from her husband, whom she succeeded in winning to her point of view. Nevertheless, navy regulations were clear—no woman was to be carried on any government ship without special authorization. The cat was soon out of the bag, but by then the *Uranie* was already far at sea. Rose de Freycinet knew how to keep her place, and she rapidly won the admiration and respect of all. During the voyage, she wrote an account of the expedition for a friend, but it was not published until 1927.

For about a month, the *Uranie* sailed the Mediterranean from Toulon to Gibralter. Quoy and Gaimard began their investigation of marine fauna,

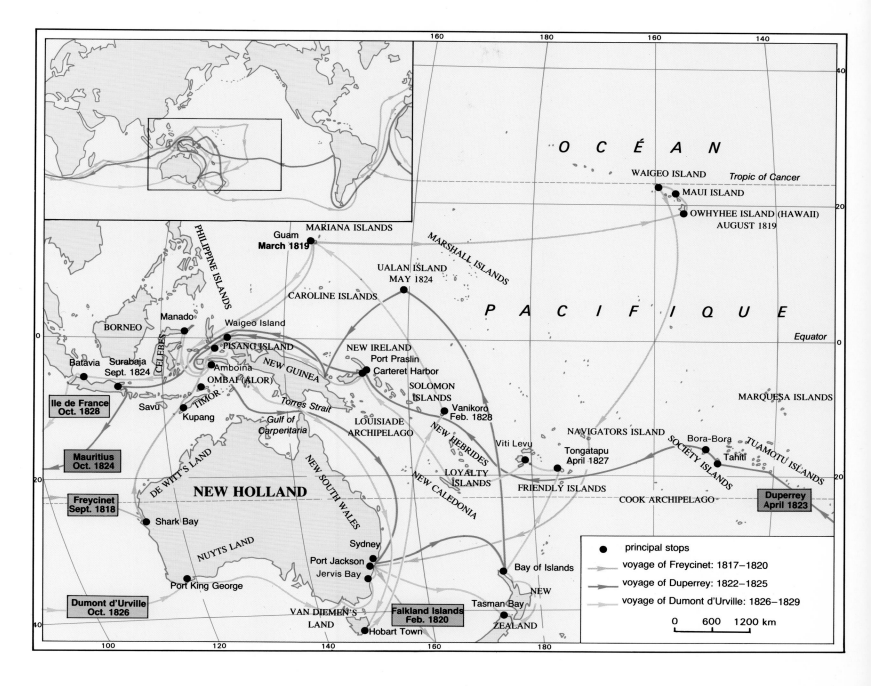

OCÉAN

PACIFIQUE

WAIGEO ISLAND   *Tropic of Cancer*
MAUI ISLAND
OWHYHEE ISLAND (HAWAII)
AUGUST 1819

MARIANA ISLANDS
Guam
March 1819

MARSHALL ISLANDS

UALAN ISLAND
MAY 1824

CAROLINE ISLANDS

Equator

PHILIPPINE ISLANDS

BORNEO
Manado
Waigeo Island
PISANG ISLAND
Amboina
OMBAI (ALOR)
Batavia Surabaja
Sept. 1824
CELEBES
Savú
TIMOR
Kupang

NEW GUINEA

NEW IRELAND
Port Praslin
Carteret Harbor

SOLOMON
ISLANDS

Vanikoro
Feb. 1828

MARQUESA ISLANDS

**Ile de France
Oct. 1828**

Torres Strait
Gulf of
Carpentaria

LOUISIADE
ARCHIPELAGO

NEW HEBRIDES

Viti Levu

NAVIGATORS ISLAND

Tongatapu
April 1827

Bora-Bora
Tahiti

SOCIETY ISLANDS

TUAMOTU ISLANDS

**Mauritius
Oct. 1824**

DE WITT'S LAND

NEW HOLLAND

NEW SOUTH WALES

NEW CALEDONIA

LOYALTY
ISLANDS

FRIENDLY ISLANDS

COOK ARCHIPELAGO

**Duperrey
April 1823**

**Freycinet
Sept. 1818**

Shark Bay

NUYTS LAND

Port King George

Sydney
Port Jackson
Jervis Bay

Bay of Islands

NEW

**Dumont d'Urville
Oct. 1826**

VAN DIEMEN'S
LAND

**Falkland Islands
Feb. 1820**

Tasman Bay

ZEALAND

Hobart Town

• principal stops
→ voyage of Freycinet: 1817–1820
→ voyage of Duperrey: 1822–1825
→ voyage of Dumont d'Urville: 1826–1829

0   600   1200 km

as a result of which the field was to be given new impetus. On November 22, the *Uranie* anchored at Tenerife, whose governor demanded that she be kept in quarantine. At Freycinet's urging, he reduced the quarantine first to ten days and then to eight, but after the fifth day the ship set sail again. On December 6, the *Uranie* came in sight of Rio de Janeiro, "where enormous and almost continuous downpours" hindered the experiments with the pendulum and the investigations into magnetism, thus forcing Freycinet to remain for almost two months (December 6, 1817, to January 29, 1818). Though unable to leave the environs of Rio, the naturalists obtained birds and several rare plants, and they brought on board living animals whose behavior could be studied at leisure. Among these was a coati that quickly became tame, playing with the ship's dog and sleeping in the hammocks, and a sloth that amused the sailors by climbing the masts. Life aboard ship was animated by the singing and the

bright colors of the caged Brazilian birds. A striped vanga made the whole voyage and was brought back to Paris alive.

The *Uranie* next crossed the Atlantic to Cape Town, where she arrived on March 7. On the sea, Quoy kept checking the fishermen's nets and discovered unknown species of fish, mollusks, crustaceans, and worms, while Gaimard observed the flight of the giant albatrosses that followed the ship. He shot down several in order to examine the contents of their stomachs and learned that, contrary to current thinking, these sea giants did not feed on fish but only on cuttlefish and squid.

The *Uranie* remained at Cape Town for twenty days, which Freycinet devoted to "gathering interesting data on magnetism and the shape of the globe." Shortly before the ship left, Kotzebue's *Rurik* appeared in Table Bay. Chamisso came on board the *Uranie*, where he was welcomed by the naturalists to whom he gave information about the places

The great French scientific voyages under the Restoration and the July Monarchy.
Voyage of Freycinet, 1817–1820.
Voyage of Duperrey, 1822–1825.
First voyage of Dumont d'Urville, 1826–1829.

the *Uranie* was going to visit and from which the *Rurik* was returning. Having left Cape Town on April 5, the *Uranie* anchored, on May 5, at Port Louis in Mauritius, formerly the Ile de France. There Freycinet met with one of his brothers, whom he had last seen at the age of twelve. The stopover in Mauritius lasted three months because the ship needed repairs. Meanwhile, the naturalists dispatched to the Natural History Museum four large lead cases containing their first harvests—among other things, seven hundred insects, including two hundred Brazilian butterflies, and a large collection of South African crustaceans.

Shark Bay and the islands of the Papuans

On September 12, 1818, one year after she had left France, the *Uranie* came in sight of the western coast of Australia and anchored in Shark Bay, which Freycinet had visited fifteen years earlier. As they were to stay for two weeks, a camp was set up on shore. The aboriginals were few in number, and it was impossible to make contact with them. In the forest, the two zoologists and the botanist found two bandicoots and a kangaroo rat that lived for several weeks aboard the *Uranie,* where they were also able to keep a carnivorous dasyure for five months. On the islands of Dorre and Bernier, Quoy and Gaimard caught a striped kangaroo and some very beautiful parakeets. Gaudichaud baptized a new shrub Keraudren, in honor of a navy medical inspector who had helped prepare the Freycinet expedition just as he had that of Baudin, seventeen years earlier. A grevillea with red flowers was to be known as *Grevillea gaudichaudi.* After leaving Shark Bay on September 27, the *Uranie* ascended north to

Reception of officers of the Uranie *at Kupang by M. Tielman, government secretary at Timor. Lithograph from an original watercolor by J. A. Pellion, navy élève. (Musée de la Marine, Paris. Photo by Michel Didier © Photeb.)*

Timor, and then to the Moluccas.

On October 5, the navigators entered "the vast bay of Kupang," where they were received by the Dutch authorities. Making several excursions into the interior, the naturalists brought back a dark-coated deer with delicate horns that were only slightly branched; the Sunda sambar, which later lived for a long time in the zoo of the Jardin des Plantes; and several birds. Leaving Kupang on October 23, the *Uranie* prepared to chart the northern coast of Timor from west to east, but contrary currents carried her north to Ombai Island. Freycinet sent a detachment to visit the village of Bituka, where the sailors found themselves confronted by warriors armored in leather decorated with banana leaves that rustled when they walked. The *Uranie* then returned to Timor and anchored at Dili, the capital of the Portuguese settlements that occupied the eastern part of the island. Welcomed by the governor, who gave several celebrations and a ball in their honor, the French renewed their provisions. During an excursion along the banks of the Dabao River, Quoy was spellbound by a fish with bulging eyes that crept along the mud—Freycinet's mudskipper. Gaudichaud, who for his part was studying the Timor pandanus, classified the climbing species as *Freycinetia.*

Once more going north, but much farther east, the *Uranie* sailed along Ceram and Amboina, passing through the Buru Strait. There she encountered the dreaded Malay pirates on their caracores. Anti-boarding nets were spread, and, under the threat of the guns, the Malays soon withdrew. Several days later, as the ship was traversing the dense Molucca Archipelago and exploring the islands of Halmahera and Gebe, more caracores appeared. This time they were filled with natives of Gebe, come as friends under the leadership of their chief, Kimalaka, who received permission to come on board and was invited to dinner. After a short stopover at Pisang, the *Uranie* reached Rawak on December 16. Here it was decided to set up an observatory. When the French were about to leave the island, they heard a warlike music of drums. It was Kimalaka's little fleet, and he was returning to see his friends and bring them presents from his own island. At Rawak, the zoologists had found a wood kingfisher and two sorts of frogmouths, or tropical nightjars, and the botanist had found other *Freycinetia* and some orchids. At Boni, a neighboring island, Gaimard made one of the best discoveries of his career—a large land bird about the size of a hen and belonging to a previously unknown species. Several months later, at Tinian in the Marianas, he found another that was somewhat different. He had discovered a new genus, perhaps even a new family of Gallinaceae, which he baptized megapodes.

Having celebrated Christmas on Waigeo Island, the navigators next traversed the Carolines, and the natives swarmed about the ship in their canoes. They were friendly and proved extremely honest traders. The clear waters of the coral reefs made it possible to see swarms of fish of unusual shapes and superb colors. Quoy's bottles began to fill up as he made a pictorial record of the bright shades of fish, crustaceans, cephalopods, and mollusks before they lost their luster.

In March, the French reached the Marianas. They were so well received there by the Spanish governor, Don José Medinilla, that Freycinet decided to make a long stay at Agana, the capital of Guam, so that the crew might recover from an outbreak of dysentery that had caused several deaths. In the Marianas, the Spanish missionaries were powerful and respected, and the sailors had to attend Holy Week services. But, in the evening, they were entertained by natives dancing under the skies.

The *Uranie* set out again on June 5, and, after sailing two months, anchored on August 8 in the bay of Karakakua (Kealakekua) in Owhyhee (Hawaii). Kamehameha I had just died, and, according to custom, his palace had been burned to ashes and pigs were being slaughtered for the funeral. As a result, Freycinet was unable to obtain food supplies. The new king, Liho-Liho, who was son and successor to Kamehameha but had not yet had his power confirmed, waited on his throne for Freycinet. He was "dressed in a blue hussar's jacket galooned with gold and sporting large colonel's epaulettes; one of his officers carried his saber. . . . It was truly a strange sight to see eight or ten masses of flesh in seminaked human form lying stretched along the ground."

During a visit aboard ship, the king's prime minister had been "struck by the chaplain's costume. Informed of the functions of this ecclesiatic, he made it known that he had long wanted to be a Christian and therefore begged to be baptized." The ceremony took place on board ship in the presence of the king and the queen mother; Freycinet was the godfather, and Gabert, his clerk, played the role of godmother. According to Arago, this Kraimoku (Kalanimoku) was a "perfidious and crafty" man who wanted to betray Liho-Liho and place the country under foreign rule. He thought that this baptism "would open his way to glory." The French then went on to Maui and Oahu, where Freycinet was able to reprovision.

During this one-month stopover in the Sandwich Islands, Gaudichaud made some discoveries—the *Santalum freycinetiana* and several new species of pandanus. Some fine mollusks and as many as six species of girellidae were fished from Hawaiian waters. Freycinet was given an enormous living leatherback by Captain Merk of the *Eagle* out of Boston. On land, Quoy and Gaimard managed to capture a native bird that had been identified during Cook's third voyage, but they noted that it had since become rare because its dazzling red plumage served as native adornments. Several other species, such as the nene, a goose, were threatened with extinction as a result of frequent stopovers by American ships. The naturalists were concerned that the arrival in these islands of white men supplied with rifles was beginning to endanger those species that were few in number.

When the *Uranie* left the Sandwich Islands at the end of August 1819, she was on her way home, but the almost year-long journey would be spent mostly on the seas. During the two-and-a-half-month crossing from the Sandwich Islands to Port Jackson, Freycinet discovered a new island in the Navigators Archipelago (Samoa); he named it Rose, in honor of his wife. While at sea, the naturalists observed several species of dolphin that were practically unknown.

In Sydney, where Freycinet stayed from November 18 to December 25, Governor Lachlan Macquarie, a popular and affable man, turned over to the French a port building, which they used as an observatory. Freycinet could hardly recognize the city, which had more than doubled in population since his first visit. Himself interested in the colony's natural history, Macquarie facilitated the naturalists' investigations. They made a long excursion in the Blue Mountains, at the foot of which stretched marshlands bordering the Hawkesbury River. Shaded by casuarinas, they were inhabited by black swans and jacanas, jabirus, white ibises, and cormorants; rainbow-colored wasps hunted insects above the waters. Higher up, on the sloping hills covered with eucalyptus, could be heard the melodious chattering of crimson parakeets and the warm and imperious voice of the lyre bird. The naturalists captured several little-known birds, including a warbler that enlivened the cabin of the captain, who took great care of it and brought it back to Paris, where it was given to the Natural History Museum. Quoy had also found several sand lizards, including a new species, the Australian black-and-yellow, blue-tongued skink, and an echidna, which he kept on board for several weeks and fed with sugar water.

Kimalaka's caracore at Gebe Island (Moluccas). Lithograph from a watercolor by A. L. Garneray, 1822. Journal of Rose de Freycinet. (Musée de la Marine, Paris. Photo by Michel Didier © Photeb.)

Traditional dance at Agana on Guam. Lithograph after an original watercolor by J. Arago. (Musée de la Marine, Paris. Photo by Michel Didier © Photeb.)

The Uranie *is shipwrecked*

Freycinet left Port Jackson on December 25; in February 1820, as the *Uranie* was approaching Tierra del Fuego, she was caught by a hurricane and helplessly pushed along Le Maire Strait. As they were passing near the Falklands, Freycinet decided to drop anchor, but "the *Uranie* hit an uncharted reef and was so badly damaged that despite four pumps she would inevitably have sunk if we had not found some suitable place to beach her." Freycinet and his men were forced to spend two months in an extremely cold climate, living the haphazard life of castaways. Food supplies began to give out. Sailors armed with sticks hunted ashy and short-winged ducks. When short of food, the French went to nearby Penguin Island, "considered as a reserve storehouse, and caught enough penguins to last two days"; but Quoy reports that it was really very bad food and good only for men who were starving.

In the wreck, the naturalists lost a large part of their collections. Gaudichaud had managed to save his herbarium, and he stubbornly dried and rescued twenty-five hundred plants. To compensate somewhat for these losses, the three naturalists made a detailed inventory of the flora and fauna of the islands. Gaudichaud was able to identify 217 species of plants and on his return published a *Flore des îles Malouines* (Flora of the Falkland Islands). The zoologists were even better served, for the archipelago was an assembly point for many birds.

It was not until April that a ship appeared—the *Mercury,* an American vessel that had been damaged at Cape Horn and was stopping in the Falklands to make repairs. The captain agreed to take the castaways to Montevideo. On the way, he suggested that Freycinet buy his ship, the crew and cargo of which would be disembarked upon arrival; the proposition was immediately accepted. Thus, at Montevideo, on May 8, 1820, the *Mercury*

became a French ship and, renamed the *Physicienne,* continued on its way, stopping at Rio de Janeiro for three months (June 20–September 13) to allow the crew to recover before the return to France. The *Physicienne* arrived at Le Havre on November 13, 1820.

Though only seven men had died, there had been thirty-eight deserters, fifteen men who had been disembarked at their request, and two others, sick, who had been left at stopovers. Freycinet had with some difficulty filled in the gaps and had, all in all, accomplished his mission. He nevertheless had to face a court-martial for the loss of the vessel, but he was acquitted and promoted to captain. However, he had a great deal of difficulty in getting the funds with which to publish his account of the voyage, a matter that was to occupy him until his death in 1842.

When the numerous cases containing the natural history specimens arrived in Paris, a scientific commission that included Cuvier, Arago, Gay-Lussac, and Humboldt was immediately charged with examining them. The report this commission presented to the Academy of Sciences was filled with praise, for the naturalists' discoveries at the very least rivaled those of Péron and Lesueur. Four of the 25 different kinds of mammals brought back were unknown, and of 313 birds, forty-five were unknown and included three new genera. Forty-five reptiles and 164 fish were counted, many of them previously unknown. Of the thirteen hundred insects representing some three hundred species, some forty were unknown, the most interesting coming from Brazil and especially from the Papuas.

But what particularly struck the scientists was the considerable number of marine invertebrates, mollusks, crustaceans, and polyps carefully preserved in alcohol and drawn from life by the expedition's naturalists and artists. They constituted the most complete collection yet brought back; it contained the first known specimens of Terebratulas and of the phyllosoma—mysterious transparent animals as flat as leaves; it was still not known that they were the larval forms of crustaceans.

Gaudichaud's herbarium included three thousand species; five hundred were not in the collection of the Natural History Museum and about two hundred were unknown. In addition, the expedition had assembled five hundred specimens. As for the iconographic documentation, it included, in addition to sketches by the naturalists, five hundred drawings by Jacques Arago representing the sites—and especially the inhabitants—of the islands visited.

In 1820, the naturalists' task was only just beginning. They now had to devote themselves to detailed examinations and classification of the new species. This long and arduous task was interrupted by the departure of Quoy and Gaimard on a new expedition, that of Dumont d'Urville on the *Astrolabe*. They were therefore not able to publish the zoology until their return. As for Gaudichaud, after having finished the botany of the voyage, in December 1830 he departed once more, this time for South America on the frigate *Herminie*.

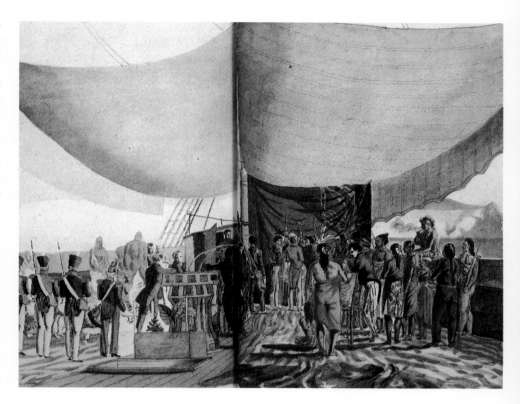

Images of a lost world

Though, by 1822, Jacques Arago was able to satisfy public curiosity with his *Promenade autour du monde* (Journey Around the World), accompanied by an atlas containing his drawings, the publication of the voyage did not begin until 1824 and continued for the next twenty years. Left incomplete as a result of Freycinet's death, it included six volumes, three of which were written by the naturalists. The illustrations filled four atlases, one of which was devoted to zoology and another to botany.

These atlases inaugurated the series of great illustrated works that henceforth accompanied the texts of the voyages; even today the plates constitute unique documentation, of a rarely equalled exactitude and beauty. After Freycinet's voyage, the creators of these plates were painters of natural history, most often attached to the museum, where they were responsible for pictorially documenting new species as they arrived. These artists thus continued the series of sumptuous vellums first commissioned by Gaston d'Orléans, the brother of Louis XIII. Under the supervision of the naturalists, they worked from specimens turned over to them. These works, which have all the delicacy of miniatures, could be very exactly reproduced thanks to the new method of lithography; some plates were later hand colored. Of course, such publications were not readily available to the general public, which was kept informed of new natural history discoveries by popular journals which were very widespread at the time, as well as by several dictionaries of natural history that appeared during this period. Thanks in particular to these great maritime expeditions, the natural sciences developed in a spectacular fashion, and in the first half of the nineteenth century they attracted a new audience.

As for the historical atlases that illustrated the history of each expedition, they are no less precious. Thanks to them, we can still enjoy a pristine image of unknown lands and, particularly, of their inhabitants, with the eyes of those who for the first time encountered fellow beings who were so different from themselves. Looking at these portraits, we can still be present at the confrontation, at the mute dialogue, between civilized man and the savage, a dialogue composed of reciprocal amazement and mutual curiosity. We can examine their body ornaments, those tattoos, those extravagant scars that were incomprehensible to those who nevertheless represented them so carefully. So much of this was soon to be forbidden by missionaries eager to impose on the "natives" their own concept of the body soiled by sin. They were fugitive visions, erased immediately after being captured—for at the same time as they recorded these practices, those intruders, the white men, made every effort to make them vanish. We now contemplate these visions with a nostalgia for virgin lands, for "primitive" beings, for everything that has since disappeared from our world.

Baptism of Kraimokou, minister of the king of Hawaii, by Abbé de Quélen on board the Uranie, *August 1819. Lithograph from a watercolor by J. Arago. (Musée de la Marine, Paris. Photo by Michel Didier © Photeb.)*

Engagement ceremony in New Holland. Engraving from a drawing by Jacques Arago. The future husband breaks his fiancée's two upper incisors before consummating the marriage. (Musée de la Marine, Paris. Photo by Michel Didier © Photeb.)

The voyage of the *Coquille*

A year after the return of the *Uranie*, Ensign Duperrey, who had just been promoted to lieutenant commander, presented the Minister of the Navy, Count de Clermont-Tonnerre, with a plan for a new scientific expedition. He was urged to take this step by his former comrade aboard the *Chevrette*, Dumont d'Urville, who had also become a lieutenant commander and who was consulted by Quoy and Gaimard when the *Uranie* was being fitted out. In 1820, d'Urville had published the account of the cruise of the *Chevrette* and, in 1822—at his own expense—a Latin work on the plants discovered during this voyage. Intelligent, cultivated, and very ambitious, he hoped to be promoted to the higher ranks very quickly, and he also wanted recognition as a true scientist; only a research expedition could make this double goal possible. Duperrey proposed an itinerary designed to complete that of the *Uranie*.

The king himself approved this project. Early in 1822, Duperrey was given the command of the *Coquille*, a 380-ton transport vessel. Equipped at Toulon and made into a corvette, she was especially refitted for the expedition. For his second in command, Duperrey chose Dumont d'Urville, who was made responsible for botany and entomology and who also served as an ethnologist and a philologist. Two other officers also came from the *Chevrette*: Lottin, who was to be the geographer and hydrographer, and Jacquinot, who was made the *Coquille*'s astronomer; the third ensign, Bérard, had sailed on the *Uranie*. The surgeon, Prosper Garnot, and his assistant, surgeon and pharmacist René Primevère Lesson, were responsible for zoology. This homogeneous team was to make the voyage an unprecedented success.

The *Coquille* left the roads of Toulon on August 11, 1822. Seventeen days later, she reached Tenerife, where she was put into an eight-day quarantine. Having crossed the Atlantic, the ship dropped anchor at Santa Catarina Island south of Brazil, in order to avoid Rio. A Portuguese officer came on board but seemed "disturbed when he saw that we were a warship and quickly fled. The next day we discovered that Santa Catarina was in a state of revolution."

Dom Joao VI, king of Portugal, chased from his throne by Napoleon, had, in 1807, taken refuge in his Brazilian possessions. In 1821, he had returned to Portugal, leaving in Rio his son Dom Pedro, who had the title of prince regent. But since the Portuguese Cortes wanted to tie Brazil closely to the mother country, in 1822, Dom Pedro had just had himself proclaimed constitutional emperor. At Santa Catarina, feeling ran high; every citizen wore on his left arm the inscription *"Independentia o la muerte."* Three *Coquille* officers were sent to the governor, but they were very coldly received; it was suspected that their ship had come to spy on the coastal defenses. Nevertheless, the Frenchmen spent two weeks in the port, where the physicists and naturalists began their work.

Descending the coast, the *Coquille* next anchored in French Bay (Berkeley Sound) in Soledad Island (East Falkland), the easternmost of the Falklands group. The observatory was set up near the ruins left by "the settlement of M. de Bougainville in 1765." At the other end of the island, one could still see "the ribs of the corvette *Uranie*." In the bay was the islet inhabited by penguins, where the castaways had gone to hunt two years earlier. "On calm evenings," wrote Lesson, "the sound coming from

Duperrey's Ship and Crew

La *COQUILLE*: 380-ton transport vessel, designated corvette; left from Toulon, 8/11/1822; returned to Marseilles, 3/24/1825; crew: 65 men; deaths: 0.

Commander: Louis Isidore Duperrey, lieutenant commander.

Second: Jules Sébastien César Dumont d'Urville, lieutenant commander.

Lieutenants: Jules Alphonse René de Blosseville; Blois de la Calante; Lesage.

Ensigns: Victor Charles Lottin; Auguste Bérard; Charles Hector Jacquinot.

Surgeon: Prosper Garnot, put ashore sick at Sydney, January 1824.

Assistant surgeon and pharmacist: René Primevère Lesson.

Draftsman: L. F. Lejeune.

it suggested that made by a crowd on a holiday." On the shores, d'Urville began an algae collection—which by the end of the voyage was to include 106 species—by harvesting laminaria that were afterward to be called *Lessonia,* whereas other species from the Chilean coast were called *Durvillea.* "The hunters spread out over territory uninhabited by man but in which a prodigious number of animals of all sorts lived in freedom." Even after the stay by Quoy and Gaimard, the zoologists still found four new species to describe.

The stay at Soledad lasted a month. "After leaving the Malouines (Falklands), for several days we saw Patagonia and Tierra del Feugo; we did not dare to approach because the sea was heavy. . . . We ran into innumerable difficulties during the voyage around Cape Horn." Having ranged the western coast of South America, on January 20, 1823, the *Coquille* arrived at Talcahuano, near Concepción. Chile was in a state of high excitement. The first president of the Chilean Republic, General O'Higgins, had had to abdicate and had just been made a prisoner. The leader of the rebellion, General Freire, was named "supreme dictator" and was preparing to enter Santiago. The province of Concepción "was plunged in great misery as a result of successive pillaging by conquerors and conquered who had made its territory an arena for their bloody battles."

Profiting from his stay, Duperrey investigated the Araucan Indians, a little-understood people whose warlike exploits had, however, made them famous even in Europe. The inhabitants of Concepción were also Indians. The mestizos had been run off at the same time as the Spaniards, and "the present generation has retained from the mother country only its religious fanaticism, its absurd superstitions, and its habits of idleness."

The investigations by the naturalists led to the discovery of new coastal species: two dolphins, two kinds of cormorants, a grebe, a puffin that was baptized the Garnot, the Peruvian diving petrel, an Inca tern shot down on the barren island of San Lorenzo, as well as numerous swallows, including several ovenbirds.

From Chile, the expedition went to Peru, staying briefly at Callao first and then at Paita. Duperrey and his officers went to Lima, some 14 kilometers from Callao. Peru was the last vice-royalty from which the Spanish troops had been expelled. They had fallen back to Callao, whose garrison was not to surrender until 1826. Comparing the internal situation of Peru with that of Chile, Duperrey wrote: "I think it is even more deplorable. At the moment, the Independents who occupy Lima control only the seaboard, an uncultivated area that has in any case been ruined by the previous wars. The Spanish have all of upper Peru [present-day Bolivia]. . . . The mines are under their control."

In Paita, which was nearer the equator, Duperrey wanted to observe the diurnal variation of the magnetic needle, which Freycinet had recently demonstrated was less in the tropics than in tem-

"King Pomare III's guard was made up of handsome men, but I would rather they had been clothed in their attractive national costume than in a few old striped black jackets, no doubt the castoffs of some dead missionaries." Original wash by L. F. Lejeune. (Service historique de la Marine, Vincennes. Photo by Michel Didier © Photeb.)

perate zones. Thus he would complete the work of his predecessors by studying where he could the intensity of earth magnetism. He was the first to trace magnetic meridians and parallels. In Paita, the naturalists found several lizards, and in the big shiny black birds that hunted them they recognized a new species, which they called the Las Casas ani.

After this last stopover on the South American continent, the *Coquille* spent a month crossing the Pacific. There was only one sick man on board, but he was the surgeon. Garnot had had a first attack of dysentery in Peru and was to long suffer from this illness, which had become chronic. During the course of this extended voyage, he and Lesson observed the behavior of seals, and Lesson was to bring back important new documentation on the different species. Suddenly, in the middle of the night, the officer on duty heard the distant crash of waves breaking over reefs. It was Réao, the first of the low islands in the Dangerous Archipelago (Tuamotus); they named it for the Minister of the Navy, Clermont-Tonnerre. On landing the next morning, the navigators saw some islanders approaching, but they withdrew immediately, and it was impossible to establish contact with them. Later, the Frenchmen came to three uninhabited islands, which they called Freycinet, Augier, and Lostange.

The end of a mirage

The navigators were eager to arrive at Bougainville's New Cythera, which had not been visited by Frenchmen since his voyage. The disillusion was complete. "Not a single woman came on board. The Tahitians told us they were waiting for us under the trees. . . . We were eager to see if M. de Bougainville was telling the truth when he compared them to Venus. . . . Under the trees we found only a few men, who were very amused by our mistake. . . . The island of Tahiti is now so different from what it was in Cook's time that it is impossible to give you a complete picture of it. The missionaries of London's Royal Society have totally changed the mores and the customs of these peoples. The women are extraordinarily reserved. . . . There are few men in Tahiti who do not know how to read and write . . . and we were astonished to see the Tahitians offering to shake hands, eating with a fork . . . since we were expecting to meet savages in a state of nature."

The English missionaries had established themselves on the island in 1797; at that time, Pomare I, who had known Cook, was still alive—he was not to die until 1803. In 1807, his son, Pomare II, had converted to Christianity, but the following year he was expelled by his subjects. He did not regain power until 1809, and then undertook to convert his subjects by force. When the *Coquille* arrived, King Pomare III was only four years old and lived under the guardianship of his aunt, Pomare-Vahine. She saw to it that the child received a purely English education, and it was the missionaries who crowned him the following year.

Aware that the maps of the archipelago contained gross errors and eager to correct them, Duperrey visited several other islands, including Bora Bora, where the natives were even more reserved than the Tahitians and came on board only after

being invited to do so.

Leaving the Society Archipelago in the middle of June, the *Coquille* sailed the Pacific for two months, on the way reconnoitering islands whose position was not accurately known: the little group to the east of the Friendly Islands (Tonga), Eua in that archipelago, Ndeni or Santa Cruz in the group bearing that name, and finally Buka, the last of the Solomon Islands before New Ireland, where Duperrey arrived at Port Praslin on August 12, 1823, and stayed until the twenty-first. Blosseville, with the help of Lottin and Bérard, made a map of this port discovered by Bougainville and then charted St. George's Channel, which separates New Ireland from New Britain.

In the area around Port Praslin, Lesson gathered seven samples of chalky madreporic limestone characteristic of these islands. His mineralogical collection, which had just been increased by basaltic lavas from the Society Islands, was next enriched with samples from the Blue Mountains of Australia, and others from Tasmania, and New Zealand; meanwhile, d'Urville collected algae, lichens, and ferns. He was to bring back 145 species of ferns, many of them previously unknown. Lesson brought on board three species of flycatchers and a black-and-white coucal, but his most interesting finds were two cuscus, curious round marsupials with immense orange-colored nocturnal eyes. The naturalists hoped to bring these animals to Paris alive. They were unable to do this, but for several weeks they studied their behavior, still little known.

Fifteen days after leaving New Ireland, the *Coquille,* having explored the Schouten Islands in detail, reached Waigeo, a volcanic Moluccan island off the northern coast of New Guinea, whose in-

Tahitian costumes, May 20, 1823. Original watercolor by L. F. Lejeune. Voyage de la Coquille. (Service historique de la Marine, Vincennes. Photo by Michel Didier © Photeb.)

terior had been little explored. Waigeo was then known as the Land of the Papuans. The Malays had long been settled there and had relegated to the mountains the Alfuros with whom they had nevertheless interbred. The navigators visited the Alfuros, entering their lattice-work bamboo houses raised on piles amid marshes. At Waigeo, Lesson made a discovery that was to bring him fame on his return.

Even birds of paradise have feet

On September 8, 1522, the *Victoria,* the only remaining ship of Magellan's fleet, returned to Seville. Among the curiosities she brought back were two dead birds whose iridescent plumage, incredibly long and delicate, amazed everyone. The birds seemed too beautiful to belong to this earth; their carefully preserved bodies had neither bones nor feet. This may have been the origin of the legend started in 1596 by the Dutchman Van Lindshoten, who had traveled through the East Indies, and who wrote that the "birds of paradise," as he called them, always remained high in the sky and came down only to die. They were even hatched in the sky, the egg being laid on the back of the male and covered by the belly of the female. Of course, after the seventeenth century, some travelers and several scientists objected to these assertions; nevertheless, the birds of paradise that came from the distant islands never had feet, and the fact was that no European naturalist had ever been able to see them alive.

The first to do so was René Primevère Lesson on Waigeo in September 1823. Penetrating into a thick wood, he saw fly up into the sky a golden-yellow bird with a brilliant red plumed tail. He was amazed and delighted, and after following it with his eyes for a long time could not bring himself to shoot it down. It was a red bird of paradise. Several days later, he was able to observe at length a superb bird of paradise *(Lophorina superba)* covered with downy black, green, and violet of a metallic sheen. These birds, of course, had feet. During the stopover in Amboina, in October, Lesson had a shock. In the stall of a Chinese merchant, he saw two large emerald-green birds of paradise with large and silky light yellow tails. Naturally, he wanted to buy them, but the merchant asked 500 francs apiece and the naturalist did not have enough money and had to give up the idea. But in Sydney, in January 1824, he was able to acquire a male bird of paradise with plumage of "a bright red vermillion which shone like spun glass."

This made Lesson impatient to reach the country of these birds—New Guinea. There the *Coquille* remained in Port Dorey from July 26 to August 9, 1824. No sooner had he landed than the naturalist went hunting. From the Papuans he was able to obtain only two mutilated skins of birds of paradise with steely throats. He searched the woods in vain for this bird. A great deal of research turned

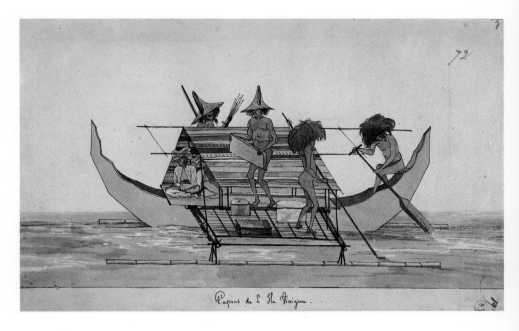

Papuans of the island of Waigeo in the Moluccas to the north of New Guinea. Original watercolor by L. F. Lejeune. (Service historique de la Marine, Vincennes. Photo by Michel Didier © Photeb.)

up three species belonging to the manucode group; two were previously unknown, and he baptized them the black manucode and the Keraudren manucode. Having been able to observe these birds in nature, he was able to bring back completely new documentation.

Little by little, the existence of these magnificent birds was strongly threatened. Initially, the feathers were used principally in the extraordinary headdresses worn by Papuans on ceremonial occasions, but eventually elegant women of the Western word took up the fashion. It soon caused a furor in Paris and London, and a profitable commerce was created through the intermediary of the Malay merchants in the Moluccas, who brought their precious booty to Singapore. This devastating hunt was not prohibited until 1924, when the fashion had passed and prices had seriously declined.

Lesson had made many other discoveries at Port Dorey: an impressive number of unknown birds, including two new species of mound birds, named for Duperrey and Cuvier; a Papuan boar; a kangaroo; and a New Guinea scrub wallaby—all of which were brought back alive. Considering that such a rich collection of animals new to science was assembled in fewer than fifteen days, it is impossible not to be as amazed as Cuvier himself was on the return of the *Coquille* by the activity and competence shown by René Primevère Lesson.

To follow him on this search, which lasted ten months, he left his companions at Waigeo. On September 23, the *Coquille* dropped anchor at Caieli (Kajeli) in Buru. As was true in many Dutch colonies, access to the port was forbidden to European ships, and Duperrey had some difficulty in obtaining permission to stay there for several days. The Frenchmen were nevertheless well received and allowed to replenish their provisions. The Presbyterian minister complained to Duperrey about the all-but-insurmountable difficulties that had blocked his attempts at conversion; the Malays were Mussulmen and intended to remain so.

PARADISIER ROUGE, FEM. (Paradisæa rubra, Lacép.)
ILE DE WAIGIOU.

Female red bird of paradise. Watercolor by Prêtre after Garnot, engraved by Coutant. (Société de Géographie, Bibliothèque nationale, Paris. Photo © Bibl. nat./Photeb.)

Male king bird of paradise from New Holland. Plate by Prêtre. Atlas de Zoologie of the Voyage de l'Astrolabe. (Bibliothèque du Muséum d'histoire naturelle, Paris. Photo © Bibl. du Muséum/Photeb.)

The French officers were able to witness their attachment to Islam when, at Caieli, they attended the inauguration of a mosque. "This festival was celebrated in honor of the death and resurrection of their prophet. On a cloth-draped platform lay a priest playing the role of Mahomet. He closed his eyes while hymns of mourning were intoned all around him. It was eight in the evening. . . . At three in the morning, he came to life and climbed ropes to the top of the mosque, from where he appeared, radiant, and then descended to the earth. . . . At that moment the young men and women began to dance . . . to the sound of a clamorous music supplied by two harmonicas and several tom-toms."

At Amboina, where the *Coquille* anchored from October 4 to 28, the welcome of Governor Merkus was gratifying. Almost all the commerce of the island was in the hands of the Chinese, whose quarter was at one of the ends of the city, the other being taken over by the *campong* of the Malays. In the Moluccas, the French caught a great number of tropical fish, including six species of magnificently colored triggerfish.

The next two and a half months were spent sailing, and Duperrey did not disembark again until Port Jackson. The *Coquille* traversed Ombrai Strait, which borders Timor, explored Volcano Island, and then—to the west of Timor—Sawu, Benjear, and the island that was given Duperrey's name. Contrary winds kept her from approaching the western coast of Australia, and, about January 10, she had to wait several days before rounding the southern part of Tasmania.

At Sydney, where Governor Brisbane gave them the best possible welcome, the navigators stayed from January 17 to March 25, a long and restful stopover. Surgeon Garnot, who had still not recovered his health, was left behind and spent his time taking notes on the natives, of whom he wrote: "The native inhabitants of New Holland are with-out doubt the most hideous peoples ever known. . . . They are generally thin and fidgety. Their hair, not woolly, is tough, black, and very thick;. . . . the upper part of their faces is flat; their noses are flattened; their mouths protrude; their lips are thick; their facial angle is from 61 to 67 degrees." Garnot embarked on the *Castle Forbes* with several large cases containing an important part of the collections, but the English ship was wrecked at the Cape in July 1824, and the cases were lost.

Meanwhile, in Australia the indefatigable Lesson explored the countryside right up to the Blue Mountains. He brought back several species of birds and the red-throated pademelon, a kangaroo that the English naturalists had not yet discovered. In the Bay of Islands, in New Zealand's North Island, where the *Coquille* stopped in April, Lesson found several other unknown birds, while d'Urville enlarged his collection of algae and ferns. At this stage of the voyage, he felt that the important thing was not only to discover new plants, but to "determine their geographic extension"—to note, for example, that a South American species was to be found in New Zealand; on his return from the voyage, he thus made an important contribution to a still very new science—geographic botany.

Duperrey next headed north and from May to July went through the extensive area of the Carolines, where he reconnoitered a great number of islands and put in to what he called Ualan (Kusaie). Observing the frigate birds, he noticed that there was not one species, as was thought, but two; he also identified several doves—to one of which he gave the name of his wife, Zoé, who had "expired at the dawn of her life"—and he obtained a number of reef fish. At the next stop, Port Dorey, he was able to finish his research on the bird of paradise.

The *Coquille* was now on the way home. She stopped at Surabaja in Java in September, reached Mauritius on October 2, put in at St. Helena in January 1825, and then at Ascension. On March 24,

she entered the port of Marseilles, having sailed 25,000 marine leagues in thirty-three months without the loss of a single man and without having run aground or sustained any damage at all.

A "scientifically exemplary" expedition

Convened in a formal session, on August 22, 1825, the Academy of Sciences received the navigators. Duperrey presented the results obtained in studies of geography, hydrography, and the contours of the globe. Cuvier then took the floor to summarize the still-unfinished inventory of the natural history specimens. The expedition, he concluded, had been "scientifically exemplary." The geological collection included three hundred typical specimens assembled by Lesson. D'Urville had harvested three thousand species of plants, of which four hundred were probably new. In the zoological collections, there were several human skulls; twelve new species of quadrupeds; 254 species of birds, of which forty-six were new and included the much-talked-of birds of paradise; sixty-three species of reptiles and amphibians, of which fifteen to twenty were new; 298 fish preserved in alcohol, seventy of them having been painted by Lesson; eleven hundred kinds of insects; and, finally, more than one thousand marine invertebrates.

The publication of the voyage in seven volumes and four large folio atlases began immediately. It was done with exceptional speed, the first volume appearing the same year as the return, the last in 1830. Duperrey assumed responsibility for the three volumes devoted to the history of the voyage, the hydrography, and the physical studies. The two-volume zoology was largely written by Lesson himself, for Garnot, whom he found in Paris, was shortly afterward named chief surgeon of Martinique. Dumont d'Urville, responsible for the botany and the entomology, set to work, but he almost immediately had to interrupt his labors to take over the command of the *Coquille,* which became the *Astrolabe;* these volumes were finished by Bory de Saint-Vincent, Brongniart, and Latreille.

On his return, Duperrey was made a frigate captain, but he was never to rise above this rank, probably because his profession was henceforth that of a scientist. After publishing several important works—particularly on magnetism—in 1842, he succeeded Louis de Freycinet at the Academy of Sciences, becoming president in 1850. Lesson returned to his native Rochefort and remained there until his death. Appointed Chief Pharmacist of the Navy in 1835, he taught botany and devoted his leisure time to the publication of works on natural history that were many in number but somewhat lacking in order and rigor. Garnot also wrote a great deal and collaborated on many publications.

Natives of New Ireland. Color engraving after L. F. Lejeune and Chazal. Voyage autour du monde sur la Coquille. Société de Géographie, Bibliothèque nationale, Paris. Photo © Bibl. nat./Photeb.)

Dumont d'Urville finds the *Astrolabe*, 1826–1829

Two months after his return, Dumont d'Urville wrote to Count de Chabrol, Minister of the Navy: "The expedition on the *Coquille* in which I have just taken part has amply proved to me that a voyage around the world is incapable of rendering real services to geography, navigation, and the natural sciences . . . I feel that the scene of these operations must be limited, and that the navigator who makes an exact study of some still unknown region of the globe will do something more worthwhile than someone whose ship has plowed through the immense spaces of the sea and only hastily visited some of the islands scattered there."

D'Urville was undoubtedly sincere, but the fact remains that he was eager to have his own command at last. At thirty-five, he had just been made a frigate captain, but his aspirations were much higher. While he was still a young student, he had bet that he would be a rear admiral by the time he was fifty, and he intended to win that bet. Given his proud and independent character, he had had difficulty accepting his subordination to his old friend Duperrey. Dumont d'Urville wanted to concentrate his activities in a limited region that was still scarcely known: the Louisiade Archipelago—neglected since Bougainville—and the largely unexplored coasts of New Guinea and New Brit-

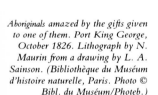

Aboriginals amazed by the gifts given to one of them. Port King George, October 1826. Lithograph by N. Maurin from a drawing by L. A. Sainson. (Bibliothèque du Muséum d'histoire naturelle, Paris. Photo © Bibl. du Muséum/Photeb.)

ain. Rossel, Director of the Depository for Navy Maps and Plans, added to his proposed program the exploration of northeastern New Zealand, the Tonga Archipelago, the Fiji Islands, and the Loyalty Islands reconnoitered by d'Entrecasteaux in 1792.

At the time of the sailing, the newspapers were full of the discovery, by the captain of a whaler, of traces of La Pérouse between the Louisiades and New Caledonia. There were still so many rumors about the fate of the lost navigators that d'Urville did not pay much attention to this news. He was nevertheless ordered to verify it on the site, and he therefore decided to change the name of the *Coquille,* which had been assigned to the expedition, to the *Astrolabe,* one of La Pérouse's ships.

The staff he assembled included two of his former comrades who had been on the *Chevrette* and then the *Coquille.* Jacquinot, made a lieutenant commander, became his second in command, and Ensign Lottin served as the astronomer; Second Lieutenant Gressien had also sailed on the *Chevrette* six years earlier. To the *Astrolabe* was also assigned as ensign the navy *élève* François Pâris—who was later to participate in two other voyages of circumnavigation—as was Lauvergne, the commander's clerk. Both men proved to be good draftsmen.

Dr. Quoy, whose work on the *Uranie* had made a name for him, asked to participate in the expedition, as did his assistant, Gaimard. Quoy, who had witnessed the shipwreck of the *Uranie,* made sure to send material to the Museum of Natural History as often as possible. The pharmacist responsible for botanical research was Pierre Adolphe Lesson, the younger brother of the *Coquille* naturalist. Thus, a team of extremely competent researchers was assembled.

The *Astrolabe* left Toulon on April 25, 1826, but contrary winds and currents forced her to anchor at Gibralter on May 21. After having landed at Algeciras, d'Urville then made a stop at Tenerife, where he hoped to meet Captain Philip Parker King, who had just left England with the *Adventure* and the *Beagle;* King had earlier made the first complete charting of the Australian coasts, and it was about this that d'Urville wanted to consult him. But the English captain had just left Tenerife, and the *Astrolabe* missed him again at the Cape Verde Islands, where she renewed her water supply. D'Urville, Quoy, and Gaimard made an ascent on

Dumont d'Urville's Ship and Crew First Voyage, 1826–1829

L'*ASTROLABE*: 380-ton corvette (former *Coquille* of the Duperrey expedition);
left from Toulon, 4/25/1826;
returned to Marseilles, 2/24/1829;
crew: 13 officers and 66 men;
deaths: 10;
deserters: 13;
left sick: some 20, including 14 from dysentery on Bourbon Island.

Commander: Jules Sébastien César Dumont d'Urville, frigate captain.

Second: Charles Hector Jacquinot, lieutenant commander.

Ensigns: Victor Charles Lottin, made lieutenant commander, 7/17/1827; Victor Amédée Gressien, made lieutenant commander, 12/31/1828; Pierre Edouard Guilbert, made lieutenant commander, 12/30/1829.

Elèves: François Pâris, made ensign, 10/29/1826; Henri Faraguet, made ensign, 1/10/1828, left sick at Bourbon, 11/24/1828; Esprit Justin Gustave Girard-Dudemaine, made ensign, June 1829.

Doctor and naturalist: Jean René Constant Quoy.

Surgeon and naturalist: Joseph Paul Gaimard, left sick at Port Jackson, 3/25/1828.

Pharmacist and naturalist: Pierre Adolphe Lesson.

Draftsman: Louis Auguste de Sainson.

Commander's clerk: Barthélemy Lauvergne.

Crimson-headed male parakeet from New Holland. Plate by Prêtre. Atlas de Zoologie of the Voyage de l'*Astrolabe. (Bibliothèque du Muséum d'histoire naturelle, Paris. Photo © Bibl. du Muséum/Photeb.)*

horseback of Tenerife's famous volcanic mountain and visited the "other side of the island," which was "a green amphitheater dotted with pretty houses that were like Provençal country farms."

On October 7, the low, barren, and savage coast of New Holland came into sight, and, after a voyage of two and a half months, the *Astrolabe* anchored at Port King George. "The natives of a pure Aboriginal type" seemed enchanted with the gifts they were given by the navigators. Having sailed along the entire southern coast of Australia by following the map made by Flinders, the *Astrolabe* anchored in the vast bay of Port Western. The closer the ship got to New South Wales, the richer the vegetation became, and the naturalists collected unknown plants and birds. Thanks to information furnished by an Englishman, d'Urville found on the east coast the entrance to Jervis Bay, which, though not far from Port Jackson, had not yet been explored.

At Port Jackson, where the *Astrolabe* anchored from December 2 to 19, the authorities were worried by the various stops the French had made; the English still feared the possibility of a French settlement in Australia, and a Sydney newspaper had even announced that the French flag had been planted at Port King George. The governor—Major-General Darling, who had only recently arrived—gave them a "polite but cool" reception. In any case, he no longer had the powers enjoyed by his predecessors; a council of five now assisted the governor and advised him. After he visited the city, d'Urville noted: "We remarked with a kind of admiration how the city had grown and improved in three years." The population of the colony, which until then had been reserved to convicts, had suddenly increased when the English government, under the pressure of public opinion, had finally decided to remove all obstacles to free immigration.

Dumont d'Urville devoted himself to a detailed on-site study of the history and present state of the colony, as well as of the physical types, characters, mores, and institutions of the aboriginals. At each stop, he made the same investigations, furnishing his government with abundant and often new documentation. He went to Parramatta and visited Reverend Samuel Marsden, who, as the leading chaplain of the colony, had lived there for more than thirty years. Marsden had also founded the first New Zealand missions, and he now furnished d'Urville with information about New Zealand that was later useful. The naturalists visited Fraser, the director of the botanical garden, who gave Gaudichaud a batch of new plants that were included in the four natural history cases sent from Sydney to the Museum of Natural History.

A little later, in New Zealand, Gaudichaud made some large collections of his own. Following on the heels of Forster and Menzies, Vancouver's companion, he discovered sixty still-unknown plants. In January 1827, the *Astrolabe* anchored in Tasman Bay on the northern coast of South Island, then in the bay of Uawa, which Cook had thought the natives called Tolaga. The Maoris who came on

Maoris doing a dance on board the Astrolabe in the bay of Uawa (New Zealand). Lithograph by A. Raffet from a drawing by L. A. Sainson. (Bibliothèque du Muséum d'histoire naturelle, Paris. Photo © Bibl. du Muséum/Photeb.)

Flying fox from Tonga (Friendly Islands). Atlas de Zoologie of the Voyage de l'Astrolabe. (Bibliothèque du Muséum d'histoire naturelle, Paris. Photo © Bibl. du Muséum/Photeb.)

board tried to persuade the French to massacre all the other islanders so that they alone could profit from the trading. When they realized that no attention was being paid to this suggestion, their attitude changed; they became respectful and eager to be of service, providing precise information about the names of the different parts of the coast, which proved useful to cartographers. At Uawa, d'Urville was the first European to observe in its natural habitat a bird still unknown to French scientists—the kiwi, which was unable to fly, covered with plumage resembling a head of hair, and provided with a very long beak. On the same site, Quoy and Gaimard discovered the New Zealand dolphin, quail, and plover, and collected numerous mollusks.

The *Astrolabe* reached the Bay of Islands in March. At Paihia, a missionary station, the commander hoped to obtain a better understanding of the attitude of the Maoris toward Europeans. Though the English clergy had made some conversions, the animosity of the natives was so great that they felt insecure. Nevertheless, they were able to reassure d'Urville that The Maoris were very afraid of cannons, so there was nothing to fear. In fact, the commander was able to note: "We had daily contacts with the inhabitants, and there is an understanding between them and us. However, they are more than ever possessed of warlike fury. . . . Despite the fact that they are cannibalistic, I persist in considering this extraordinary people as worthy of occupying the first ranks of the savage nations, as much for their physiques as for their bravery, confidence, and intelligence."

This prolonged stay in northeastern New Zealand was by no means a disinterested one. Until then, it had been unoccupied; several whalers visited the coasts, but the only permanent French settlements were the few missionary posts. The government was worried about the fate of this land that had been visited in Cook's day by Surville and

Marion du Fresne. D'Urville therefore obtained information that would be necessary should France decide on establishing settlements there.

"In the midst of disastrous events"

At the Friendly Islands, which the *Astrolabe* reached on April 20 after a month of sailing, she had just anchored at Tongatapu, when a violent windstorm caused her to lose her anchors; for three and a half days, she was buffeted about by the waves and was in danger of being lost among the breakers. On April 24, the storm ceased, and a chief came aboard the ship tied up at Pangai-Modu, solemnly carrying a kava branch that placed the *Astrolabe* under the protection of the gods. As it was thought that La Pérouse had stopped at the Friendly Islands before disappearing, the commander questioned the chiefs. They suggested he speak to a princess named Faka-Kava, who was between fifty-five and sixty years old. She remembered that shortly before the visit of the d'Entrecasteaux vessels, "two similar vessels, which also flew the white flag, had anchored together at Anamoka [Anamouka, Annamooka], that they had stayed there for ten days, and had then left sailing west . . . This information suggested that on leaving Botany Bay La Pérouse headed for the Friendly Islands, as he had planned, and anchored at Anamoka." While this investigation was going on, the naturalists visited the island and brought back a large bat, the Tonga flying fox, and some very beautiful morays—the starred moray and the circled moray—as well as numerous reef fish.

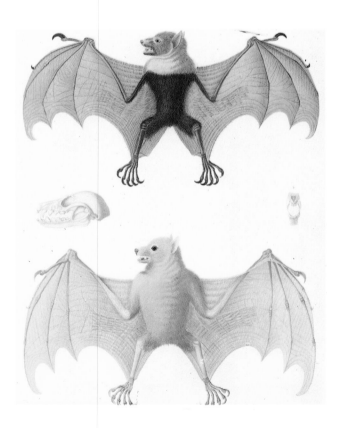

D'Urville was getting ready to lift anchor when an incident that was to have dramatic consequences occurred. A boat sent ashore came into conflict with men belonging to Chief Tahofa, and its crew was made prisoner. A detachment was sent to its aid but had to retreat before the host of hostile armed natives. The corvette then took up a position before Mafanga, a particularly venerated holy place, and d'Urville threatened to reduce it to ashes if the men were not released. Hostilities continued for a week, and Tahofa's troops, entrenched in their fortifications, threw back every attack. On the French side, there was one death, and, when the natives finally released their prisoners, two of them deserted. Since they were known troublemakers, the commander decided against looking for them.

They were not the first deserters. There had already been two at Port Jackson, but they had been retaken. D'Urville himself wrote that almost all the sailors wanted to leave the ship at one or another of his stopovers. Dr. Quoy was indignant, noting that, not only were there numerous desertions, but other sailors "then became pusillanimous and clamorous, constantly complaining . . . despite the fact that no crew had ever been better treated and fed." The fact was that, even though he was stubborn and sometimes hotheaded, d'Urville rarely resorted to punishments and always looked after the welfare of his crew. Perhaps Gaimard furnished an explanation for this rebellious attitude when he wrote that, in the future, no expedition should be fitted out from Toulon, since the men recruited there were almost all undisciplined and thieving; on the *Astrolabe,* they appropriated objects collected by the naturalists: A dozen seals that had been brought alive from Port Western disappeared and were only recovered because they could be heard bleating in the hold.

D'Urville's Fijian friend

From Tongatapu, the *Astrolabe* went west to the Viti or Fiji Archipelago. At Ono (Viti-Levu), a medal around a native's neck drew the attention of the French, and a Russian inscription on the back showed that it had been given to the man by the Russian navigator Bellingshausen, commander of the *Vostok,* who had discovered the island in 1820. Thanks to Tambua-Nakoro, the son of the chief of Viti-Levu, who offered himself as a guide and remained aboard the *Astrolabe* during the entire exploration, from May 24 to June 11, d'Urville was able to chart the position of more than 120 islands, most of which had not yet been discovered. The commander befriended this man "whose manners were gentle, whose body was attractive, and whose nature was agreeable. In my eyes he was superior to all the savages I had observed previously." On leaving him, Dumont d'Urville presented Tambua-Nakoro with a fawn-colored ermine, 3 ells of blue cloth, and a bronze medal of the expedition—

gifts that obviously pleased him greatly.

Of the Fijians, Dr. Quoy wrote: "The hundred and fifty natives we have seen are in general very handsome men. . . . Their skin is black, tending to chocolate. The top of their faces is wide, the nose and lips are broad. . . . Their hair is like that of the Papuans, very thick and curly. . . . It is naturally black, but they increase the intensity of the color with charcoal; that is what most do, but others redden it with lime, or sometimes whiten it by making it blondish, which increases the thickness of the hair and makes it look like frizzy horsehair. . . . Their tattooing is in relief, which is to say that they groove the arms and chest with holes which they quicken until a scar is formed, swelling to the size of a small cherry."

The next objective was the small Loyalty Archipelago that bordered the east coast of New Caledonia. There, the *Astrolabe* explored several islands situated south of Beautemps-Beaupré Island discovered by d'Entrecasteaux in 1793. The *Astro-*

Ornithoptera priami (New Guinea) and Danaus lotis (Borneo), butterflies collected by Quoy and Gaimard. Drawings by A. Ch. Vauthier. (Bibliothèque du Muséum d'histoire naturelle, Paris. Photo © Bibl. du Muséum/Photeb.)

Facade and details of sacred building in Port Dorey (New Guinea). Drawing and engraving by L. A. Sainson. Atlas historique of the Voyage de l'Astrolabe. (Bibliothèque du Muséum d'histoire naturelle, Paris. Photo © Bibl. du Muséum/Photeb.)

labe was scheduled to go to the south coast of New Guinea next, but the loss of some of her anchors made it imprudent to traverse the Torres Strait. She therefore went north and, on July 5, anchored at Carteret Harbor in New Ireland.

The waters were infested with large sea crocodiles—some were almost 6 meters long—which the crew hunted from a launch. The naturalists collected butterflies whose wings were so immense they were often taken for birds—for example, the *Ornithoptera urvillianus,* a superb species of changeable blue-green; some polyparia; and some holothurians caught near Cocos Island. After exploring the southern coast of New Britain, the *Astrolabe* charted the northern coast of New Guinea, where she discovered several small islands.

The next stop was Port Dorey, which d'Urville and two of his officers had already visited in 1824. The Papuans were inhospitable, and the French found it difficult to reprovision themselves, for the only acceptable payment was Spanish piastres, which "these savages made into bracelets, causing a considerable waste of this precious metal. . . . Ugly, filthy, and badly made, they wore up to three or four bracelets on each arm, depending on their wealth."

D'Urville left in a boat to visit the tribe of Ayakis, who were considerably more welcoming than the inhabitants of Port Dorey, who had been their enemies. When they were about to leave and were taking on water, a sailor was hit by an arrow and seriously wounded. A veritable panic followed. However, the naturalists were quite content with this stop at which they had caught two new marsupials, the Aru or Aroe kangaroo and the flat-quilled bandicoot; one of the most beautiful birds of paradise, the great emerald; some golden green beetles; a giant spider, the Quoy mygale; and some orchids. On examining some of the holothurians that had been caught for them, they observed an amazing phenomenon: Some of these sea cucumbers had

in their abdominal cavity one or sometimes two fish belonging to the genus *Fierasfer.* The holothurians did not seem to suffer from this forced cohabitation. At about the same time, Mertens, the naturalist on the *Senyavin* commanded by Lütke, was making identical observations.

At Amboina, the Dutch administrator Moreen placed himself at the disposition of the French, who remained on the island from September 25 to October 10. The *Astrolabe* having been repaired, Dumont d'Urville was able to traverse Torres Strait and sailed along the Australian coast to Tasmania, where he stopped at Hobart Town from December 19, 1827, to January 6, 1828.

The ghost of M. de La Pérouse

It was there he learned some news he could scarcely believe. Peter Dillon, the captain of an English vessel, had just discovered the remains of La Pérouse's ship on Vanikoro Island, one of the Santa Cruz group to the north of the New Hebrides, the south of which the *Astrolabe* had visited several months earlier.

A seaman since childhood, Dillon had been born in Martinique but raised in Ireland, afterward settling in Calcutta. In 1813, during an expedition to the Fiji Islands on the *Hunter,* he had barely escaped a massacre in which several of his companions perished. Later, he took over command of the cutter *Elizabeth,* which had joined up with the *Hunter* at Sandalwood Island. Horrified by the scenes they had witnessed, several Europeans begged Dillon to take them back to their homes on Bow Island. Among these was a Prussian named Martin Bushart, who had tried to escape his fondness for alcohol by living the precarious but sober life of the Polynesians. The *Elizabeth* was unable to stop at Bow Island, and so it set Bushart and his native wife ashore at Tikopia in the Santa Cruz group. On his return to Calcutta, Dillon married and had a ship built on which he sailed the Southern Seas. In 1826, the *St. Patrick* touched at Tikopia, and there Dillon met up again with Bushart. During the course of his visit, the English captain noticed in the possession of the natives several intriguing items, most notably a silver sword guard. From Bushart he learned that, thirteen years earlier, when he had landed in Tikopia, he had seen several other objects that could only have come from a European ship. The natives had brought them from neighboring Vanikoro Island. Bushart's companion, a sailor named Joe who had been on Vanikoro six years earlier, maintained that he had met there two very old white men, the sole survivors of a shipwreck. From this, Dillon concluded that the ship must have been one of La Pérouse's. He went to Vanikoro with the Prussian, but bad weather kept him from landing there and he returned to Calcutta.

On the basis of the information provided by Dillon and Bushart, who showed the sword guard found on Tikopia, the governor of Bengal turned over to Dillon a ship, the *Research,* to see if there might still be some survivors of La Pérouse's crews. On reaching New Zealand, Dillon learned that Dumont d'Urville had recently been there, and he tried in vain to overtake him.

On August 28, 1827, the *Research* anchored at Tikopia and was given a warm welcome. The sailor Joe came on board accompanied by an interpreter named Rathea. According to some old men from Vanikoro, one morning, after a violent nocturnal storm, a large unknown ship had been discovered on a reef. The crew had gone ashore and with wreckage from the ship built a small boat, which some seven to ten moons later had left the island and sailed west; nothing more was heard of them. In some tales, there was talk of a second ship that had also been wrecked on the rocks; the few survivors had been massacred when they reached shore. Dillon was also told of two castaways who had remained on the island; one was dead and the other had gone off with natives who had picked him up.

The unhealthy climate on Vanikoro forced Dillon to leave on October 8, 1827, but he took with him many objects that were thought to have come from the wrecks, including a bronze ship's bell, a wooden fragment of a frigate's superstructure, and another bell ornamented with a crucifix and carrying the French inscription *"Bazin m'a fait"* (Bazin made me). On his return to Calcutta, April 7, 1828, Dillon set sail for Paris, where he was received by Charles X, who indemnified him and awarded him a life-long pension by appointing him to the Legion of Honor.

From Hobart Town, the *Astrolabe* immediately left for Tikopia, arriving on February 10. Bushart had just returned, and agreed to accompany the French to Vanikoro; but the next morning he changed his mind. D'Urville had to content himself with taking along two British deserters who had been on Tikopia for nine months; one of them "spoke the language of the islands fluently."

At Vanikoro, where they anchored from February 21 to March 17, the investigation ran into difficulties. The reefs on which the vessels had struck were on the other side of the island. "Our people saw scattered at the bottom of the sea, at a depth of three or four fathoms, anchors, launches, cannon balls, ingots, and especially a great quantity of lead plates, the only lasting proofs of this terrible catastrophe." The "natives seemed to have agreed on a system of disclaimers." No doubt they feared that the French had come to avenge the massacre of their compatriots. Fever broke out among the crew. Vanikoro's climate was indeed deadly to Europeans but also to natives, who generally died young. By the end of the stay, nine out of ten men on the *Astrolabe* were sick, including the doctors. D'Urville, unable to obtain new information and carrying with him only a few unimportant items left behind by Dillon, decided to quit this inhospitable island. Before leaving, however, he raised a monument to the memory of La Pérouse. Suffering from a violent fever, he was unable to officiate at the inauguration ceremonies and was replaced by Jacquinot. When the musket salutes were fired, "the

Landing of Dumont d'Urville on the beach of Tikopia on February 10, 1828. Watercolor by L. A. Sainson. (Société de Géographie, Bibliothèque nationale, Paris. Photo © Bibl. nat./Photeb.)

Aru scrub wallaby, kangaroo captured in New Guinea by Quoy and Gaimard. Atlas de Zoologie *of the* Voyage de l'Astrolabe. *(Bibliothèque du Muséum d'histoire naturelle, Paris. Photo © Bibl. du Muséum/Photeb.)*

Various types of helmet shells from the South Seas brought back on the Astrolabe. *Lithograph from drawings by Blanchard.(Bibliothèque du Muséum d'histoire naturelle, Paris. Photo © Bibl. du Muséum/Photeb.)*

savages, cold with fear, ran off in all directions."

On the return to France, the objects brought back were shown to Lesseps, the only survivor of the La Pérouse expedition, who identified them as belonging to Fleuriot de Langle's *Astrolabe*. The following year saw the publication of Dillon's account and, in 1831, of a new edition of La Pérouse's *Voyage* by Lesseps. The latter noted that of all the items collected, not one came from the *Boussole*. The mystery was therefore only partly cleared up. It was not until 1964 that the wreck of the *Boussole* was found and searched, and that the 1788 tragedy could finally be reconstructed; this last version basically confirms the information collected by Dillon. The *Boussole* had sunk first and all her crew must have perished; caught on a coral reef, the *Astrolabe* had been unloaded and taken apart. The lifeboat later constructed on shore left for the west and was probably wrecked in one of the Solomon Islands.

Scurvy and dysentery

When Dumont d'Urville's *Astrolabe* set sail from Vanikoro on March 17, 1828, she had become a "floating infirmary." Only a third of the crew was fit for duty. After sailing for forty-five days in punishing heat, the ship, having traversed the Carolines, came to Guam, in the Marianas, on May 2, and had to remain there until June 30 while the crew recovered its health. Luckily, the Spanish governor, Don José Medinilla, placed his own Umata Palace at the disposition of the commander and his officers, and turned over a former convent for use as a hospital. Gaimard was among the thirty-nine patients installed there. Quoy and Lesson looked after them, but Lesson, himself seriously ill, had to interrupt his botanical studies. Only Quoy

was still more or less healthy, and he was able to study the anatomy of a young dugong that had been caught.

Twenty-eight days later, when the ship set sail again, most of the patients were still feverish. The convalescent malaria victims had enormous appetites, and dysentery soon broke out among them. The *Astrolabe* stopped at Buru in June and then at Amboina from June 30 to July 6. At Amboina, d'Urville had asked that he be provided with some horned hogs, which were lacking at the Museum of Natural History, but, in the interval, the natives had sold them to a passing European ship. The governor of the Moluccas, Merkus, therefore told d'Urville that if he were willing to accompany him to Manado, he would turn over two of the horned hogs he had there. He added that he would set the whole population to work helping to meet the naturalists' needs. On July 29, d'Urville was ceremoniously received at Celebes, where he and his officers paraded on horseback between two ranks of Dutch soldiers; Quoy and Gaimard followed on a palanquin. Merkus kept his promises generously; in addition to the two horned hogs, the French embarked three antelopes "similar to the buffalo," no doubt nilgais; birds; snakes; and a great many fish. But the health situation did not improve, and d'Urville decided to return home.

After a four-day stopover at Batavia, the *Astrolabe* reached Mauritius, where she stayed for a month and a half in order to allow the crew to recover completely; however, there were still cases of scurvy aboard. At Bourbon (Réunion), in Novem-

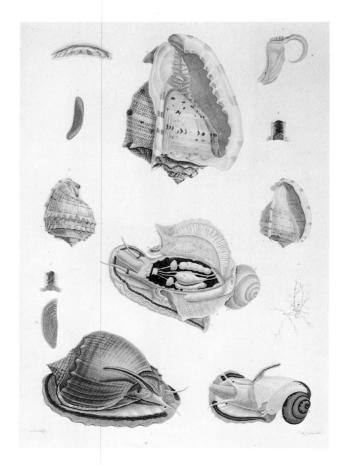

ber, fourteen men—including Gaimard and Ensign Faraguet—had to be put ashore. They were repatriated by the *Bayonnaise,* which arrived there two weeks later and reached Marseilles on March 19, 1829. The *Astrolabe* had arrived on February 24.

Ten of its seventy-eight men had died—eight of dysentery, one in an accident, and another killed in Tonga; there had also been thirteen desertions. But d'Urville brought back documentation that was as rich as it was precise, and political as well as geographic and ethnographic; it filled fourteen volumes and five large atlases, which began to appear in 1830 and continued for five years.

Thanks to Quoy's foresight, the scientists of the Museum of Natural History had received five large shipments before the return of the *Astrolabe.* These had already been inventoried when, on October 26, 1829, Cuvier presented to the Academy of Sciences a report written by a commission that included the zoologist Geoffroy Saint-Hilaire; the entomologist Latreille; and Duméril, a specialist in snakes and fish. Cuvier emphasized that Quoy and Gaimard had brought back a larger collection than had all their predecessors—or even than they themselves had brought back from their previous voyage on the *Uranie.* To this was added the six thousand drawings and the six thousand copies made lest the originals be lost; this represented an average of twelve drawings a day.

The botany of the voyage was done by A. Lesson. In addition to descriptions of species little or completely unknown, including a dozen orchids, it contained a very complete *Essai d'une flore de la Nouvelle-Zélande* (Study for a New Zealand Flora). Quoy and Gaimard took a great many pains with the zoology, which was published in 1833. It was during that time that Quoy became an intimate friend of Cuvier, about whom he wrote some interesting memoirs that have never been published. Named Chief Physician of the Navy, he later withdrew to Rochefort, where this modest man lived in retirement and was completely absorbed in his work. He died in 1869 at the age of seventy-nine. A younger man, Gaimard later made several other voyages.

Named captain, Dumont d'Urville presented himself for the Academy of Sciences seat left vacant by the death of Rossel. He felt that he had a right to this succession, but he was not elected. Mortified—and even more indignant—he was ready to put in for retirement when the government of Charles X, who had so inadequately compensated him for his services, collapsed. By a curious irony of fate, it was to d'Urville that the government entrusted the task of taking the dethroned king and his family to England. It was not until 1837 that the government of Louis-Philippe gave Dumont d'Urville permission for another voyage. Promoted to corvette captain, Jacquinot went with him.

Consuls, missionaries, and scientists, 1824–1840

LE CALLOCÉPHALE AUSTRAL, Mâle.

Male austral callocephal. Lithograph by Coutant from Pancrace Bessa. Journal de la navigation de la Thétis et l'Espérance by H. de Bougainville. (Musée de la Marine, Paris. Photo by Michel Didier © Photeb.)

These scientific expeditions were paralleled by other voyages of circumnavigation that were political in nature. The aim was to renew relations with the French missions established in Cochin China in the seventeenth century but neglected since the collapse of the *ancien régime,* and to repossess establishments in India recently restored by the British; in addition, it was important to be in a position to fight British expansion in the islands of Oceania as well as in the South American nations that had recently won their independence.

Such were the goals of the missions that were successively entrusted to Hyacinthe de Bougainville, oldest son of the famous navigator, who had left on the *Thétis* and the *Espérance* in 1824–1826; to frigate captain Pierre-Théodore Laplace in 1829–1832 on the *Favorite,* and then in 1837–1840 on the *Artémise;* to corvette captain Nicolas Vaillant in 1836–1837 on the *Bonite;* and, finally, to Captain Abel Aubert Dupetit-Thouars in 1836–1839 on the *Vénus.*

At the time of each of these voyages, the medical officers on board were given the responsibility of procuring on site the animal and vegetable species missing from the museum holdings. Some of them brought back large collections—as did, for example, Eydoux, surgeon on the *Favorite* and then the *Bonite,* on which he was accompanied by the pharmacist-botanist Gaudichaud-Beaupré, who twenty years earlier had taken part in the Freycinet expedition.

Despite its short duration—it lasted only twenty-one months—the voyage of the *Bonite* was exemplary in this matter. The naturalists tried to bring back as many living animals as possible, including twenty mammals, and so transformed the deck into a veritable menagerie; seven reached the zoo of the Jardin des Plantes in good health. After having examined the collections brought back, the members of the Academy of Sciences and the professors of the museum declared that they were much larger than they had dared hope for. There were monkeys, marsupials, and rodents; three hundred species of birds out of a total of nine hundred; snakes and amphibians; 417 specimens of fish from the China Seas; and, above all, so many marine invertebrates of all kinds that their study had to be turned over to a specialist who spent ten years completing his task. It is thus easily understandable that the publication of the voyage begun in 1840 was not completed until 1866; it included eighteen volumes plus three large atlases—a record that was not surpassed until the thirty volumes of Dumont d'Urville's second voyage, published several years later.

Chevalier boa. Colored engraving after P. L. Oudart. Atlas de Zoologie *of the* Voyage de la Bonite *by Vaillant. (Musée de la Marine, Paris. Photo by Michel Didier © Photeb.)*

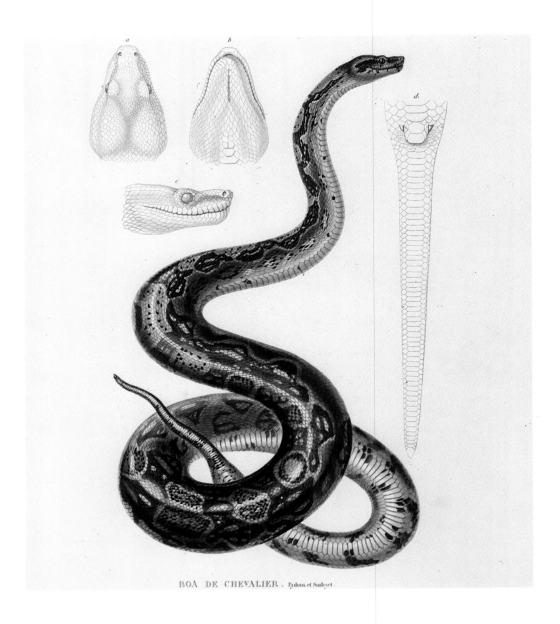

BOA DE CHEVALIER . Eydoux et Souleyet .

The
British scientists
on the seas,
1825-1842

From Nature by B. Waterhouse Hawkins.

Day & Haghe Lith.rs to the Queen

BRACHYTELES FRONTATUS.

The voyage of the *Blossom,* 1825–1828

At the termination of Flinders's voyage in 1803, Great Britain was completely absorbed in the struggle against Napoleon and was unable to undertake new voyages around the world. Nevertheless, the hope of finding in the extreme north of the American continent the passage that supposedly led from the Atlantic to the Pacific was not abandoned. In 1818, Parliament promised a large reward to whomever discovered it or pushed the search to the North Pole.

In May 1818, an expedition commanded by Captain John Ross and including the *Isabella* and the *Alexander* set sail. Ross was accompanied by his nephew, James Clark Ross, and Lieutenant William Edward Parry. After passing through Lancaster Sound, however, he found himself faced with what he believed was a chain of impenetrable mountains; beating a retreat, he contented himself with exploring the west coast of Greenland. That same year, a second expedition left to search for the passage, but this time north of Spitsbergen. Commanded by Captain John Franklin, who at the age of fifteen had been a cabin boy on the *Investigator,* and by Captain David Buchan, this expedition was equally unfruitful. From 1819 to 1827, there were four other searches commanded by Captain Parry. In 1824, for his third expedition, William Edward Parry made a new attempt by leaving from Prince Regent Inlet, which separated Baffin's Island from Somerset Island.

On February 16, 1825, accompanied by the naturalist Dr. John Richardson, Franklin left Liverpool for a second voyage, during the course of which he was to explore the Arctic coasts of Canada between the Mackenzie and Coppermine Rivers. In 1829, Dr. Richardson published a *Fauna boreali-americana,* with which the scientific study of animal life in Canada began. The botanist Thomas Drummond, assistant naturalist on the expedition, also made important discoveries. Parry and Franklin having joined up, they were to return through the Bering Strait after their provisions ran low, but Parry's *Hecla* was locked in by ice and returned to England alone in October 1825.

The frigate *Blossom,* charged with the responsibility for reprovisioning them and on the way exploring the Arctic Ocean, left Spithead on May 19, 1825. She was commanded by Captain Frederick William Beechey, who had in 1818 participated in

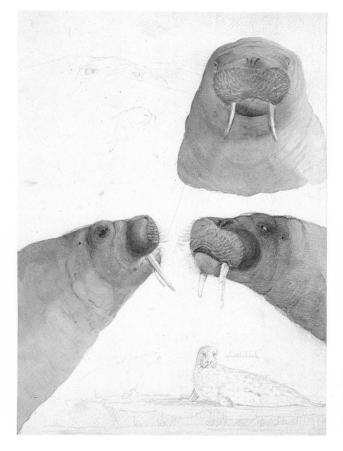

Atlantic walrus. Original watercolor by F. W. Beechey, done in 1819 during the first Parry expedition. ("Arctic" University of Calgary, Canada. Photo © The Arctic Institute of North America, Calgary/Photeb.)

Franklin and Buchan's expedition to Spitsbergen and, in 1819, during Parry's first campaign, penetrated as far as 113° 54′ 43″ into the polar Arctic Circle. An excellent geographer and a good draftsman, he was also a competent zoologist. The botanist George Tradescant Lay had also embarked on the *Blossom,* and he was assisted by the surgeon Alexander Collie, who was given meteorological and geological responsibilities. The second lieutenant, Edward Belcher, was to make significant paleontological discoveries during this voyage. To complete the team, in addition to Beechey, there were two other draftsmen among the officers.

The *Blossom* reached Tenerife and then stopped at Rio de Janeiro from July 4 to August 4; having gone around Cape Horn, she then stopped at Concepción from October 9 to 20 and at Valparaiso from October 20 to November 2. Lay established an inventory of Chilean avifauna that was extremely rich

Facing page: Brachyteles frontatus, spider monkey killed by Belcher at Cubrera (Costa Rica) in March 1838. Lithograph after B. Waterhouse Hawkins. The Zoology of the Voyage of H.M.S. Sulphur. (British Museum, Natural History, London. Photo by courtesy of the trustees, British Museum/Photeb.)

Preceding page: FitzRoy's Beagle at anchor in Beagle Channel, Tierra del Fuego, May 1834. Watercolor by Conrad Martens. (National Maritime Museum, London. Photo © the museum/Photeb.)

in marine species, and he identified penguins, diver birds, several species of pelicans and cormorants, sea gulls, and terns.

Having reconnoitered Sala y Gomez, the English dropped anchor at Easter Island on November 16. Lieutenant George Peard disembarked and, finding himself surrounded by thieving natives, had to beat a retreat under a hail of large stones. During the course of the musket fusillade that followed, the chief who had led his men in the assault was killed. Continuing westward, the *Blossom,* on December 4, reached Pitcairn Island, where Beechey was to make inquiries about the *Bounty* mutiny. The crew ran into great difficulty when their boats tried to land. Inaccessible cliffs protected the bay, and large reefs bordered the coasts. The inhabitants, having constructed their village inland, had been careful to shield it behind a thick grove of palms that prevented it from being seen from the sea. Nevertheless, Beechey and his companions were well received.

The Bounty *mutineers*

The last surviving mutineer, John Adams, no longer had to fear the consequences of a crime that went back some forty years, and he therefore gave a detailed account of it to the *Blossom*'s officers. Under the command of Lieutenant William Bligh, who had been master of the *Resolution* during Cook's third voyage, the *Bounty,* in 1787, with forty-four men, had left England to pick up breadfruit trees in Tahiti and transport them to the Antilles. The sailors grew very fond of Tahiti, where they stayed for five months and made many friends. Bligh, authoritarian and a martinet, was hated by his officers; as a result, on the return journey, one of them, Fletcher Christian, aided by Alexander Smith—who on Pitcairn Island was to take the name John

Inland scene on Pitcairn Island. Engraving by E. F. Finden from a drawing by F. W. Beechey, December 1825. "The little village was composed of five houses built more solidly than elegantly on a patch of cleared land." (Bibliothèque du Muséum d'histoire naturelle, Paris. Photo © Bibl. du Muséum/Photeb.)

Beechey's Ship and Crew

The *BLOSSOM:* 26-cannon frigate, only 16 for the voyage;
left from Spithead, 5/19/1825;
returned to Spithead, 10/12/1828;
crew: 110 men, reduced to 100, 10 sailors having been disembarked as unfit.
deaths: 15.

Commander: Frederick William Beechey, captain.

Lieutenants: George Peard; Edward Belcher, responsible for hydrographic and geological research; John Wainwright, responsible for astronomical observations.

Ensigns: J. F. Gould, left sick at Rio; William Smyth, draftsman; James Wolf.

Midshipmen: John Rendall; Richard B. Beechey, draftsman.

Master: Thomas Elson.

Purser: George Marsh.

Surgeon: Alexander Collie, responsible for meteorology and geology.

Assistant surgeon: Thomas Neilson.

Naturalist: George Tradescant Lay.

Adams—decided to seize the ship and return to Tahiti.

On April 28, 1789, Bligh was set adrift in a launch with the eighteen men who had supported him. After a harrowing 6,7000-kilometer voyage in the Pacific, the survivors reached Timor. Meanwhile, with twenty-five men aboard, the *Bounty* sailed for the Society Islands. The mutineers tried to establish themselves on Tubuai, but, faced with the hostility of the natives, decided to return to Tahiti, where sixteen of them disembarked. They were arrested and several died following the shipwreck of the *Pandora,* which was bringing them back to England. The others, with Christian and Smith, decided to try their luck elsewhere. By means of a ruse, they succeeded in taking with them twelve Tahitian women and six Tahitian men. Christian led them to Pitcairn, a deserted island discovered by Carteret in 1767, which seemed to suit their purposes. The mountains were so difficult to reach, and the passages so narrow, that several men could defend them against an entire army.

After destroying their ship, the nine Englishmen divided up the island, but the Tahitians, having received nothing, rebelled; quarrels inevitably followed and brought fighting and massacres in their train. Christian and four of the mutineers died, and Adams was critically wounded. At the end of several years, of the nine original mutineers, only Adams and a man called Young were alive. When the latter died, Adams was the master of the island and devoted himself to the education of the nineteen children, many of them resulting from unions between the sailors and the Tahitian women. It was not until 1808, eighteen years after they had settled there, that the refuge of the *Bounty* mutineers was discovered by an American ship that happened to stop at Pitcairn. When the *Blossom* arrived, there were thirty-six men and thirty women in the little colony, which was relatively prosperous. The houses, built of wood and thatched with palms, were mostly one story high. Breadfruit trees, coconut palms, banana trees, taro, sweet potatoes, and sugarcane provided an adequate diet and, given the mild climate, required little looking after. The islanders were tall, sturdy, and healthy.

On his return to England, Beechey filed a most favorable report, and the little colony henceforth enjoyed the protection of the crown. Several attempts were made to resettle the population of Pitcairn on other Pacific islands, but the islanders always stubbornly returned, and to this day their descendants still live there. The information gathered by Beechey about this astonishing story excited public opinion in England and was used as a basis for Sir John Barrow's celebrated *The Eventful History of the Mutiny and the Piratical Seizure of H.M.S.* Bounty, published in 1831.

Leaving Adams and his people on December 20, 1825, Beechey set sail for the Gambier Islands, sighting as he went first Oeno and then Timoe. When a launch attempted to land at Timoe, the natives tried to seize it. Beechey wrote that he was confirmed in his opinion that the nature of these people completely disinclined them from establishing relations with foreigners, and that only fear could keep them from committing acts of violence. However, the navigators were able to renew their water supplies and to find a good anchorage.

In January 1826, the reception given the English in the Gambier Islands was considerably more friendly. Though according to their custom the natives rubbed noses with the new arrivals, they nevertheless tried to steal whatever they could lay their hands on. Beechey discovered three new islands and gave them the names of his lieutenants. Because of the slopes, the earth—which was the result of the decomposition of basaltic rocks—was firm only in a few places; but it was extremely fertile and well irrigated by mountain streams. Despite this, the islanders did not engage in farming and had no domestic animals. Their nourishment consisted basically of fish caught with lines or nets from rafts formed by tree trunks bound together; they had no boats.

The population, of Polynesian origin, was extremely mixed and showed great variations in complexion and features. They were good-natured enough, Beechey wrote, when they were content, inoffensive if they were not irritated, and though obsequious when their numbers were inferior, they were otherwise arrogant. Lieutenant John Wainwright, having remained alone, was attacked by the

natives, and the English had to open fire to save him. The men were covered with tattoos, some of which imitated the blue trousers of the English seamen who had previously visited the islands; the women had few tattoos.

Continuing her route along the Pacific from January to March 1826, the *Blossom* reconnoitered Lord Hood's Island (Marutea), thus named by Captain James Wilson in 1797, and then, traversing the Tuamotus, stopped at Clermont-Tonnerre (Réao), Serle Island (Pukaruha), and Queen Charlotte's Island (Nukutavake). There the naturalists found numerous coral reef fish belonging to the genus *Chaetodon*. Beechey next discovered three islands which he named after men in the Admiralty—Barrow (Vanavana), Cockburn (Ahunui), and Byam Martin (Nganati). A splendid collection of shells, holothurians, and starfish was found on the last-named island, on which were some shipwrecked Tahitians who begged the English to take them back to their country. Beechey agreed, but first he visited Gloucester Island (Pararo) and Bow Island (Hao) and discovered the islands of Melville (Hikueru) and Crocker (Heraiki).

The *Blossom* remained at Tahiti from March 26 to April 26. The king at the time was Pomare III, who was six years old. The regent, his aunt Pomare-Vahine, came on board, and later Beechey visited her at Papeete. "A completely romantic spot," he noted, but one which, as he saw it, the puritanism of the ministers covered with gloom and unhappiness by prohibiting the usual distractions, including dancing; the dance that the seamen witnessed was done by New Zealanders.

Shortly after the *Blossom* left, dysentery broke out, and one of its victims was the naturalist Lay, who had to be put ashore at the next stop, Oahu in the Sandwich Islands. The surgeon Collie was given his responsibilities. At Oahu, Beechey visited King Lio-Lio (Rio-Rio) and his minister Kraimokou (Kalanimoku), who had been nicknamed Pitt. The harvests having been bad, Beechey was

Natives of the Gambier Islands attack Lieutenant Wainwright, who had remained alone. Engraving by E. F. Finden from a drawing by R. B. Beechey. (Bibliothèque du Muséum d'histoire naturelle, Paris. Photo © Bibl. du Muséum/Photeb.)

165

unable to reprovision and went to Onihau (Niihau), but food was in short supply there too.

The *Blossom* next headed for Kamchatka and, on June 28, anchored at Petropavlovsk, where the *Krotky*, commanded by Baron Wrangel, was also at anchor. The Russians gave the Englishmen a warm reception and facilitated the research of the naturalists, but the latter soon found that the animals to be observed there were already described in the *Arctic Zoology* published by Thomas Pennant in 1792. Dispatches awaiting Beechey announced the return of the Parry expedition, and he now had to hasten toward Kotzebue Sound on the American coast, where he had to be on July 15 in order to rendezvous with Franklin.

In search of Franklin

On July 16, the *Blossom* anchored at St. Lawrence Island in the Bering Sea and then entered Kotzebue Sound. Beechey recorded that they were soon visited by several bidars carrying ten to thirteen men, who had come to propose some trading; they all wore in their lips ornaments made of bits of ivory, stone, or glass, which they slid from the hole to offer for sale. When the English expressed their disgust at this sight, they laughed at them, sticking their tongues through the hole and blinking their eyes.

At six in the morning on July 25, the ship reached Chamisso Island, ten days late. Beechey disembarked supplies and messages for Franklin on this island, where ten years earlier Eschscholtz had discovered bone fossils. On visiting the site, Collie unearthed teeth, jaws, and curled tusks of mammoths; aurochs' horns; and the bones of large deer and horses. Beechey then explored the sound. Traveling up Cape Thompson, they discovered a tongue of land that jutted west-northwest into the sea. Beechey called it Point Hope. A tender commanded by Mr. Elson went much farther north in search of Franklin but returned without having found him; Elson had, however, sighted the farthest spit of land that the expedition's people were to reach; "It was the most northern point that had been discovered on the American continent," Beechey noted. This point was given the name of the secretary of the Admiralty, Sir John Barrow. Before reaching it, the tender had been caught in floating ice and dragged toward the shore in Peard Bay. The Eskimos who came along seemed hos-

tile, and he was greatly relieved when the wind changed, and the ice began to melt; the ship was finally able to regain the open sea.

The season was well advanced, and ice was beginning to form in the sea. In September, Beechey had to resign himself to leaving Kotzebue Sound and go south toward the Spanish missions at San Francisco in order to repair the ship and renew his provisions. The crew was able to rest there from November 6, 1826, to January 5, 1827. In February, the navigators put into Oahu in the Sandwich Islands, where Lay came back on board, and, on April 10, they anchored at Macao.

No sooner had he arrived than Beechey received orders from the Chinese authorities to leave after a few days, which he did after reprovisioning. He wanted next to explore the sea beyond Loo-Choo Island in order to check the charting of the Arzobispo and Malabrigos islands that were to be found on Spanish maps. However, contrary winds forced him to stop from May 15 to 27 at Loo-Choo, which was then Chinese; it was not to become Japanese and be called Okinawa until 1895. An official came on board and informed him by means of gestures that it was forbidden to anchor in the roads. He was followed by a host of curious onlookers. Beechey asked permission to disembark his sick, and an important-looking little man wearing a large pair of Chinese spectacles came on board; it was the doctor. He asked permission to take their pulse, and the sick men were later allowed to go ashore provided they did not enter the city.

In June, Beechey was finally able to reach the Bonin Islands, which were none other than the Spaniards' Islas de Arzobispo. The island on which he disembarked was given the name of the Home Secretary, Sir Robert Peel, and a group of neighboring islands was given Parry's name. The naturalists discovered several unknown birds and a bat, the hairy-footed flying fox.

On July 2, 1827, the *Blossom* was once again at Petropavlovsk, from which she went to Bering Island. Elson, taking the large boat, explored the coast as far as Kotzebue Sound, looking to the east of Cape Prince of Wales for a passage that had been mentioned by Eskimos the previous year. After finding a well-sheltered port, Elson rejoined the expedition at Chamisso Island. In the large boat, Lieutenant Edward Belcher went north to the region explored in 1826 while Beechey reconnoitered the harbor discovered by Elson; he found a second one, Port Clarence, which could serve as a shelter for ships incapable of crossing the Bering Strait once

Inhabitant of the Alaskan coast wearing sunglasses, August 1826. Voyage of the Blossom. *(Bibliothèque du Muséum d'histoire naturelle, Paris. Photo © Bibl. du Muséum/Photeb.)*

Coral reef fish. Left to right: Chaetodon vinctis, strigangulus, and vittatus. Lithograph after J. D. C. Sowerby. Zoology of Voyage of the Blossom. *(British Museum, Natural History, London. Photo by courtesy of the trustees, British Museum/Photeb.)*

the bad weather set in.

When the *Blossom* returned to Chamisso Island, Beechey was surprised not to find Belcher. The large boat had visited the northern coast, going beyond Icy Cape, but Belcher had found no trace of Captain Franklin; the supplies left during the previous cruise had not been touched. On his return to Chamisso Island, Belcher was collecting wood with his men when suddenly he noticed that the sea had become heavy; they went back to the boat, which soon broke up. Four men were drowned while the Eskimos, who had been watching, made no effort to rescue them. Belcher and the survivors, having gathered up the debris of the wreck, took refuge at Garnet, where Beechey had to come looking for them.

On October 6, the expedition sailed from Port Clarence and, on the twenty-ninth, reached Monterey on the California coast; among other things, Lay discovered a stunningly beautiful ceanothus with pale blue flowers and, in the desert, several species of plants with elegant flowers that were later called *Layia*. The *Blossom* then sailed to San Blas on the west coast of Mexico, where she remained from December 14, 1827, to January 27, 1828. Lay, who had gone off to visit the interior as far as Tepic, brought back a large collection of new plants and was able to observe various animals, including the coyote, which had only recently been recognized as a distinct species. In February, the navigators were at Mazatlan and, in March, at Acapulco. On May 25, they reached Coquimbo on the coast of Chile

and, on July 21, after having rounded Cape Horn, Rio. On October 12, the *Blossom* reentered Spithead after a voyage that had lasted three years and almost five months. Of the hundred men in the crew, fifteen had died.

Eighteen days earlier, Sir John Franklin had landed at Liverpool after two years and seven and a half months of absence. On August 18, 1826, he had reached Return Reef, the westernmost point of his voyage; at the time he was 160 miles from Cape Barrow, which had just been discovered by Elson, who had gone to look for him on the *Blossom*'s big launch. The two men might very well have met, but Franklin had been obliged to sail east in order to rejoin at Fort Franklin, on September 21, the other group led by Richardson. Though, in the final analysis, the expedition of the *Blossom* had been of no use to Franklin, it had nevertheless been profitable. Beechey had discovered several islands in the Pacific and rediscovered the Arzobispos of the Spanish; he had also completed the reconnaissance of the western coast of America. The natural sciences also benefited. The zoology of the voyage written up from the collections and notes assembled by Beechey himself, Richardson, and several other scientists—as well as the botany written by W. J. Hooker and Walker-Arnott working with the herbarium of Lay and Collie—contained a significant number of new species; the geology made use of important paleontological discoveries made by Belcher on Chamisso Island.

"A large junk left the port surrounded by a great number of boats. She was decorated with flags of all sorts and sizes. It was the junk which every year brought the tribute from Loochoo to Fechien." Engraving by E. F. Finden from a drawing by William Smyth. (Bibliothèque du Muséum d'histoire naturelle, Paris. Photo © Bibl. du Muséum/Photeb.)

Darwin on the *Beagle*, 1831–1836

Portrait of Darwin at age thirty-one by George Richmond, 1840. (Photo from the collection of George P. Darwin.)

On December 27, 1831, a small 240-ton brig left the roads of Devonport. Lieutenant Robert FitzRoy, the commander, had been given the mission of completing an earlier study of the coasts of Patagonia and of Tierra del Fuego, begun under the command of Captain King in 1826–1830, with two ships, the *Adventure* and the *Beagle*. The captain of the *Beagle* having committed suicide in his cabin, his post had fallen to FitzRoy, who was then only twenty-two. Born in 1805, he belonged to an illustrious family that traced its roots to an illegitimate child of King Charles II of England; his father was a lord and his grandfather a duke; his uncle, Viscount Castlereagh, had played a leading role in the congresses of the Holy Alliance.

In 1831, FitzRoy departed again on the *Beagle* to complete the work begun by King, as well as to chart the coasts of Chile, Peru, and several Pacific islands, and to make a series of chronometric observations around the world. Though the presence of a naturalist on board was thought necessary, the Admiralty had not provided any compensation for him. J. S. Henslow, a Cambridge botany professor, had been considered, but he had refused for family reasons and instead suggested one of his students, Charles Darwin. On that occasion, Henslow wrote to Darwin that he did not consider him a "*finished* naturalist, but as amply qualified for collecting, observing, and noting, anything new to be noted in Natural History."

And the truth was that this twenty-two-year-old student would only become a naturalist during the course of the voyage, which would be an apprenticeship and initiation for him. Later, he would write: "The voyage of the *Beagle* has been by far the most important event in my life and has determined the whole of my existence."

The son of a rich and respected doctor in Shrewsbury, Shropshire, Charles Darwin, born on February 12, 1809, had begun his medical studies in Edinburgh when he was very young, but, unable to bear the sight of blood, he had had to give them up. In any case, his inclination was more toward the natural sciences. From an early age, the young boy had begun to collect butterflies and plants, minerals and shells. The personality of his paternal grandfather, dead before Charles's birth, may have played a role in the genesis of this precocious passion. Dr. Erasmus Darwin was indeed

FitzRoy's Ship and Crew

The *BEAGLE*: 240-ton brig with 10 cannons; left from Devonport, 12/27/1831; returned to Falmouth, 10/2/1836; crew: 74 men, including 8 marines.
Commander: Robert FitzRoy, lieutenant commander, promoted to captain, March 1835.
Lieutenants: John Clements Wickham; Bartholomew James Sulivan; John Lord Stokes, hydrographer.
Surgeon: Robert MacCormick, disembarked at Rio, April 1832.
Assistant surgeon: Benjamin Bynoe, promoted to surgeon, April 1832.
Naturalist: Charles Darwin.
Painters: Augustus Earle, put ashore sick in Montevideo, April 1833; Conrad Martens, embarked at Montevideo, April 1833.
Purser: George Rowlett, died at sea, July 1834.
Midshipmen: Philip Gidley King; Arthur Mellersh.
Master: Edward Main Chaffers.
Commander's clerk: Hellyer, died in the Falklands, February 1833.
Passengers: York Minster, Jemmy Button, and Fuegia Basket—Fuegians disembarked at Tierra del Fuego, January 1833; Richard Matthews, missionary, disembarked at the Bay of Islands, New Zealand, November 1835; Charles Musters, volunteer, died in Rio, June 1832.

an inquisitive type. A medical doctor, he was in addition a physiologist, botanist, and poet—in fact, he was curious about everything. His poems had won him a certain fame, but his reputation was even more based on his works on botany, in which could be seen the vague outline of the evolutionism that was to make his grandson famous.

When, after three years of studies in Edinburgh, Charles returned to Shrewsbury, his father had to give up the idea of making a doctor of him. He therefore suggested that Charles become a minister; the young man agreed unenthusiastically and was sent to Christ's College, Cambridge. There, as in Edinburgh, he made friends, becoming particularly close to two professors, Henslow and the geologist Adam Sedgwick. These two men were not only eminent naturalists but also clergymen, and this proved to young Darwin that the two vocations were not incompatible.

Darwin was stupefied when, in August 1831, he received, through Henslow's good offices, the offer to leave on a great voyage around the world; despite his father's reservations, he accepted. On September 5, he met FitzRoy in London. Scarcely older than Darwin—at the time he was twenty-six—FitzRoy already had solid experience behind him and received the postulant with the charming affability that was natural to him. The voyage would last two years, perhaps even longer, but the naturalist signed on would be free to quit the ship at stopovers and to make long excursions on land. In his enthusiasm, several days after their meeting, Darwin wrote to FitzRoy that a new life would begin for him with their departure. "It shall be as a birthday for the rest of my life."

Everything on the *Beagle* was new and interesting to Darwin. Though small—hardly 30 meters long, it would have to accommodate seventy-four men—the ship had been carefully refitted for the voyage. Darwin's future companions were young and sympathetic. The assistant surgeon, Benjamin Bynoe, who had been with FitzRoy on the previous *Beagle* expedition, was enthusiastic about natural history; he was later to become Darwin's assistant. But most unusual of all were the three Fuegian passengers: Three years earlier, they had been brought to England by FitzRoy, who had had them taught at his own expense. Now FitzRoy was taking them back to their tribe dressed in the latest fashion and provided with a supply of European utensils; he was convinced that they would spread among their people the principles of civilization and Christianity. In this task, they would be aided by a young missionary who had agreed to share their destiny.

No sooner were they on the sea than Darwin's enthusiasm was put to a strong test; he had just discovered sea sickness, and there was to be no cure for him. Another cause of discomfort surfaced: the impossibility of privacy. At night, Darwin shared his cabin with Midshipman Philip King, a warmhearted youth with whom he got along quite well; during the day, the commander offered him the hospitality of his cabin.

As was usual, each man's life aboard ship was carefully regulated. They drank only water, never wine or alcohol. On Sunday mornings, FitzRoy would assemble the crew for religious services during which he would read and comment on a passage from the Bible.

After a few days, Darwin began to know these men with whom he was to spend more than four years of his life. His relations with FitzRoy were always friendly. (He was to discover that behind a courteous facade and a rigidity and severity in the performance of his duties, there hid a sensitive, nervous, and unstable man.) Everybody on board liked this young and modest naturalist who was always ready to welcome and profit from other people's experience.

After ten days at sea, the *Beagle* reached Tenerife. Because a cholera epidemic was then raging in Europe, the men were not allowed to disembark, but, in the Cape Verde Islands, a twenty-three-day stopover gave Darwin the opportunity to make his first personal examination of a volcanic island.

From top to bottom: Jemmy Button in 1833, on his return from England; in 1834 as he was reencountered by the Beagle. Drawings by FitzRoy. (Service historique de la Marine, Vincennes. Photo M. Didier © Photeb.)

Sunday religious services aboard the English frigate H.M.S. Hyperion. Watercolor by Augustus Earle, 1820. (Rex Nan Kivell Collection, National Library of Australia, Canberra. Photo © National Library of Australia/Photeb.)

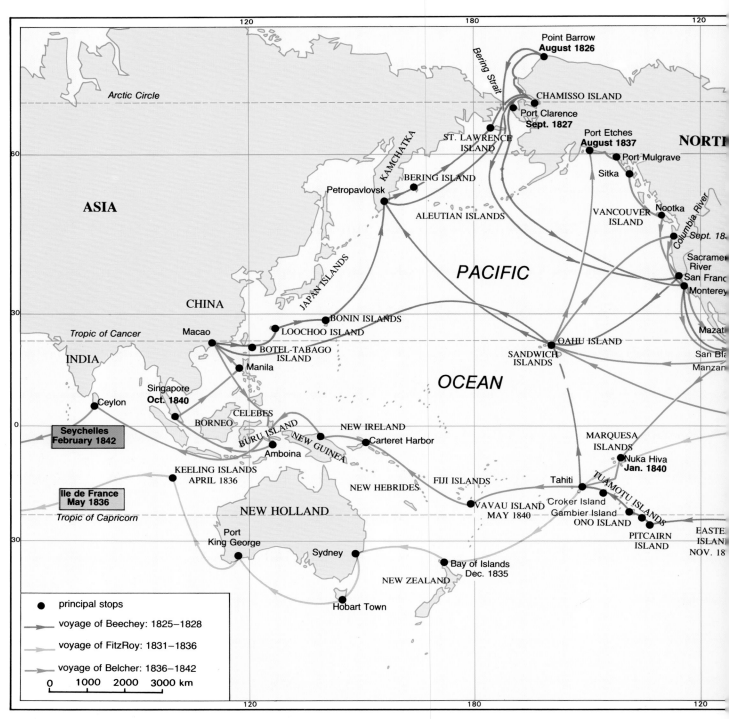

British scientists on the seas,
1825–1842.
Voyage of Beechey, 1825–1828
Voyage of FitzRoy, 1831–1836
Voyage of Belcher, 1835–1842

The magic of the great forest

On February 28, after a sixty-three-day voyage, the *Beagle* entered All Saints Bay before the picturesque city of Bahia (Salvador), in the environs of which Darwin discovered the Brazilian forest. "To a person fond of natural history, such a day as this brings with it a deeper pleasure than he can ever hope to experience again." On March 18, the ship continued her way south, and, on the morning of April 4, Darwin was able to contemplate the wonderful bay of Rio de Janeiro. Because the brig had some hydrographic studies to make along the Brazilian coasts, she did not leave until July 5.

For Darwin, their arrival was a great day—his mission was beginning. As soon as he was on shore, he reached an agreement with an Irishman named Patrick Lennon, who was to visit his coffee plantation some 200 kilometers north of Rio. Soon the little troop of horsemen penetrated the forest of vine-smothered giant trees with brilliant orchids shining on their branches. The silence was broken only by the sharp cries of toucans and parrots. Metallic-colored butterflies floated in the green light. The young naturalist went from find to find, enchanted, in a state close to ecstasy, but also horrified by the terrible struggle that was continuously going on among these strange species and fascinated in particular by the ferocity of the giant spiders as well as by the imitative characteristics of insects, who, to escape their enemies, simulated green

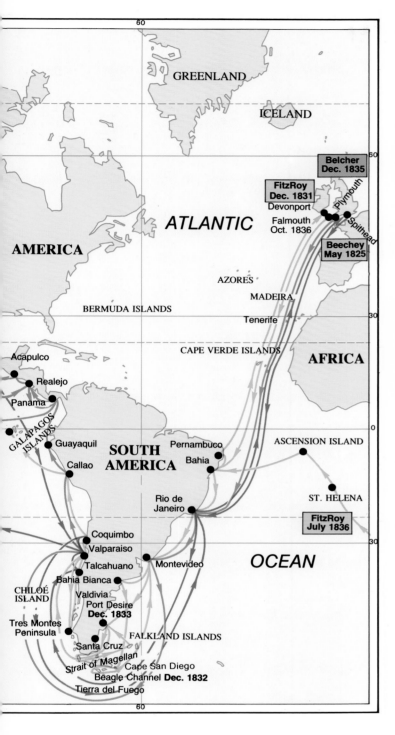

once more with FitzRoy aboard the *Beagle,* he made his sentiments known. FitzRoy's reaction was disconcerting. For him slavery was actually a necessity. Why, it even figured in the Bible; and once FitzRoy had said *Bible,* he had said all, and there was no use arguing with him. As Darwin maintained his point of view, a violent argument followed, and FitzRoy flew into a rage. Given the situation, he announced, it would be impossible for him to continue sharing his cabin with a man whose views were opposed to his own. Darwin, who was also in a temper, replied that he could do better than that—he could leave the ship. Shortly after, embarrassed at having given way to anger, the commander apologized to the naturalist and asked that he continue to use his cabin; Darwin immediately agreed.

Luckily, the two men were going to separate for several weeks. While the *Beagle* continued her hydrographic mission to the north of Rio, Darwin established himself at the foot of the Corcovado with the painter Augustus Earle and Midshipman King. During these weeks of freedom, with the help of his two companions, he collected and preserved spiders, butterflies, birds, and shells, which he shipped to his teacher, Henslow, who wrote back that Darwin was accomplishing "miracles."

Early in July, Darwin returned to the bay of Rio, and, on the fifth, the ship set sail. After a stopover at Montevideo, it reached Bahia Blanca, south of Buenos Aires, on September 7, 1832.

The Punta Alta fossils

At some distance from his little port, in a wild and desolate site, the naturalist suddenly noticed fossilized bones embedded in a soft rock. He immediately decided to prospect this lode methodically, and as the stop was to be brief, he would sometimes spend the night on the site and work twenty-four hours at a stretch with the help of Sims Covington, his cabin boy, who, after the return of the *Beagle,* was to remain in Darwin's service for several years.

At first, Darwin wondered what these bones he was extracting one by one—a tusk, an enormous pair of claws, a skull that resembled that of a hippopotamus, a petrified carapace—could be. Until then, paleontological discoveries in South America had been extremely rare. Initially disconcerted, at the end of a few days Darwin was jubilant. The bones must belong to species still unknown to zoologists and extinct for tens of thousands of years.

As strange as they might be, these fossilized animals nevertheless somewhat resembled present-day smaller species, whose ancestors they might have been. He was convinced that this marvelous relationship between living and dead animals on the same continent must inevitably throw light on beings that had once lived on Earth, as well as on how they had come to vanish. Later, Darwin was to make other paleontological discoveries in Pata-

or dead leaves, dry branches, lichens, budding flowers, thorns, bird excrement, or even other insects. He discovered an unknown world, and what might have been a handicap for him turned out to be useful, for Darwin was an amateur, not a professional or a specialist. He did not limit himself to a single aspect of the question but saw it whole; above all, he had the amateur's undulled curiosity. He studied the general conditions of life in the environment under observation, the relations between vegetable and animal life, the interdependence of species—everything that was to become the major theme of his future work.

When the little troop reached Lennon's plantation, Darwin indignantly witnessed the cruel treatment of the black slaves. Several weeks later,

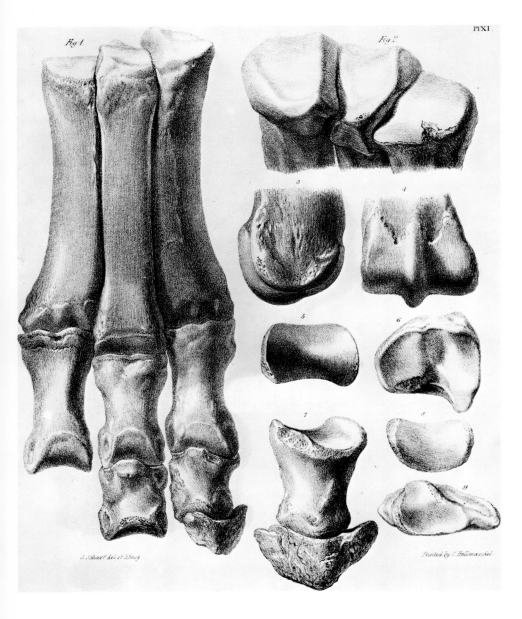

Fig 1.   Fig 2   PI XI

Bones of the front right foot of Macrauchenia, *fossil discovered by Darwin at Punta Alta in September 1832. Drawings and lithograph by G. Scharf. (Bibliothèque du Muséum d'histoire naturelle, Paris. Photo © Bibl. du Muséum/Photeb.)*

something" to it. The austral summer had come, and, in November, the brig headed for the southern tip of the South American continent.

Tierra del Fuego

Even in the middle of the Southern Hemisphere summer, which was when the *Beagle* was there, the climate of Tierra del Fuego was one of the worst in the world. The glaciers came right up to the shore, the sea was swept by continuous storms, and the winds were violent and icy. On December 17, 1832, the *Beagle* entered Le Maire Strait and went along the coast. In a letter, Darwin wrote that he had been plunged into extreme amazement by a strange apparition—the sight of a wild man. It was a naked Fuegian; his long hair floated in the wind, and on his painted face could be read an expression that Darwin believed would seem incredibly savage to those who did not consider this man's total aspect. He was standing on top of a crag, gesticulating and uttering guttural cries that made those of domestic animals seem almost comprehensible. In his journal he added: "It was without exception the most curious and interesting spectacle I ever beheld: I could not have believed how wide was the difference between savage and civilized man . . ." Seeing these men, it was hard not to believe that they were creatures of a completely different world. Darwin was not to forget the shock he received at Tierra del Fuego. From that day on, the dizzying problem of human origins began to preoccupy him, but he waited almost forty years before giving the public the results of his long reflections in *The Descent of Man, and Selection in Relation to Sex,* a work for which he was to be violently attacked.

Nevertheless, three years had been enough to modify completely the Fuegians that FitzRoy was returning to their country. The education they had received in England had made of Jemmy Button, only seventeen, a veritable dandy; and of Fuegia Basket, as young as he, a pretty, modest, and reserved young lady who was counting on marrying York Minster, the third Fuegian. But York, who was an adult, had remained morose, taciturn, and subject to violent rages.

Before the ship could reach Ponsonby Sound, where the three Fuegians wanted to be set ashore, she was hit by a violent storm on January 11, 1833. "At noon a great sea broke over us, and filled one of the whale-boats, which was obliged to be instantly cut away. The poor *Beagle* trembled at the shock, and for a few minutes would not obey her helm; but soon, like a good ship that she was, she righted and came up to the wind again. Had another sea followed the first, our fate would have been decided soon, and for ever."

On January 19, in clear and calm weather, four launches commanded by FitzRoy entered Ponsonby Sound, where they were greeted by some men on an overhanging cliff. "Springing from the

gonia and Uruguay. What could account for the disappearance of so many species? What connection could be made between this disappearance and the Flood, between it and the Creation—which, as every Christian knew, had taken place at nine in the morning on Sunday, October 23, 4004 B.C.? Darwin began to question everything he had learned.

Back on ship, he discussed this with FitzRoy, who had no doubts about the matter: These animals were antediluvians. The Bible was literal truth. Darwin did not agree, though he was unwilling to irritate the commander, to whom he could offer no decisive arguments opposing this view; above all, he was wary of bringing his own Christian education in question. However, his investigative spirit already saw before it a path of passionate research. He would have to launch into an on-site study of the continent's geological history. His discussions with FitzRoy became more and more spirited until they were in complete opposition. Nevertheless, their friendship in no way suffered. In 1832, Charles Darwin had finally found his vocation. He decided to devote his whole life to natural history, hoping that he might someday be able to add "a little ground, they waved their arms round their heads, and sent forth the most hideous yells." When the Englishmen disembarked with gifts, however, they succeeded in calming these men. There were soon about a hundred of them watching the sailors put up three wigwams, one for Richard Matthews, the missionary, one for Jemmy Button, and one for York Minster and Fuegia Basket. The news of the landing had spread, and, a few days later, Jemmy's mother, two sisters, and four brothers arrived. "The meeting was less interesting than that between a horse turned out into a field, when he joins an old companion," Darwin wrote.

When FitzRoy returned ten days later (February 6), Matthews came running up and gasped out his tale, which Darwin reports as follows: "From the time of our leaving, a regular system of plunder commenced; fresh parties of the natives kept arriving: York and Jemmy lost many things, and Matthews almost everything which had not been concealed underground. . . . Matthews described the watch he was obliged always to keep as most harassing; night and day he was surrounded by the natives, who tried to tire him out by making an incessant noise close to his head. . . . It was quite melancholy leaving the three Fuegians with their savage countrymen; but it was a great comfort that they had no personal fears. York, being a powerful, resolute man, was pretty sure to get on well, together with his wife Fuegia. Poor Jemmy looked rather disconsolate, and would then, I have little doubt, have been glad to have returned with us." FitzRoy decided to take Matthews back on board.

A year later, on March 5, 1834, the *Beagle* again dropped anchor in the bay at Woollya. A small boat approached; one of the men in it was busy washing the paint off his face. "This man was poor Jemmy,— now a thin haggard savage, with long disordered hair, and naked, except a bit of a blanket round his waist. . . . As soon, however, as he was clothed, and the first flurry was over, things wore a good appearance. . . . He told us . . . that his relations were very good people, and that he did not wish to go back to England: in the evening we found out the cause of this great change in Jemmy's feelings, in the arrival of his young and nice-looking wife."

Jemmy had brought his friends what was most precious to him, and he left the *Beagle* loaded down with gifts. Returning the next morning, he remained on board until the vessel set sail. All that the three Fuegians had learned from their contacts with the white men served only—as was seen later— to make their lives among their own people more difficult. By the end of the nineteenth century, the three Fuegian tribes were almost extinct.

Pampas and Gauchos

At the end of February 1833, the *Beagle* left Tierra del Fuego and, after a stopover in the Falkland Islands, went on to Maldonado, a peaceful little city situated near the mouth of the Rio de la Plata.

Given the almost constant storms, the *Beagle* was inadequate for FitzRoy's mission to chart the coast. He therefore made an on-site acquisition of an American ship that he rebaptized the *Adventure*. FitzRoy should have obtained the previous consent of the Admiralty, but he could not wait the several months it would take to get a response to his request. He went to work, going back and forth along the coasts of Argentina from April 28 to July 23.

During these three months, Darwin remained at Maldonado. After a two-week excursion into the interior accompanied by an armed escort—the country was extremely dangerous—on his return he began packaging his collections for shipment to England. Dispatching 1,529 specimens preserved in alcohol, he noted that his collection of regional quadrupeds and birds was becoming more or less complete.

At the end of July, the *Beagle* returned to pick him up and then set sail for the village of El Carmen on the banks of the Rio Negro in Patagonia. El Carmen was then the southernmost outpost of the colonial penetration into the still unexplored pampas. More and more confident in his own powers, Darwin decided to traverse some thousand kilometers of this territory. FitzRoy got him to agree that he would stop at Bahia Blanca, where the *Beagle* would meet up with him; then, if everything had gone well, he could continue on his way.

Accompanied by a guide and an armed escort of six gauchos, on August 11, Charles Darwin entered the vast desert plains. He was soon quite at ease among these gauchos, for whom he had felt immediate sympathy and admiration, and he easily accommodated himself to the harshness of their

Portraits of Fuegians drawn by R. FitzRoy; from top to bottom: a woman, a man, a young boy. (Service historique de la Marine, Vincennes. Photo by Michel Didier © Photeb.)

Darwin's nandu, or rhea. Plate from the Zoology of the H.M.S. Beagle. (Bibliothèque du Muséum d'histoire naturelle, Paris. Photo © Bibl. du Muséum/Photeb.)

The Beagle beached at the mouth of the Santa Cruz (April 13–May 12, 1834). FitzRoy and Darwin profited from this stop to go up the river toward the Andes. Engraving by Thomas Landseer after C. Martens. (Bibliothèque du Muséum d'histoire naturelle, Paris. Photo © Bibl. du Muséum/Photeb.)

lives. On the way, he continually made notes on the fauna of the pampas. One of his most memorable encounters was with a new species of nandu, the South American ostrich, *Rhea darwini*.

After several days, the little troop arrived at the camp of General Rosas, commander of the Argentinean forces on the Rio Colorado. The camp looked more like a bandits' hideout than the headquarters of an army, and Rosas was respected all the more because at the slightest indiscretion he had the guilty party shot. Having become the governor of Buenos Aires in an 1828 coup d'état, Juan Manuel Ortiz de Rosas was at the time the undisputed master of the Argentine republic. He was to prove himself a bloody tyrant whose dictatorship would last until 1852, when he was defeated by the neighboring countries with the aid of Great Britain and France. Though Darwin could not help but feel great esteem for this man who was both intelligent and energetic, he was horrified by the atrocities that he witnessed, for to conquer new territories, the army had launched a pitiless extermination campaign against the Indians.

On September 20, 1833, Darwin arrived safely in the Argentinean capital, but he spent only one week there. On September 27, he left for the north so as to reach Santa Fé by following the Rio Paraná. There he had his first attack of fever and had to spend a week in bed. After that, he had to hasten to Montevideo, where he was to join up with the *Beagle* on October 21. The return voyage was a dramatic one. In the interval, Rosas had decided to overthrow the government, and the entire country was in a state of revolution. Darwin got back to the brig just as she was about to leave the mouth of the Rio de la Plata and once more head south. The crew was exhausted. For more than a year it had lived amid storms and cold. Earle had had to leave the *Beagle*; at Montevideo his place was taken by Conrad Martens, a young and enthusiastic landscape painter who was to remain with the expedi-

tion until the end. The *Beagle* and the *Adventure* had to make long stopovers along the inhospitable Patagonian coast—at Port Desire and then at San Julian—before she once more reached Tierra del Fuego (January 29–March 7) and the Falklands (March–April). In June, the *Beagle* traversed the Strait of Magellan. This time it was winter, and the ship advanced with difficulty through the continuous storms. The deck was covered with snow, and the rigging was iced over. Enormous blocks of ice detached themselves from the cliffs with ominous rumbles.

The Andes

On July 23, the *Beagle* dropped anchor in Valparaiso Bay. In the city, Darwin encountered an old boarding school friend, Richard Corfield, who was eager to be of service to him.

On August 14, he left Valparaiso on horseback for a six-week excursion that was to prove most fruitful. The higher up into the Cordilleras he went, the better he felt; his geological observations became more and more enlightening, and explanations came spontaneously to his mind. At 4,000 meters, he discovered a thick seam of shells and, a bit lower, a small forest of petrified pines. Thus, little by little was revealed to him the "marvelous history" of this fold that had surged from the waters, forming first a series of islands covered with forests and, finally, a chain of mountains. All this orogenic movement was accompanied by earthquakes and volcanic eruptions that were still going on.

When he returned to Valparaiso on September 27, Darwin was radiant but exhausted; as soon as he got back he had to take to bed in his friend Corfield's house, and he was unable to leave his room until the end of October.

During this time, consternation reigned on board the *Beagle*. The commander had just received a letter in which the Admiralty refused to take responsibility for the purchase of the *Adventure*, and he was ordered to sell the ship as soon as possible. For a man as proud as FitzRoy, this decision was an outrage, and, after an initial outburst of fury, he sank into a state of despair. He was going mad, he told his distressed officers; "there was insanity in the family." Though everybody on board tried to calm him, FitzRoy remained inflexible and felt henceforth unable to lead the expedition. Darwin was dumbfounded; for him the voyage was only beginning, and he believed himself on the verge of important discoveries. If the *Beagle* returned to England, he would remain behind to complete his research, even if it required a year or two. Proceeding with intelligence and prudence, First Lieutenant Wickham managed to save the situation. Little by little, FitzRoy allowed himself to be convinced. Finally, the *Adventure* was resold, even bringing in a slight profit, and FitzRoy agreed to resume command. On November 1834, the *Beagle* anchored at San Carlos, the capital of Chiloé Island, off the coast of Chile. She then visited the many small islands forming the Chonos Archipelago and reached Valdivia on February 8, 1835.

The earthquake

At the beginning of 1835, there were many earth tremors in Chile, and Darwin was able to study them attentively. On the night of January 19, 1835, from Chiloé he had witnessed the eruption of the Osorno: "Dark objects, in constant succession, were seen, in the midst of a great glare of red light, to be thrown up and to fall down." Afterward, Darwin was to learn that many other volcanoes had become active at the same time.

Four weeks later, while the brig was anchored at Valdivia, Darwin noted, on February 20: "This day has been memorable in the annals of Valdivia, for the most severe earthquake experienced by the oldest inhabitant." The center of the quake was much farther north, and it was not until he got to Talcahuano, near Concepción, that the naturalist was able to measure the extent of the disaster twelve days earlier. Talcahuano and Concepción "presented the most awful yet interesting spectacle I ever beheld." He was aware that it was an unusual opportunity for him, a budding geologist, to witness at first hand the enormous forces that had fashioned the surface of the Earth; he never forgot what he had seen and felt in Chile, and he made use of it in his writing.

On March 11, 1835, the *Beagle* was once more at Valparaiso, where Darwin again met his friend Corfield. Two days later, he left for the Andes, convinced that the season was now favorable for crossing the Cordillera by the highest and most dangerous route. By means of the Portillo Pass, it was possible to reach the other side and get to the little city of Mendoza at the foot of the Andes across the border that separated Chile from Argentina. It was the longest and most difficult climb he had ever made, but it was so exciting that he managed it without great fatigue.

After twenty-four days spent high in the mountains, Darwin arrived at Santiago (April 8) in such good health that he noted: ". . . never did I more deeply enjoy an equal space of time." A few days later, he was back in Vaparaiso. In his journal (March 25) he had recorded: "We slept in the village of Luxan, which is a small place surrounded by gardens, and forms the most southern cultivated district in the Province of Mendoza." Earlier, he had noted: "At night I experienced an attack (for it deserves no less a name) of the *Benchuca,* a species of Reduvius, the great black bug of the Pampas. . . . No pain was caused by the wound. It was curious to watch its body during the act of sucking, as in less then ten minutes it changed from being as flat as a wafer to a globular form." In this state, he wrote, it is easily crushed.

On April 27, he left again with four horses and two mules, this time going along the northern coast. Sleeping under the sky and cooking over camp fires, the little expedition reached Copiapo, some 700 kilometers from Valparaiso, where FitzRoy was to pick Darwin up. In the meantime, the commander had received good news from England; the Admiralty, fearing that it had reacted too quickly to the purchase of the *Adventure,* had promoted him to the rank of captain. Though FitzRoy would not admit it, he was very proud of this promotion, and his morale became excellent.

The bay of Valparaiso in August 1834. Watercolor by Conrad Martens. (Rex Nan Kivell Collection, National Library of Australia, Canberra. Photo © National Library of Australia/Photeb.)

Ruins of the cathedral of Concepción after the earthquake of February 20, 1835. Engraving by S. Bull after a drawing by Lieutenant J. C. Wickham. (Service historique de la Marine, Vincennes. Photo by Michel Didier © Photeb.)

On July 12, the *Beagle* reached the coast of Peru at Iquique, and, on July 19, at Callao, where she remained until September 7. Though the situation in Chile—where, in 1833, a constitution had been proclaimed that was to remain in force for almost a century—was relatively stable, the same could not be said for Peru, which had been plunged into anarchy by a power dispute among four armed parties. Since the crew was forbidden to disembark, all Darwin could do was visit Lima and its immediate environs.

The Galapagos, or living prehistory

In July, Darwin had written from Lima to his cousin William Darwin Fox in England that he was eager to see the Galapagos, those islands interesting him more than any other place they would visit during the voyage. Indeed, at the Galapagos he was to make a methodical study of the many adaptations of animals to new natural surroundings, and even to observe the formation of species better armed to confront a hostile environment. His hopes high, on the morning of September 17, he landed on Chatham Island (San Cristobal), one of the ten islands in the archipelago. His first impression was hardly favorable. "Nothing could be less inviting than the first appearance. A broken field of black basaltic lava, thrown into the most rugged waves, and crossed by great fissures, is everywhere covered by stunted, sunburnt brushwood, which shows little signs of life. The dry and parched surface, being heated by the noonday sun, gave to the air a close and sultry feeling, like that from a stove . . ." Courageously setting to work, he collected plants and animals of all sorts, even spending the night amid "black truncated cones," the miniscule craters with which the islands were dotted.

The ship moved from island to island. It was on James Island (San Salvador) that Darwin made his most important observations. Supplied with tents and provisions, he landed there on October 8 with Bynoe, Covington, and two seamen; he remained

a week. By the time FitzRoy returned to pick him up again, he had crossed the island in every direction and completed a more or less exhaustive study. No doubt he was interested in everything he saw, but soon his attention focused particularly on the giant tortoises, two kinds of iguanas, and, finally, the finches, the close observation of which was to provide some surprises.

At the time, giant land tortoises could be found in unimaginable quantities; completely approachable, they were very easy to observe. Some attained a considerable size and weighed more than 100 kilos. But more amazing still were the large sea iguanas that looked like miniatures of the dragons that populated the Earth well before the appearance of man. These "hideous-looking creatures" more than a meter long moved very slowly on land, but they could swim quite well. The iguanas did not feed on fish but, as Darwin ascertained, on "minced seaweed (Ulvae)," which they tore from submerged rocks. Even more plentiful were the land iguanas. In fact, they were so numerous that Darwin and his companions "could not for some time find a spot free from their burrows on which to pitch our single tent. . . . In their movements they are lazy and half torpid." The birds, of which on James Island alone Darwin procured twenty-six land species, were less disconcerting; but in examining the finches, whose aspect seemed quite ordinary at first glance, the naturalist found a singular phenomenon. Extremely abundant, all these birds greatly resembled one another, but their beaks differed considerably. Sometimes they were as developed as those of the hawfinch, sometimes as delicate as those of warblers. Better yet, between these two extreme sizes there were intermediate ones so clearly defined that thirteen species could be established. The reason for these variations was obvious: Some of the Galapagos finches were granivorous and others insectivorous. Among the former, some fed on large, hard seeds that only a strong beak could crush, and others on seeds that were smaller and not as tough.

Here was a typical example of adaptation to an environment; it could be assumed that all these birds descended from a common ancestor that had emigrated from the nearby continent. Food resources being extremely limited on these islands, in order not to enter into competition, their descendants had undergone different transformations so as to be able to exploit these resources as completely as possible. Darwin's conclusion about the finches was later to be confirmed by science, but for a twenty-six-year-old naturalist who had just entered the profession its consequences were so audacious that he only briefly mentioned the finches in his journal. It was not until much later, after mature reflection, that Darwin utilized the finches as an argument in favor of his theory of natural selection. But in the Galapagos he had already been struck by the then-profoundly revolutionary idea that the variation of species stems from common ancestral forms. He had discovered the process of speciation. His studies made him so enthusiastic, he wrote to

his sister, that, at night, he was unable to sleep.

A long promenade

Darwin's observations were now more or less finished, as was FitzRoy's mission. All that remained was to make a chronometric reconnaissance across the world. As a result, when the *Beagle* left the Galapagos on October 20, 1835, the atmosphere on board was considerably more relaxed; the voyage was not taking on the character of a careless promenade around the globe. After sailing for twenty-five days, on November 15, the *Beagle* dropped anchor in Matavai Bay, where the navigators were warmly received. Darwin was won over by the beauty of the landscapes and by the cordial hospitality of the Tahitians, but he was disappointed by the appearance of the women, who

seemed far from deserving the reputation given them by previous travelers.

After three weeks at sea, the *Beagle* anchored in the Bay of Islands. The Maoris did not make as good an impression on Darwin as the Tahitians had. They were filthy savages whose faces disappeared under symmetrical tattooing that gave "a disagreeable expression to their countenances." In addition, they were inhospitable, and one did not feel safe among them. On the other hand, Darwin waxed nostalgic at the sight of the English colonial gardens. The work done by the missionaries in Tahiti, and especially in New Zealand, so impressed him that he agreed to collaborate on a memorandum, suggested by FitzRoy but to be written and signed by both of them, that asked the British government to give increased aid to missions established in the Pacific. Curiously enough, this memorandum was printed in the *South African Recorder* (September 1836) and is Darwin's first signed publication. When the *Beagle* got to the Bay of Islands, Richard Matthews disembarked to stay with his brother, who, like himself, was a missionary.

On December 30, the *Beagle* headed for Australia. The development and prosperity of Sydney amazed Darwin. It was really a country to settle in if one wanted to make money. However, there was a shadow to the picture: All that wealth came from the labor of convicts, and the sight of these wretches slaving away while their masters lived in idleness was intolerable to him. As for the aboriginals, their number was shrinking alarmingly, and they had become strangers in their own country. The same could be said for the extraordinary Australian fauna. "A few years since this country abounded with wild animals; but now the emu is banished to a long distance, and the kangaroo is become scarce; to both the English greyhound has been highly destructive. It may be long before these animals are altogether exterminated, but their doom is fixed." On February 3, 1836, the *Beagle* began a twelve-day stopover in Hobart Town, Tasmania, where the fate of the natives was even worse. The navigators again disembarked in Australia, at King George Sound, from March 3 to 14. There, Darwin was lucky enough to witness a "corrobery." "It was a most rude, barbarous scene. . . . We have beheld many curious scenes in savage life, but never, I think, one where the natives were in such high spirits, and so perfectly at their ease."

On April 1, the *Beagle* reached the Cocos Islands (Keeling Islands) in the middle of the Indian

Giant land tortoises. Very abundant in the Galapagos in Darwin's time, they are now threatened with extinction. Engraving by K. Jahrmangh after G. Mützel for Les Merveilles de la Nature *by A. E. Brehm. (Bibliothèque du Muséum d'histoire naturelle, Paris. Photo © Bibl. du Muséum/Photeb.)*

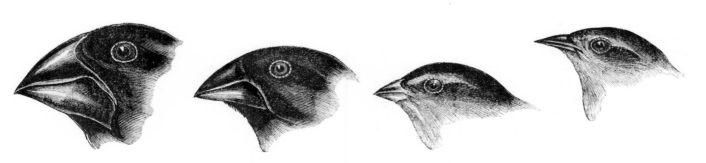

Four types of Darwin's finch (from the Galapagos). From left to right: big beak, medium beak, miniscule, and olive finch. Extract from Voyage d'un naturaliste autour du monde *by Darwin, 1875. (Bibliothèque nationale, Paris. Photo by Jeanbor © Arch. Photeb.)*

Three species of Brazilian palms. Drawing by P. Oudart after d'Orbigny; engraving by Breton. Voyage dans l'Amérique méridionale by Alcide d'Orbigny. Atlas of 1847. (Bibliothèque nationale, Paris. Photo by Michel Didier © Photeb.)

Ocean. If the Galapagos resembled Hell, this was Eden. Darwin was finally able to resolve a problem that had been bothering him for some time—the formation of the coral islands. As he saw it, the missing clue sought by geologists could only be found by observing the living polyp. Accompanied by FitzRoy, he made a boat trip around the exterior reef of an atoll and took a number of soundings along its slopes. It seemed that the coral formations were the final stage of a very long process of complementary interactions: first the emergence of an island due to underwater volcanic movements, then the colonization of its slopes by myriads of polyps, and finally—when the weight of this artificial growth overloaded the Earth's crust—an inverse movement, called subsidence, in which the island gradually sank into the ocean. Little by little, the polyps continued their constructions upward, while the volcanic relief sank. At the end of this process, which probably took at least a million years, there was no longer anything but a coral ring surrounding a lagoon—in other words, an atoll. Once more the instability of the Earth's crust and the changes it had undergone in the course of time were demonstrated. Darwin's explanation of the formation of coral reefs, discredited at the beginning of the twentieth century, has been completely confirmed by deep soundings made since then.

On April 29, the *Beagle* reached Mauritius, where, until May 9, Darwin was the guest of the general administrator, Captain Lloyd, who caused a sensation by bringing him back to the ship perched on his personal elephant, the only one on the island. Until then the weather had been good, but on the way to Cape Town, it turned nasty, and the pace

of the *Beagle* was slowed, so that she did not reach her destination until May 31. She left again on June 15 but did not reach St. Helena until July 8. At Ascension, Darwin found letters from England. One of them informed him that Professor Sedgwick, who had taught him geology, had just declared that henceforth Charles Darwin would have to be counted among the scientific authorities. After having read that letter, Darwin scrambled up the mountains, his geologist's hammer ringing out on the volcanic rock.

England was drawing near when suddenly FitzRoy decided to complete his chronometric observations by making a detour to the South American coast. To Darwin, this zigzag progress was extremely painful. He acknowledged that he hated the sea, was horrified by it, loathed both it and all the ships on it. After brief stopovers in Bahia and Pernambouc, the *Beagle* came in sight of the English coast on October 2. It was a Sunday, so FitzRoy held a final religious service to thank God for having allowed the *Beagle* and her crew to return home safely.

Darwin leaped ashore as soon as the brig was at the Falmouth quay. Without having been announced, on October 5, he erupted into the family home just as his father and sisters were having breakfast. Amid the cries of the young girls, Dr. Darwin could be heard rumbling: "The shape of your head is quite altered."

The consequences of the voyage

Six months after his return, in May 1837, Darwin visited the *Beagle*, which was to leave for Australia in a week. It seemed strange to see her and to think that he would not be leaving with the others. Only seasickness kept him from being tempted to go along. If he had, he would have found on board, if not FitzRoy—who after ten years of almost continuous navigation now wanted to publish the results of his voyages—at least several of his former companions. In the interval, First Lieutenant John C. Wickham had been promoted to captain and succeeded Captain King, who had led the first expedition of the *Adventure* and the *Beagle* in 1826–1830, as commander of the naval forces in Australia. In his new capacity, Wickham immediately set up and entrusted to the *Beagle* a mission to explore the Australian coasts. He was to have taken charge of it himself, but he fell sick and designated John Lord Stokes, the former third lieutenant of the *Beagle,* to replace him. Benjamin Bynoe, now chief surgeon, took part in the expedition. He was also to fill the office of naturalist left vacant by Darwin, whose student he had been. As for Second Lieutenant James B. Sulivan, after having been named governor of the Falkland Islands in 1857, he became Chief Naval Officer in the maritime department of the Board of Trade, one of the most important posts to which a navy officer could aspire. Unfortunately, there was another competitor—

FitzRoy himself, who found it hard to accept that a man who had twenty-five years earlier been his subordinate was preferred over him.

Robert FitzRoy had had bad luck. The publication of his voyage in 1839 had been respectfully received, but it was eclipsed by the appearance that year of the third volume of the account, which had been written by Darwin. The publisher, John Murray, immediately suggested that Darwin make of his volume a separate edition, which came out in 1845 and has since then been translated into many languages. Extremely sensitive, FitzRoy took offense. However, the two men had little occasion to meet. In 1841, the captain was elected to the House of Commons, where he remained until 1843, the year in which he was named the governor of New Zealand. But he remained in Auckland only a short time; the position he took favoring the natives won him the enmity of the colonists, who managed to have him recalled. Nevertheless, FitzRoy had gained a reputation for his meteorological work, and as a compensation for his disappointment in 1857, he was made rear admiral, just as he was thinking of resigning from the navy. At Darwin's invitation, he came to spend two days with him in the country, following which the naturalist wrote to his sister that FitzRoy had "the most consummate skill in looking at everything and everybody in a perverted manner." At the time, FitzRoy was an exhausted and embittered man. On Sunday, April 30, 1865, Rear Admiral Robert FitzRoy committed suicide by cutting his throat, just as his uncle, the minister Castlereagh, had done forty-three years earlier on the very day he was to leave for the Congress of Verona.

Named secretary of the Geological Society of London in 1838, Charles Darwin married his cousin and childhood friend, Emma Wedgwood, in 1839. A year older than he, she was an intelligent and gay young woman with a talent for music. As soon as they were able to, the Darwins went to live in the country in Kent, some 25 kilometers from London, in a large, simple, but comfortable house called Down House, where Darwin was to remain until his death. There, ten children were born, including four sons who survived him. The Darwins were a happy and close-knit family. Sheltered from financial worries thanks to the fortune he had inherited, the success of his books, and prudent financial management, Darwin enjoyed complete independence. At Down House he adopted an extremely regular way of life from which he never departed.

Following his return in 1836, he set to work classifying the enormous collections he had assembled. Immmediately after having written his account of the voyage, he undertook his *Journal of Researches into Geology and Natural History of the countries visited during the Voyage of H.M.S. "Beagle" around the world, under the command of Capt. Fitz-Roy, R. N.,* which was published in 1840. Included in it was his famous study on "The Structure and Distribution of Coral Reefs," which had taken him twenty months to complete. Concurrently, he had

Patagonian pampas cat. Plate of the Zoology of the Voyage of the H.M.S. Beagle, by Darwin. (Bibliothèque du Muséum d'histoire naturelle, Paris. Photo © Bibl. du Muséum/Photeb.)

undertaken the laborious polishing of the *Beagle*'s zoology, the five volumes of which appeared between 1839 and 1843. Though the work on it had been divided among several specialists, Darwin was in charge and himself wrote several of the studies. All these tasks devoted to the results of his voyage had taken ten years, but after 1844, Darwin wrote to his friend, the botanist Joseph Dalton Hooker: "At last gleams of light have come, and I am almost convinced (quite contrary to the opinion I started with) that the species are not (it is like confessing to a murder) immutable, unchangeable."

As he continued to work, Darwin reluctantly elaborated the theory that was to make him famous. He was still hesitating over the publication of the results of his slow and prudent reflections when, in June 1858, he received a letter sent from Ternate by the naturalist Alfred Russel Wallace. The latter sent an essay entitled "On the Tendency of Varieties to Depart Indefinitely from the Original Type" and asked him if he thought it good enough to submit to Charles Lyell. Darwin immediately sent it to the great geologist with a warm recommendation, but he could not resist sighing that "all my originality, whatever it may amount to, will be smashed . . ." The truth was that Wallace had come to the same conclusions that he had. But Lyell and Hooker felt that this was no reason for Darwin to refrain from publishing his own theory, and that he ought to make it known at the same time that Wallace's was. They even arranged for the two theses to be jointly presented before the Linnean Society.

The following year, Darwin finally decided to publish his *On the Origin of Species,* which caused a sensation and went into three successive printings. The clergy was aroused, and in June 1860, at the meeting of the British Association in Oxford, there was a fiery public debate that was to stir up all England. Darwin had excused himself on the grounds of ill health, but he was represented by his former teacher, Henslow, assisted by T. H. Huxley and

Tangara darwinii, one of the South American birds discovered by Darwin. Plate by John Gould. Zoology of the Voyage of H.M.S. Beagle. *(Bibliothèque du Muséum d'histoire naturelle, Paris. Photo © Bibl. du Muséum/Photeb.)*

J. D. Hooker, who supported his point of view against fierce opposition led by the Bishop of Ox-ford, S. Wilberforce, and the anatomist Richard Owen, who, twenty years earlier, had collaborated on the zoology of the *Beagle*. By a curious coincidence, the day before this debate, FitzRoy had presented to the same meeting a paper on meteorology.

Charles Darwin never went back to sea. Since his return, his health had continued to decline. After 1842, he had to give up traveling of any kind. After 1859, he even avoided appearing in public. In 1871, he noted that he had never spent a day without feeling ill. Permanently exhausted, Darwin suffered from gastrointestinal problems accompanied by vomiting, somnolence, and heart trouble. The doctors were unable to ascribe this incurable illness to any organic cause. At the time, it was believed to be a form of hypochondria. Some gossips claimed that the naturalist was prey to remorse for having dared to attack the very bases of Christian faith.

In fact, the origin of his sickness went very far back into the past. In March 1835, he had been bitten by bugs in the Andes; currently known as *Triatoma infestans,* these are now recognized as carriers of *Trypanosoma cruzi,* the agent of Chagas's Disease, which is common in the Andes and whose symptoms completely correspond to those experienced by the founder of Evolutionism. However, this disease was not described until 1909—twenty-seven years after Darwin's death.

The interminable cruise of the *Sulphur,* 1835–1842

While the *Beagle* was still anchored in the Bay of Islands in New Zealand and getting ready to return to England, a new expedition was leaving. It was commanded by Captain Beechey, who, in 1831, had published the account of his previous voyage. He was leaving again on the *Sulphur,* a 308-ton vessel, accompanied by the *Starling,* a 109-ton schooner commanded by Lieutenant Henry Kellett. The two ships got under way at Plymouth on December 24, 1835. Beechey's mission was to continue the exploration and hydrographic survey of the western coasts of America in order to complete the work done by King and FitzRoy in 1826–1830, as well as that which he himself had done between 1825 and 1828. For the natural history research, Beechey was assisted by the surgeon of the *Sulphur,* Richard Brinsley Hinds. This was not to be a true voyage of discovery: The expedition was particularly commissioned to verify, rectify, and complete the data assembled by previous navigators. This perhaps explains the length of the mission and, in part, the apparently capricious nature of the voyage—the comings and goings from one point to another being determined by weather that was more or less favorable according to the season.

The hydrographic work was to begin at Valparaiso, where the two ships arrived on June 9, 1836, after stopovers in Madeira, Tenerife, Rio de Janeiro, and Montevideo. But Beechey fell so seriously ill at Valparaiso that he had to be sent back to England, leaving the command to Kellett. In August, the latter reached Callao and Paita in Peru, and then Guayaquil, the port of Ecuador, where the navigators remained until the end of the year in order to chart the Guayaquil River.

Ascending north, the expedition reached Panama on January 29, 1837. There it was rejoined by Belcher, Beechey's lieutenant on the *Blossom,* who had been promoted to captain and put in charge of the operations, into which his arrival infused new spirit. Belcher was personally interested in natural history, and his cabin soon looked like the annex of a museum; he did everything he could to increase the natural history work in regions that had been little prospected, and he himself took an active part in the research.

In April 1837, the *Sulphur* stopped in Realejo, Nicaragua, and then in Libertad, from which point Belcher and Kellett went by mule to San Salvador.

From May 27 to June 10 the ship anchored at San Blas on the Mexican coast, and a group that went to Tepic, in the interior, made some excellent botanical harvests. Leaving the American coast, the navigators then went to the Sandwich Islands and dropped anchor in Honolulu on July 9, a few days before the *Vénus* of Dupetit-Thouars. After reprovisioning, the Englishmen sailed to the northwestern coast of America in order to complete and verify the cartographic work done by Vancouver in 1790–1795.

Operations began in August, when the weather was humid and uncomfortable in the Gulf of Alaska. The *Starling* dropped anchor at Port Mulgrave (Yakutat) in order to determine the position and the altitude of mounts St. Elias and Fairweather. Meanwhile, the *Sulphur* was at Port Etches, Hinchinbrook Island, in Prince William Sound, where the Russian-American Company had a post. Initially alarmed, the Russians received the Englishmen well and showed them their fur warehouses and fisheries. Methodically visiting this much-indented coast fragmented into a multitude of islands, Belcher was able to rectify Vancouver's many errors.

In September, the two ships went farther south to Sitka, the principal Russian fur-trading establishment. Relations between the Russians and the Indians had not improved since Lütke's stay in 1827. When the natives asked permission to visit the *Sulphur,* their bizarre accoutrements surprised the sailors; some wore wooden helmets carved in the shapes of birds or fish. The naturalists collected numerous jellyfish, mollusks, and several interesting birds.

From Sitka the ships went to Friendly Cove

Stem of a New Guinea war boat. Anonymous engraving from Voyage of the Sulphur. *(Bibliothèque nationale, Paris. Photo by Michel Didier © Photeb.)*

Coryphilus dryas, small parrot from the Marquesas. Lithograph by B. Waterhouse Hawkins from a drawing by John Gould. Zoology of the Voyage of the Sulphur. (British Museum, Natural History, London. Photo by courtesy of the trustees, British Museum/Photeb.)

in Nootka Bay, where Cook and then Vancouver had made their observations. Belcher intended to reconnoiter the Columbia River but was prevented by bad weather. He was to return there in 1839. Instead of going to Yerba Buena, he was able to complete his exploration of the Sacramento and reach the point at which the river ceased to be navigable. On December 2, the ships reached Monterey, California. Dupetit-Thouars had just renewed his supplies there, and they were to come across him two weeks later at San Blas in Mexico. At Monterey, the navigators learned that a seventeen-year-old queen named Victoria had just been crowned at Westminster Abbey.

After having charted the Gulf of Tehuantepec, in February 1838, the expedition was back in Realejo; accompanied by Hinds, Belcher went off to visit the mountains (Volcano Viejo, 1,626 meters), then, via the small city of Léon, Lake Managua, along whose shores they traveled. Back in Realejo, in March Belcher explored the Papagayo Gulf—with some difficulty, since the information he had was almost completely wrong. On March 25, after having long searched for it, he found the magnificent harbor of Culebra in Costa Rica. On the shore he bagged a fine monkey, all limbs and tail, belonging to the spider monkey family. With Hinds's help he assembled a large collection of plants and animals—made up principally of bats, rodents, and birds—that was sent to England directly from Panama.

The two ships then descended to Callao, the port of Lima. The summer and autumn of 1838 were devoted to charting the Peruvian and Ecuadorian coasts, as well as to making numerous magnetic and meteorological observations. Then once more back to Realejo, exploring on the way the gulfs of Fonseca and Nicoya (December 1838–January 1839). Since it was the rainy season and they could not resume charting the northwest coast, in May–June Belcher was back at the Sandwich Islands. As soon as the weather allowed, the *Sulphur* and the *Starling* began exploring the Columbia River right up to Port Vancouver. The Hudson Bay Company had its main western base there and twice a year—in March and September—communicated with the east coast by means of expeditions that took more than three months to cross the continent. Having completed their work in California and Mexico, the two ships finally left the American coasts in December 1839, heading west for Europe and thus completing the circumnavigation of the globe.

Belcher visited Nuka Hiva, one of the Marquesas, Bow (Hao) Island, Tahiti and Huahine, Rarotonga Island in the Cook Archipelago, and Vavau in the Tongas; in traversing the Fijis, the English ran across the American expedition led by Charles Wilkes, and after having stopped in the New Hebrides and Carteret Harbor in New Ireland, in July 1840, they reached the northeast coast of New Guinea, whose small bordering archipelagos they charted. On all these islands, Hinds's investigations were fruitful. Even though these areas had been prospected several times, he had discovered a number of new plants, birds, and especially fish, of which he was to bring back more than two hundred specimens.

By the way of Caieli on Buru Island, and Macassar in the Celebes, the ships reached Singapore on October 16, 1840. There Belcher found orders to go to south China, where the first of the "Opium Wars" was under way; having broken out a year earlier when some officials had tried to curb the activities of English merchants who were illegally introducing this drug to the Chinese market. The English had responded by sending an expeditionary force from India. The *Sulphur* immediately made for the Canton River, where, on December 20, it was joined by the *Starling,* which had been damaged in a storm and had stopped in Manila for repairs. The two ships took an active part in the fighting—especially the capture of Hong Kong. Nevertheless, Belcher had time to survey the Chinese coast, and Hinds was able to enrich his collections with several Chinese plants, including a decorative bamboo with olive-green stalks, *Arundinaria hindsi.* In November, a typhoon had seriously damaged the mast of the *Sulphur,* and so she now returned to England. On his way home, Belcher again passed Buru Island; visited Ceylon and the Seychelles; explored Mozambique Channel, touching Madagascar, where Hinds was able to procure a rare species of lemurian; and by the way of the Cape of Good Hope reached Spithead on July 19, 1842. On August 29, a vanquished China ceded Hong Kong to Great Britain and opened five of its ports to international commerce.

The voyage of the *Sulphur* had lasted six years and eight months. The results were published from 1843 to 1845; Belcher had written the account of his navigation, and Hinds had taken care of the zoology and—with the aid of G. Bentham—the botany.

In 1843, Belcher left on the *Samarang* for a new three-year cruise in the China Seas and Borneo. In 1852–1855, he led an Arctic expedition sent to search for Sir John Franklin, from whom there had been no news for several years. At that time, Belcher commanded the *Blossom,* on which he had once been a lieutenant. But this new expedition was a failure and led to his disgrace. Though he no longer sailed the seas, he ended his days as an admiral.

The French, Americans, and English discover the Antarctic, 1837-1843

Dumont d'Urville's last exploit, 1837–1840

After 1774, when, during the course of his second voyage, Captain Cook reached the lowest latitude ever attained, 71° 11′ S, whalers and sealers began to fish in the Antarctic waters. In February 1819, the Englishman William Smith rounded Cape Horn as far south as possible to take advantage of favorable winds and discovered an island on which he managed to disembark. He called it South New Britain. During the following summer, sailing on the frigate *Andromache,* his compatriot Edward Branfield reconnoitered all the neighboring islands—which he called the South Shetlands—and indicated that there were more lands farther south. In December 1820 and January 1821, Bellingshausen discovered the islands of Peter I and Alexander I. About this same time, Captain Nathaniel Palmer, an American, sighted the long mountainous point of the Antarctic continent facing Cape Horn. It was given his name, but he was only able to approach it. More impressive was the exploit of the English sealer James Weddell, who, in January 1823, found the South Orkney Islands and on February 18 broke the latitude record by reaching 74° 15′ S by 34° 16′ W. In 1824, Weddell published his *Voyage Towards the South Pole,* which caused a sensation. In it he claimed that it was possible to reach the South Pole because beyond a certain point the temperature grew milder and the sea was almost free of ice. Finally, in 1831, Biscoe and Avery charted Enderby Land and then Graham Land—which extended Palmer Land toward the south—and on its west flank the Biscoe Islands, but the sealer was only able to get a glimpse of these islands.

France had taken no part in any of these bold enterprises. Louis-Philippe was therefore eager to have her finally establish her presence in the Antarctic and, if possible, to discover new territories.

In 1836, Captain Dumont d'Urville, who was forty-six and had not been to sea for six years, felt that his career was over. After 1830, he had devoted himself to the publication of the account of his first voyage and then had undertaken a compilation, *Voyage pittoresque autour du monde* (Picturesque Journey Around the World). He was thinking seriously of retiring, but before doing so he made one last effort; in January 1837, he contacted the new Minister of the Navy, Claude de Rosamel, and proposed a new expedition. He was told that for the moment nothing could be done about his

Orthoptera, including two leaf insects (center) collected in Triton Bay, New Guinea. Original drawing by E. Blanchard. Manuscript of Voyage au pole Sud. *(Bibliothèque du Muséum d'histoire naturelle, Paris. Photo © Bibl. du Muséum/Photeb.)*

proposal, and he was therefore greatly surprised when, shortly thereafter, Rosamel suggested he take over command of the *Astrolabe.* He understood somewhat better when, in February 1837, he was given an audience by King Louis-Philippe, who was aware of the English expeditions, and was asked to explore the South Pole. This was something that d'Urville had not foreseen. "I was old, suffering from a cruel disability [he had gout], completely disenchanted and without illusions." If he accepted the royal mandate, it was only because he considered it his last chance.

He was to leave with two ships—the *Astrolabe,* on which he had already sailed around the world, and a 300-ton corvette, the *Zélée,* the command of which he turned over to his faithful Charles Hector Jacquinot. Both ships were already old; neither was spacious or comfortable; and both were completely unsuitable for a polar expedition. D'Urville was faced with an additional disappointment when he recommended his former lieutenants

Facing page: "The Astrolabe *springs a leak on an ice floe, February 6, 1838." Lithograph by E. de Laplante after L. Le Breton, extract from* Voyage au Pole Sud et dans l'Océanie sur l'Astrolabe et la Zélée. *(Musée de la Marine, Paris. Photo © the museum/Photeb.)*

Preceding page: Dumont d'Urville's Astrolabe *and* Zélée *run aground in Torres Strait, May–June 1840. Painting by Louis Le Breton, the draftsman of the expedition. (Peabody Museum, Salem. Photo by Mark Sexton © the museum.)*

Dumont d'Urville's Ships and Crews
Second Voyage, 1837–1840

L'*ASTROLABE* and LA *ZELEE;*
left from Toulon, 9/7/1837;
returned to Toulon, 11/7/1840;
total of crews: 165 officers and men;
deaths: 22;
deserters: 13;
disembarked: 8;
left sick: 6.

L'*ASTROLABE:* 380-ton corvette;
crew: 84 men.

Commander: Jules Sébastien Dumont d'Urville, captain.

Lieutenants: Louis François Marie Auguste de Roquemaurel, second, made corvette captain, 12/20/1840; François Edmond Eugène Barlatier-Demas.

Ensigns: Joseph Antoine Duroch, made lieutenant commander, 8/20/1839; Jacques Marie Eugène Marescot-Duthilleul, died on board, 11/23/1839; Jean Marie Emile Gourdin, died on board, 12/8/1839; Auguste Elie Aimé Coupvent-Desbois, made lieutenant commander, 12/20/1840.

Hydrographer: Clément Adrien Vincendon-Dumoulin.

Surgeon and naturalist: Jacques Bernard Hombron.

Assistant surgeon and naturalist: Honoré Jacquinot.

Surgeon's aide: Louis Le Breton, draftsman.

Assistant naturalist: Pierre Marie Alexandre Dumoutier.

Painter: Ernest Auguste Goupil, died at Hobart Town, 1/4/1840.

Elèves: Louis Emmanuel Le Maistre-Dupard, put ashore sick at Rio, 11/13/1837; Charles François Eugène Gervaize, made ensign, 8/20/1837; Pierre Antoine Lafond, made ensign, 8/20/1839, put ashore sick at Semarang, 11/25/1839; Joseph Emmanuel Prosper Boyer, made ensign, 8/10/1839, put ashore sick at Bay of Islands (New Zealand), 4/29/1840.

La *ZELEE:* 300-ton corvette;
crew: 81 men.

Commander: Charles Hector Jacquinot, corvette captain.

Lieutenants: Joseph Fidèle Eugène du Bouzet, 2nd, made corvette captain, 12/20/1840; Charles Jules Adolphe Thanaron.

Ensigns: Tardy de Montravel, made lieutenant commander, 3/20/1839; Tony de Pavin de La Farge, died aboard ship, 11/20/1839; Antoine Auguste Thirin.

Surgeon and naturalist: Elie Jean François Le Guillou.

Assistant surgeon and naturalist: Jules Grange.

Elèves: Jean Edmond Gaillard, made ensign, 3/6/1839, left sick at Bourbon, 7/2/1840, where he died in 1842; Germain Hector Perigot, left sick at Valparaiso, 5/29/1838; Paul François René de Flotte, embarked at Tahiti, 11/15/1838, made ensign, 8/20/1839.

Scytothalia jacquinotii *seaweed collected in the Antarctic Ocean. Original watercolor by Alfred Riocreux, 1842. Manuscript of* Voyage au pole Sud. *(Bibliothèque du Muséum d'histoire naturelle, Paris. Photo © Bibl. du Muséum/Photeb.)*

for the post of second in command; they all refused. He finally had to accept officers he did not know. "And what happened? Some retained to the very end the zeal, enthusiasm, and ardor that had made them undertake the voyage. . . . As for the others, soon disgusted with this kind of navigation and the privations it brought with it, some contented themselves with coldly carrying out their duties and ceased taking an interest in the operations, while others, more exasperated by the disappointments they encountered, were hostile to their leader's efforts and spoke with disdain of the expedition to which they unfortunately found themselves attached."

Luckily, at the request of the commander, the excellent hydrographer Vincendon-Dumoulin was assigned to the voyage. In April and May, d'Urville visited London so that he could inform himself about the recent English expeditions to the Antarctic, but he learned nothing more than what he already knew of Biscoe's voyage. He turned to the Museum of Natural History, but he had enemies there and so got no help. The physiologist and phrenologist Dumoutier offered his services and was accepted as

assistant natural historian. Once again, the navy medical department filled the vacant posts by appointing J. B. Hombron as the *Astrolabe*'s surgeon and Honoré Jacquinot as his assistant; on the *Zélée,* the surgeon was to be Le Guillou, assisted by Jules Grange. Hombron and Jacquinot were to be responsible for zoology and botany; Le Guillou was to focus on entomology; Grange served as the mineralogist and geologist; and Dumoutier was to do the anthropological research. But Dumont d'Urville's troubles were by no means over. The fitting out of the corvettes at Toulon was interminable, and the crew offered him seemed unsuited for such a voyage; he had to accept young and inexperienced sailors, many of whom were to fall sick or desert. One of the men exclaimed on seeing the commander: "We won't get far with this fellow!"

Finally, on September 7, 1837, the *Astrolabe* and the *Zélée* set sail from Toulon three weeks behind schedule. On September 30, they were at Tenerife, where they remained until October 7, but they had to make an unscheduled stop at Rio de Janiero to disembark an *élève* who was very sick. As delays accumulated, the commander began to fear that he would miss the season best suited for exploring the glacial seas. In the Strait of Magellan, d'Urville set up camp at Port Famine, where he remained from December 15 to 28. The ships put out sea anchors in low waters and brought up quantities of marine animals which were studied by Hombron. For the Museum of Natural History he prepared the skin and skeleton of a cross-bearing dolphin previously described by Quoy and Gaimard. At Tierra del Fuego they saw some guanacos, the wild form of the llama. The commander took an active part in this research. When he saw the plants collected by Hombron, he recognized certain species that were in Commerson's herbarium—which he had once studied at the museum—and set himself to collecting plant specimens. "I had irrevocably promised myself to encourage all the various branches of science whenever this could be done without compromising the principal operations that had been assigned to me." This activity rejuvenated him, as the entries in his journal show.

Since the officers were disappointed at not finding any Patagonians at Port Famine, the ships left to anchor at Peckett Haven from January 5 to 18, 1838. Here the Patagonians, gentle and peaceful people, were extremely friendly. Living among them was a Swiss clockmaker who had tried to make his fortune in the United States. He had obviously failed to do so, since he had accepted the attractive offer of an American sealer, which had eventually abandoned him on this desolate coast along with six companions in misfortune. Five of them had left and never showed up again. The Swiss and an Englishman had remained among the Patagonians, who had given them wives and shared their meager existence with them. Nevertheless, the two castaways asked to be taken on board.

Confronting the ice floe

Having sailed south from Port Famine on January 8, d'Urville distributed the supplementary clothing that had been provided. The first ice appeared on January 9. A few days later, at 59° 30' S, "an immense block in the form of a triangular prism" could be seen glistening when the fog lifted. "At the sight of this unusual spectacle the sailors were greatly excited. It was, indeed, the advance guard of the formidable enemy they were to fight against." Shortly afterward, d'Urville noted: "Our task is becoming gloomy and painful." A glacial rain and melting snow fell. Some white petrels flew over the ships, which were surrounded by dorsal-finned whales. Soon there was no real night, but only a kind of twilight that lasted two hours—from 11 P.M. to 1 A.M.

Dumont d'Urville's instructions were to follow the route indicated by Weddell. "The latter's reading of 74° 15' having been accepted as authentic, there was nothing to do but see how far beyond this latitude we could penetrate." As had been agreed with the Minister of the Navy, d'Urville

Group of Patagonians from Peckett Haven, January 1838. Drawing and lithograph by A. J.-B. Bayot. Voyage au pole Sud. (Musée de la Marine, Paris. Photo by Michel Didier © Photeb.)

announced to his men that a bonus of 100 francs would be given to each of them if they got to 75° S, and a supplement of 20 francs would be added for every degree below this parallel. The ships reached 65°, where they were confronted by an impenetrable ice floe. "To the limits of the horizon on both the east and west spread an immense plain of blocks of ice piled up and jumbled together in confusion. Their average height was hardly more than four or five meters." D'Urville and his officers contemplated this "marvelous spectacle. More severe and grandiose than can be expressed, even as it lifted the imagination it filled the heart with a feeling of involuntary terror; nowhere else is one so sharply convinced of one's impotence. The image of a new world unfolds before us, but it is an inert, lugubrious, and silent world in which everything threatens the destruction of one's faculties."

The first reconnaisance of the ice floe took place on January 22, 1838. Several days later, the ships went around the South Orkneys. The polar route that Weddell claimed was open remained impenetrable, and deciding that he could go no farther south, d'Urville sailed up to the South Shetlands—a region already traversed by his predecessors but never hydrographically charted. For a month, the *Astrolabe* and the *Zélée* wandered in the ice and fog. Before leaving the area, d'Urville wanted to make an attempt to force a passage through the ice. "The sailors complained: 'Hasn't the commander had enough of this ice? When is he going to get us out of here?'"

With curiosity and excitement the crew observed the penguins skilfully swimming about; unattackable in the water, on land they looked like "old gentlemen in evening clothes." On the ice blocks the seals, "stupid and passive," emotionlessly watched what they could not understand. Among them the naturalists distinguished three species, including a new one—the crabeater seal. They also studied the still relatively unknown behavior of the giant fulmar that flew around the ships in great bands. With the help of the sailors, who caught spotted petrels, puffins, and albatross, on their return Hombron and Jacquinot were able to present an *Essai d'une classification de procellaridés* (Study for a Classification of Procellariidae).

Stirred by the boldness of a commander resolved to proceed despite all obstacles, the sailors lost their fear and became enthusiastically determined to make the expedition a success. On February 9, the *Astrolabe* was caught in the ice. "We were solidly locked in the ice pack, and the abundantly falling snow could only weld the ice together more firmly. . . . Every conceivable effort was made to move the corvette forward. . . . The crews happily leapt onto the ice and then, running out the lines, broke up and separated the ice ahead, lustily towing us forward; our two ships slowly but constantly advanced toward the open sea." Hungry after these efforts, they "feasted on seal meat, despite the fact that it is black, oily, and tough." The same maneuver worked three times, and the *Astrolabe* and the *Zélée* were able to enter and leave the floe. Nevertheless, they had not reached the latitude attained by Weddell and had not even gone beyond 65° S. They had, however, reconnoitered two new land masses: one, which was high and extended indefinitely toward the southwest, was called Terre Louis-Philippe; the other, which had a low-lying coast, was dedicated to the Prince of Joinville, one of the king's sons and the family sailor. Actually, these two land masses were part of what had already been sighted by Palmer in 1820 and Biscoe in 1831. Scurvy broke out; there were eleven victims on the *Astrolabe* and twenty-nine on the *Zélée;* all were exhausted, and the commander himself, overcome by listlessness, could swallow nothing.

On March 7, the two ships left the South

The Astrolabe *caught in an ice pack and hauled by the sailors, February 9, 1838. Watercolor by A. E. F. Meyer. (Mitchell Library, Sydney. Photo by courtesy of the Mitchell Library/Photeb.)*

Shetlands, and, on April 6, they reached the vast bay of Talcahuano in Chile, where they stayed until May 23. There were now forty scurvy cases on the *Zélée,* more than half of the crew. An English frigate, the *President,* lay at anchor in the port, and the English and French sailors feted one another. Civil war had broken out in Chile. General Freire, dictator from 1823 to 1826, had tried to seize power again and been defeated; taken prisoner, he shortly afterward went into exile. The country had also just been struck by a terrible earthquake that had destroyed Concepción, the nearby large city whose ruins d'Urville went to visit. From excursions by the naturalists into the surrounding area, Dumoutier brought back a large catch of birds, including a condor. When the ships set sail for Valparaiso, two of the scurvy victims were dead, and six who were gravely ill had to be left behind. Eight men asked to be disembarked, and eight others failed to show up and had to be considered deserters. There were therefore great gaps in the crew, and these were not

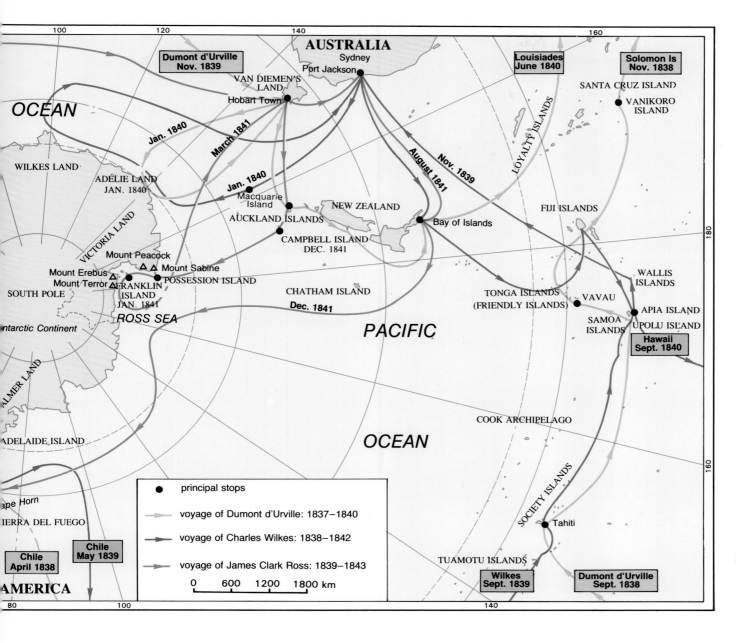

The French, Americans, and English discover the Antarctic.
2nd voyage of Dumont d'Urville, 1837–1840.
Voyage of Wilkes, 1838–1842.
Voyage of Ross, 1839–1843.

easy to fill. Arriving at Valparaiso on May 24, d'Urville found a letter from his wife; their oldest son, who was twenty, had died a month after his father's departure. Everything conspired to overwhelm him.

From Mangareva to Hobart Town

From Valparaiso to Mangareva, which the ships reached at the end of July, the crossing was painful and slow. There had been no European visitors to the Gambier Archipelago, discovered by Wilson in 1797, since the stopover made there in 1826 by Captain Beechey of the *Blossom*. D'Urville noticed with amusement that the epaulettes worn by the English officers had drawn so much attention that the natives now wore them—but tattooed on their skin. In 1834, two French priests had established the first mission at Mangareva; in 1838, it had as its head an apostolic vicar, the bishop of Ni-

lopolis. The missionaries had gotten the natives to burn their temples, so the navigators could visit only the charred ruins. As for the mission, it had become so prosperous that it had sent to Tahiti two priests, who were soon expelled by Reverend George Pritchard, the British missionary. D'Urville undertook to rectify the situation. Thanks to the welcome by the missionaries, the French stay on Mangareva was most gratifying. The commander was given an audience by Mapu-Teoa, who reigned over the island's sixteen hundred inhabitants, and attended a high Mass celebrated by the bishop on August 15. Immediately afterward, the *Astrolabe* and the *Zélée* weighed anchor; they reached Nuka Hiva, in the Marquesas, on August 26.

As had happened thirty-four years earlier to Krusenstern's ships, the French vessels were immediately surrounded by canoes filled with women eager to board the ships. The commander had anti-boarding nets spread, but the women clung to them in such stubborn clusters that, like Krusenstern, he

189

had to cede; "to console the poor creatures I had them told that I would allow them on board the ships at night." He himself was not insensible to the charms of the Marquesan women. Unfortunately, since the arrival of Westerners, many of the women were covered with hideous sores caused by venereal disease.

The *Astrolabe* and the *Zélée* dropped anchor at Tahiti on September 9, and Dumont d'Urville learned that the *Vénus* had arrived ten days earlier. Dupetit-Thouars had already taken the steps demanded by his government, and the presence of three French warships at the island incited d'Urville to support his intervention. Accompanied by their officers, the two captains therefore went to see Pomare. "In her tent, we found the queen dressed in a simple peignoir-like robe and holding her child in her arms; she was seated on a kind of rug. Near her was her husband, Prince Pomare-Tane, her aunt, her sisters, her cousins—young women, some of whom were pretty—and finally the queen's orator, a kindly faced and grave personage charged with speaking for Her Majesty, for such was the national etiquette." In a severely worded reprimand, d'Urville once again expounded France's complaints. The reply he received made it clear that Pomare was under the control of the Protestant missionaries, whose leader, Pritchard—a virulent adversary of the French—"lived like the real king of the island." This duty accomplished, it remained only to enjoy the site's pleasures. Hombron gathered numerous mollusks on the reefs, while Le Guillou completed a collection of coleoptera that was to increase at each stop.

Leaving Tahiti on September 16, the two ships dropped anchor at Apia (Upolu) in the Samoas. The island, which was covered with luxuriant vegetation, struck the sailors as being even more beautiful than Tahiti. Since the Samoas were little known, the Polynesian inhabitants, who wore extremely elaborate tattoos—though only on the thighs—were examined with great curiosity. The naturalists and the commander himself were very busy enumerating the local fauna, which was as rich as it was interesting. They captured fox bats, pigeons, beautiful red-and-green parakeets, a sort of boa that reached lengths of 3 meters, and magnificent harp shells, which were extremely common there. The last of the scurvy victims had recovered, and the crew was then in good health.

Next the ships headed southwest in order to visit Vavau, one of the Friendly Islands. There D'Urville encountered Father Thomas, whom he had known ten years earlier on Tonga, and learned what had happened to Simonet, the *Astrolabe* deserter. This rascal had threatened to kill the missionary, and Father Thomas now asked that the commander take the deserter with him. D'Urville had Chief Tahofa bring Simonet on board bound hand and foot, and then placed him in irons; but he released him shortly thereafter, thinking that the information he had acquired might be useful. Indeed, Simonet, who at his own request was put ashore two years later at the Bay of Islands in New Zealand, served as an interpreter at the following stop, Pao Island in the Fijis, where d'Urville had a painful mission to fulfill.

Four years earlier, the inhabitants of the village of Piva had murdered Captain Bureau, commander of the French ship the *Aimable Joséphine*. D'Urville now burned the village to the ground, and this act of vengeance sowed terror on the island; the inhabitants had to be convinced that this punishment having been meted out, the French remained the friends of the Kai-Viti. The population gathered on the beach, where they crouched unarmed. "The look of this assembly was truly imposing. On one side were the white-headed senators (they wore large white turbans), on the other the people in silent rows meditatively observing the results of this conference; in the middle, our rich uniforms, our weapons shining under a brilliant sun; everything contributed to an ensemble lacking in neither dignity nor grandeur." To solemnize this reconciliation, kava was ceremonially offered to the officers. Louis Le Breton made a drawing of the scene.

D'Urville then went on to complete the exploration of the archipelago begun during his previous voyage. These high lands were extremely fertile and densely populated, but decimated by the incessant wars carried on by chiefs whose power was limitless. The commander asked for news of the Fijians who had helped him ten years earlier: The charming Tambua-Nakoro, who had been his guide, had been killed in one of those battles that were most often designed to provide the victors with human flesh, the Fijians being cannibals. On the death of a chief, several of his women were immolated near his tomb; as a sign of mourning, many of his subjects would then cut off a section of a toe or finger, but this gesture was by no means disinterested since the chief's heirs would see to it that an indemnity was paid. In the Fijis, sick old people were put to

Reception of the French at Pau, in the Fiji Islands, October 1838. Lithograph by A. J.-B. Bayot after L. Le Breton. (Musée de la Marine, Paris. Photo by Michel Didier © Photeb.)

death. A pit was prepared into which the victim descended on his own and was clubbed over the head.

Continuing westward, d'Urville traversed the Santa Cruz Islands. He wanted to see Vanikoro again, but the islanders fled at his approach. On the way he reconnoitered Banks and Ndeni Islands before reaching the Solomons. Navigation was difficult because the ships were often becalmed and immobilized in suffocating heat. On November 18, they dropped anchor at Isabel Island. His predecessors having emphasized the perfidy and ferocity of the natives, d'Urville was surprised to find them so peaceable, although they seemed terrorized by the cannon and muskets. Several officers, having spent the night on shore and attended dances by the women and then by the men, brought back somewhat macabre stories picked up from a native who was otherwise extremely sympathetic. "Nothing is as delicious as the body of an enemy killed in combat, and when this happy event occurs, the Pentahi nation sings joyfully all through the night; the body is brought out and they proceed as follows: the skull is opened and the chiefs, whose palates are the most delicate, plunge bananas into the brain and eat it raw; only when there is nothing left do they begin to eat the thighs, then the hands, and then the lower belly and back. . . . Finally, what remains is turned over to the people, except for the private parts, which are spread with banana leaves and baked in an oven, then offered to the leading chiefs."

On December 22, the navigators reached the Hogoleu (Truk) Islands in the Carolines. The ships were immediately surrounded by some thirty canoes filled with eager natives making a deafening noise. The officers spent a day and a night on shore with them, where the islanders sang and danced and asked the French to do the same. The latter broke into some songs by Béranger and then into the "Marseillaise," which made a great impression. Lafond, an *élève,* began to dance, but his clothing hindered his movements and the natives insisted that he remove it. "Soon we saw him *in naturalibus,* dancing by himself among the savages." On January 1, 1839, d'Urville was again at Guam in the Marianas, where he had stopped ten years earlier. Governor Medinilla was dead, but his successor received the French courteously. Until the end of the month, they reconnoitered the Yap and Palau groups in the Carolines, and, after having stopped at Mindanao, went to Ternate, with its "delicious woods and cool, pleasant houses." The sultan gave them a reception during the course of which women dancers, all of them ugly, put on a pantomime to the accompaniment of martial music. In February, at Amboina, the French received traditional Dutch hospitality. "Every day was marked by a new celebration given in our honor." During a brief stopover at Banda, the Dutch resident gave the naturalists a dugong preserved in a hogshead of arrack, and a small black living kangaroo.

On March 27, the *Astrolabe* and the *Zélée* anchored off the north coast of Australia in Raffles

Pirogue of the Fiji islanders. Anonymous lithograph from Voyage au pole Sud. *(Musée de la Marine, Paris. Photo © the museum/Photeb.)*

Bay, then at Port Essington, where Commodore Bremen was establishing the foundations of Victoria Town. The English were most welcoming; they took the travelers on a tour of the plateau where the new town was being constructed, and made them a gift of several rare animals, including a phalanger, the flying squirrel; but the sailors were disappointed by the aridity of the countryside and even more by the hideousness of the aboriginals, who had thin limbs and big bellies. In April, d'Urville stopped at the Aru (Aroe) Islands, where Honoré Jacquinot killed a boa that was 11 feet long and whose flesh was delicious. The next stop was in Teluk Triton in New Guinea, where the tall trees reverberated with the hoarse cries of the birds of paradise and the underwood was alive with parrots, giant slow-flying calaos, and all sorts of strange and magnificent birds.

From there the French went on to Ceram in the Moluccas, and then to Macassar (Makasar) in the Celebes. On June 8, they reached Batavia, where mail was waiting for the navigators—but not the bonuses that Dumont d'Urville had requested for his officers. This increased his ill humor, and he had an attack of gout. From Batavia, the French went to Singapore and then, in July, to Borneo. They had made a brief stop there in June, and during that time H. Jacquinot had collected more than twenty species of birds, including the graceful sunbird, a little blue-headed parakeet, a black-and-vermillion flycatcher, and a rust-colored woodpecker. During this second stop the naturalists captured a large female proboscis monkey with an enormous swollen nose—a type characteristic of Borneo.

After circling in the region interminably, the *Astrolabe* and the *Zélée* went to Solo in the Philippines. The sultan had indicated that he was eager to

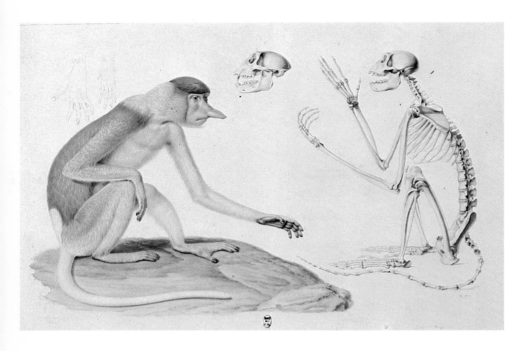

Borneo proboscis monkey brought back by the Dumont d'Urville expedition. Original drawing by J. C. Werner, 1843. (Bibliothèque du Muséum d'histoire naturelle, Paris. Photo © Bibl. du Muséum/Photeb.)

sign a commercial treaty with France, but d'Urville became aware that he had no real authority over this people who were given to plundering. The negotiations ended with nothing more than a celebration amid the tumult and excitement of the Malays. Once more passing near Borneo, the French succeeded in capturing six proboscis monkeys in the islands. The commander stopped wherever the naturalists could add to their collections, but the crew was suffering from the humid climate. In November, there were sixteen sick men on the *Astrolabe* and thirteen on the *Zélée.* "From November 1 to December 12," wrote d'Urville, "our ships were a scene of death and mourning." Four died on the *Astrolabe,* five on the *Zélée.*

With great difficulty and a sense of relief, they reached Hobart Town, the capital of Tasmania, where the governor, the celebrated seaman and explorer Sir John Franklin, received the French warmly and put a temporary hospital at their disposition. At Hobart, d'Urville met with Captain John Biscoe, who in 1831 had discovered Enderby Land and had just come from Sydney, where Charles Wilkes's American expedition was. This reinforced d'Urville's decision to once again go farther south. "One discovery remained to be made, that of the magnetic pole." The crew was decimated—the painter Goupil, not yet twenty-five, had just died—and so the commander wanted to leave with only the *Astrolabe;* but Jacquinot, insistent on following his commander to the very end, angrily objected.

Adélie Land

The two ships set sail on January 1, 1840. Those who were sickest were left behind at Hobart Town, where they were to be picked up on the way back. There were still several cases of dysentery on board and four men were lost, but then all the others recovered and it was with gaiety of heart that

the French crossed the polar circle, organizing a celebration with masks, a banquet, songs, and dances.

This time they touched on a completely different region, situated between 140° and 160° E. At about 64° S, the ships were suddenly surrounded by icebergs that seemed to have recently detached themselves from the coast. The continent must have been close, and swarms of petrels wheeled about the ships. On January 19, land was seen. It was completely covered with snow and so high that it was impossible to see the summit. Initially, the French thought they were dealing with a mirage, and it was only after several hours that everybody on board became convinced that it was really the Antarctic Continent. The corvettes had the greatest difficulty approaching the land and had to advance amid enormous floating blocks of ice that could at any moment crush and overturn them. Taking symbolic possession of the land in the name of France, d'Urville gave this coast his wife's name and called it Terre Adélie. There the naturalist found penguins with black heads and white bellies—a new species, the Adélie penguin. For several days, the ships sailed along this inhospitable coast until a storm made further navigation too dangerous. They crossed the *Porpoise,* a brig of the expedition led by Wilkes, who later accused d'Urville of failing to respond to the signals sent him. This incident was to give rise to a controversy between the French and the Americans about the priority of the discovery.

On January 30, Dumont d'Urville gave the name of Côte Clarie to a large wall of ice that was never afterward rediscovered. He had established the approximate position of the magnetic pole. "I felt that our task had been accomplished." In his account, the commander then went on to praise the behavior of all aboard, saying that they had been "courageous and enthusiastic," but he made no mention of the fact that there had been three more deaths.

On his return to the Tasmanian capital, d'Urville took the hospitalized sick men back on board. Though the city looked "extremely pleasant and animated . . . with its exquisitely clean houses," the atmosphere was made heavy by the presence of convicts. "The contempt felt and expressed by the free population for the slave population excited feelings of hate in the latter. . . ." In passing, d'Urville regretted that France had neglected its opportunities in Tasmania; it had been Baudin's expedition that had determined the English to settle there, and since the same process had just been repeated in New Zealand, he concluded: "We always arrive too late." The naturalists had brought back to the ship a carnivorous marsupial, the Tasmanian devil, that reached the Museum of Natural History alive.

The English settle in New Zealand

On February 25, the *Astrolabe* and the *Zélée* set sail for the Auckland Islands to the south of New

Zealand. There they once again met up with the Americans of the *Porpoise*. The ships then went up the coast of New Zealand and stopped in Otago Harbor. The Maoris, d'Urville wrote, "were far from having profited from contact with the whalers. In general, they were dressed in the European manner, and this costume under which they incompletely hid their lack of cleanliness made them look like beggars clothed in rags. . . . Their women, piled on the decks of these ships, indulge in almost public prostitution."

On April 29, the navigators reached the Bay of Islands. Facing their anchorage was the village of Korora-Reka, with thatch-covered cottages inhabited by English emigrants and adventurers from every country, including some from France. The commander immediately paid a visit to the Catholic mission, where he was informed of recent events. On January 29, a Captain Hobson had arrived on the corvette *Herald* with eighty soldiers and landed in the bay. The next day, he called together the inhabitants of Korora-Reka and read them a document making him governor in the name of the queen of England. Both Wilkes and d'Urville refused to recognize him. American and French interests were endangered; foreign ships which until then had anchored in the ports without charge would henceforth have to pay stiff anchorage fees. In addition, the French were called on to renounce the attempts at colonization undertaken by compatriots such as Captain Langlois de Rochefort, who had landed in New Zealand in 1840 and had bought Banks Peninsula from the Maoris.

Before leaving the Bay of Islands, the sailors attended Mass. One still saw there, wrote d'Urville, "those noble faces of warriors, whose fine and concise tattooing attested to their rank and dignity. Some of these men were draped in large mats of New Zealand flax covered with dog skins." This was the traditional Maori costume, which was no longer in use. As the commander was going aboard ship, a native offered him two kiwis. He had first seen these strange birds, prehistorical survivors incapable of flight, in Tolaga Bay in 1827, but had been unable to procure any. He considered it a stroke of fortune to be able to take back a species that was still unknown in France.

The *Astrolabe* and the *Zélée* were now on the way home. D'Urville reconnoitered and named several islands in the Loyalty group and the Louisiades. In the redoubted Torres Strait, the corvettes became stuck on reefs, and, as a precaution, supplies and the natural history collections were unloaded. When the sea rose, however, the ships were able to break loose and continue on their way. The exhausted crew needed rest badly, and for several days in June d'Urville anchored in Kupang Bay, Timor. From there he headed first for Bourbon Island and then for St. Helena, where several weeks later the Prince of Joinville was to come to pick up Napoleon's coffin.

On November 7, 1840, the two ships entered the roads of Toulon. Dumont d'Urville could con-

New Zealand kiwis brought back to France by Dumont d'Urville. Drawing and lithograph by J. and E. Gould for Birds of Australia 1840– 1848. (Bibliothèque du Muséum d'histoire naturelle, Paris. Photo © Bibl. du Muséum/Photeb.)

gratulate himself on having scrupulously carried out his instructions. True, he had not been able to penetrate the Antarctic Continent, and his discovery of Adélie Land was contested by Wilkes; however, it could be established that the latter had arrived in the area several days after the French. The cost of the voyage had been high; there had been more than twenty deaths aboard ship, not counting those who died after being left at ports of call, and twenty-one crew members who had deserted; but the scientific results obtained in every category were highly praised by men of learning.

Dumont d'Urville had won his bet. He was not yet fifty when he was made rear admiral a month after his return. Jacquinot was promoted to captain. D'Urville immediately set to work preparing an account of the discoveries made during the voyage. The natural history collections, richer than any brought back by any other single expedition, included numerous mammals and marsupials, some proboscis monkeys, the Samoan flying fox, spiny anteaters, several kangaroos, some seals, some dolphins, and other cetaceans whose skins and skeletons had been preserved, three hundred different species of birds among the seven hundred collected, 160 species of reptiles and four hundred of fish, thirteen hundred species of insects, and finally numerous marine invertebrates of all kinds.

Dumont d'Urville had just written the first three volumes of the history of the voyage and begun the fourth when he was suddenly struck down by death, after having so often narrowly escaped it. On May 8, 1842, on his way to Versailles with his wife and second son, he and they perished in a railway accident at Bellevue. This pointless death caused great excitement. A few days later there was an official funeral attended by two admirals and eleven rear admirals. Jacquinot, who had just been given the command of the *Généreux,* had to give it up and devote himself to the publication of the *Voyage au pole Sud et dans l'Océanie* (Voyage to the South Pole and Oceania), which took until 1854 and was the largest of its type: twenty-three octavo volumes and seven folio atlases; largely due to Prêtre, Oudart, and Prévost, the plates of the natural history atlases were the most successful work in the genre. The history of the voyage was completed by the hydrographer of the *Astrolabe,* Vincendon–Dumoulin, who also wrote the volumes devoted to physics and hydrography. However, one of the members of the team refused to participate. The surgeon of the *Zélée,* Elie Le Guillou, given the responsibility for the entomological collections, had not gotten along well with his leader. On his return, he published an account of the voyage in which he violently attacked him; he was no more flattering to his companions, who unfailingly answered in kind.

Giant clam shells set out by Torres Strait natives in order to collect rain water; the trees are screw pines. (Musée de la Marine, Paris. Photo © the museum/Photeb.)

The first American voyage around the world, 1838–1842

During the course of his long voyage, Dumont d'Urville had crossed the ships of Lieutenant Charles Wilkes, who had left Norfolk, in Chesapeake Bay, on August 18, 1838. At the instigation of its ninth president, Andrew Jackson, the United States, home to increasing numbers of immigrants from England and Ireland, initiated an expansionist policy. The pioneers were slowly invading the Western half of America and the Indians were systematically being expelled; Texas, which until then had been Mexican, had proclaimed its independence and was immediately recognized by the United States, which was preparing to annex it. Henceforth, the government was to protect the enterprises of its nationals anywhere in the world.

For some time, American whalers and sealers had been exploiting the resources of the southern hemisphere, and on several occasions ships had penetrated the Antarctic. It was now felt that the time had come to challenge France and England and to establish American rights in the area. Congress decided to dispatch an expedition. The Secretary of the Navy, Mahlon Dickerson, gave command of it to Lieutenant Wilkes, who had already sailed the South Seas and commanded the *Vincennes,* a 780-ton sloop of war that had been transformed into a "small frigate" for the expedition. This appointment, which surprised Wilkes himself, was sorely contested. Wilkes was not always equal to the situation, and his officers found it difficult to tolerate his impetuous and authoritarian behavior.

The expedition, to which six ships had been assigned, was provided with exceptional scientific support. There were six scientists, a gardener, a taxidermist, and even an instrument maker on the *Vincennes.* Another sloop of war, the 650-ton *Peacock,* carried a second team, which included a geologist, a naturalist, and a philologist. On the *Relief* there were a botanist and a painter, and this brought to twelve the number of scientists and draftsmen. There were, in addition, a 32-ton brig, the *Porpoise,* and two schooners, the 110-ton *Sea Gull* and the 96-ton *Flying Fish.* Nevertheless, this powerful expedition had been badly organized. The ships chosen for it proved ill adapted for such a voyage; none of them had been adequately protected against ice and rough seas, and large open portholes and gunports permitted the entry of icy Antarctic waters. In addition, Wilkes was to com-

Lupus gigas *and* Lupus occidentalis. *Plate by T. R. Peale for* The U.S. Exploring Expedition, *edition of 1858. These are in fact two large types of the common wolf. (Bibliothèque du Muséum d'histoire naturelle, Paris. Photo © Bibl. du Muséum/Photeb.)*

plain bitterly about the shoddiness of the clothing meant to protect the sailors against the Antarctic cold.

While the *Relief* went directly to Rio de Janeiro, the other ships made their first call (September 16) at Funchal, Madeira, where the naturalists immediately set to work, then at Port Praia in the arid Cape Verde Islands.

On November 24, the American flotilla reached Rio, leaving on January 6, 1839, for Viedma, at the mouth of the Rio Negro in Argentina, and, by way of Le Maire Strait, Tierra del Fuego. There, on February 16, Wilkes established at Orange Harbor, not far from Cape Horn, a camp that was to serve as a base for the expedition during its first cruise in the Antarctic regions. The nesting season was in full swing, and numerous small Magellan penguins had gathered there busily plucking feathers from one another; when they were disturbed in this occupation, they unhesitatingly attacked the sailors. The naturalists were also able to study the sheathbills, all white with large yellow beaks, which were very trusting. They captured a leopard seal, some geese, and some plovers, and they killed two Magellan wolves, a male and a female.

195

Wilkes's Ships and Crews

left: 8/18/1838, from Norfolk;
returned: 8/9/1842, to New York;
total of crews: 83 officers, 12 civilians, 345 men, 240 replacements;
deaths: 23;
deserters: 127;
disembarked: 88.

The *VINCENNES:* 780-ton sloop of war.

Commander: Lieutenant Charles Wilkes, commanding the expedition.

Lieutenants: Thomas T. Craven, Overton Carr, Robert E. Johnston, James Alden, William L. Maury (the 3 1st lieutenants in turn took over several commands during the course of the voyage).

Scientific team: Charles Pickering, naturalist; Joseph Drayton, draftsman; J. D. Brackenridge, gardener and assistant botanist; John G. Brown, scientific instrument maker; John W. W. Dyer, assistant taxidermist; Joseph P. Couthouy, naturalist, left at Sydney.

The *PEACOCK:* 650-ton sloop of war, shipwrecked 7/18/1841.

Commander: Lieutenant William L. Hudson.

Scientific team: James D. Dana, mineralogist; T. R. Peale, naturalist; Horatio Hale, philologist; F. L. Davenport, interpreter.

The *RELIEF:* transport ship, new supply vessel sent from Callao, June 1839.

Commander: Lieutenant A. K. Long.

Scientific team: William Rich, botanist; Alfred T. Agate, draftsman.

The *PORPOISE:* 32-ton brig.

Commander: Lieutenant Cadwallader Rhinggold.

The *SEA GULL:* 110-ton schooner, disappeared off Cape Horn about 5/1/1839.

The *FLYING FISH:* 96-ton schooner, sold at Singapore in February 1842.

On February 25, at Orange Harbor, the expedition split up. The *Peacock* and the *Flying Fish* headed west—to the areas where, in 1773, Cook had been the first to pass 60° S—to see if the ice wall had advanced since that time. The *Vincennes* remained at Orange Harbor while Wilkes, with the *Porpoise* and the *Sea Gull,* left to explore the Antarctic Sea between the South Orkneys and Palmer Land. He charted 30 miles of the coast until the cape that he named Hope, then visited the South Shetlands, following more or less the same route that Dumont d'Urville had taken the previous year but going farther down to 69° S. Pushing toward the west, Wilkes followed the route taken by Weddell, but at about 100° W, he too found himself faced by an impenetrable wall of ice. The weather remained good during the thirty-six days (March–April 1839) of this voyage.

On her own, the *Porpoise* then went up the coast of South America as far as Valparaiso, where she stopped from May 15 to May 29. When Wilkes had been there in 1821, it was no more than an overgrown village of six thousand; now the city had thirty thousand inhabitants. Order reigned, and crime was always punished. Manufactured goods from Great Britain, the United States, and France could be found in the shops. Using Santiago as a base, the naturalists made excursions into the Andes and brought back some guanacos and several species of little-known birds. At Valparaiso, Wilkes learned that the *Relief* had lost her anchors and had had to go to Callao. She was such a wretched ship that the leader of the expedition ordered her to re-

turn to the United States by way of the Sandwich Islands and Sydney, where she was to disembark supplies destined for the other ships. In the meantime, the *Vincennes* and the *Flying Fish* had reached Valparaiso, but not the *Sea Gull,* which had disappeared off Cape Horn on about May 1 and was never to be seen again. The expedition made a long stop at Callao, from May 30 to July 6. Wilkes went to Lima, which the Chileans had treacherously invaded two years earlier while Bolivia was again separating from Peru. Despite this, the atmosphere there was peaceful. The naturalists visited the impressive ruins of the Pachacamac temples and then left to explore the high Inca country, where they ran into caravans of llamas.

On July 13, the *Vincennes,* the *Peacock,* the *Porpoise,* and the *Flying Fish* left Callao for the Tuamotus. Wilkes read his instructions to the men: They were in no way to trouble the customs and beliefs of the Oceanic peoples or to make any show of superiority to them. Arriving at Clermont-Tonnerre (Reao) Island on August 13, the four ships landed at Serle (Pukarua), a miniscule coral islet, and then at the group making up Byron's Disappointment Islands, twenty-eight in all. The rejection given them by the islanders was far from friendly. At Whytohee, the Americans were prevented from disembarking until they were authorized to do so by old Chief Koroja, who came on board. At Raraka, Wilkes was amazed to find a Tahitian preaching the Bible. He estimated that the total population of this multitude of islands could not be more than ten thousand. Nature there was rich, and an incredible number of birds were found. Frigate birds' nests covered the branches of the trees, and the air was criss-crossed by swarms of gannets, tropic birds, and terns. Busy bands of crabs circulated on the beaches, and enormous sharks swam near the shore. The naturalists discovered several species of snakes, magnificent reef fish, some large eels, thick-shelled mollusks, some spiders, and some rare butterflies.

In September, the four ships entered Matavai Bay in Tahiti. Queen Pomare, who was pregnant, lived in retirement, and the Americans were received by Tana, governor of the Matavai district, and by Reverend Wilson, who took them to visit the Protestant missions. Wilkes was gratified by the work of the missionaries, thanks to whom the Tahitians were finally decently clothed. Consul Blackle asked him to intervene with the authorities: Tahitians had captured an American ship whose crew had been mistreated, and they refused to turn over to their commanders the many sailors who had deserted. When Wilkes called together a council of chiefs, the latter profited from the occasion to complain about the power exercised over the queen by the English missionaries and their leader, George Pritchard. The next stop was Eimeo, and, compared to Tahiti, this island seemed still savage. There the Americans were the guests of Reverend Simpson and his wife, who headed a missionary school.

The *Porpoise* had already left to explore that part of the ocean between the Society Islands and the Samoas. The *Vincennes* joined her in October at Rose Island, and then went to Tutuila and Olo-Onuga, where the old chief greeted Wilkes by rubbing the back of his hand over his nose. These islands also abounded in sea birds, and the naturalists made large catches. Wilkes noted with satisfaction that the English missionary residing there, a man of great piety, saw to it that the Sabbath was strictly observed. As for the *Porpoise,* after having disembarked at Savaii the officers assigned to observe the tides, she dropped anchor at Upolu, where the *Peacock* and the *Flying Fish* joined her. Despite their reputation resulting from the massacre of de Langle during the La Pérouse expedition, the Samoans struck the Americans as being cheerful, intelligent, hospitable, and eager to be helpful.

Having completed the reconnaisance of the Samoas, the little squadron sailed for Sydney, where Wilkes, who was supplied with excellent maps, decided he could do without the services of a pilot. On the morning of November 29, the inhabitants of Port Jackson were surprised to find four anchored ships flying the American flag. Wilkes had to apologize to the governor, Sir George Cripps, for conduct so little in keeping with custom. Sydney seemed just like a growing American city to him; it boasted 24,000 inhabitants, and the colony as a whole had a population of 120,000. Unfortunately, drunkenness was widespread, and little attempt was made to hide it.

The second exploration of the Antarctic

Before heading south in order to reach the lowest possible latitude, the expedition's commander put his scientists ashore at Sydney. The naturalist Joseph Couthouy was dismissed, and the geologist James D. Dana was given responsibility for research into marine fauna. The weather was fine and the winds favorable, but on January 2, 1840, they ran into fog and the ships were separated. Several days later, they joined up again at the Macquarie Islands. Among the myriads of birds that inhabited it were penguins—yellow-crested rock hoppers who looked like "an army of Lilliputian soldiers." On January 10, at 61° 8′ S and 162° 32′ E, the first icebergs appeared. At 64°, a vast plateau of ice was seen, its steep slopes forming an unbroken wall. Wilkes was the first to be convinced that it was a continent. On January 23, the *Vincennes* went on alone into a large indentation in the coast that was named Disappointment Bay since they had hoped it would penetrate farther. The *Peacock,* having lost her anchors, collided with an iceberg. Captain Hudson barely managed to avoid catastrophe, but the damage was so extensive that the sloop had to be sent back to Sydney, where everyone was amazed that she had been able to sail in such condition. From the very beginning of the cruise, the *Flying Fish* had been unable to meet the demands of the weather and had given up the attempt to follow the other ships.

However, the *Vincennes* and the *Porpoise* continued their exploration, running into several storms that put them at the mercy of icebergs and often finding themselves caught in the ice. In the sea swam numerous whales, in the air circled the gray and the spotted petrels from the Cape, and on the ice the penguins were drawn up—a giant-sized king pen-

"King Zeapot and His Two Wives." Drawing done by George F. Emmons in New South Wales during the Wilkes expedition. (Yale University, New Haven. Photo © Beinecke Rare Books and Manuscripts Library, Yale University/Photeb.)

guin was caught. On January 29, the Americans entered a bay in which they were able to land on exposed rock and take samples of basalt and red sandstone. The next day, the *Porpoise* saw two chips: They were the *Astrolabe* and the *Zélée*. At about 100° W, the *Vincennes* and the *Porpoise* came to the very spot at which, in 1773, Cook had been stopped by a wall of ice; beyond, it swung to the north. There were fifteen men sick from exhaustion on board the *Vincennes,* and Wilkes, feeling it would only be a waste of precious time to continue west, decided to head for New Zealand, where a rendezvous with the entire squadron had been arranged.

He went by way of Sydney, where he found the *Peacock* being repaired, and he gave orders for her to go directly to Tongatapu, where all the ships were to meet in April. After giving his crew a month of rest, on March 19, he left for the Bay of Islands, where the *Flying Fish* and the *Porpoise* were waiting. The latter had on the way stopped at the Auckland Islands, where she had met up with Dumont d'Urville's expedition. The officers of the two ships had arrived at the Bay of Islands just in time to witness the ceremonies accompanying the signing by the Maori chiefs of the treaty that placed them under the rule of the English lieutenant-governor, Hobson. However, when Wilkes arrived, he decided not to recognize this arrangement, which seriously threatened American commerce in New Zealand.

On April 22, the *Vincennes* arrived in the Friendly Islands and anchored first off Eua and then at Tongatapu. Wilkes visited the Protestant missions established there since 1829 and was hospitably received by a chief known as King George, a dignified, athletic type. The *Porpoise* and then the *Peacock* having rejoined the *Vincennes,* they sailed to the Fijis, which they explored for four months (May 6–August 11, 1840). Wilkes's men were charmed by the Fijians, who were even handsomer than the inhabitants of Tongatapu. Though the common people were thin, badly nourished, and enslaved, the chiefs were tall, well built, and demonstrated a love of finery. Their hair, kept in order by a personal barber, was a sort of "immense wig"; anyone bold enough to copy the style was immediately put to death. On Totoya Island, there was a surprise encounter with a white man named David Whippy, who, to escape the treatment he had been subjected to on a ship—despite the fact that it was commanded by his own brother—had sought refuge on the island. He had been living there for eighteen years, serving as a royal messenger, and was highly considered by the chiefs. Nevertheless, he warned the Americans against the Fijians, whom he described as thieving, treacherous, fierce, and withal very cowardly. This judgment seemed unjust until the day when a *Vincennes* cutter was attacked without provocation; two officers were killed and several men were wounded. After carrying out reprisals, the expedition left the Fijis on August 10. The naturalists had made some fine harvests, particularly their capture of some superbly colored fruit

doves, genus *Ptilnopus*.

On September 22, the ships reached Oahu Island in the Sandwich Islands. Since they had been looking forward to finding a "perfect garden," the Americans were disappointed by the look of this bare and rocky island. Wilkes was received by Kamehameha III, a distinguished and courtly man elegantly dressed in a blue jacket and white pants of European manufacture; he was eager to have his power officially recognized by the Westerners.

At Oahu, the ships separated once again. The *Vincennes* went to the other islands of the archipelago, whose volcanoes were visited by the officers and scientists; setting up a camp on the edge of the Mauna Loa crater, they spent three weeks there. Meanwhile, the *Porpoise,* which had sailed for the Tuamotus on November 16, was mapping islands whose position was uncertain and charting the ocean bottom. In January 1841, after a stop at Tahiti, she visited Flint and Penrhyn Islands. In December 1840, the *Peacock* and the *Flying Fish* once again stopped in the Samoas, completing their hydrographic mission and naming several islands; they then went to the Gilbert and Ellice Islands south of the Fijis. On April 5, 1841, all the ships were together and set sail for the North American coast along with the brig *Wave,* which was loaded with supplies.

Some Americans discover America

Cape Disappointment was sighted on April 28, and the squadron went to the head of the Columbia River but was unable to cross the bar created by a line of reefs. They therefore dropped anchor at Port Discovery in Juan de Fuca Strait, which separates the Olympic Peninsula from Vancouver Island. This region, which now forms the border between the United States and Canada, was at the time almost unknown. Only a few nomadic Indians lived in the area. Wilkes had been ordered to explore these territories, which were coveted by the United States. Once again, the expedition split up into reconnaisance groups with different missions. One unit went up the Columbia River until the first falls, about 120 miles from its mouth. On July 18, the *Peacock* having been wrecked in Juan de Fuca Strait, Wilkes raced to her aid and found that the crew had taken refuge at Astoria. To replace this ship, he bought the *Oregon,* a brig that had been stationed at the entrance to the Columbia.

Then the *Vincennes* set out for San Francisco, where the much-weakened Spanish missions were suffering from the aftershock of events in the mother country. After a lengthy stay had made it clear that this port "could become one of the best if not the best port in the world," the ship went up the Sacramento. During this time, a detachment was traversing the vast area between the Columbia and the Sacramento, an exhausting undertaking that nevertheless made it possible to gather precise information about this part of Oregon and that also enriched the natural history collections.

By October 28, the different teams were back in San Francisco, and the expedition set sail for Honolulu so that the men might rest up in a better climate. The ships separated on leaving the Sandwich Islands, then joined up again at Manila on January 13, 1842. On the way, the expedition had reconnoitered an isolated island to the north of the Marshalls and named it Wake. (It was, in fact, San Francisco Island, discovered by Mendaña in 1529.) After exploring a new volcano in the Philippines, the Taal—celebrated for its frequent eruptions—the Americans signed with the sultan of Solo a commercial treaty similar to the one Dumont d'Urville had given up on three years earlier. The sultan was a slender man with betel-blackened teeth and eyes bloodshot from the abuse of opium. The terrible effects of opium were seen even more clearly when they visited Singapore, where they spent a month (Jan. 19–Feb. 26, 1842). The opium dens were a "disgusting spectacle" from which staggered haggard addicts whose health had been sapped. On the other hand, the Americans were amazed by the activity of the port, into which crowded European and Oriental ships. Along the streets they saw a strange mixture of peoples—Chinese, Armenians, Parsees from India, Arabs, and Kaffirs. The naturalists obtained numerous specimens of exotic flora, including two species of insectivorous plants belonging to the genus *Nepenthes*. The *Flying Fish,* in too wretched a state to make the return journey to America, was sold at Singapore; finally, after an eventful voyage that had lasted almost four years, the *Vincennes,* the *Porpoise,* and the *Oregon* arrived in New York on August 9, 1842.

The expedition had lost three out of six ships; of the 345 men who had set sail, only 221 returned home: twenty-three were dead, forty-seven had deserted, and sixty-two had been disembarked in different ports. To replace the missing, 240 men had been taken on, but only 126 of these reached New York. There had been 127 desertions—22 percent of the crews.

Scientifically, the expedition had been a success, as the twenty volumes of the *United States Expedition* published between 1845 and 1876 were to demonstrate. It had made first-rate contributions not only in geography, hydrography, and physics, but also in geology, mineralogy, zoology, botany—the plant collection included more than five thousand species—and finally anthropology. The most remarkable studies had been done by Dana, who devoted fourteen years to their publication. Not only did he write the geology and the two volumes on mollusks, but, in 1846, he published *Zoophytes,* an in-depth study. He had, indeed, brought back 261 actinoid zoophytes (Coelenterata), almost all (203)

new species, and 483 coral zoophytes (229 new species). Thanks to the Wilkes expedition, Dana had become one of the greatest naturalists of his time, just as had Darwin on the *Beagle,* not long since.

Yet Wilkes's troubles were by no means over. The loss of his three ships had already made a bad impression. On his return, he was immediately accused by his collaborators—Lieutenant Robert F. Pinkney, commander of the *Flying Fish;* Dr. Charles F. Guillou, surgeon of the *Porpoise*—for failures in conducting the expedition, abuse of power, and false declarations as to his discoveries in the Antarctic, which were strongly contested by Dumont d'Urville and James Clark Ross. Wilkes was court-martialed but acquitted. He was later to distinguish himself during the course of the Civil War, when he commanded the James River flotilla that destroyed City Point. Promoted to rear admiral, Wilkes retired in 1866 and died eleven years later at the age of seventy-nine.

La Pérouse's fruit doves captured at Upolu (Samoas) by naturalists of the Wilkes expedition. Watercolor by T. R. Peale. (Bibliothèque du Muséum d'histoire naturelle, Paris. Photo © Bibl. du Muséum/Photeb.)

James Clark Ross:
The *Erebus* and the *Terror*, 1839–1843

Portrait of Captain James Clark Ross by John R. Wildman. (National Maritime Museum, London. Photo © the museum/Photeb.)

Though the English were the last to set out, they were the best prepared. Endowed with somewhat romantic names—Erebus was the Greek hell—the *Erebus* and the *Terror* had been specially built for navigation in the polar seas. The ships were small, slow, and heavy; they had sturdy hulls, decks of double planking, and watertight bulkheads that would prevent flooding in case of collision with an iceberg. The expedition thus enjoyed a freedom of maneuver not available to its predecessors, but, most important, it was commanded by a man whose entire life had been spent at sea.

Nephew of Captain John Ross, who had distinguished himself by his discoveries in the Arctic, James Clark Ross already had a well-established scientific reputation, and he was also considered "the handsomest man in the Royal Navy." At eighteen, he had accompanied his uncle and Lieutenant W. E. Parry on their 1818 voyage to discover a passage between the Atlantic and the Pacific. From 1819 to 1827, he had taken part in Parry's four cruises and in the search for this passage, and then, in 1828–1833, in his uncle's second expedition. The *Victory*, immobilized on the coast of the Boothia Peninsula, had spent three winters there; after that, the crew had had to abandon her and go by boat to Lancaster Sound, where, by chance, they were picked up by a whaler and brought back to England in 1833.

On May 31, 1831, James Clark Ross had determined the exact position of the magnetic North Pole that had been so long looked for. It was in the Boothia Peninsula, some 1,000 miles from the geographic North Pole. Perfectly aware of the difficulties he would encounter, Ross saw to it that his crew was provided with warm, weatherproof clothing, and that the ship was provisioned with adequate quantities of preserved food. Before leaving England, he had met with John Balleny, the commander of a sealer, who had recently discovered a group of islands beyond the Antarctic Circle and had found the sea free of ice until 69° S.

Ross's second in command, Francis R. M. Crozier, appointed commander of the *Terror,* had been with him on Parry's third cruise in 1824–1825. Having been the naturalist on his previous voyages, Ross had become an "accomplished zoologist," and, in 1823, he had discovered the very rare Ross's gull in the Arctic. During the new expedition, he was personally to assemble large natural

history collections with the help of the two surgeons, Robert McCormick on the *Erebus* and John Robertson on the *Terror*. The botanical work was turned over to two twenty-two-year-old scientists, David Lyall and Joseph Dalton Hooker. The latter was the son of the botanist William Jackson Hooker, who, in 1841, was to become the director of the celebrated Kew Gardens. J. D. Hooker was also a friend of Darwin; the latter, on the return of the *Beagle,* had consulted with him about the publication of his Voyage. An excellent physicist, Ross had studied magnetism in Great Britain in the three preceding years, and he was given the responsibility of making observations on the variations of the magnetic needle in different parts of the globe.

When the *Erebus* and the *Terror* set sail from Chatham, a military port near London, on September 19, 1839, Dumont d'Urville was in Java and Wilkes in Tahiti. After stopovers in Madeira and Porto Praia, the expedition reached St. Helena on January 13, 1840, and spent a month there while Ross made his first magnetic readings, which were continued at Cape Town from March 16 to April 6. The navigators next went to the Kerguelen Islands. Off Marion Island, Hooker encountered the "first botanical phenomenon" of the voyage: the extraordinary abundance in the sea of *Macrocystis pyrifera,* giant algae that were up to 50 meters long. On May 8, the English dropped anchor at Christmas Harbour, where, until July 20, they made the first complete exploration of the Kerguelens. The naturalists studied the life of colonies of emperor penguins—the largest of the genus—that weighed an average of 30 kilos. Several were captured and brought back to England, where a precise identification of the species could be made. A few months later, Ross was to discover two other species, much smaller, at the Campbell Islands: the Papuan penguin of the Macquaries and, in the Antarctic, the Victoria rock hopper, which had a small yellow crest and a red beak.

On August 16, Ross reached Hobart Town, where he was welcomed by Sir John Franklin. Neither man could guess that five years later Franklin would in turn leave with the *Erebus* and the *Terror* and never return. At Hobart Town, Ross learned that Dumont d'Urville had just discovered Adélie Land and Wilkes a part of what he called the Antarctic Continent. The American made available to

James Clark Ross's Ships and Crews

The *EREBUS:* 370-ton vessel, armed with new-model large-caliber mortars.
left from Chatham, 9/19/1839;
returned to Folkestone, 9/4/1843;
crew: 64 officers, sailors, and soldiers.

Commander: James Clark Ross, captain.

Lieutenants: Edward Joseph Bird, John Sibbald, James F. L. Wood.

Purser: Thomas R. Hallett.

Master: Charles T. Tucker.

Assistant master: Henry B. Yule

Midshipmen: Alexander J. Smith, Henry Oakeley, Joseph Dayman.

Surgeon: Robert McCormick, responsible for zoology and geology.

Assistant surgeon: Joseph D. Hooker, responsible for botany.

The *TERROR:* 340-ton vessel;
left from Chatham, 9/19/1839;
returned to Folkestone, 9/4/1843;
crew: 64 officers, sailors, and soldiers.

Commander: Francis Rawdon Moira Crozier, captain.

Lieutenants: Archibald McMurdo, Charles G. Phillips, Joseph W. Kay.

Master: Pownall P. Cotter.

Assistant master: John E. Davis, draftsman.

Midshipmen: Peter A. Scott, Thomas E. L. Moore, William Molloy.

Surgeon: John Robertson, responsible for zoological and geological research.

Assistant surgeon: David Lyall, responsible for botanical research.

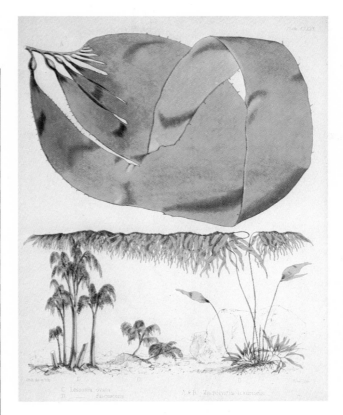

Giant seaweed collected by J. D. Hooker in the Antarctic Ocean. Macrocystis luxurians *(above and bottom right),* Lessonia ovata *(center), and* Lessonia frutescens *(left). Drawing and lithograph by Fitch in* The Zoology of the Voyage of H.M.S. Erebus *and* Terror. *(Scott Polar Research Institute, Cambridge. Photo © Scott Polar Research Institute/Photeb.)*

his English rival the map he had drawn of it. Ross was in a somewhat embarrassing situation, for it was precisely in that region that he hoped, according to his calculations, to find the magnetic pole. He decided to sail farther to the east than his predecessors had, and he was not to regret this decision.

Ross planned things so as to make excellent use of the three months he was to spend in Tasmania. Eager to set up the permanent observatory, he was overjoyed to find that the materials needed in its construction had been ready for several months. Nor did Hooker waste his time. He made a more or less complete inventory of Tasmanian flora, which was known only through the collections made by Robert Brown thirty-five years earlier. Thanks to the help of two Englishmen who had settled in Tas-

mania—William Archer and Ronald Campbell Gunn—Hooker identified 1,203 species, the best known of which was the *Eucalyptus gunnii.* On November 12, the *Erebus* and the *Terror* began their descent toward the south, stopping at the Auckland Islands and then at the Campbell Islands, two archipelagos situated between New Zealand and the Antarctic Ocean. On the principal Auckland Island, which was mountainous and woody, Hood identified 370 plant species, most of which were unknown; seals and wattled cormorants were found there also.

Sailing through a sea thick with floating ice, the ships crossed the Antarctic Circle on January 1, 1841. Colliding with masses of ice that had all but destroyed Wilkes's ships, they valiantly continued beyond where the French and Americans had had to stop. At about 60° 32′ S, they reached the edge of an ice floe that rose to about 60 meters above the water. However, it did not rest on land, since the bottom could not be found at 410 fathoms; "no doubt it was only attached to land at its sides." Moving out to sea, the ships once again found the ice floe somewhat farther east and sailed alongside it, but wind and currents soon pushed them toward the ice. Penetrating the pack, they managed to break the crust and sail some 200 miles through previously inaccessible regions. On January 9, the open sea appeared before them; no land was in sight.

Ross gave the order to continue full southwest in the hope of reaching the magnetic pole. On January 11, the officer of the watch reported land ahead of the *Erebus.* Soon they could see mountains completely covered with perpetual snow and rising from 2,000 to 3,000 meters above sea level. In some spots, the glaciers that descended from the sum-

Eucalyptus gunnii *species discovered in Tasmania by J. D. Hooker. Drawing and lithograph by Fitch. The Botany of the Voyage of* H.M.S. Erebus *and* Terror.*(Bibliothèque du Muséum d'histoire naturelle, Paris. Photo © Bibl. du Muséum/Photeb.)*

mits and filled the valleys advanced several miles into the sea. The highest, which was more than 3,700 meters, was called Mount Sabine in honor of the physicist with whom Ross had studied the magnetism of Great Britain. The ships reached 71° 15′ S.

Victoria Land

The next day, favored by the weather, they managed to approach a little island. The shores were covered with ice, but after a great deal of effort Ross and a detachment managed to land. The island was named Possession Island. Accompanied by Captain Crozier, as a crowd of fascinated penguins looked on, Ross claimed this coastal zone for Great Britain and baptized it Victoria Land in honor of the young queen of England. As mountains appeared while the ships sailed along the east coast and continued their way south, Ross gave them names: Peacock, in honor of Wilkes; and then Whetwell and Lloyd, for the scientists; and Robinson, for the admiral of that name. The *Erebus* and the *Terror* had already beaten Weddell's record and were still continuing south. On January 27, the navigators were able to land at 76° 8′ S and 168° 12′ E on a volcanic island which was named in homage to Sir John Franklin. January 28, on another island, they came upon a high mountain from the summit of which escaped sudden jets of flame and black smoke; at intervals, the smoke would disperse and they could see the completely denuded crater. The sailors were amazed by this active volcano in the middle of the ice. It was named Mount Erebus, and the nearby extinct crater was called Mount Terror; the island was called Ross Island.

The ships were following along the north shore of this island in hopes of finding a passage toward the magnetic pole when, to the east, a low white line extending as far as the eye could see came into view. "It presented an extraordinary appearance, gradually increasing in height as we got nearer to it, and proving at length to be a perpendicular cliff of ice, between one hundred and fifty and two hundred feet above the level of the sea, perfectly flat and level at the top, and without any fissures or promontories on its even seaward face." Ross had just discovered what is now known as the Ross Ice Shelf, a more or less impenetrable obstacle consisting of an immense floating platform, from 200 to 300 meters thick, from which icebergs flat as tables detached themselves. He followed the barrier for more than 600 kilometers and reached 78° 4′ S, the highest latitude he was to achieve. After that one could go no farther south. Ross noted in his journal: "We might with equal chance of success try to sail through the cliffs of Dover, as to penetrate such a mass." He turned east in hopes of finding a passage, but, on February 5, the ice made all movement impossible and the ships had to return in the direction of Victoria Land. On February 17, they reached 76° 12′ S and 164° E. They were no more than 160 miles from the magnetic pole, but on that day, Ross had to give up hopes of reaching it.

Ascending north, the expedition went to reconnoiter the islands John Balleny had discovered in 1839. On March 4, it was near the land that Wilkes had called the Antarctic Continent, but, on March 6, reaching the area where the American navigator had reported a mountain chain, the English found only the open sea; Ross was convinced that Wilkes had been the victim of a mirage. On April 6, the *Erebus* and the *Terror* were at Tasmania, where the crew was able to rest for three months. During the course of this first Antarctic cruise, McCormick and Robertson had captured unknown sea birds—among them the Antarctic fulmar—and several species of seals, including the crabeater, the Weddell seal, and the Ross seal, which was not rediscovered again until 1898 and has since been only rarely captured. Hooker had everywhere made a detailed inventory and was able to describe eighteen Antarctic plants, none of which had flowers.

At Port Jackson, where the expedition remained from July 14 to August 5, the naturalists worked with colleagues on the site and were able to bring aboard several Australian rodents belonging to the genera *Conilurus* and *Leporillus,* and an especially fine collection of lizards, including the giant varan—which was more than 2 meters long—the mangrove varan, the rough-necked varan, and spiny and rugose skinks. But the find that was to set the scientific world agog was not made until a little later, in New Zealand: the *Sphenodon punctuatum,* the tuatara of the Maoris, a large lizard having a crest formed of mobile scales and which is actually a living fossil, the only animal that has more or less retained intact the anatomical characteristics of reptiles of the Permian Period (primary era). At Dusky Sound in New Zealand's South Island, another strange animal had been discovered—the kakapo or owl parrot, which is almost incapable of flight and lives a withdrawn life in the forested mountains. In New Zealand, where the ships anchored in the Bay of Islands from August 18 to November 23, Hooker, with the aid of the missionary and botanist William Collenso, gathered 1,767 plants, thus breaking the record of all his predecessors. In the Bay of Islands, as in Sydney, Ross pursued his magnetic observations.

In December 1841, the *Erebus* and the *Terror* once again left for the south. Having crossed the Antarctic Circle, they returned to the ice floe. Despite the circumstances, the New Year was greeted by all with confidence and enthusiasm. The men spent half the day in various games on the ice, and the celebration closed with an imaginative great ball on the ice. If his friends in England had been able to see them, Ross wrote, they would have thought themselves—and in a sense it was true—in the presence of a joyous band. Hooker and Davis had sculpted an ice statue of Venus, and on the surface of the floe they had made a ballroom decorated with figures of Bacchus and Britannia. The ships entered the Ross Sea, but the weather was not as favorable as it had been the previous year, and they soon found themselves surrounded by floating blocks of ice that threatened to lock them in.

On February 2, they had to abandon the attempt at 67° 28′ S and head east, following along the Antarctic Continent at some distance; heading north, they reached the Falkland Islands on April 6, 1842. Unwilling to admit defeat, Ross was determined to attempt a third cruise, which had not been scheduled. He wrote of his plans to the Admiralty and, while he awaited a reply, established camp in the Falklands from April to December, making expeditions to Tierra del Fuego and Hermite Island. From the former, Ross had transplanted to the Falklands, which lacked trees, several hundred standing Antarctic beeches *(Nothofagus)*. In these

regions that had already been prospected by previous navigators, the zoologists nevertheless made several discoveries—the sociable plover, and a seal that was named in honor of Hooker. The latter had established a herbarium of some one thousand species. In November, Ross received the authorization he had requested, and, on December 17, the *Erebus* and the *Terror* crossed the Antarctic Circle for the third time.

The commander intended to explore the east coast of Graham Land and thus to go as far as possible into the Weddell Sea. The always changing weather was to decide things otherwise. The ice pack had come much farther forward than in previous years. The wind blew constantly, and the ships moved through fog and snowstorms. During the night, the sailors remained on the alert, ready to respond to the cry "Berg ahead!" and to the immediately following command "All hands on deck!" Captain Crozier did not spend a single night in his cot during the cruise. Blocked in the ice from January 9 to 16, Ross profited from the situation to make soundings, but this time he had to resign himself to no more than completing the charting done by Dumont d'Urville on the coasts of Terre Louis-Philippe and Joinville; he sighted new mountains, Haddin and Penny, and discovered two islands of volcanic origin, Paulet and Cockburn, where the English were able to land.

On March 5, 1843, the *Erebus* and the *Terror* reached the highest latitude they were to attain during the course of this third cruise, 71° 30′. The weather was overcast and some snow was falling. White petrels, ordinarily the sign of a nearby ice floe, were seen in the sky. In the afternoon, the officer of the watch announced that it was no more than a few meters away, but covered by fierce waves. It was impossible to proceed. On March 19, at the place where Bouvet claimed to have discovered Cape Circumcision, the two ships narrowly escaped collision with icebergs being swiftly pushed along by

The Erebus *and the* Terror *in sight of Mount Erebus, January 28, 1841. Original watercolor by J. E. Davis. (National Maritime Museum, London. Photo © the museum/Photeb.)*

Capture of emperor penguins on the Antarctic Continent, January 1841. Engraving from a drawing by J. D. Hooker. (Bibliothèque nationale, Paris. Photo © Bibl. nat./Photeb.)

currents; waves over 25 meters high were breaking over these icebergs. Even ships as well equipped as his could have sunk, and Ross had to sail farther north.

On April 4, the navigators arrived at Cape Town, and, on May 13, they reached St. Helena, where Ross repeated the magnetic observations made on the way in. On September 14, the *Erebus* and the *Terror* dropped anchor at Folkestone after having spent four years less fifteen days at sea.

This time the losses in men were low, and Ross had done better than his predecessors. He had not only completed their discoveries and gone around the greater parts of the Antarctic Continent, but he had managed to explore the coasts closest to the pole. During the course of the expedition, he had put a boat into the sea. A 38-kilo weight had been attached to the end of a hemp rope wound around an enormous reel. When the boat was several meters from the *Erebus,* Ross gave orders for the ballast to be thrown overboard. The line spun out rapidly, but it took more than an hour before the weight touched bottom; 4,800 meters of cord had been played out. James Clark Ross had made the first abyssal sounding and found a depression in the bed of the ocean that was almost equivalent to the height of Mont Blanc. On many occasions, he also had the temperature of deep waters taken, and found that it was the same at all latitudes. These experiments made Ross a precursor in oceanography.

The results obtained in the domain of the natural sciences were equally remarkable; the work that followed, and the publications based on it, went on for more than thirty years. Among the animals brought back were seven species of seals, three of

bats, some twenty rodents, more than twenty craniums and skins of cetaceans, about 150 species of birds, as many species of reptiles, thirty species of crustaceans, several hundred marine invertebrates, and finally three hundred species of fish—all the more precious in that until that time there was little knowledge of any that lived beyond the fiftieth parallel.

To prepare the zoology of the voyage, which appeared from 1844 to 1871, a team of scientists had to be recruited, and it included the famous Dr. Richardson, who had been Franklin's companion. The botany was written entirely by Hooker; it is a gigantic work in six volumes, describing more than three thousand species and illustrated with 530 plates. If Hooker was not able to finish the last volume until 1859, it was because in the interval he had gone to explore the Himalayas. He was never to cease traveling, even though, in 1865, he succeeded his father as director of Kew Gardens. When he retired in 1885, his duties were assumed by his son-in-law, who retired in 1905. For more than sixty years, three generations of Hookers had reigned over the famous garden, which had expanded considerably thanks to their care. Hooker was still working when, at the age of ninety-four, he died on December 10, 1911.

Knighted on his return, Ross was to direct a new expedition to the polar seas to search for Sir John Franklin, who, on May 19, 1845, had left with the *Erebus* and the *Terror*—the latter still under the command of Captain Crozier—in order to find the much-talked-of Northwest Passage that no navigator had yet managed to discover. When he got to Somerset Island, Ross spent the winter of 1848–1849 there, and then a rescue expedition went on foot with sleds pulled by men over more than 3,000 kilometers in the Canadian far north; no trace was found of Franklin, and the mystery of his disappearance was not cleared up until 1858. After 1849, Ross no longer went to sea; named rear admiral in 1856, he died in 1862.

After Ross's return in 1843, the silence of the Antarctic was temporarily resumed, since the seal population had been decimated by the hunters' massacres. Toward the end of the century, it was the whalers who again haunted the Antarctic Ocean; northern whales had become rare, and the harpoon guns that had come into use made it easier to take the southern whales, which were otherwise more difficult to hunt. The whalers were soon followed by the explorers, the interests of scientists having once more turned to the extreme south, made more accessible by technical progress.

Grandeur and decline of the circumnavigators

Ross's voyage concluded the first reconnaissance of the Antarctic Continent and put a final period to the long quest, begun three-quarters of a century earlier, that had led the circumnavigators to the ends of the Earth. The long journey was over. Henceforth, the blank spaces that had still existed in the maps of the world in 1768 could be filled in. No doubt there were others, even staggering ones, in the interior of continents—for example, in 1843, Africa had been little explored—but on the seas there were only discoveries of details to be made.

An irritating problem remained, however—that of the northern passage supposedly linking the Atlantic and Pacific. For more than three centuries, it had been searched for, sometimes in the East and sometimes in the West; but neither Cook nor his successors had found it. On May 19, 1845, the *Erebus* and the *Terror,* having returned a year and a half earlier from the Antarctic, left for the far north. This time the expedition was led by Sir John Franklin; Crozier once more took command of the *Terror.*

Since 1818, Franklin had searched in vain for the passage; in 1845, having decided to find it at whatever cost, he left with two ships that had been tested in the polar seas, taking supplies for three years. He was not heard from after the summer of 1847, and in 1848–1849, three groups were sent in vain to look for him. It was not until 1859—after still other attempts, including that of Belcher in 1852–1854—that traces of the expedition, which had perished in the ice, were found. The Northwest Passage did exist, but it was situated between Davis Strait and the Bering Strait and was much too far north to be usable. It was traversed for the first time in 1903–1906 by the Norwegian Roald Amundsen.

By a significant coincidence, 1843, the year of Ross's return, saw the first crossing of the Atlantic by a screw propeller ship—the English vessel *Great Britain.* This was the result of a slow evolution. The first satisfactory attempts to use steam as a means of propelling ships had been made between the death of Cook and the departure of La Pérouse: Jouffroy d'Abbans's steamship went up the Saône in 1783. But it was not until after 1840, with the adoption of the propeller and of iron construction, that decisive progress was made—and it would still be some time before steamships become commonplace and finally replaced sailing vessels.

Initially, they were not faster, and their use, particularly over long distances, posed problems that were only slowly solved; chief among the latter was that of obtaining coal at ports of call. However, since their mode of autonomous propulsion removed the major defect of sail navigation—being at the mercy of the winds—the future belonged to them. In 1872, twenty-nine years after Ross's return, the first large modern scientific voyage around the world was organized—that of the *Challenger,* which inaugurated oceanographic cruises.

When, in 1843, voyages of circumnavigation came to a halt, the spirit that had been behind the expeditions of Bougainville, of Cook, and of their immediate successors already belonged to the past. The enthusiasm with which new lands and peoples had been discovered, and the idealistic humanitarianism that had presided over relations with the latter, had long since changed. They had given way to the more interested, more materialistic preoccupations of the middle classes—the merchants and businessmen who first in England and then in France had progressively assumed power.

The development of industry and international commerce gave prime importance to the opening of new markets; little by little, economic factors took precedence over political ones. Great Britain was in the forefront in this area as in exploration. Immediately after the discovery of these new lands, she sent there simultaneously both convicts, who were the first colonists, and missionaries. Increasingly active, after 1789 the Protestant missionaries invaded the Pacific isles from the Society Archipelago to the Sandwich Islands and were there at the founding of New South Wales and New Zealand. Shortly thereafter, Great Britain began to establish along the maritime routes strategic points and commercial trading posts: Singapore was annexed in 1819, and New Zealand in 1840. Only France could challenge such expansion, and she tried to establish herself around the world by supporting her merchants and especially by becoming the protector of the Catholic missions that were the rivals of the Protestant missions. Over a period of time, this settlement laid the groundwork for the attachment of the colony to France. This was done in 1842 when Dupetit-Thouars annexed the Marquesas and occupied Tahiti.

This evolution was reflected in the character

and conduct of the men charged by their governments with leading voyages of circumnavigation. Certainly the generosity and gentleness Cook had shown to the natives long served as a model. The relations of the members of the Kotzebue expedition with the inhabitants of Ratak, and those of Dumont d'Urville with the Fijians during his first voyage, still remained exemplary. But reprisal operations soon began. Though he sorely regretted it, even Dumont d'Urville considered himself obliged to carry such operations out at Pau, also in the Fijis, during his second voyage; and the energy—not to say the brutality—of Dupetit-Thouars foreshadowed the violence that was to become uppermost.

Ethnography took its initial steps with Cook in a climate of relative and initially favorable confidence that had accompanied the first discoveries. Those who continued along the path he outlined were missionaries, and what is more they were Protestants. The cultures they were studying began to decline and then to disappear because of the oppressive authority—often supported by force—that these missionaries exercised in the name of Christian morality.

During this same period, animal species discovered by the circumnavigators began to disappear, massacred either by the crews of the ships to which the navigators had opened the way or as the result of the introduction of the European animals they had been the first to transport. Nevertheless, the voyages of circumnavigation had spread the field of the natural sciences over the entire world. The vast systems conceived by Linnaeus and Buffon just before these expeditions began were completed thanks to the voyages, which also simultaneously filled in the gaps on the maps of the Earth. The editions of Linnaeus's *Systema naturae* and Buffon's *Histoire naturelle* succeeded one another at a rapid pace during the last years of the eighteenth century and continued doing so until the middle of the nineteenth. They registered new discoveries as they came along, resolving the new questions they posed—that, for example, of the Australian marsupials—and permitting more ample syntheses such as Cuvier's *Règne animal distribué d'après son organization* (The Animal Kingdom Distributed According to Its Organization), 1815–1829, completed by his *Histoire des progrès des sciences naturelles depuis 1789 jusqu'à ce jour* (The History of the Progress of the Natural Sciences from 1789 to Our Day), 1834–1838. Thanks to the naturalists who took part in these voyages—men who were often surgeons or even ship's officers—zoology and botany aroused tremendous enthusiasm, even among the general public, that made this period the Golden Age of Discovery.

Appendices

Biographical dictionary of navigators, scientists, and artists

ANDERSON William. Born in 1750. 1772–1775, surgeon's mate on the *Resolution*, Cook's 2nd voyage. 1776–1779, surgeon and naturalist on the *Resolution*, Cook's 3rd voyage. Dies of tuberculosis off coast of Alaska, 8/3/1778.

ANSON George. Born in Shrugborough Park (Staffordshire), 4/23/1697. 1712, joins the Navy. 1723, made captain. 1724–1735, leads 3 expeditions to South Carolina and founds a city bearing his name. 1735–1739, makes several voyages to the coast of Guinea and to America. 1740–1744, commands an expedition to attack the Spanish in South America. 1745, member of the Admiralty staff; 1755, becomes the assistant director. 1757, defeats a French fleet; is made vice admiral and baron. 1761, admiral and First Lord of the Admiralty. Dies at Moor Park (Hertfordshire), 6/6/1762.

ARAGO Jacques. Born in Estagel (Pyrénées-Orientales), 1790. Brother of the astronomer François Arago. 1818–1820, official "writer" and draftsman aboard the *Uranie*, Freycinet expedition. 1822, publishes *Promenades autour du monde*. Has several plays produced. 1835, directs theater in Rouen. 1837, becomes blind. 1838–1840, publishes *Voyage autour du monde*. 1855, dies in Brazil.

AURIBEAU Alexandre Hesmivy d'. 1791–1792, second in command to d'Entrecasteaux on the *Recherche*; becomes head of the expedition following d'Entrecasteaux's death. Dies in Semarang (Java), 8/23/1794.

BANKS Sir Joseph. Born in London, 12/15/1743. Son of a rich Lincolnshire doctor. Educated at Eton, Harrow, and Oxford. 1761, on the death of his father, inherits a fortune that permits him to devote himself to natural history, and begins to assemble important collections. 1763, collects plant specimens in Newfoundland and Labrador. 1768–1771, he and an entire team participate in Cook's 1st voyage; on his return, Banks is received as a hero. 1772, at his own expense he organizes a scientific expedition to the Hebrides and Iceland. 1778, elected president of the Royal Society. 1781, baronet. 1797, state councillor and member of the Privy Council. Royal advisor for Kew Gardens until his death, Banks was helpful to all British exploration missions and extended his patronage to naturalists of all countries, even those Great Britain was at war with. His botanical collections, preserved by R. Brown, form the basis of the British Museum, Natural History. Dies in London, 5/19/1820.

BARET Jeanne. Born about 1740 in Burgundy. 1764, enters the service of Commerson, a widower, to look after his son.

1766–1768, disguised as a valet, she accompanies Commerson on the *Etoile* during the Bougainville expedition; disembarks with him on the Ile de France, 12/12/1768. After Commerson's death (1773), marries a rich Ile de France smith. Widowed, she bequeaths her wealth to Commerson's son, whom she raised, and dies in about 1788.

BAUDIN Charles. Born in Sedan in 1784. Son of a man who represented the Ardennes at the the National Convention. 1800–1804, midshipman on the *Géographe*, Baudin expedition. Loses his right arm during a campaign against the British under the Empire. After Waterloo, lends himself to Napoleon's plans to escape to America. 1814, put on the inactive list, he starts a commercial concern at Le Havre. 1830, reenters the Navy. 1838, as a rear admiral he commands an expedition to Mexico. 1841, Minister of the Navy. 1841–1847, maritime prefect of Toulon. 1847, commands the Mediterranean squadron. 1854, promoted to admiral, he dies several days later at Ischia.

BAUDIN François André. Born about 1770. 1800, lieutenant on board the *Géographe*, Baudin expedition; 4/25/1801, left behind at the Ile de France because of illness; 12/29/1801, returns to Rochefort on the American ship the *Philanthrope*. 1808, rear admiral. 1810, baron. 1817, major general at Brest. 1826, officer of the Legion of Honor. 1828, commands the port of Brest. Dies about 1838.

BAUDIN Nicolas. Born Ile de Ré in 1754. 1793–1795, makes two cruises to the Far East for the Museum of Natural History: to China, the Sunda Isles, and India; and another to the Antilles. Is shipwrecked and leaves the salvaged natural history collections on the Spanish island of Trinidad. 1796–1798, departs to pick up his material on the *Belle Angélique* but is un-

able to; he therefore makes a scientific expedition to the Antilles and to South America, bringing back many dried plants and seeds, as well as 207 cases of living plants and shrubs. 1800–1803, as a captain he commands the expedition of the *Géographe* and the *Naturaliste*. Dies at Port Louis, Ile de France, 9/16/1803.

BAUER Ferdinand Lucas. Born in Feldsberg, Austria, 1/20/1760. Son of the painter Lukas Bauer; student of P. Boccius and N. von Jacquin, he specializes in drawing plants. 1786–1787, accompanies J. Sibthorp to Greece. 1801–1803, natural history artist on the *Investigator*, Flinders expedition. 1803–1805, remains with R. Brown at Port Jackson, visits Norfolk Island. 1806, begins publication of Sibthorp's *Flora graeca* in 10 illustrated volumes. 1812, settles in Hietzing, near Schoenbrunn. 1813, publication in London of the illustrations of the *Flora Novae Hollandiae* of R. Brown. Dies in Hietzing, 3/17/1826.

BEAUTEMPS-BEAUPRE Charles François. Born in La Neuville-du-Pont (Marne), 1766. 1785, hydrographer responsible for making maps of the Baltic. 1791–1794, chief engineer on the *Recherche*, d'Entrecasteaux expedition; back in France 1796. Responsible for all the great hydrographic undertakings during the Empire and the Restoration; nicknamed the "Father of Hydrography." 1808, publishes the Atlas of the *Voyage d'Entrecasteaux*. 1810, member of the Academy of Sciences. Publishes the *Nouveau pilote français*. Dies in Paris, 3/15/1854.

BEECHEY Frederick William. Born in London, 2/17/1796. Son of Sir William Beechey, court painter. 1811, joins the navy. 1818, accompanies the Franklin and Buchan expedition to Spitzbergen. 1819, is part of the Parry expedition to the Arctic. 1821–1822, with his brother explores the Barbary coast to the east of Tripoli. 1825–1828, captain in command of the expedition on the *Blossom*. 1836, commands the expedition on the *Sulphur*, but, falling sick, returns to England. 1837, maritime director of the Board of Trade. Devotes his leisure to natural history, publishing two works on botany and zoology. 1854, rear admiral. 1855, president of the Geographical Society. Dies in London, 11/29/1856.

BELCHER Sir Edward. Born in Halifax (Nova Scotia), 1799. 1812, joins the navy. 1816, midshipman on the *Superb*, he takes part in the bombardment of Algiers. 1818, lieutenant commander, makes a voyage to the north Pacific and then is ordered to hydrograph the north and west coasts of Africa. 1825–1826, hydrographer on the *Blossom*, Beechey expedition. 1835, captain. 1837–1842, takes command of the expedition on the *Sulphur*, which he picks up at Panama. 1843–1846, commands the *Samarang* in the China Seas and at Borneo. 1852–1855, on the *Blossom*, commands an Arctic expedition in search of the remains of the Sir John Franklin expedition; fails to show sufficient authority and is too quick to abandon his ships, one of which frees herself from the ice floe and is found in the open sea. This failure brings disgrace, and he is never again assigned active service, though he is made rear admiral (1861), vice admiral (1866), and admiral (1872). Dies in London, 3/18/1877.

BLIGH William. Born in Tyntan (Cornwall), 9/9/1754. 1776–1780, master on the *Resolution*, Cook's 3rd voyage. 1782, takes part in the British rescue expedition to Gibraltar. 1787, as lieutenant is in command of the *Bounty*, charged with bringing breadfruit trees from Tahiti to the Antilles. 1789, following a mutiny, Bligh and 19 men are abandoned in a launch that sails 6,700 kilometers before reaching Timor. 1791–1793, commands a second expedition on the *Providence*, which manages to bring 300 breadfruit trees to Jamaica. 1795–1805, as captain commands several vessels; bombards Copenhagen in 1801. 1806, as governor of New South Wales, his extreme severity provokes a rebellion among the colonists and he is recalled in 1808. 1810, rear admiral. 1814, vice admiral. Dies in London, 12/7/1817.

BOUGAINVILLE Hyacinthe Yves Philippe Potentien, Baron de. Born in Brest, 12/26/1782. Eldest son of L. A. de Bougainville. 1798, student at the Ecole Polytechnique. 1800–1804, midshipman on the *Géographe*, Baudin expedition. 1805, attached to the staff of Admiral Bruix at Boulogne. 1808, lieutenant commander on the *Charlemagne*. 1809, commands the corvette *Hussard*. 1811, frigate captain. 1817–1819, serves on the frigate *Cybèle*, commanded by Kergariou, in Indochina and Malacca. 1820, commands the corvette *Seine*, which goes to the United States. 1821, captain. 1824–1826, commands the expedition of the *Thétis* and the *Espérance*. 1827, publishes *Journal de la navigation autour du globe* . . . 1828, commands the *Scipion*. 1838, rear admiral. Dies in Paris, 10/18/1846.

BOUGAINVILLE Louis Antoine de. Born in Paris, 11/11/1729. Son of a notary at Chatelet. Becomes lawyer. 1751, student of d'Alembert's. 1753, assistant medical officer for the Picard regiment. 1754–1756, publishes a *Traité du calcul intégral*. 1758, as Montcalm's aide-de-camp, he is wounded during the attack on Fort Carillon. 1759, as colonel he negotiates the surrender of Quebec. 1760, sent back to France to defend French interests in America. 1763, switches to the navy with the rank of captain. 1763–1766, establishes a French settlement in the Falklands. 1766–1769, voyage on the *Boudeuse* and the *Etoile*. 1771, publishes his *Voyage autour du monde*. 1772, proposes an expedition to the north pole and is turned down. 1779, participates in the American Revolution as a squadron commander. 1781, in Brest, he marries Flore de Longchamp-Montendre. 1782, is defeated by Hood at Martinique and is court-martialed; in disgrace, he withdraws to

Sénart. Birth of his 1st son, Hyacinthe (he was to have 3, born in 1785, 1788, and 1796). 1789, member of the Academy of Sciences. 1790, commands the Brest squadron. 1792, refuses the rank of vice admiral. 1793, withdraws to his farm in Anneville (Calvados). 1794, imprisoned in Coutances from 7/4 to 9/4/1796. Member of the Institute and the Central Astronomical Office. 1798, member of the commission preparing the Egyptian campaign. 1799, senator. 1804, officer of the Legion of Honor. 1808, count of the Empire. Dies in Paris, 8/31/1811, and is given a state funeral at the Pantheon (9/3/1811).

BROWN Robert. Born in Montrose (Scotland), 12/21/1773. 1794, assistant surgeon in a Scottish regiment. 1798, is presented by the botanist Correa da Serra to J. Banks, who recommends him to Flinders. 1801–1803, naturalist on the *Investigator*, Flinders expedition. August 1803, remains behind at Port Jackson with F. Bauer and stays in Tasmania for 10 months. October 1805, returns to England. 1810, librarian and curator of the Banks collections; publishes *Prodromus Florae Novae-Hollandiae*, containing 2,200 species, of which 1,700 are new. 1811, member of the Royal Society. 1823, inheriting the herbarium and library belonging to Banks, he has them transferred to the British Museum (1827), where he becomes curator. 1827, discovers the "Brownian movement." 1832, corresponding member of the Academy of Sciences in Paris. Dies in London, 6/10/1858.

BURNEY James. Born in London, 1750. 1760, cabin boy in the Navy. 1770, voyage to Bombay as a seaman. 1772–1775, 2nd lieutenant on the *Adventure*, Cook's 2nd voyage; on return, presents Omai to London society and to his sister Fanny, a writer who was later to become famous. 1776–1780, 1st lieutenant on the *Discovery*, Cook's 3rd voyage. 1782, captain. 1784, no longer goes to sea. 1804–1816, publishes a chronological history of South Seas discoveries which is greeted as "a masterpiece of fundamental erudition." 1806, member of the Royal Society. 1816, writes a history of buccaneers in America. 1819, publishes a history of discoveries in the Northeast and of the first Russian expeditions to the East. 1821, rear admiral. Dies in London, 1821.

BUSSEUIL François Louis. Born in Nantes, 11/2/1791. Becomes a doctor. 1824–1826, surgeon on the *Thétis*, expedition by H. de Bougainville. Next, voyages on the *Terpsichore* to Brazil, the South Seas, and Madagascar, and on the *Flore* to Senegal. Dies in Gorée, 6/14/1835. One of the pioneers in marine fauna of the South Atlantic.

BYRON John. Born 11/8/1723 at Newstead Abbey, 2nd son of the 4th Baron Byron and grandfather of the poet Lord Byron. 1740, midshipman on the *Wager*, Anson expedition. 1741, shipwrecked on the coast of Patagonia. 1745, returns to Great Britain and publishes his account of the loss of the *Wager*. 1758, distinguishes himself in battles against France and is appointed commodore. 1764–1766, voyage on the *Dolphin* and the *Tamar*. 1767, publishes *An Account of a Voyage round the World in the Years 1764, 1765, and 1766*. 1769, governor of Newfoundland. 1775, rear admiral. 1778, vice admiral. 1779, con-

voying an army of reinforcements to America, he encounters the worst recorded storms in the Atlantic and is given the nickname "Foul Weather Jack," because each time he goes to sea he meets

John Byron in his captain's uniform. Painting by Sir J. Reynolds. (National Maritime Museum, London. Photo © the museum/Photeb.)

with bad weather. Commander-in-chief in the West Indies (Antilles). Dies in London, 4/10/1786.

CARTERET Philip. 1764–1766, 1st lieutenant on board the *Tamar*, Byron expedition. 1766–1769, commands the *Swallow*, Wallis expedition. 1794, vice admiral. Dies in Southhampton (Hampshire), 7/21/1796.

CHAMISSO DE BONCOURT Louis Charles Adélaïde called Adelbert von. Born at the Château de Boncourt (Champagne), 1781. 1792, immigrates with his family to Holland, then to Würtzburg. 1796, page of the queen of Prussia in Berlin. 1798, ensign, then in 1801 lieutenant of von Gütze's infantry regiment. 1802, his family returns to France, but he remains in Prussia. 1804, with Varnhagen founds an *Almanac of the Muses*. 1808, leaves the army and goes to France, where he meets Mme. de Staël, whom he follows to Coppet, where he remains 1811–1812. 1812, at the University of the Berlin botanical gardens; marries and eventually has seven children. 1821, publishes "Ideas and Remarks" in Kotzebue's *Reise um die Welt*. 1827, *Observations on Botany and the Vegetable Kingdom*. 1829, *Salas y Gomez*. 1830, *Frauenliebe und Leben*. 1832, director of the Royal Herbarium in Berlin. 1833, member of Prussia's Academy of Sciences. 1835, publishes *Voyage Journal*. 1836–1837, works on a Hawaiian grammar. Dies in Berlin, 8/21/1836.

CHESNARD DE LA GIRAUDAIS François. Born in St. Malo in 1727. Goes to sea with his father at the age of 5. 1759, commands the *Machaut* in a convoy for Canada in which Bougainville sails on the *Chézine*. 1761, frigate lieutenant. 1763, commands the *Sphinx* in the Bougainville expedition to the Falklands. 1767–1769, commands the *Etoile* in the Bougainville voyage around the world.

CHORIS Louis. Born in Iekaterinoslav, 3/21/1795, into a German family established in Russia. 1813, painter of the scientific expedition of Marshall von Biber-

Adelbert von Chamisso. Lithograph by Oldermann from a drawing by Ritschel.(Bibliothèque nationale, Paris. Photo © Bibl. nat./Photeb.)

stein to the Caucasus. 1815–1818, draftsman on the *Rurik*, Kotzebue expedition. 1819–1827, lives in Paris, frequents scientists and artists, works in the studio of Gérard and learns lithography. Illustrates his *Voyage pittoresque autour du monde* (1823–1826) and publishes *Vues et paysages des régions équinoxiales* (1825). 1827, lives in New Orleans. On 3/19/1828, leaves from Veracruz for an expedition to the interior of Mexico and dies several days later in an ambush.

CLERKE Charles. Born in Weatherfield (Essex), 1743. 1755, enters the Navy. 1764–1766, on board the *Dolphin*, Byron expedition. 1766, serves in the Antilles. 1768–1771, midshipman on the *Endeavour*, Cook's 1st voyage. 1772–1775, 2nd lieutenant on the *Resolution*, Cook's 2nd voyage. 1776–1779, frigate captain, commands the *Discovery*, Cook's 3rd voyage; on Cook's death, commands the expedition on the *Resolution*. Dies of tuberculosis off Kamchatka, 7/22/1779.

COMMERSON Joseph Philibert. Born in Châtillon-les-Dombes (Ain), 11/18/1727. Son of a notary. 1747, doctor of medicine in Montpellier; corresponds with Bernard de Jussieu and Linnaeus, who commissions him, for the queen of Sweden, to study Mediterranean fish. 1755, at Fernet, meets Voltaire, who wants to keep Commerson with him as his secretary and the agricultural administrator of his estates; he refuses. 1760, marries. 1762, his wife dies in giving birth to a son. 1764, takes Jeanne Baret into his service; called to Paris by B. de Jussieu. 1766, king's naturalist and botanist. 1766–1768, naturalist on the *Etoile*, Bougainville expedition. 12/12/1768, lands on the Ile de France, where he works with P. Poivre. 1770–1771, the king asks him to make a study of Madagascar, where Commerson stays 6 months. Works on the Ile de France with the painter Jossigny. Dies there of pleurisy, 3/13/1773.

Jules Sébastien César Dumont d'Urville in undress. Anonymous lithograph. (Bibliothèque nationale, Paris. Photo © Bibl. nat./Photeb.)

COOK James. Born in Marton-in-Cleveland (Yorkshire), 10/27/1728. As 2nd of 9 children of a poor peasant, lives in a thatched cottage. 1741, leaves school to help his father. 1742, apprenticed to a grocer in Staithes. 1743, cabin boy on the *Freelove* at Whitby. 1755, 2nd in command on a collier, he joins the Royal Navy on the *Eagle*. 1757, deep-sea pilot on the *Pembroke*. 1758, commissioned by Admiral Saunders to sound the St. Lawrence from Quebec to the sea. 1760, returns to

England. 1762, marries Elizabeth Batts. 1763, leaves for Newfoundland as hydrographer with Palliser. 1768, on the advice of Palliser, Sir Edward Hawke, First Lord of the Admiralty, recommends him for the command of the astronomical expedition of the Royal Society. 1768–1771, 1st voyage on the *Endeavour*. 1771, named commander. 1772–1775, 2nd voyage on the *Resolution* and the *Adventure*. 1775, ship's captain; 4th captain of the Greenwich Hospital, member of the Royal Society. 1776–1779, 3rd voyage on the *Resolution* and the *Discovery*. Dies on Owhyhee (Hawaii), 2/14/1779.

CROZIER Francis Rawdon Moira. Born in Ireland in 1796. 1810, joins the navy. 1821, lieutenant, accompanies Parry on his 2nd expedition. 1824–1825, participates in Parry's 3rd expedition in the Arctic. 1831–1835, serves on the coasts of Portugal. 1835, makes a cruise to Baffin Bay. 1839–1843, captain, commands the *Terror*, in J. C. Ross expedition. 1845, commands the *Terror* in the Franklin expedition sent to search for a Northwest Passage. 1847, on the death of Franklin, takes command of the expedition. Spring 1848, dies of starvation with all his men.

DANA James Dwight. Born in Utica (New York), 2/12/1813. 1838–1841, geologist and mineralogist on the *Peacock*, Wilkes expedition; responsible later for marine zoology. 1842–1856, at government expense, publishes his discoveries on geology, crustaceans, zoophytes, and coral islands. 1873, a correspondent of the Paris Academy of Sciences. Dies in New Haven (Connecticut), 4/14/1895.

DARONDEAU Benoît Henri, called **Benoni.** Born in Paris, 1805. 1826, graduates from the Ecole Polytechnique. 1826–1829, takes part in a project to sound the harbors and ports of France's western coast, then in 1831–1835, hydrographs the northern coast. 1836–1837, hydrographer on the *Bonite*, Vaillant expedition. Publishes several important works on hydrography and earth magnetism. Dies in Paris in 1869.

DARWIN Charles. Born in Shrewsbury (Shropshire), 2/12/1809. Son of Dr. Robert Darwin and grandson of Dr. Erasmus Darwin. 1817, mother dies. 1825–1827, begins his medical studies at the University of Edinburgh, but soon gives them up to devote himself to geology and natural history. 1828–1831, theological studies at Christ's College, Cambridge; becomes friendly with the botanist Henslow and the geologist Sedgwick. 1831–1836, naturalist on the *Beagle*, FitzRoy expedition. 1838, secretary of the Geographical Society. 1839, marries his cousin Emma Wedgwood; publishes the 3rd volume of FitzRoy's voyage. 1839–1843, zoology of the *Beagle*. 1842, settles with his family at Down House (Kent). Publishes *On the Origin of Species by Means of Natural Selection* (1859); *The Variation of Animals and Plants under Domestication* (1868); *The Descent of Man, and Selection in Relation to Sex* (1871). Dies at Down House, 4/19/1882; is buried in Westminster Abbey.

DUCLOS-GUYOT Pierre Nicolas. Born in St. Malo, 12/14/1722. 1734, apprentice in Merchant Service on the *Duchesse*. 1742–1743, ensign and then lieutenant on the

Saint-Michel of the British East India Company. 1759, with Bougainville, on the *Chézine*, which goes to Quebec. 1763, lieutenant on the *Aigle*, Falklands cruise. 1764, fire-ship captain. 1765, commands the *Lion*; returning from Lima, he rediscovers the island discovered by La Roche and named South Georgia in 1775 by Cook. 1766–1769, Bougainville's 2nd in command on the *Boudeuse*. 1777, captain of the port of the Ile de France. 1784, leaves the service for health reasons. 1792, recalled to active duty, made captain. Dies at Saint-Servan, 3/10/1794.

DUMONT D'URVILLE Jules Sébastien César. Born in Condé-sur-Noireau (Calvados), 5/23/1790, into a noble but poor family. 1797, his father dies. 1804–1807, excellent student at the *lycée* of Caen; bets with a friend that at 50 he will be a rear admiral. 1807, apprentice midshipman, Brest. 1810, midshipman 1st class, Toulon. 1812, ensign. 1815, marries. 1817, does not manage to embark on Freycinet's *Uranie*. 1819–1821, ensign on Captain Gauthier's *Chevrette*, he hydrographs the Mediterranean islands, the Dardanelles, and the Black Sea; announces the discovery of the *Venus de Milo*. 1821, Legion of Honor, lieutenant commander, continuation of his botanical studies at the Museum of Natural History. 1822, publishes at his own expense *Enumeratio plantarum quas in Insulis Archipelagi . . .* 1822–1825, Duperrey's second in command on the *Coquille*. 1824, frigate captain. 1826–1829, commands the *Astrolabe* expedition. 1829, captain, presents his candidacy to the Academy of Sciences but is not elected. 1830, made responsible for conveying Charles X and his family into

exile on the cargo boat the *Seine*. Publishes, in 1830–1835, the *Voyage de l' Astrolabe*; in 1834–1835, *Voyage pittoresque autour du monde*, a general summary of voyages of discovery since Magellan. 1837–1840, commands the expedition of the *Astrolabe* and the *Zélée*. 1841, rear admiral, begins writing *Voyage au pôle Sud . . .* 5/8/1842, he dies along with his wife and son in a railroad accident at Bellevue.

DUPERREY Louis Isadore. Born in Paris, 10/21/1786. 1803, enters the navy. 1809, makes a hydrographic survey of the coasts of Tuscany. 1817–1820, ensign on the *Uranie*, Freycinet expedition. 1821, cruise on the *Chevrette* with Dumont d'Urville. 1822–1825, commands the expedition on board the *Coquille*. 1825, frigate captain. 1825–1830, publication of the Voyage of the *Coquille*. Afterward publishes numerous works on physics, geography, and magnetic observations. 1831, establishes the "map of movements of waters on the surface of the Great Ocean," in which he shows the origin of the Humboldt Current that brings cold waters to the coasts of Peru. 1842, succeeds Freycinet at the Academy of Sciences, of which he becomes the president in 1850. Dies in Paris in 1865.

DUPETIT-THOUARS Abel Aubert. Born at La Fessardière, near Saumur, 8/3/1793. Nephew of the botanist Louis Marie Dupetit-Thouars and of naval Captain Aristide Dupetit-Thouars. 1805, joins the Boulogne fleet of the Navy. 1829, takes part in the Algiers expedition, which he prepares. 1830, commands the brig *Griffon* in the South Seas. Distinguishes himself at Callao by his energetic handling of the troubles between France and Peru; captain, commands the *Créole*. 1836–1839, commands the expedition aboard the *Vénus*. 1841, rear admiral. 1842, commander of the frigate *Reine Blanche*, annexes the Marquesas, occupies Tahiti—expelling Pritchard—but is disavowed by the French government. 1846, vice admiral. 1849, deputy representing Maine-et-Loire. 1855, member of the Academy of Sciences. Dies in Paris, 3/17/1864.

ENTRECASTEAUX Antoine Raymond Joseph de Bruni, Chevalier d'. Born in the château d'Entrecasteaux (Var), 1737. His father presided at the *parlement* of Provence. 1754, marine guard under the command of the bailiff of Suffren, a relative of his. 1756, distinguishes himself at the battle of Minorca. 1770, lieutenant commander. 1779, assistant director of Ports and Arsenals. Following a murder committed by a nephew, wants to leave the service; is named commander of the naval station of the Indies. 1787–1789, governor of the Ile de France. 1789, division chief. 1791–1794, commands the expedition of the *Recherche* and the *Espérance*. 1791, rear admiral. 1792, vice admiral, but he dies of scurvy while still at sea (7/21/1793) before he receives word of his promotion.

ESCHSCHOLTZ Johann Friedrich. Born in Dorpat (Livonia), 11/12/1793. Doctor of medicine in Dorpat. 1815–1818, doctor and naturalist on the *Rurik*, Kotzebue expedition. 1823–1826, doctor and naturalist on the *Predpriyatiye*, 2nd Kotezebue expedition. Published *Entomographies* (1823), *System der Acalephen* (1829), *Zoologischen Atlas* (1829–1833). Dies 5/19/1831.

EYDOUX Fortuné. Born in 1802. Medical doctor. Makes a scientific voyage to Tangiers. 1830–1832, surgeon and naturalist on the *Favorite*, 1st Laplace voyage. 1834–1835, cruise on the frigate *Victoire* to the African coasts. 1836–1837, surgeon and zoologist on the *Bonite*, Vaillant expedi-

tion. Dies of yellow fever at Martinique, 1841.

FITZROY Robert. Born at Ampton Hall (Suffolk), 7/5/1805. Descendant of a liaison between King Charles II and the Duchess of Cleveland. Son of Lord Charles FitzRoy, grandson of the Duke of Grafton and of the 1st Marquess of Londonderry, nephew of the minister Castlereagh. 1819, enters the Royal Naval College. 1826–1830, accompanies Captain King on a hydrographic exploration of the coasts of South America; 1828, replaces on the *Beagle* Captain Stokes, who committed suicide in his cabin. 1831–1836, lieutenant, then captain, commands the *Beagle* expedition. 1839, publishes the voyage of the *Adventure* and the *Beagle*, and then various works on astronomy and meteorology. 1841–1843, member of Parliament. 1843, governor of New Zealand. Heads the Meteorology Department of the Board of Trade. 1852, his wife and his oldest daughter, age 16, die. 1857, rear admiral. 1861 publishes a treatise on meteorology. Commits suicide in Norwold (Surrey), 4/30/1865.

FLEURIOT DE LANGLE Paul Antoine Marie. Born in the château of Kerlouet, at Quimper-Guézennec, 1744. Makes several voyages under the orders of Rosily and Lamotte-Picquet, notably to San Domingo. Member of the Naval Academy, of which he becomes the director in 1783. 1778, takes part with the Duke of Chartres in the battle of Ushant. 1781, transports to America the U.S. envoys Loreins and Penn. 1782, commands the *Astrée* in the raid on Hudson Bay directed by La Pérouse. 1785, captain; having probably refused command of the expedition in favor of his friend La Pérouse, he commands the *Astrolabe*. Massacred at Tutuila (Samoa), 12/12/1787.

FLINDERS Matthew. Born in Donnington (Lincolnshire), 3/16/1774. 1789 enters the navy and serves on the *Bellerophon*. 1791–1792, accompanies Captain Bligh on his 2nd expedition on the *Providence*. 1795, midshipman, leaves for New South Wales with Governor Hunter and George A. Bass. 1796–1797, visits with Bass the southeast coast of Australia. 1798, with Bass, finishes the exploration of Bass Strait and sails around Tasmania. 1801–1803, frigate captain, commands the expedition on the *Investigator*. In December 1803, he is imprisoned on the Ile de France. 1810, returns exhausted to England; prepares the publication of his voyage. Dies in London, 7/19/1814.

FORSTER Johann Georg Adam. Born in Nassenhuben, near Danzig (Gdansk), 11/27/1754. Son of J. R. Forster. 1765, accompanies his father to Russia. 1772–1775, with his father, naturalist on the *Resolution*, Cook's 2nd voyage. 1777–1778, publishes in London *Voyage Round the World . . .* and *Observations*, by J. R. Forster. 1778, goes to Paris, where he would like to remain, but he does not stay. 1779, returns to Germany. 1780, professor of natural history at Kassel and, in 1784, at Wilna, where he gets his doctor's degree in medicine. 1788, librarian of the Elector of Mayence. 1790–1791, voyage with A. von Humboldt to Belgium, Holland, England, and France. 1792, is deputized by the people of Mayence to ask the National Convention to attach this city

to the republic, but he meets only with indifference on the part of the leaders of the Revolution. 1793, denounced as a traitor in Germany. Dies in despair and poverty in Paris, 1/12/1794, while the Terror is at its height.

FORSTER Johann Reinhold. Born in Dirschau (Polish Prussia), 10/22/1729. Pastor and preacher in Prussia. 1765, makes a scientific voyage on the *Volga*. 1766, settles in London. 1771, publishes *Flora Americae septentrionalis* and *Novae species insectorum*; 1772, translates Bougainville's voyage. 1772–1775, naturalist on the *Resolution*, Cook's 2nd voyage. 1776, in Gottingen, in Latin, publishes *Description of Species of Plants Collected During the Voyage in the South Seas*; in 1778, in London, his *Observations Made During a Voyage Round the World*. 1780, Frederick II has him come to Halle as a professor of natural history and director of the botanical gardens. 1787, publishes a history of discoveries and voyages made in the North. The latter part of his life is saddened by the death of his sons. Dies in Halle, 12/9/1798.

FREYCINET Louis Claude de Saulces de. Born in Montélimar, 8/17/1779. 1794, midshipman with his brother, Louis Henri, on the *Hepreux*. 1800–1804, ensign on the *Naturaliste*, Baudin expedition. 1801, lieutenant commander; 1802–1803, commands the *Casuarina*. 1804–1805, commands the brig *Voltigeur*, but, still exhausted, is assigned to the Map Depot. 1811–1816, is charged with continuing his friend Péron's *Voyage aux terres australes*. 1813, correspondent of the Institute. 1817–1820, frigate captain, commands the *Uranie* expedition. 1820, captain. 1821, one of the founders of the Société de Géographie. 1824, publishes an augmented edition of Baudin's Voyage. 1824–1842, publishes *Voyage autour du monde sur l' Uranie. . . .* 1826, member of the Academy of Sciences. 1830, replaces Rossel as director of maps and charts. 1832, retires, is saved from cholera by Gaimard; death of his wife, Rose Pinon. Dies at Freycinet, near Loriol (Drôme), 8/18/1842.

Johann Reinhold Forster and his son Johann Georg. Anonymous engraving.(Bibliothèque nationale, Paris. Photo © Bibl. nat./Arch. Photeb.)

FREYCINET Louis Henri de Saulces, Baron de. Born at Montélimar, 1777. Older brother of Louis Claude. 1794, midshipman on the *Hepreux*, takes part in Mediterranean battles. 1800–1804, ensign on the *Géographe*, Baudin expedition; 1801, lieutenant commander. 1804–1805, under the command of Louis Claude on the *Voltigeur*. 1806, commands the *Phaéton*; loses his right arm. 1811, frigate captain, commands the *Elisa* and stands up to an entire English division near Martinique; has a leg shattered. 1816, captain. 1821–1826, governor of Bourbon Island. 1826, rear admiral. 1827, governor of French Guyana. 1828, bafon. 1829, governor of Guadeloupe. 1830, major general at Toulon. 1834, maritime prefect of Rochefort, where he dies in 1840.

FURNEAUX Tobias. Born in Stoke Damerel (Devon), 1735. 1755–1766, sails on various ships: Antilles, African coasts, the English Channel. 1766–1768, 2nd lieutenant on *Dolphin*, of Wallis, his cousin. 1772–1775, commander of the *Adventure*, Cook's 2nd voyage. 1775, captain. Dies in Swiley, 9/18/1781.

GAIMARD Joseph Paul. Born in Saint-Zacharie (Var), 1796. 1817–1820, assistant surgeon and zoologist on the *Uranie*, Freycinet expedition. Makes several trips to Holland, Belgium, and Great Britain to study the scientific establishments of the navy. 1826–1829, surgeon and naturalist on the *Astrolabe*, Dumont d'Urville expedition. 1831–1832, goes to study a cholera epidemic in Poland, Prussia, Austria, and Russia for the Academy of Sciences. 1835–1836, surgeon on the *Recherche* in Greenland; 1836, president of the Scientific Commission of Iceland. 1837, voyage to Sweden, Norway, and Denmark. 1838–1839, makes 2 cruises to Iceland on the *Recherche*. 1839, directs the scientific commission for expeditions to the Polar Seas, but no longer goes to sea. 1844, publishes *Voyage en Islande et au Groenland*; 1847, *Voyage en Suède, en Scandinavie et au Spitzberg*. 1848, retires. Dies very poor in Paris, 1858, and is buried at the expense of the government.

GAUDICHAUD-BEAUPRE Charles. Born in Angoulême, 10/4/1789. Studies botany at the Museum of Natural History with L. Cl. Richard and Desfontaines. 1811–1814, pharmacist of the naval forces in Antwerp. 1817–1820, pharmacist on the *Uranie*, Freycinet expedition. 1825, publishes *Flore des îles Malouines*. 1826, botany of the *Uranie*. 1828, correspondent of the Academy of Sciences. 1830–1832, pharmacist and botanist on the *Herminie*; visits Brazil, Chile, and Peru, then stays in Rio, explores the Mato Grosso and the province of Sao Paulo, and brings back 3,000 plants. 1836–1837, pharmacist and botanist on the *Bonite*, Vaillant expedition. 1837, member of the Academy of Sciences. From his voyages he brings back more than 10,000 plants, of which 1,200 to 1,400 are new. Dies in Angoulême, 1/6/1854.

GORE John. Born in America, about 1730. 1755, joins the navy. 1764–1766, assistant master on the *Dolphin*, Byron expedition. 1766–1768, midshipman on the *Dolphin*, Wallis expedition. 1768–1771, 2nd and then 1st lieutenant on the *Endeavour*, Cook's 1st voyage. 1772, takes Banks to Iceland. 1776–1780, 1st lieutenant on the *Resolution*, Cook's 3rd voyage; after the death of Clerke, takes command of the expedition and brings it to a conclusion. Captain, he takes over the post left vacant by Cook at Greenwich Hospital. Dies in Greenwich, 8/10/1790.

HAMELIN Jacques Félix Emmanuel. Born in Honfleur, 10/13/1768. 1786–1788, a sailor, despite family objections, embarks on the *Asie* for the coast of Angola. 1792, assistant helmsman on the *Entreprenant*. 1793, ensign on the *Proserpine*. 1795, lieutenant on the *Minerve*; seriously wounded in the leg during the capture of the *Bewick*. 1796, frigate captain on the *Révolution*, then commands the *Fraternité*. 1800–1804, commands the *Naturaliste*, Baudin expedition. 1805, captain, commands part of the Boulogne fleet commissioned at Le Havre. 1806, on the *Vénus*, breaks the blockade at Le Havre and Cherbourg. 1808, crosses the Indian Ocean. 1810, in the battle at Grandport (Ile de France) takes or destroys four British frigates. Baron of the Empire and rear admiral, commands an Escaut (Schelde) division, then a Brest squadron. 1818, major general at Toulon, then commander of the Mediter-

ranean naval forces. 1832, director general of the Map Depot. Dies in Paris, 11/25/1839.

HODGES William. Born in London, 1744. Student of Richard Wilson, paints theater decors and landscapes. 1772–1775, painter on the *Resolution*, Cook's 2nd voyage. 1775, goes to India, where he makes his fortune. 1777, begins to show at the Royal Academy. Dies in Brixham (Devon), 3/6/1797.

HOOKER Sir Joseph Dalton. Born in Halesworth (Suffolk), 6/30/1817. 1839, doctor of medicine in Glasgow, becomes friendly with Darwin. 1839–1843, assistant surgeon on the *Erebus*, J. C. Ross expedition. 1844–1847, publishes *Flora antarctica*. 1846–1847, botanist of the Geological Survey of Great Britain. 1847, member of the Royal Society. 1847–1851, travels in the Himalayas for Kew Gardens. 1853–1855, publishes *Flora Novae Zelandiae*. 1855, assistant director of Kew Gardens. 1855–1859, publishes *Flora Tasmaniae*. 1860, botanical voyage to Palestine. 1865, director of Kew Gardens. 1873–1878, president of the Royal Society. 1874, explores the Moroccan Atlas Mountains; 1877, the Rocky Mountains. 1885, leaves Kew Gardens. Dies in Sunningdale (Berkshire), 12/10/1911.

HUON DE KERMADEC Jean Michel. Born in Brest, 1748, into a family of Breton sailors. Takes part in the battles led by Orvilliers and Lamotte-Picquet. 1786–1787, vice chief of naval staff with d'Entrecasteaux on the *Résolution* at the time of voyage to China. 1791–1794, captain, commands the *Espérance*, d'Entrecasteaux expedition. Dies during a stop in Balade (New Caledonia), 5/6/1793.

JACQUINOT Charles Hector. Born in Nevers, 3/4/1796. 1822–1825, ensign on the *Coquille*, Duperrey expedition. 1826–1829, lieutenant commander, 2nd in command to Dumont d'Urville on the *Astrolabe*. 1837–1840, corvette captain, commands the *Zélée*, Dumont d'Urville's 2nd voyage. 1840, captain. 1842, commands the *Généreux*. 1842, begins publishing Dumont d'Urville's voyage. 1852, rear admiral, commands the Levant division. 1855, commands the Piraeus expedition, is named vice admiral. Dies in Toulon, 1879.

JURIEN DE LA GRAVIÈRE Pierre Roch. Born in Gannat (Allier), 11/5/1772. 1786, apprentice in Merchant Service on the corvette *Favorite*, then on the brig *Héros*. 1791–1794, *volontaire* on the *Espérance*, d'Entrecasteaux expedition; is made ensign. 1798, frigate captain. 1803, captain. 1809, in the battle of Sables d'Olonne with three frigates forces the withdrawal of 6 British vessels. 1814, takes possession of Bourbon Island. 1817, rear admiral and viscount. 1830, vice admiral and peer of France. 1848, retires. Dies in Paris, 1/15/1849. *Souvenirs d'un amiral* (1860) was assembled from his writings by his son, Rear Admiral J. B. E. Jurien de La Gravière.

KING James. Born in Clitheroe (Lancashire), 1750. 1765–1770, serves under Palliser in Newfoundland, then in the Mediterranean. 1774–1776, studies in Paris, then at Oxford. 1776–1780, 2nd lieutenant on the *Résolution*, Cook's 3rd voyage; 1779, after the death of Clerke, commands the *Dis-*

covery. 1780, captain. 1782, member of the Royal Society. 1783, gets tuberculosis, goes to Nice, where he dies in October 1784.

KOTZEBUE, Otto von. Born in Revel (present-day Tallinn, Estonia), 12/30/1787. 2nd son of the German writer A. F. F. von Kotzebue. 1803, student at the St. Petersburg school for cadets when Krusenstern takes him on his expedition. 1815–1818, lieutenant, commands the *Rurik*. Captain-lieutenant of the *gardes-marine*. 1821, publishes his *Reise um die Welt*. 1823–1826, commands the 2nd expedition on the *Predpriyatiye*. 1830, *Neue Reise um de Welt in 1823, 1824, 1825, und 1826*.

KRUSENSTERN Adam Ivan (Johann) Ritter von. Born in Haggud (Estonia), 11/19/1770. 1787–1789, serves in the navy during the Russo-Swedish War. 1793, serves on a British ship. 1797–1799, travels to the Indies and to Canton on a British merchant ship. 1803–1806, commands the expedition aboard the *Nadezhda* and the *Neva*. 1810–1814, publishes *Voyage Around the World, 1803–1806*, and in 1814 *Contribution to the Hydrography of the Great Ocean*. 1815, expedition to the Arctic in search of the Northwest Passage. 1824–1827, *Atlas of the Pacific Ocean*. 1826, rear admiral and director of the naval academy, member of the scientific committee of the Ministry of the Navy, of the St. Petersburg Academy of Sciences, corresponding member of the Paris and Stockholm Academies of Science. 1829, vice admiral. 1841, admiral. Dies on his estate of Asz, near Revel (Estonia), 8/24/1846.

LA BILLARDIERE Jacques Julien Houtou de. Born in Alençon, 10/23/1755. 1772, studies medicine and botany at Montpellier. 1780, works in the Jardin du Roi with Desfontaines and Lemonnier, who send him to Kew Gardens, where he meets Banks. 1786–1788, botanical voyage to the Levant. 1790, publishes *Icones plantarum Syriae rariorum*. 1791–1794, botanist on the *Recherche*, d'Entrecasteaux expedition; 1794, prisoner at Semarang. 1796, returns to France. 1799, publishes *Relation du voyage . . . ;* member of the Academy of Sciences. Republican and anti-Bonapartist, lives in retirement, spending the summers in a cottage near Paris. Dies in Paris, 1/8/1834.

LAMANON Robert de Paul, Chevalier de. Born in Salon-de-Provence, 1752. Initially a seminary student. 1774, begins walking tours through Provence, Switzerland, the Alps, and the Pyrenees. 1779, in a cellar on Rue Dauphine in Paris he discovers the skeleton of a fossil whale. 1780–1782, publishes studies on the fossils, geology, and mineralogy of the Midi. 1785, physicist, mineralogist, and meteorologist on the *Boussole*, La Pérouse expedition. Is killed at Tutuila (Samoa), 12/1/1787.

LANGSDORFF Carl Heinrich, Baron von. Born in Wollstein (Rhenish Hesse), 4/18/1774. 1797, doctor of the Prince of Waldeck, whom he accompanies to Portugal. 1803, naturalist on the *Nadezhda*, Krusenstern expedition, which he leaves in July 1804 to cross Siberia. 3/16/1808, arrives in St. Petersburg. 1812, publishes *Bermerkungen auf einer Reise um die Welt in den Jahren 1803 bis 1807*. 1813, Russian consul general in Brazil, where he collects plants with Freyreiss. 1821–1830, di-

Sir Joseph Dalton Hooker, photograph taken in about 1855. (National Portrait Gallery, London. Photo Maull and Polyblank © the museum/Photeb.)

rects a great Russian expedition to the unexplored territories of the Amazon Basin and Mato Grosso. Dies at Freiburg (Baden), 6/29/1852.

LA PÉROUSE Jean François de Galaup, Comte de. Born in the château de Gua (Albi), 8/23/1741, into an old merchant family ennobled in the 16th century. 1756, as a *garde de la marine* he participates in the Seven Years War. 1759, is wounded and taken prisoner by a British squadron. 1762, sails for America. 1764, navy ensign. 1767, commands the *Adour*. 1773–1775, takes part in the campaigns of Bengal, India, and China. 1775, on the Ile de France, falls in love with a young Creole, Eléonore Broudou, and wants to marry her; his family objects. 1778, lieutenant commander. 1779, as commander of the

DE LA BILLARDIÈRE,
(Jacques Jules)

Amazone, he takes part in the attack on Savannah, capturing a British raider and a frigate. 1780, captain. 1781, as commander of the *Astrée*, with La Touche-Tréville, he captures 2 British ships at Cape Breton. 1782, commander of the *Sceptre*, is ordered to attack the English posts in Hudson Bay; destroys the forts of York and Prince of Wales. 1783, marries Eléonore Broudou. 1785–1788, commands expedition on the *Boussole* and the *Astrolabe*.

LAPLACE Cyrille Pierre Théodore. Born "at sea," 11/7/1793. 1809, *élève* in the imperial navy. 1812, ensign. 1819, lieutenant commander. 1828, corvette captain. 1829–1833, commands the expedition of the *Favorite*. 1830, frigate captain. 1833–1839, publication of his *Voyage autour du monde . . .* 1834, captain. 1834–1836, commander of the *Artémise* in the Martinique observation squadron. 1837–1840, commands expedition on the *Artémise*. 1841, rear admiral. 1841–1854, publishes *Campagne de circumnavigation de l'Artémise.* 1844–1847, commands the naval division of the Antilles. 1853, vice admiral. 1854, member of the Admiralty Council, publishes *Observations sur l'émancipation des Noirs.* Dies in Brest in 1875.

LAUVERGNE Barthélemy. Born in Toulon, 7/4/1805. 1826–1829, secretary to the commander on the *Astrolabe*, 1st Dumont d'Urville expedition. 1830–1832, secretary to the commander and draftsman on the *Favorite*, 1st Laplace expedition. 1836–1837, painter on the *Bonite*, Vaillant expedition. 1838–1849, shows his paintings at the Salon. Dies in Carcès (Var), 11/16/1871.

LESSEPS Jean-Baptiste Barthélemy, Baron de. Born in Sète, 1/27/1766. Son of the consul general of France in St. Petersburg. 1783, vice consul in Kronstadt. 1785–1787, Russian interpreter aboard the *Astrolabe*, La Pérouse expedition; disembarks 10/7/1787 at Petropavlovsk, arrives at Versailles 10/17/1788. 1789, consul in Kronstadt. 1790, publishes the account of his voyage from Siberia to France. 1793, consul general in St. Petersburg. 1798, chargé d'affaires in Constantinople, is thrown into prison at the time of the Egyptian Expedition. 1802–1812, general commissioner of commercial relations with Russia. 1814, consul general and chargé d'affaires in Lisbon. 1831, publishes a new edition of La Pérouse's voyage "containing all that has been discovered since the shipwreck . . ." Dies in Lisbon, 4/6/1834.

LESSON René Primevère. Born in Rochefort, 3/20/1794. 1816, medical officer and then pharmacist, in charge of the Rochefort botanical garden. 1817, his first wife dies. 1822–1825, assistant surgeon and pharmacist on the *Coquille*, Duperrey expedition. 1829, publishes *Voyage médical autour du monde.* 1830, publishes *Journal d'un voyage pittoresque . . .* Professor of botany at the naval school in Rochefort, where he is to remain the rest of his life, writing numerous works on natural history. 1835, chief pharmacist in the navy. His 2nd wife dies, and, in 1838, his 15-year-old daughter. Dies in Rochefort, 4/28/1849.

LESUEUR Charles Alexandre. Born in Le Havre, 1/1/1778. 1800–1804, assistant gunner on the *Géographe*, Baudin expedition; distinguishes himself as a draftsman and is relieved of his regular duties to become Péron's assistant; makes more than 1,500 drawings and paintings. 1807–1815, works on the *Voyage aux terres australes* with Péron, then Freycinet. 1815, sails for the United States and settles in Philadelphia, from where he sends many things to the Paris Museum of Natural History; voyage on the Mississippi, meets Audubon, prepares a work on North American fish. 1836, returns to France, directs the Museum of Natural History at Le Havre. Dies in Le Havre at end of 1857.

LUTKE Fedor Petrovich, Count. Born in St. Petersburg, 9/17/1797. Studies at the school for naval cadets. 1817–1819, on the *Kamchatka*, Golovnin voyage. 1821–1824, on the *Apollo* in the Arctic seas. 1825, aide-de-camp of Nicolas I. 1826–1829, captain-lieutenant, commands the *Senyavin* expedition. 1835, publishes *Voyage Around the World . . .*; rear admiral. 1843, vice admiral. 1850, maritime governor of Revel, then in 1853 of Kronstadt. 1855, admiral and member of the Council of State. 1861, corresponding member of the Paris Academy of Sciences. 1866, president of the St. Petersburg Academy of Sciences. Dies in St. Petersburg, 8/8/1882.

MERTENS Karl Heinrich. Born in Bremen, 1796. Son of the botanist F. K. Mertens. 1820, doctor of medicine. 1826–1829, surgeon and naturalist on the *Senyavin*,

Lütke expedition. 1829–1830, sails again on the *Senyavin* for the coast of Iceland. Dies on his return to St. Petersburg, 9/17/1830.

MILIUS Pierre Bernard. Born in Bordeaux, January 1773. Son of a shipbuilder. 1787–1793, apprentice in the merchant service; makes several voyages to the Antilles. 1793, serves on the frigate *Précieuse*; his heroism wins him rank of ensign. 1796, promoted to lieutenant. 1800, lieutenant on the *Naturaliste*, Baudin expedition. 1801, frigate captain; after the death of Baudin (1803), takes command of the *Géographe*, which he brings back to France. 1805, commands the *Didon*, is taken to Great Britain as a prisoner. 1806, freed on giving his word that he will not return to active service. 1811, captain, commands the port of Venice. 1814, chief of the naval mission charged with retaking possession of Martinique and Guadeloupe. 1818–1821, governor of Bourbon Island. 1821, baron. 1822, commander and administrator of Cayenne, French Guiana. 1827, rear admiral. Dies of paralysis at Bourbonne-les-Bains, 8/11/1829.

NASSAU-SIEGEN Charles Henri Nicholas Othon, Prince d'Orange et de. Born in Paris, 1/6/1745. 1761, 2nd lieutenant, captain of dragoons; obtains authorization to accompany Bougainville. 1766–1769, on the *Boudeuse*. 1778, takes part in the American Revolution, raising a legion in his name. 1783, enters the Russian navy. 1788, defeats a Turkish fleet in the Black Sea. 1789, admiral, commands the Russian fleet in the Baltic, defeats the Swedish squadron commanded by Gustavus III. 1792, sent by Catherine II to the banks of the Rhine in order to organize the war against revolutionary France. Dies in the Ukraine, 1808.

NELSON David. Gardener-botanist of Kew Gardens, a protegé of Banks. 1773–1774, takes part in an expedition to the Arctic coasts of America. 1776–1780, midshipman on the *Discovery*, Cook's 3rd voyage. 1787, botanist on the *Bounty*, Bligh expedition. 1789, is disembarked with Bligh at the time of the mutiny. Dies of fever in Kupang (Timor), 6/20/1789.

Portrait of Krusenstern. Engraving by F. Lehmann, 1812, in Voyage Around the World. (*Bibliothèque du Muséum d'histoire naturelle, Paris. Photo © Bibl. du Muséum/Photeb.*)

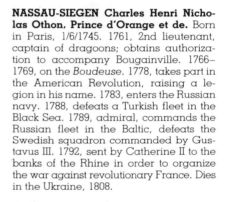

J. J. de La Billardière in 1799. Engraving by Julien Boilly, 1831. (Bibliothèque nationale, Paris. Photo © Bibl. nat./Photeb.)

C. A. Lesueur on the Géographe, resting on a cage containing fowl. Self-portrait in pencil. (Muséum d'histoire naturelle, Le Havre. Photo © the museum/Photeb.)

PARIS François. Born in Brest, 1806. 1820, enters the naval academy at Angoulême. 1826–1829, *élève* on the *Astrolabe*, 1st Dumont d'Urville expedition; is made ensign. 1830–1832, frigate lieutenant on the *Favorite*, 1st Laplace expedition. 1837–1840, lieutenant commander on the *Artémise*, 2nd Laplace expedition. Makes numerous drawings during these voyages. 1846, captain, has an arm amputated as a result of an accident. 1858, rear admiral. 1862, member of the Academy of Sciences. 1864, vice admiral. 1875, on his retirement becomes the curator of the naval museum in the Louvre. Publishes several important works. Dies in Paris in 1893.

PERON François. Born in Cérilly (Allier), 1775. 1792, gives up his studies in theology to enlist in the Allier battalion. Is discharged after losing his right eye. His fiancée leaves him. Following this disappointment, he studies medicine in Paris. A. L. de Jussieu has him appointed zoologist of the Baudin expedition (1800–1804). 1806, unanimously elected a member of the Institute. 1807, publishes the 1st volume of *Voyage aux terres australes*. Dies in Cérilly, 12/14/1810.

PICKERSGILL Richard. Born in West Tanfield (Yorkshire), 1749. 1766–1768, apprentice aboard the *Dolphin*, Wallis expedition. 2nd petty officer and then master of the *Endeavor*, Cook's 1st voyage. 1772–1775, lieutenant on the *Resolution*, Cook's 2nd voyage. 1776, commands the schooner *Lion*, voyage to Baffin Bay. On return is court-martialed for drunkenness and other irregularities. Given no assignment by the Admiralty, he agrees to command a privateer. Drowns in the Thames in July 1779.

QUOY Jean René Constant. Born in St. Jean de Liversay (Charente-Maritime), 1790. 1806, medical studies at Rochefort; student of Vivès. 1808, first cruise on the corvette *Département des Landes*, to the Antilles and Réunion. 1817–1820, surgeon and zoologist on the *Uranie*, Freycinet expedition. 1830, publishes the zoology of the *Uranie* with Gaimard. 1826–1829, doctor and naturalist on the *Astrolabe*, first Dumont d'Urville expedition. 1832–1835, professor of medicine at the Rochefort naval school. 1833, publishes the zoology of the *Astrolabe* with Gaimard. Dies in Rochefort, 1869.

RICHE Claude Antoine Gaspard. Born in Chamblet (Beaujolais), 8/20/1762. Doctor in Montpellier. 1788, first secretary of the Philomathic Society. 1791–1794, naturalist on the *Espérance*, d'Entrecasteaux expedition. 1797, very ill, returns to France and goes to take the cure at Mont-Dore, where he dies, 9/5/1797.

ROSS Sir James Clark. Born in London, 4/15/1800. 1812, joins the navy. 1818, accompanies his uncle, John Ross, and Parry on their voyage in search of a Northwest Passage by way of Baffin Bay. 1819–1827, participates in four cruises by Parry in search of this passage. 1828–1833, J. Ross's second on his 2nd Arctic expedition. 1835–1838, with Sabine and Lloyd he is assigned to make a magnetic study of Great Britain. 1839–1843, captain, commands the Antarctic expedition on the *Erebus* and the *Terror*. Made a peer on his return; mar-

ries. 1847, publishes his *Voyage of Discovery . . . .* 1848, member of the Royal Society. 1848–1849, directs one of the groups sent to look for Sir John Franklin, then ceases to go to sea. 1856, rear admiral. Dies in Aylesbury (Buckinghamshire), 4/3/1862.

ROSSEL Elisabeth Paul Edouard, Chevalier de. Born in Sens, 9/11/1765. 1780, *garde de la marine*. 1785, accompanies d'Entrecasteaux to India. 1791, lieutenant on the *Recherche*, d'Entrecasteaux expedition; July 1794, takes command of the expedition. 1795, embarks at Surabaja on a Dutch vessel. Is made prisoner by the English and not released until 1802. 1808,

publishes *Voyage d'Entrecasteaux. . . .* 1811, member of the Central Astronomical Office. 1812, member of the Academy of Sciences. 1814, assistant director general and in 1826 director general of maps and charts. 1828, rear admiral. 1st president of the Geography Society. Dies in Paris, 11/20/1829.

SOLANDER Daniel Carl. Born in Piteå (Nordland, Sweden), 2/19/1736. 1750, enters the University of Uppsala to study theology but becomes a student of Linnaeus. 1753–1766, botanical voyages to Lapland, Russia, and the Canary Islands. 1760, Linnaeus, who wants to make him into his successor, sends Solander to London to demonstrate his system. 1763, joins the British Museum and becomes the assistant curator in 1766. 1768–1771, assistant to Banks aboard the *Endeavour*, Cook's 1st voyage. 1772, accompanies Banks on his expedition to the Hebrides and to Iceland. 1773, curator of the natural history department of the British Museum. Dies in London, 5/13/1782.

SPARRMAN Anders. Born in Uppland (Sweden), 1747. 1764, assistant surgeon on voyage to India and China. 1768, at the University of Uppsala he studies medicine and is a student of Linnaeus. 1770, doctor of medicine. 1772, is sent by the Swedish government on a botanical mission to Cape Town. 1772–1775, assistant naturalist on the *Resolution*, Cook's 2nd voyage. 1775, explores South Africa, where he studies the fauna and the bush-

men. 1778–1779, president of the natural history collection of Stockholm's Academy of Sciences. 1783, publishes his *Voyage*. 1787, makes a stay in Senegal. Dies in 1820.

STOKES John Lort. 1826–1830, midshipman on the *Beagle* under the command of his father, Captain Pringle Stokes, then of FitzRoy, King expedition. 1831–1836, 3rd lieutenant on the *Beagle*, FitzRoy expedition. Governor of the Falkland Islands. 1857, chief of the maritime department of the Board of Trade.

VAILLANT Auguste Nicolas. Born in Paris, 7/2/1793. Begins as an apprentice. 1810, midshipman 2nd class in Helder's naval forces. 1813, midshipman 1st class; with a "pistol in his hand," he commands the sloop *Texel*, which has a Dutch crew. 1814, lieutenant in infantry and then artillery in Holland. 1816, is dismissed from officers' ranks as a Bonapartist after being denounced. 1818, ship's ensign, he follows Milius to Guiana. 1824, ship's lieutenant, commands the *Estafette* in the Levant. 1828–1830, chief of Admiral de Rigny's staff in the Peloponnesus expedition. 1831, corvette captain, commands the *Actéon*. 1836–1837, commands the expedition of the *Bonite*. 1838, captain, participates in the Mexico and La Plata campaigns. 1848, prefect of the 4th maritime district. 1849, rear admiral. 1851, Minister of the Navy; governor general of the Antilles, then of Martinique. 1853, returns to France for health reasons. Dies in Paris, 11/1/1858.

VANCOUVER George. Born in King's Lynn (Petersham, Surrey), 6/22/1757. 1772–1775, midshipman on the *Resolution*, Cook's 2nd voyage. 1776–1780, midshipman on the *Discovery*, Cook's 3rd voyage. 1780, lieutenant commander; 1781–1789, in the squadron of Admiral Rodney in the Antilles. 1789, responsible for the Jamaica naval station. 1791–1795, commands the exploration expedition to the North Pacific of the *Discovery* and the *Chatham*. Dies of exhaustion in Richmond (Surrey), 5/10/1798; the same year sees the publication of his *A Voyage of Discovery to the North Pacific*, published by his brother.

WALLIS Samuel. Born in Fentonwood, 1728. 1755, lieutenant commander. 1757, captain. 1758, command in Canada, where he participates in the capture of Louisbourg. 1766–1768, commands the expedition of the *Dolphin* and the *Swallow*. 1772, resigns from active service. 1780, navy commissioner. Dies in London, 1/21/1795.

WEBBER John. Born in London, 10/6/1752. Son of a Berne sculptor settled in London. 1769–1770, in Paris for his artistic education. 1771, completes his studies at the Royal Academy, London. 1776–1780, painter on the *Resolution*, Cook's 3rd voyage. 1780–1792, exhibits in London. 1787–1792, publishes 16 color views of Cook's 3rd voyage. 1792, member of the Royal Academy. Dies in London, 4/29/1793.

WESTALL William. Born in Hertford, 10/12/1781. Student of his older brother, Richard, historical painter. 1801–1803, landscape painter on the *Investigator*, Flinders expedition. 1803, after the shipwreck of the *Investigator*, he goes to China, then Bombay, returning to En-

François Péron on his return from the Baudin expedition. Engraving by Tardieu from a drawing by C. A. Lesueur. (Bibliothèque nationale, Paris. Photo © Bibl. nat./Photeb.)

gland in 1805. Shows his work—especially topographic watercolors—in London until his death. Dies victim of an accident in St. John's Wood, 1/22/1850.

WICKHAM John Clements. 1826–1830, midshipman, then lieutenant on the *Adventure*, King expedition. 1831–1836, 1st lieutenant on the *Beagle*, FitzRoy expedition. 1837, replaces King as chief of the naval station in Australia.

WILKES Charles. Born in New York, 4/3/1798. 1818, enters the navy as a midshipman. 1826, lieutenant commander. 1830, heads the Division of Instruments and Maps. 1829–1835, makes several voyages to the South Seas. 1838–1842, commands the first American scientific expedition. 1845–1876, publishes the account of the voyage. 1844, commander. 1862, commodore. During the Civil War, commands the James River fleet. 1866, rear admiral, retires. Dies in Washington, D.C., 2/7/1877.

WILLAUMEZ Jean-Baptiste Philibert. Born in Le Palais (Belle-Ile), 8/17/1763. Son of a gunner, he serves in the ranks before 1789. 1791–1794, ensign on the *Espérance*, d'Entrecasteaux expedition. 1795, captain. 1802, participates in the expedition to San Domingo. 1804, commands the Brest squadron, successfully battling the British at Cape Town and in the Antilles. Rear admiral. 1819, vice admiral. 1820, publishes a very complete *Dictionnaire de la marine*. 1837, count and peer of France. 1844, retires. Dies in Suresnes, 5/17/1845.

Charles Wilkes as a U.S. Navy commander. Engraving by R. W. Dodson from a drawing by Thomas Sully. (Bibliothèque nationale, Paris. Photo © Bibl. nat./Photeb.)

Geographical Dictionary

Amboina: The marketplace of the Malay quarter. Anonymous engraving from the Atlas historique *of Dumont d'Urville's first voyage. (Bibliothèque du Muséum d'histoire naturelle, Paris. Photo © Bibl. du Muséum/Photeb.)*

ADMIRALTY ISLANDS. 2°10′S–147°E. Archipelago of MELANESIA situated N of NEW GUINEA. It was discovered in 1616 by the Dutchmen Le Maire and Schouten. Carteret, who visited it in 1767, gave the islands their present name. Stop by d'Entrecasteaux (1792). The Admiralty Islands, occupied by the Germans from 1885 to 1914, were afterward placed under an Australian mandate.

ALASKA. Large peninsula at the extreme NW of North America, it is prolonged by the ALEUTIAN ISLANDS and situated between 71° and 54°N and between 130° and 176°W. It was discovered in 1741 by Bering and Chirikov, who took possession of it in the name of the emperor of Russia. At the end of the 18th century, the peninsula and the surrounding continental territories were exploited for furs by the Russian-American Company. Cook went along the coasts in 1778 during his 3rd voyage. La Pérouse anchored there in 1786. Lisiansky's *Neva* stayed there in 1804–1805; Kotzebue was there in 1816 and 1817, and Lütke in 1827. Beechey stopped there in 1826 and 1827, and Belcher in 1837. In 1867, Alaska was sold by Russia to the United States.

ALEUTIAN ISLANDS. 52°N–176°W. String of islands forming a regular curve 2,300 kilometers long between ALASKA (North America) and KAMCHATKA (North Asia) and bounding the N of the Pacific Ocean and the S of the BERING SEA. The archipelago was discovered by Bering, who in 1741 died on the island bearing his name. Cook went along it in 1778 at the time of his 3rd voyage (see UNALASKA). The Aleutians belonged to Russia until the sale of Alaska.

AMBOINA. 3°43′S–126°12′E. Small island of the MOLUCCA ISLANDS. Discovered in 1512 by António de Abreu, it was occupied by the Portuguese from 1564 to 1605. The Dutch seized it and began growing spices (cloves and nutmeg), of which they maintained a monopoly. The island was occu-

pied by the English from 1796 to 1802, then from 1810 to 1817, and afterward returned to Holland. Stopovers by d'Entrecasteaux (1792), Duperrey (1823), Dumont d'Urville (1827 and 1828), and Belcher (1840).

ASCENSION ISLAND. 7°57′S–14°22′W. Situated in the South Atlantic, facing the African coast, 1,330 kilometers N of ST. HELENA, it was discovered on Ascension Day 1502 by the Spaniard Juan de Nova and annexed by England in 1815. Ships on the way north often stopped there after putting into St. Helena.

AUCKLAND ISLANDS. 51°S–166°30′E. Group of uninhabited islands, situated S of NEW ZEALAND, discovered by the whaler Bristow in 1806. Dumont d'Urville, Wilkes, and Ross stopped there in 1840.

AUSTRALIA. See NEW HOLLAND.

BANKS ISLANDS. 13°50′S–167°30′E. Archipelago of MELANESIA, situated between the NEW HEBRIDES and the SANTA CRUZ ISLANDS. It was sighted in 1606 by the Spaniard Queiros but not discovered until 1788 by Captain Bligh, who gave it the name of Sir Joseph Banks.

BATAVIA. Present-day Djakarta. 6°10′S–106°48′E. Capital of the island of Java. Founded in 1619 by Jan Coen, governor-general of the Dutch East India Company, on the site of the former city of Jacatra, it became the center of the Dutch empire of the East Indies. Most of the circumnavigators stopped there after crossing the Pacific Ocean and before entering the Indian Ocean. There they found the European civilization with which they had lost contact for months—letters from their families were often waiting—but the unhealthiness of the climate took its toll, especially in the form of dysentery victims.

BERING SEA. 60°N–175°W. Secondary sea N of the Pacific between ALASKA on the E and Siberia on the W. It communicates on the N with the Arctic Ocean by the BERING STRAIT and is bounded on the S by the curve of the ALEUTIAN ISLANDS. It was explored by Bering in 1728–1729 and 1740–1741.

BERING STRAIT. 65°30′N–169°W. Arm of the sea that separates the NE end of the Asiatic continent from the NW end of the American continent and links the Arctic Ocean and the BERING SEA. It was reconnoitered in 1728 by Vitus Bering, a Danish navigator in the service of Russia.

BISMARCK ARCHIPELAGO. See NEW BRITAIN.

BONIN ISLANDS. Japanese name Ogasawara. 27°N–142°10′E. Group of islands off the Japanese island of Kyūshū. Sighted in the 16th century by the Spaniards, who

called them Islas del Arzobispo, then reconnoitered in 1639 by the Dutchman Mathieu Quast, the Bonins were rediscovered by Beechey in 1827, then by Lütke in 1829. Long uninhabited, in 1875 these islands were recognized as belonging to Japan.

BORA BORA. See SOCIETY ISLANDS.

BOURBON ISLAND. Present-day Réunion. 21°06′S–55°36′E. Volcanic and mountainous island, the westernmost of the MASCARENE ISLANDS, in the Indian Ocean about 700 kilometers to the E of Madagascar. Discovered in 1528 by the Portuguese Pedro Mascarenhas and at that time uninhabited, it was occupied by some French in 1638, annexed by the French East India Company under the name of Bourbon in 1665, and then became a possession of the French crown. Conquered by the English in 1810, it was returned to France in 1814. Named Réunion Island under the Revolution—to recall the "reunion" of the Marseilles forces with the National Guard in 1792—then renamed Bonaparte Island, after 1848 it was once again called Réunion. French circumnavigators stopped there: Freycinet (1818), H. de Bougainville (1824), Dumont d'Urville (1828 and 1840), Laplace (1830 and 1837), Vaillant (1837), and Dupetit-Thouars (1839).

BURU ISLAND. See MOLUCCA ISLANDS.

CANARY ISLANDS. 26°N–15°30′W. Mountainous volcanic archipelago in the Atlantic 100 kilometers from the W coast of Africa. It includes, in order of size, 7 inhabited islands: Tenerife, Fuerteventura, Grand Canary, Lanzarote, La Palma, Gomera, and Hierro, as well as several small uninhabited islands. Already visited by the Phoenicians, in 1479 the Canaries were annexed by Spain. Most voyages of circumnavigation made this their first stop, often anchoring in the port of Santa Cruz de Tenerife.

CAPE HORN. 56°S–65°16′W. Promontory forming the S tip of South America at the extremity of the southernmost island of TIERRA DEL FUEGO. The sea around this vertical cliff more than 600 meters high is made very dangerous by reefs and shallows, winds, and coastal currents. Sighted by the Englishman Sir Francis Drake in 1578, Cape Horn was reconnoitered in 1616 by the Dutchmen Le Maire and Schouten. They gave it the name of one of their ships, the *Hoorn*, which was also the name of their native city.

CAPE OF GOOD HOPE. 34°S–18°30′E. Promontory at the W of the southern end of the African continent. It was discovered in 1486 by the Portuguese Bartolomeu Diaz, who named it *Cabo Tormentoso*, Cape of Storms. It was afterward called Good Hope by King Joao II of Portugal, who was aware that his mariners had reached the entrance of the sea that led to the Indies. The Cape of Good Hope was rounded for the first time by Vasco da Gama in 1497.

CAPE TOWN. 33°55'S–18°22'E. Vast port on Table Bay at the foot of Table Mountain at the southern end of Africa. Founded by Dutch settlers in 1652 and made the capital of the colony, the city was occupied by the English from 1795 to 1802, and definitively retaken by them in 1806. Cape Town was an obligatory stop for all European ships going to the Indian Ocean or returning from there to Europe. They stayed a long time to reprovision and to let their crews rest.

CAPE VERDE ISLANDS. 16°N–24°W. Atlantic archipelago 500 kilometers from western Africa off the coast of Cape Vert—promontory of the coast of Senegal—it is composed of many islands. Discovered in 1450 by the Genoese Antonio de Noli, who was in the service of Portugal, it remained Portuguese until its independence in 1975. Circumnavigators, especially those from England, often made it their first stop after MADEIRA.

CAROLINE ISLANDS. 8°N–147°E. Archipelago of MICRONESIA that extends 2,800 kilometers between the PHILIPPINE ISLANDS on the W, the MARIANAS in the N, and the MARSHALL ISLANDS in the E. It includes more than 450 small, low, and flat islands, the principal ones being Kusaie, Yap, Truk, and Ponape. Sighted in 1527 by the Portuguese Diego da Rocha, then by the Spaniard Villalobos in 1543, they were afterward forgotten. Rediscovered in 1686 by the Spaniard Francisco Lazeano, who gave them the name of his master, King Charles II, the Carolines remained Spanish possessions until 1898. Sold at that time to Germany, they were placed under a Japanese mandate in 1919 and have been occupied by the United States since 1945. The islands were visited by Duperrey (1824), Lütke (1827 and 1828), and Dumont d'Urville (1838).

CELEBES ISLAND. Indonesian name Sulawesi. 2°S–121°E. Large island situated E of Borneo—from which it is separated by the Makasar Strait—W of the MOLUCCA ISLANDS, and S of the PHILIPPINE ISLANDS, from which it is separated by the Celebes Sea. A central mountain mass, from which detach volcanic chains, forms 4 peninsulas. The island was discovered by the Spanish in 1526 and conquered by the Dutch in 1607. Carteret stopped at Makasar and then at Bonthain in 1767–1768. Stops by Dumont d'Urville in 1828 and Belcher in 1840. Since 1950, Sulawesi has been part of the Republic of Indonesia.

CERAM. See MOLUCCA ISLANDS.

COOK ISLANDS or **HERVEY ISLANDS.** 20°S–158°W. Archipelago of POLYNESIA to the N of the Tropic of Capricorn and SW of the SOCIETY ISLANDS. In 1606, the Spaniard Queiros discovered Rakahanga Island in the N of the archipelago. Cook landed in 1773 on the island he called Hervey, and he visited it again in 1775. The other islands are Rarotonga, Manahiki, and Penrhyn. The archipelago became a British protectorate in 1888 and came officially under NEW ZEALAND in 1901.

Ten years later they became part of New Zealand and in 1965 gained independence.

COOK STRAIT. See QUEEN CHARLOTTE SOUND.

DANGEROUS ARCHIPELAGO. See TUAMOTU.

DAVIS LAND. Hypothetical territory supposedly discoverd in 1687 by the Englishman Edward Davis, commander after William Dampier of the *Bachelor's Delight.* Long looked for by circumnavigators, it was never refound.

DESOLATION ISLANDS. See KERGUELEN ISLANDS.

EASTER ISLAND. Native name Rapa Nui. 27°08'S–109°23'W. Triangular volcanic island 118 square kilometers, the easternmost island of POLYNESIA, situated under the Tropic of Capricorn off the coast of South America. It was discovered on Easter Sunday, April 5, 1722, by the Dutchman Jacob Roggeveen. In 1770, a Spanish expedition commanded by Felipe Gonzalez took possession of it. In 1774, Cook made a brief stop there. In 1786, La Pérouse introduced new crops and domestic animals (sheep and pigs). In 1805, the American ship *Nancy* managed to kidnap from the island 12 men and 10 women for use in seal fishing. Stops by Kotzebue (1816), Beechey (1825), and Dupetit-Thouars (1838). In about 1860, Peruvians went there to capture slaves for their guano trade; in 1862, one of their expeditions ravaged the island and more than 1,000 islanders were taken away. Chile took possession of the island in 1888.

FALKLAND ISLANDS. 51°45'S–59°W. Known to the French as the Malouines, this archipelago of the South Atlantic is situated off the eastern coast of South America; it includes 2 principal islands—West Falkland and East Falkland, or Soledad—and 200 islets or reefs. Discovered in 1592 by the Englishman John Davis and visited in 1683 by the Englishman Dampier, who gave them the name of the treasurer of the navy, Viscount Falkland, the archipelago was colonized by the Acadians under the leadership of Bougainville, who, supported by the shipbuilders of St. Malo, called them the Malouines. Visited by Byron in 1765, the islands were ceded by France to Spain in 1767 and in 1771 went to Great Britain, which established a colony there in 1833. Freycinet's *Uranie* was shipwrecked there in 1820. Duperrey sojourned there in 1822. FitzRoy stopped there in 1833 and 1834, and Ross in 1842.

FIJI ISLANDS. 18°S–175°E. Archipelago in POLYNESIA, it is composed of several volcanic islands, including Viti Levu, Vanua Levu, and a multitude of madreporic islands and islets that are largely uninhabited. Discovered by the Dutchman Abel Tasman in 1643, then visited by the Englishmen Bligh (1789), Barber (1794), and Wilson (1797). The Russian Bellingshausen reconnoitered some 20 islands in 1820. Dumont d'Urville in 1827 and again in 1838 made the 1st systematic reconnaissance, which was completed by the Wilkes expedition in 1840. The archipelago was then evangelized by English Methodist mis-

sionaries. Fiji was annexed by Great Britain in 1874. It became independent in 1970.

FRIENDLY ISLANDS. Present-day Tonga Archipelago. 20°S–175°W. Archipelago of POLYNESIA, situated N of NEW ZEALAND, W of the NEW HEBRIDES, E of the SOCIETY ISLANDS. Covering an area of 997 square kilometers, it includes 180 islands or islets, some of which are volcanic though most are coral. The principal island is Tongatapu (607 square kilometers). The archipelago was discovered by the Dutchmen Le Maire and Schouten in 1615 and visited by Tasman in 1643. They gave Dutch names to the islands reconnoitered: Middleburg (Eua), Amsterdam (Tongatapu), and Rotterdam (Anamooka). Wallis discovered 2 islands in 1767. Cook, who stayed there for a long time in 1773, 1774, and 1777, called them the Friendly Islands. In 1788, La Pérouse stopped there before disap-

Celebes: The Tondano road. Drawing by Sainson from the Atlas historique *of Dumont d'Urville's first voyage. (Bibliothèque du Muséum d'histoire naturelle, Paris. Photo © Bibl. du Muséum/Photeb.)*

pearing. In 1793, d'Entrecasteaux anchored at Tonga, and Malaspina traversed the archipelago. Dumont d'Urville stayed in Tonga in 1827 and 1838, and Wilkes in 1840. Long a British protectorate, the Tonga archipelago became independent in 1959.

GALAPAGOS ISLANDS. 0°30'S–90°30'W. Volcanic archipelago in the Pacific Ocean, situated 950 kilometers W of Ecuador. Visited by Vancouver in 1795, it was annexed by Ecuador in 1832. FitzRoy and Darwin stayed there for some time in 1835. The Galápagos were next visited by Vaillant in 1836 and Dupetit-Thouars in 1838.

GAMBIER ISLANDS. 23°8'S–137°20'W. Archipelago in POLYNESIA situated to SE of TUAMOTU and including a dozen volcanic islands surrounded by coral reefs. The principal island is Mangareva. The archipelago was discovered in 1797 by the Englishman Wilson, who was transporting missionaries to Polynesia on the *Duff*; he gave it the name of Admiral Gambier, who had distinguished himself in the wars against Napoleon. Beechey stopped there in 1825–1826. In 1834, 2 French priests founded a mission, which soon prospered. Dumont d'Urville stopped in 1838. The Gambier Islands were annexed by France in 1881.

GILBERT ISLANDS. Present-day Kiribati. 0°30'S–174°E. Archipelago in MICRONESIA, situated SE of the MARSHALL ISLANDS; composed of several volcanic islands and madreporic islets and peopled with a mixture of Papuans and Polynesians. In 1765, Byron discovered Nikunau Island, to which his name was given, but the archipelago was not explored until the Englishmen Marshall and Gilbert did so in 1788. The exploration was completed by Wilkes in 1840–1841. A protectorate and then a British colony, the archipelago became independent in 1979 under the name Kiribati.

GUAM ISLAND. See MARIANAS.

Kamchatka: View of Petropavlovsk. Lithograph by Emile Lassalle after Mesnard. Voyage autour du monde sur la *Vénus*, 1836–1839. *(Musée de la Marine, Paris. Photo by Michel Didier © Photeb.)*

HAWAIIAN ISLANDS. See SANDWICH ISLANDS.

HERVEY ISLANDS. See COOK ISLANDS.

HUAHINE ISLAND. See SOCIETY ISLANDS.

ILE DE FRANCE. Present-day Mauritius; French, Maurice. 20°17'S–57°33'E. Volcanic island in the MASCARENE ISLANDS in the Indian Ocean. Found deserted by the Portuguese navigator Pedro Mascarenhas in 1507, it was occupied after 1598 by the Dutch, who gave it the name of *stathouder* Maurice of Nassau, then abandoned by them in 1711. Recolonized by the French from Bourbon Island, in 1721 it became the Ile de France. Baudin stopped there in 1801 and died there in 1803. Flinders was imprisoned there from 1803 to 1810. Conquered by the English in 1810 and recognized as a British possession by the 1814 Treaty of Paris, it went back to its old name, becoming independent in 1966. Stops were made there by Freycinet (1818), Dumont d'Urville (1828), Laplace (1830, 1837), and FitzRoy (1836).

ISLE OF PINES or **ILE DES PINS.** Part of the archipelago of NEW CALEDONIA and situated to the SE of Grande Terre, it was discovered by Cook in 1774. Having become French, from 1872 to 1875 it served as a penal colony for those condemned to deportation after the French Commune.

JUAN DE FUCA, STRAIT OF. See VANCOUVER ISLAND.

JUAN FERNANDEZ ISLANDS. 33°S–80°W. 3-island archipelago some 600 kilometers from the SW coast of South America. Discovered in 1563 by the Spaniard Juan Fernandez, soldier in Pizarro's army, they were visited by buccaneers in the 17th century. On one of the islands, Mas à Tierra, Woodes Rogers, in 1708, picked up the Scottish sailor Alexander Selkirk, who had been shipwrecked and had lived there alone for more than four years. Selkirk's adventures inspired Daniel Defoe's *Robinson Crusoe*. The archipelago belongs to Chile.

KAMCHATKA. 56°N–158°E. Mountainous and volcanic peninsula of northeast Siberia bathed on the W by the OKHOTSK SEA and on the E by the BERING SEA. Discovered in 1696 by the Russians, who built the port and the city of Petropavlovsk (Saint Peter and Saint Paul), it was linked to Russia by the sea for the 1st time in 1716. The *Resolution* and the *Discovery*, commanded by Clerke after Cook's death, anchored there in 1779, as did La Pérouse in 1787. Later stops by Krusenstern (1804, 1805), Kotzebue (1816), Beechey (1826, 1827), Lütke (1827, 1828), and Dupetit-Thouars (1837).

KERGUELEN ISLANDS or **DESOLATION ISLANDS.** 49°15'S–69°10'E. Southern archipelago of the Indian Ocean, situated about halfway between South Africa and Australia. In 1772 and 1774, Kerguelen de Trémarec discovered one of these islands and took possession of it in the name of the king of France. In 1776, Cook became aware that there was an archipelago. In 1840, Ross made the 1st exploration. The Kerguelens have been French since 1772.

KURIL ISLANDS. 50°50'N–156°36'E. Archipelago of the northern Pacific extending 1,200 kilometers between the S point of KAMCHATKA and the Japanese island of YESO. Partly explored in 1643 by the Dutchman De Vries on the *Kastrikum*, the Kuriles were visited by La Pérouse in 1787. Initially occupied by the Russians, they were ceded (1875) to Japan in exchange for the S part of SAKHALIN. The Japanese ceded them to the USSR after World War II.

LE MAIRE STRAIT. 54°50'S–65°W. It links the Atlantic and the Pacific between TIERRA DEL FUEGO and STATEN ISLAND. It was discovered by the Dutch navigators Jakob Le Maire and Willem Schouten.

LOUISIADES. 11°S–153°E. Archipelago in MELANESIA to the SE of NEW GUINEA. It is composed of islands and coral reefs scattered from the NW to the SE along a 390-kilometer stretch. Discovered in 1606 by the Spaniard Torres, then sighted in 1768 by Bougainville, who gave it the name of the king of France, the archipelago was explored by La Pérouse in 1787 and visited by Dumont d'Urville in 1840. It is now part of Papua New Guinea.

LOYALTY ISLANDS or **LOYAUTE ISLANDS.** 21°S–167°E. Small island group that is a dependency of NEW CALEDONIA, from which it is separated by a passage 150 kilometers wide. It was discovered in 1792 by d'Entrecasteaux, and was for some time under British rule. Dumont d'Urville reconnoitered it in 1840. It has been a French possession since 1864.

MACQUARIE ISLANDS. 54°36'S–158°55'E. Volcanic archipelago of the southern Pacific, near the Antarctic Circle. Its principal island bears the name of Lord Macquarie, governor of NEW SOUTH WALES from 1809 to 1821. It was visited by Bellingshausen in 1820. These islands are a dependency of Tasmania.

MADEIRA. 32°40'N–16°45'W. Island situated in the Atlantic 545 kilometers to the W of Africa. Capital: Funchal. It is the center of a small archipelago including Porto Santo and the 2 uninhabited islands of Desertas and Selvagens. Discovered in the 14th century by the Portuguese when it was uninhabited, Madeira was surveyed in 1419 and then settled by Portuguese colonists. The circumnavigators, especially the English, often made this their 1st stop, for reprovisioning and to load on Madeira wine, which did not spoil easily.

MAGELLAN, STRAIT OF. 54°S–71°W. It links the Atlantic and the Pacific between the tip of South America on the one hand and TIERRA DEL FUEGO and the Magellan Archipelago on the other. It consists of a succession of fiords that forms a vast curve. Reconnoitered by Magellan in 1520, it was often used by circumnavigators to avoid a detour around the feared Cape Horn.

MAGELLAN ARCHIPELAGO. See TIERRA DEL FUEGO.

MALOUINES. See FALKLAND ISLANDS.

MARIANAS. 16°N–145°30'E. Archipelago in MICRONESIA, situated in the E of the Pacific Ocean, to the E of the PHILIPPINE IS-

LANDS and the N of the CAROLINE ISLANDS. It is composed of 15 volcanic islands subject to eruptions and quakes. The principal island is Guam. The archipelago was discovered in 1521 by Magellan, who gave the name of Ladrones, or Thieves Islands, to 2 of these islands, probably Guam and Rota. The Spaniard Legaspi took possession of it in the name of Philip II in 1565. In the 17th century, the islands received the name of the queen of Spain, Mariana of Austria, who sent missionaries there. The Englishman Dampier landed in Guam in 1684. After the 18th century, the cruelty of Spanish rule had all but depopulated the islands. Since the end of World War II, the Marianas have been administered by the United States. They were visited by Byron (1765) and by Wallis (1767). Stops by Malaspina (1792), Kotzebue (1817), Freycinet (1819), Dumont d'Urville (1828, 1839).

MARION-AND-CROZET. 46°S–52°E. Small archipelago in the S of the Indian Ocean. It was discovered by Marion du Fresne and Crozet in 1772 and visited by Cook in 1776. Often referred to as the Crozet Islands or the Marion Islands.

MARQUESA ISLANDS. 9°S–139°30′W. Volcanic archipelago in POLYNESIA situated in the eastern Pacific to the S of the equator, 1,200 kilometers to the E of TAHITI. It extends from the NW to the SE for about 360 kilometers. The principal islands are, from north to south: Eiao, Nuku Hiva (present departmental center), Ua Huka, Ua Pu, Hiva Oa, Tahuata, and Fatu Hiva. Discovered in 1595 by the Spaniard Mendaña, who visited Magdalena (Fatu Hiva), Santa Cristina (Tahuata), and Dominica (Hiva Oa) and called the archipelago Las Marquesas de Mendoza for the viceroy of Peru, who had organized the expedition he was directing. The islands were visited in 1774 by Cook, who called Fatu Hiva Hood Island. In 1791, Captain Ingram, an American, discovered another group, which he called the Washington Islands. Several months later, the Marquesas were visited by France's Etienne Marchand, who discovered Nuku Hiva—which for a time bore his name—and baptized the archipelago Iles de la Révolution. Stops by Krusenstern (1804), Dupetit-Thouars and Dumont d'Urville (1838), and Belcher (1840). The Marquesas were annexed to France in 1842 by Dupetit-Thouars and served as a prison colony until 1865.

MARSHALL ISLANDS. 9°N–168°E. Archi-

pelago in MICRONESIA to the E of the CAROLINE ISLANDS, it is composed of 3 islets of volcanic origin and some 30 large atolls. It was discovered in 1528 by the Spaniard Alvaro de Saavedra, visited by Wallis in 1767, then explored in 1788 by the Englishmen Marshall and Gilbert. On the *Rurik* in 1816–1817 and the *Predpriyatiye* in 1824, Kotzebue discovered several islands. A German possession from 1885 to 1914, the Marshalls were in 1919 placed under a Japanese mandate and became American after World War II.

MASCARENE ISLANDS. Indian Ocean archipelago composed of the islands of Réunion (see BOURBON ISLAND) and Mauritius (see ILE DE FRANCE), and the islets of Rodriguez and Cargados. The name comes from the Portuguese navigator Pedro Mascarenhas, who discovered Réunion in 1528.

MAURITIUS. See ILE DE FRANCE.

MELANESIA (from the Greek *melas*, "black," and *nesos*, "island"). Collective name for Oceanic islands situated NE of Australia and E of Malaysia, thus named because of the dark complexion of the inhabitants, the Melanesians, of whom the Papuans are typical. Other than NEW GUINEA to the W, Melanesia includes, to the NE of the latter, the ADMIRALTY ISLANDS, the Bismarck Archipelago or NEW BRITAIN, the SOLOMON ISLANDS, the LOUISIADES, the SANTA CRUZ ISLANDS, the NEW HEBRIDES, NEW CALEDONIA, and finally the FIJI ISLANDS.

MICRONESIA (from the Greek *micros*, "small," and *nesos*, "island"). Collective name of the Oceanic islands of the intertropical Pacific, situated between the PHILIPPINE ISLANDS and the MOLUCCA ISLANDS to the W, MELANESIA to the S, and POLYNESIA to the E. Most of these island are atolls. Micronesia from west to east includes the MARIANAS, the CAROLINE ISLANDS, and PALAUS, the MARSHALL ISLANDS, and the GILBERT ISLANDS.

MOLUCCA ISLANDS. 2°S–128°E. Archipelago of the western Pacific, situated between the CELEBES ISLANDS and NEW GUINEA, and including 2 groups of islands: the northern Moluccas, linked to the Celebes by the Sula or Soela Archipelago, with the volcanic islands Gilolo or Halmahera (the largest), Tidore, Obi, Ternate, and Waigeo; and the southern Moluccas, which are granitic and very mountainous—the large island of Ceram and the smaller islands of Buru, AMBOINA and Banda. The population is for the most part Malaysian. The Moluccas were discovered by the Italian navigator Ludovico de Varthema in 1502, then visited in 1511 by the Portuguese Francisco Serrão. The Portuguese settled there but were replaced after 1605 by the Dutch. Bougainville stopped at Caieli (Buru) in 1768. The d'Entrecasteaux expedition stayed at Waigeo and then at Caieli in 1793. Freycinet reconnoitered several islands of the archipelago in 1818–1819. Duperrey put in there in 1823. Du-

The Marquesas: Village in the bay of Madre de Dios. Lithograph by L. P. A. Bichebois and Bayot after Mesnard. Voyage sur la Venus. *(Musée de la Marine, Paris. Photo by Michel Didier © Photeb.)*

The Falklands: Hunting party on Penguin Island. Original wash by Jules Lejeune. Voyage de la Coquille. (Service historique de la Marine, Vincennes. Photo by Michel Didier © Photeb.)

View of Nootka. Engraving after a wash by Suria done during the Malaspina expedition, 1789–1794. (Museo Naval, Madrid. Photo by Oroñoz © Photeb.)

New Britain: Port Praslin waterfall. Watercolor done in July 1768 by Ch. Routier de Romainville, cartographer of the Bougainville expedition. (Archives Nationales, Paris. Photo by Michel Didier © Arch./Photeb.)

mont d'Urville anchored at Ternate and Ceram in 1839, and Belcher at Caieli in 1842.

NAVIGATORS ISLANDS. See SAMOA.

NEW BRITAIN. 5°S–150°E. Archipelago of MELANESIA, situated off the NW coast of NEW GUINEA. It includes the islands of New Britain, New Ireland, New Hanover, and the ADMIRALTY ISLANDS. The southern island was discovered and named Nova Britannia by William Dampier in 1690. In 1767, Carteret baptized the northern island New Ireland and a 3rd island New Hanover. In 1768, Bougainville anchored in New Ireland in the roads which he called Port Praslin. Stops by d'Entrecasteaux in Carteret Harbor (1792), Duperrey at Port Praslin (1823), Dumont d'Urville (1827), and Belcher (1840) in Carteret Harbor. After it became a German possession in 1885, the archipelago was called Bismarck, New Britain became New Pomerania, and New Ireland became New Mecklenburg. The archipelago has been under an Australian mandate since 1921.

NEW CALEDONIA. 21°30'S–165°30'E. Group of islands comprising part of MELANESIA, situated in the Pacific some 1,500 kilometers E of Australia, immediately N of the Tropic of Capricorn and S of the NEW HEBRIDES. In addition to the island of the same name also known as Grande Terre (400 kilometers long and 50 kilometers wide), the archipelago includes many smaller islands: the Chesterfield group to the NW, the Belep and Huon Islands to the N—like Grande Terre, they are protected by a long coral barrier—the Loyauté, or LOYALTY ISLANDS, group to the E, and the Ile des Pins, or ISLE OF PINES, to the SE. These islands are inhabited by Kanakas—Melanesians interbred with Polynesians. New Caledonia was discovered and named by Cook in 1774. D'Entrecasteaux stayed in the bay of Balade in 1793. New Caledonia was annexed by France in 1853.

NEW GUINEA. 6°S–150°E. Covering 810,000 square kilometers, it is the largest island in the world after Greenland. Situated immediately to the N of Australia, from which it is separated by the TORRES STRAIT, it is inhabited principally by Papuans. Its discovery is attributed to the Portuguese Antonio de Abreu (1511). It was visited by the Spaniard A. de Saavedre in 1528. In 1605–1606, the Dutchman Willem Jansz, or Janszoon, went around it from the south. In 1606, the Spaniard Luis Vaez de Torres, a lieutenant of Queiros's, hav-

ing discovered to the S the strait that bears his name, demonstrated that it was an island. The Englishman Dampier explored the N coast in 1700 and Cook landed on the S coast. Sonnerat stopped there and in 1776 published a *Voyage to New Guinea*. In 1792, d'Entrecasteaux sailed along the coasts. Duperrey stayed at Port Dorey in 1824. Dumont d'Urville explored the N coast in 1827 and 1839. Belcher made a stop there in 1840. Since 1973, the eastern part of New Guinea has been an autonomous state, a member of the Commonwealth; the west of the island is part of the Indonesian Republic.

NEW HEBRIDES. 16°S–167°E. Archipelago in MELANESIA, situated between NEW CALEDONIA to the SW and the SOLOMON ISLANDS to the NW. It includes 37 islands and extends over 820 kilometers. In 1605, Pedro Fernandes de Queiros, a Portuguese pilot in the service of Spain, disembarked on the island he called Tierra Australia de Espiritu Santo, thinking he had taken possession of the "Southern Continent." The archipelago was partly discovered in 1768 by Bougainville, who named it the Grandes Cyclades, and then in 1774 by Cook, who visited Mallicolo (Malekula), Eromanga, and Tanna; he gave it the name it has to this day. The New Hebrides were annexed by France in 1885, then ruled by a Franco-British condominium after 1887. A member of the Commonwealth since 1980, the islands took the name of Vanuatu.

NEW HOLLAND. 25°S–135°E. Name given to Australia from the time of its discovery by Dutch navigators at the beginning of the 17th century until the publication in 1814 of *Voyage to Terra Australis* by Flinders. The N coasts of the Australian continent, situated to the S of TIMOR and NEW GUINEA, were reconnoitered by the Portuguese as early as the 16th century, but the Dutch began the first exploration. In 1605–1606, Willem Jansz discovered the NW coast, which he baptized New Holland. Endracht's Land on the W was reconnoitered by Dirke-Hertoge, commander of

the *Eendragt* in 1616. In 1642, Abel Tasman discovered VAN DIEMEN'S LAND and in 1644 visited the northwest coast. William Dampier was, in 1687, the first Englishman to disembark on Australian soil; in 1699, he returned to the W coast and afterward published one of the first known texts on the country, its inhabitants, its flora, and its fauna. However, the true exploration of the continent did not begin until the 1st voyage of Cook, who in 1770 took possession of a fragment of the E coast. After the founding of NEW SOUTH WALES, La Pérouse stayed in Botany Bay in 1788 before he disappeared. In 1791, Vancouver took possession of King George Sound; d'Entrecasteaux explored the coast of Nuyts Land in 1792. Bass and Flinders discovered (1798) the strait that separated Tasmania from Australia. From 1801 to 1803, the Baudin expedition visited the W and S coasts, while Flinders explored the coasts from W to SE and then from SE to the Gulf of Carpentaria, in the N of the continent. Almost all the circumnavigators anchored in Port Jackson.

NEW SOUTH WALES. 33°S–146°E. The first of the 6 original states of the Commonwealth of Australia, situated to the SE of the continent between Queensland to the N and Victoria to the S. The coast was discovered and explored by Cook in 1770. Botany Bay, the British colony, was established in New South Wales in 1787; the following year, Arthur Phillip landed with 1,500 colonists, of whom 800 were convicts, and founded Sydney in the bay of Port Jackson.

NEW ZEALAND. 41°S–174°E. Archipelago in POLYNESIA situated 1,600 kilometers to the SE of Australia and composed of 2 large islands separated by Cook Strait (see QUEEN CHARLOTTE SOUND). North Island has an irregular coast, whereas South Island is rectangular and more massive. A cordillera of volcanic origin runs through both islands; its summit, Mount Cook, on South Island, is more than 3,700 meters high. New Zealand was discovered in 1642 by the Dutchman Tasman, who gave it its present name; but it was not until 1769 that it was explored by Cook, who returned several times. In the interval, the Frenchmen Surville (1769) and Marion du Fresne (1772) had also visited the archipelago. Vancouver anchored there in 1791. In 1814, the 1st English missionaries arrived from Australia. The following circumnavigators stopped in New Zealand: Duperrey (1824), Dumont d'Urville (1827), Laplace (1831), FitzRoy (1835), and Dupetit-Thouars (1838). In 1840, the archipelago was annexed by Great Britain, but neither Wilkes nor Dumont d'Urville recognized this claim. Ross stayed there in 1841. Between 1840 and 1850, British colonists began arriving in great numbers, and there were long wars with the Maoris. In 1907, New Zealand became a dominion of the British Commonwealth.

NOOTKA. 49°32'N–126°42'W. Island off the coast of British Columbia (Canada), separated from the S of VANCOUVER ISLAND by the Sound discovered by Cook in 1778. British fur-trading post in 1786, occupied in 1789 by the Spanish, who turned Nootka over to Vancouver in 1792.

OKHOTSK SEA. 53°N–150°E. Secondary sea formed by the Pacific and bounded on the W by the coast of Siberia and on the E by the KURIL ISLANDS and KAMCHATKA.

PALAUS or **PELEWS**. Archipelago in MI-CRONESIA, near the CAROLINE ISLANDS and extending in a circular arc over some 900 kilometers. Discovered and claimed by the Spanish, these 26 small islands were sold to Germany in 1899 and came under a Japanese mandate in 1919; they are now administered by the United States. The archipelago was reconnoitered by Du-mont d'Urville in 1839.

PATAGONIA. 44°S–68°W. SE part of South America, bounded on the W by the Cordillera of the Andes, on the E by the Atlantic, and on the S by TIERRA DEL FUEGO. Patagonia was divided between Chile and Argentina in 1880. In 1741, the *Wager* of the Anson expedition was wrecked there. Stops by Byron (1764), Bougainville (1768), La Pérouse (1786), and FitzRoy (1833–1834).

PAUMOTU. See TUAMOTU.

PENRHYN ISLAND. See COOK ISLANDS.

PETROPAVLOVSK. See KAMCHATKA.

PHILIPPINE ISLANDS. 12°N–123°E. Archipelago in the W of the Pacific, situated above the CELEBES ISLAND, to the N of the equator, and bounded on the E by the South China Sea. It includes 3 principal islands: Luzon in the N, Mindanao in the S, and Palawan to the SE, as well as more than 7,000 other islands or islets. Mountainous and volcanic, the Philippines have an almost entirely Malaysian population. The archipelago was discovered in 1521 by Magellan, who called it St. Lazarus. In 1542, the Spaniard Villalobos took possession of the archipelago and gave it the name of the future king, Philip II. Manila was founded in 1571 on the island of Luzon and became the center of Spanish commerce with the Far East. Galleons transported its crops either to Acapulco in Mexico or directly to Europe. Manila—and especially Cavite, a port situated in Manila Bay—served as a stopping place for a great number of circumnavigators: La Pérouse (1787), Malaspina (1792), Kotzebue (1818), H. de Bougainville (1824), Lütke (1829), Laplace (1830, 1838), Vaillant (1836), Dumont d'Urville (1839), and Wilkes (1842). Ceded by Spain to the United States in 1898, the Philippines are now an independent republic.

New Zealand: English missionary settlements at Kidikidi in the Bay of Islands. Anonymous engraving from the historical Atlas of the Voyage de la Coquille, *1822–1825. (Société de Géographie, Bibliothèque nationale, Paris. Photo © Bibl. nat./Photeb.)*

PITCAIRN ISLAND. 25°04'S–136°06'W. Small island of POLYNESIA (5 square kilometers), situated to the S of the Tropic of Capricorn and to the SE of the GAMBIER IS-LANDS. It was discovered in 1767 by Carteret, who gave it the name of the young officer who had first sighted it. Initially uninhabited, it was colonized in 1790 by some of the mutineers of the *Bounty*. In 1825, Beechey went there to investigate. Pitcairn has since become a British colony and is administered from Wellington.

POLYNESIA (from the Greek *polus*, "numerous," and *nesos*, "island"). Vast complex of islands dispersed in the Pacific between MICRONESIA, MELANESIA, and Australia on the one hand, and the W coast of America on the other. These islands are divided into several groups in a vast triangle bordered by NEW ZEALAND to the SE, the SANDWICH ISLANDS to the NW, and EASTER ISLAND to the SW. To the W, near Micronesia and Melanesia, are the FRIENDLY IS-LANDS, SAMOA, the Tokelau Islands, the Phoenix Islands; on either side of the equator, about halfway between the Sandwich Islands and TAHITI, are the Line Islands and, to the SE of these, the MAR-QUESA ISLANDS. The SOCIETY ISLANDS form almost the center of the triangle, with the GAMBIER ISLANDS and TUAMOTU to the E and a scattering of several isolated islands like PITCAIRN ISLAND and the Austral (Tubuai) Islands.

PORT JACKSON. See NEW SOUTH WALES.

QUEEN CHARLOTTE SOUND. 41°14'S–174°30'E. Arm of the sea separating North Island from South Island of NEW ZEALAND. It was named by Cook in honor of Sophie Charlotte of Mecklenburg-Stelitz, wife of George III. Afterward it was named Cook Strait.

REUNION ISLAND. See BOURBON ISLAND.

ROSS SEA. 76°S–175°W. Part of the Antarctic Ocean to the S of the polar circle and situated between Victoria Land and Edward VII Peninsula, it is bounded on the S by the Ross Ice Shelf. It was named in 1902 by Scott in memory of James Clark Ross, who had explored it in 1842.

ST. HELENA. 45°31'N–75°32'W. Greatly indented volcanic island in the Atlantic, below the equator; 1,200 kilometers to the S of ASCENSION ISLAND and 1,800 kilometers off the W coast of Africa. Discovered by the Portuguese in 1502 on the feast of St. Helena (August 18), it became a place to which deportees were sent. Annexed (1633), then occupied (1645) by the Dutch, it was ceded by them to the English in 1659. Reoccupied in 1673 by the Dutch, it was retaken in 1675 by the English, who made it a citadel on the route to the Cape. Numerous navigators stopped there on their return, after visiting CAPE TOWN.

SAKHALIN or **SAGHALIEN**. 51°N–143°E. Large island of the north Pacific, near the NE coast of the Asiatic continent, from which it is separated by the Tartar Strait,

New Holland: Port Jackson in 1803. Drawing by C. A. Lesueur. Historical Atlas of the Voyage aux terres australes, *1807–1816. (Bibliothèque du Muséum d'histoire naturelle, Paris. Photo © Bibl. du Muséum/Photeb.)*

Philippines: Taal volcano on the island of Luzon. Drawing and lithograph by L. Choris. Voyage pittoresque autour du monde sur le Rurik, 1815–1818. *Bibliothèque nationale, Paris. Photo © Bibl. nat./Photeb.)*

and to the N of the Japanese island of YESO. It is bathed on the north by the OKHOTSK SEA and on the SW by the Sea of Japan. Discovered in 1643 by the Dutchman De Vries, it was recognized as an island by La Pérouse in 1787, then visited by Krusenstern in 1804. Explored by Nevelsky in 1849–1852, it was occupied by the Russians in 1857, 1st in the north and then entirely when Japan ceded (1875) the S part in exchange for the KURIL ISLANDS.

SAMOA. 14°S–171°W. Archipelago of POLYNESIA, to the S of the equator and to the NE of the FRIENDLY ISLANDS. It is composed of 14 islands, all volcanic, surrounded by a barrier of madreporic atolls. The principal islands are Savaii, Upolu, Tutuila, and Tau. The Samoas were discovered by the Dutchman Roggeveen in 1722 and visited in 1768 by Bougainville, who called them the Navigators' Archipelago. La Pérouse came to Manua (Tutuila); Dumont d'Urville to Upolu (Lipolu) in 1838; Wilkes discovered several of the islands in 1839 and 1841. In 1899, a common protectorate was established under Great Britain, the United States, and Germany. Today, the Samoas are controlled by the United States except for the western part, which, after having been under a New Zealand mandate, became independent in 1962.

Sandwich Islands: Queen Kinau accompanied by her ladies in waiting in Honolulu. Lithograph by L. P. A. Bichebois and Bayot from a drawing by Masselot. Voyage sur le Vénus, 1836–1839. *Musée de la Marine, Paris. Photo © the museum/Photeb.)*

SANDWICH ISLANDS. Present-day Hawaiian Islands. 20°N–157°W. Archipelago in E POLYNESIA, it is the closest one to North America, under the Tropic of Cancer. It includes some 20 basaltic islands and islets with several summits higher than 4,000 meters and several craters that are still active. The most important islands are Hawaii, Maui, Oahu, Kauai, and Molokai. In 1778, Cook discovered the westernmost islands of the archipelago but did not see the principal island, Owhyhee (Hawaii). He landed there the following year in Kealakekua Bay and was killed on February 14, 1779. Cook had given the archipelago the name of the Earl of Sandwich, First Lord of the Admiralty. After 1789, the Sandwiches were visited by the American explorer Robert Gray. In 1792, 1793, and 1794, Vancouver stayed there and received Kamehameha I's homage to the kind of England. Whereas the former lived on Owhyhee, his son, Lio-Lio, who succeeded him in 1819, settled at Honolulu on Oahu, which after 1820 became the center first of English and then of American missionaries. Stops by Krusenstern (1804), Kotzebue (1816, 1817) Freycinet (1819), Beechey (1826), Vaillant (1836), Dupetit-Thouars (1837), Laplace and Belcher (1840), and Wilkes (1841). More and more frequented by American ships and missionaries, the Hawaiian Islands were annexed by the United States in 1898; since 1959, Hawaii has been the 50th state in the union.

SANDWICH LAND. 57°45′S–26°30′W. Group of icy islands, situated to the W of CAPE HORN, discovered by Cook in 1775 and named by him Sandwich Land or Southern Thule.

SANTA CRUZ ISLANDS. 10°30′S–166° W. Archipelago in MELANESIA, situated between the SOLOMON ISLANDS and the NEW HEBRIDES. The most important of these volcanic islands are Santa Cruz or Ndeni, Vanikoro, and Tikopia. They were discovered in 1596 by the Spaniard Alvaro Mendana de Neira, who called them Santa Cruz (Holy Cross) and died there. Queiros stopped there in 1605. In 1767, Carteret landed on Santa Cruz Island; he named the island Egmont Island and the group to which it belonged the Queen Charlotte Islands. In 1793, d'Entrecasteaux sighted Ile de la Recherche (Vanikoro), but he did not visit it. It was there that in 1788 La Pérouse lost the ships that d'Entrecasteaux was later sent to find. The remains of the *Astrolabe* were found in 1826 and 1827 by Peter Dillon, and then by Dumont d'Urville in 1828.

SAVU or **SAWU.** 9°40′S–120°E. Principal and northernmost island of an archipelago that is a dependency of TIMOR and formed of 3 islands. Cook came there in 1770.

SEYCHELLES. 4°35′S–55°40′E. Archipelago in the Indian Ocean, 1,100 kilometers from Madagascar and 1,600 kilometers from Mauritius. Discovered by French coasters in 1741, the Seychelles were occupied by order of Mahé de La Bourdonnais, whose name was given to the principal island. In 1756, the French East India Company gave the archipelago the name of the comptroller-general of finances, Moreau de Séchelles. The islands were settled by colonists from the ILE DE FRANCE, who came with their black slaves. Taken over by the English in 1810, the Seychelles were ceded to them by France in 1814; they became independent in 1976. Laplace visited them in 1830 and 1837, Belcher in 1842.

SITKA. 57°03′N–135°14′W. Island of ALASKA, separated from the continent by the Sitka Strait. The Russian-American Company, which called it Baranov, had at the end of the 18th century established there a fort and a settlement named Novo-Arkangelsk. Lisiansky's *Neva*—part of the Krusenstern expedition—stayed there in 1804–1805; Lütke was there in 1827, and Belcher in 1837.

SOCIETY ISLANDS. 17°S–150°W. Group of islands of volcanic origin situated to the E of POLYNESIA, about 5,000 kilometers from the closest continental coasts. They were divided into 2 groups: to the SE the Iles du Vent (Windward Islands)—TAHITI, Moorée, and Makatéa; to the NW the Iles sous le Vent (Leeward Islands)—Huanine, Raiatea, Bora Bora, and Tahaa. After Wallis, who discovered Tahiti in 1767, and Bougainville, who in 1768 dubbed the archipelago Bourbon, these islands were visited by Cook, who stopped there during each of his 3 voyages and called them the Society Islands in honor of London's Royal Society. See also TAHITI.

SOLOMON ISLANDS. 8°S–159°E. Archipelago of MELANESIA, to the E. of NEW GUINEA, situated between NEW BRITAIN and the NEW HEBRIDES. Constituted of mountainous volcanic islands and surrounded by simple atolls, it was discovered in 1568 by the Spaniard Mendaña de Neira, who thought he had refound the Bible's Ophir and therefore named it for King Solomon. Forgotten for 2 centuries, the archipelago was rediscovered in 1767 by Carteret, in 1768 by Bougainville (the Bougainville and Choiseul Islands), in 1769 by Surville, who thought that it was a single island and baptized it Terre des Arsacides ("assassins"), and in 1788 by the Englishman Shortland. All these navigators thought they had discovered a new archipelago, and it was not until 1792 that d'Entrecasteaux realized that these were the Solomons of Mendaña. Stops by Duperrey (1823) at Buka Island and Dumont d'Urville (1838) at Santa Isabel. Conquered by Germany in 1885, the Solomons became a British protectorate in 1893. Since 1978, they have been independent within the framework of the Commonwealth.

SOUTH GEORGIA. 54°15′S–36°45′W. Situated in the South Atlantic far in the N of the WEDDELL SEA. Traversed by high mountains covered with glaciers, it was sighted as early as 1675 by Antoine de la Roche, a London merchant of French descent, but discovered and named by Cook in 1775.

STATEN ISLAND or **ISLA DE LOS ESTA-DOS.** 55°S–64°W. Barren island bristling with high mountains; situated to the E of TIERRA DEL FUEGO, from which it is separated by the LE MAIRE STRAIT. Discovered in 1616 by the Dutch navigator Jakob Le Maire, it is now part of the territory of Argentina. Cook stopped there in 1774–1775.

SYDNEY. *See* NEW SOUTH WALES.

TAHITI or **OTAHEITI.** 17°37′S–149°27′W. The largest of the SOCIETY ISLANDS, formed of 2 volcanic islands united by an isthmus: West Tahiti (Tahiti Nui) and East Tahiti (Tahiti Iti), or the Taiarapu Peninsula. The island, which may have been sighted in 1605 by Queiros, who named it Sagittaria, was discovered on June 23, 1767, by Wallis, who called it King George III Island. The following year, Bougainville baptized it New Cythera. Cook stayed there for some time in 1769, 1773–1774, and 1777. In 1772, 1774, and 1775, the Spaniard Domingo de Boenéchea, commander of the *Aguila*, tried to found a settlement with colonists, soldiers, and missionaries, but he failed; the 2 missionaries who remained behind tried for 11 months to evangelize the population. In 1788, the *Bounty* commanded by Bligh stopped there for 5 months. The following year, 16 mutineers of the *Bounty* disembarked there but were arrested. In 1791–1792, Vancouver stopped there.

Between Cook's 2nd and 3rd voyages, the island had been divided into 2 kingdoms, which were later reunified by Otoo. He took the name of Pomare and founded a new dynasty which extended his rule as far as TUAMOTU. In 1797, the first missionaries of the London Missionary Society established themselves on Tahiti. With the support of the Pomares, they held the real political power until the arrival of the French Catholic missionaries in 1836. This counterbalanced the Protestant influence and gave rise to a troubled situation—rivalry between Protestants and Catholics, English and French, supported by local chiefs who were partisans of the different groups. Stops by Bellingshausen (1820), Duperrey (1823), Beechey (1826), FitzRoy (1835), Dupetit-Thouars and Dumont d'Urville (1838), Laplace and Wilkes (1839), and Belcher (1840).

In 1842, Dupetit-Thouars managed to obtain an agreement establishing a French protectorate over Tahiti, but he failed to gain his government's support and in 1843–1844 the "Pritchard affair" almost led to serious consequences between France and Great Britain. It was followed in 1845–1846 by an insurrection caused by Pritchard. Nevertheless, in 1847 Dupetit-Thouars's agreement was confirmed. In 1880, Pomare V signed an act turning the Society Islands over to France. Tahiti became the center of French rule in Oceania.

TASMANIA. *See* VAN DIEMEN'S LAND.

TENERIFE. *See* CANARY ISLANDS.

TIERRA DEL FUEGO. 54°S–69°W. Large island situated at the S end of South America—from which it is separated by the Magellan Strait (see MAGELLAN, STRAIT OF)—and surrounded by islands forming the MAGELLAN ARCHIPELAGO (the principal ones being STATEN ISLAND, Desolación Island, Hoste Island, Wollaston Islands), and by CAPE HORN. It was discovered in 1520 by Magellan, who saw the fires lit by its inhabitants, the Fuegians, on the shore, and gave it their name. These islands, which represent a total surface of 71,500 square kilometers, are today divided between Argentina (the east of Tierra del Fuego) and Chile (the west and the Magellan Archipelago). Stops by Cook (1769 and 1774), FitzRoy (1832, 1833, and 1834), Dumont d'Urville (1838), and Wilkes (1839).

TIMOR. 8°35′S–126°E. The last large island at the E of the Indonesian islands. Discovered by the Portuguese Fernao Perez de Andrade in 1532, in the 17th century it was divided between the Portuguese and the Dutch. The latter occupied the western part with Koepang (Kupang) as their capital; Dili on the NE coast was the principal city of the Portuguese settlements. The island often served as a port of call for the circumnavigators: Baudin (1801, 1803), Flinders (1803), Freycinet (1818), and Dumont d'Urville (1840).

TONGA ARCHIPELAGO. *See* FRIENDLY ISLANDS.

TORRES STRAIT. 10°25′S–142°10′E. Sep-

arating the NE point of Australia (Cape York Peninsula) from the S coast of NEW GUINEA, it was discovered by the Spaniard Torres in 1606. Its difficult passage caused many wrecks. The ships of Dumont d'Urville ran aground there in 1840.

TUAMOTU, or **PAUMOTU,** or **DANGEROUS ARCHIPELAGO.** 19°S–142°W. Archipelago in POLYNESIA, situated to the E of the SOCIETY ISLANDS and composed of numerous atolls. In 1520, Magellan probably landed on Caroline Island. The Spaniards Queiros and Torres visited the archipelago in 1605, and Roggeveen came in 1721. In 1765, Byron, having been unable to land, called them Islands of Disappointment. In 1767, Wallis put in there, then Carteret, who gave several islands the names of members of the English royal family. In 1768, Bougainville, who saw these low-lying islands surrounded by reefs before arriving at TAHITI, called them the Dangerous Islands. Stops by Cook (1769); Kotzebue (1816, 1824); Bellingshausen, who discovered some 20 islands (1820); Duperrey—who gave Clermont-Tonnerre its name—and Beechey (1826); Wilkes (1839); and Belcher (1840). In 1842, the western islands were placed under a French protectorate, and in 1881 the entire archipelago was annexed by France.

UNALASKA. 53°52′N–166°32′W. One of the ALEUTIAN ISLANDS. Stops by Cook (1778), Kotzebue (1816, 1817), and Lütke (1827).

VANCOUVER ISLAND. 49°45′N–126°W. Large island off the coast of British Columbia (Canada), from which it is separated by several arms of the sea crowded with islands: Juan de Fuca Strait, Strait of Georgia, and Queen Charlotte Strait. Discovered in 1774 by the Spaniards Perez and Martinez, visited in 1775 by Quadra, all coasts of the island were explored by Vancouver in 1792. A post of the Hudson Bay Company from 1849 to 1859, the island became part of British Columbia in 1866.

Tahiti: View of the valley that begins at Matavai Bay. Watercolor by William Ellis. Cook's third voyage. (Rex Nan Kivell Collection. National Library of Australia, Canberra. Photo © National Library of Australia/Photeb.)

Sitka: The arsenal and the Novo-Arkangelsk lighthouse. Engraving in Voyage round the World, 1836–1842, *by Belcher. (Bibliothèque nationale, Paris. Photo by Michel Didier © Photeb.)*

Timor: Domestic pursuits, child's cradle, threshing rice, making coconut oil. Watercolor by Pellion. Freycinet expedition, 1817–1820. (Musée de la Marine, Paris. Photo by Michel Didier © Photeb.)

VAN DIEMEN'S LAND. Present-day Tasmania. 42°S–147°E. Large island situated to the S of Australia. It was discovered in 1642 by the Dutchman Abel Tasman, who saw no inhabitants; he gave it the name of Anthony Van Diemen, governor-general of the Dutch East India Company, who had organized his voyage. It retained that name until 1853.

VITI ISLANDS. See FIJI ISLANDS.

WAIGEO ISLAND. See MOLUCCA ISLANDS.

WALLIS ISLANDS. 13°18'S–176°10'W. Archipelago in POLYNESIA, to the NW of the FRIENDLY ISLANDS. The only important island is Uvéa, which is volcanic and surrounded by small coral islands. Discovered by Wallis in 1767, visited by Wilkes in 1839, the archipelago became a French protectorate in 1866; it has been French overseas territory since 1959.

WEDDELL SEA. 72°S–45°W. Part of the Antarctic Ocean, to the south of the polar circle, bounded on the E by Coats Land and on the W by CAPE HORN and the South Shetland Islands. In 1823, the English sealer James Weddell discovered this sea, which was at the time free of ice.

YESO. "Land of the Barbarians." Present-day Hokkaido. 44°N–143°E. The northernmost island of the Japanese archipelago, separated from SAKHALIN in the N. by the La Pérouse (Soya) Strait and from Hondo in the S by the Tsugaru Strait. It was visited by La Pérouse (1787) and by Krusenstern (1805).

Van Diemen's Land: View of the Hobart Town roads. Lithograph by F. A. Saint-Aulaire, from a drawing by Sainson. The first Dumont d'Urville voyage, 1826–1829. (Bibliothèque du Muséum d'histoire naturelle, Paris. Photo © Bibl. du Muséum/Photeb.)

Bibliography

General works

Abrégé de l'histoire générale des voyages par Laharpe, 24 vol., Paris, 1801–1815.

Aldus Encyclopedia of Discovery and Exploration, 8 vol., London, 1971.

AUBERT DE LA RAÜE, *L'Homme et les îles*, Paris, 1956.

BÉRIOT (A.), *Essai sur les sources documentaires concernant les voyages de circumnavigation entrepris par la marine française*, thèse dactylogr., Paris, 1958.—*Grands Voiliers autour du monde. Les voyages scientifiques 1760–1850*, Paris, 1962.

BONNEFOUS ET PÂRIS, *Dictionnaire de la marine à voile et à vapeur*, 2 vol., Paris, 1848.

BROSSARD, contre-amiral R. DE, *Histoire maritime du monde*, Paris, 1974.

CÉLÉRIER (H.), *Histoire de la navigation*, Paris, 1946.

CHARLIAT (P.J.), *Le temps des grands voiliers*, in *Histoire universelle des explorations*, t. III, Paris, 1956.

CHEVALLIER (E.), *Histoire de la marine française, 1773–1815*, 2 vol., Paris, 1886.

DAVY DE VIRVILLE (A.), *Histoire de la Botanique en France*, Paris, 1954.

DEBENHAM (F.), *Discovery and Exploration*, Library of Congress, Washington, 1960.

DECHAMPS (H.), *Histoire des explorations*, Paris, 1969.

DUHAMEL DU MONCEAU (H.L.), *Avis pour le transport par mer des arbres et des plantes vivaces, des semences et de diverses autres couriosités d'histoire naturelle*, Paris, n.d.—*Traité de la conservation de la santé des équipages des vaisseaux*, Paris, 1769.

Earth's Last Frontiers. A History of Discovery and Exploration, London, 1971.

EYRIÈS (J.B.B.), *Abrégé des voyages modernes depuis 1780 jusqu'à nos jours*, 14 vol., Paris, 1822.

GUÉRIN (L.), *Histoire maritime de la France*, 6 vol., Paris, 1863.

JAL (A.), *Glossaire nautique. Répertoire polyglotte des termes de marine anciens et modernes*, Paris, 1848.

LACOUR-GAYET (A.), *La marine militaire sous le règne de Louis XV*, Paris, 1905—*La marine militaire sous le règne de Louis XVI*, Paris, 1910.

LA ROUËRIE (G.) et VIVIELLE (J.), *Navires et Marins, de la rame à l'hélice*, Paris-Brussels, 1931.

LA RONCIÈRE (C.G. BOUREL DE), *Histoire de la marine française*, Paris, 1899.

LE GENTIL (G.), *Découverte du monde*, Paris, 1954.

LE SAINT (L.), *Illustrations de la marine française*, Tours, 5th ed., 1891.

LOTURE (R. DE), *La Navigation à travers les âges*, Paris, 1952.

MARGUET (F.), *Histoire de la navigation du XVe au XXe siècle*, Paris, 1931.

MAURO (F.), *L'Expansion européenne (1600–1870)*, Paris, 1964.

MERRIEN (J.), *La vie quotidienne des marins au temps du Roi-Soleil*, Paris, 1964.

MOLLAT (M.), dir. *Les aspects internationaux de la découverte océanique aux XVe et XVIe siècles*, Paris, 1966.

MONTÉMONT (A.), *Bibliothèque universelle des voyages autour du monde*, Paris, 1833–1837.

NEUVILLE (D.), *Les établissements scientifiques de l'ancienne marine*, Paris, n.d.

REUSSNER (A.), NICOLAS (L.) et BELOT (R. DE), *La puissance navale dans l'histoire*, 3 vol., Paris, 1958, 1963.

ROBINSON (Ch. N.), *The British Fleet*, London, 1894.

ROUCH (J.), VICTOR (P.-E.), TAZIEFF (H.), *L'Époque contemporaine*, in *Histoire universelle des explorations*, t. IV, Prais, 1958.

ROUX (F.), *L'Album de marine du duc d'Orléans*, Paris, 1980.

SAVERIEN, *Dictionnaire historique, théorique et pratique de marine*, Paris, 1758.

TOUSSAINT (A.), *La Route des îles*, Paris, 1967.

VAN LOON (H.), *La Conquête des mers*, Paris, 1935.

Voyages et Découvertes. Des voyageurs naturalistes aux chercheurs scientifiques. Catalogue of the exposition at Muséum d'histoire naturelle, Paris, 1981.

WILLAUMEZ (vice-admiral J.B.P.), *Dictionnaire de marine*, Paris, 1820.

ZOBEL (M.), *Les naturalistes voyageurs et les grands voyages maritimes aux XVIIIe et XIXe siècles*, Paris, 1961.

Chapter 1

Narratives of the voyages

ALAUX (J.-P.), *Magellan, le premier voyage autour du monde par le navire la Victoire, d'après le récit de Antoine Pigafetta, gentilhomme vicentin et chevalier de Rhodes (. . .)*, Paris, 1925.

ANSON (G.), *A voyage round the World in the Years MDCCXL, I, II, III, IV, to the South Seas*, London, 1748—*Voyage autour du monde fait dans les années 1740 à 1744*, Amsterdam, 1751.

AVEZAC (A. D'), *Campagne du navire l'Espoir de Honfleur, 1503–1505. Relation authentique du voyage du capitaine de Gonneville ès terres nouvelles des Indes, publié intégralement pour la première fois*, Paris, 1869.

DAMPIER (W.), *A New Voyage around the World*, London, 1697.—*Nouveau voyage extraordinaire à la Nouvelle-Hollande et aux Terres australes*, Amsterdam, 1701, new ed., 6 vol., 1712.

FLEURIEU (P. CLARET DE), *Voyage fait par ordre du roi en 1768 et 1769 à différentes parties du monde pour éprouver en mer les horloges marines inventées par M. F. Berthoud*, Paris, 1773.

FRÉZIER (A.), *Relation du voyage de la mer du Sud aux côtes du Chili et du Pérou, fait pendant les années 1712, 1713 et 1714*, Paris, 1716.

GONNEVILLE (LE PAULMIER DE), *Relation du voyage du capitaine de Gonneville aux Indes (1503–1505)*, ed. by Ch. A. Jullien, in J. Cartier, *Voyages au Canada*, «La Découverte», Paris, 1981.

NARBOROUGH (J.), *Voyage to the South Sea*, 2 vol. London, 1711.

Narrative (The) of the hon, John Byron containing an account of the great distresses suffered by himself and his companions on the coast of Patagonia from the year 1740 till their arrival in England, 1746, (. . .) with (. . .) a relation of the loss of the Wager man of war (. . .), London, 1768.

PIGAFETTA (A.), *Premier voyage autoûr du monde de Magellan (1519–1522)*, L. Peillard, Paris, 1964.

PINGRÉ (A.G.), *Mémoire sur les découvertes faites dans la mer du Sud avant les derniers voyages des Français autour du monde*, Paris, 1778.

ROGGEVEEN (J.), *The journal of Jacob Roggeveen*, Oxford, 1970.

SONNERAT (P.), *Voyage à la Nouvelle-Guinée*, Paris, 1776.

WOODES (R.), *A cruising Voyage around the World*, London, 1708.

History of maritime discoveries from 16th to 18th centuries

BAKER (J.N.L.), *Histoire des découvertes géographiques et des explorations*, Paris, 1949.

BEAGLEHOLE (J.C.), *The exploration of the Pacific*, London, 1947, 3rd ed., 1966.

BROC (N.), *La Géographie des philosophes. Géographes et voyageurs français au XVIIIe siècle*, Paris, 1975.

BURNEY (J.), *Chronological History of the discoveries in the South Sea or Pacific Ocean*, 5 vol., London, 1804–1816.

Collection de tous les voyages faits autour du monde par les différentes nations de l'Europe, 9 vol., Paris, 1795.

DAHLGREN (E.W.), *Voyages français à destination de la mer du Sud avant Bougainville (1695–1749)*, Paris, 1907.

DALRYMPLE (A.), *An historical Collection of the several voyages and discoveries in the South Pacific Ocean*, London, 1770–1771.

DE BROSSES (President Ch.), *Histoire de la navigation aux Terres australes*, 2 vol., Paris, 1756.

DEPREZ (E.), *Les grands voyages et les grandes découvertes jusqu'à la fin du XVIIIe siècle*, Paris, 1950.

DUNMORE (J.), *French Explorers in the Pacific*, 2 vol., Oxford, 1965–1969.

FAIVRE (J.-P.), *Savants et Navigateurs, 1750–1840*, in *Cahiers d'histoire mondiale*, U.N.E.S.C.O., Neuchâtel, 1966.

FLEURIEU (P. CLARET DE), *Découvertes des Français en 1768 et 1769 dans le sud-est de la Nouvelle-Guinée*, Paris, 1770.

HEAWOOD (E.), *A History of Geographical Discovery in the XVII th and XVIII th Centuries*, Cambridge, 1912.

DELEUZE, *Histoire du Muséum d'histoire naturelle*, Paris, 1823.

JACK-HINTON (C.), *The Search for the Islands of Solomon, 1567–1838*, Oxford, 1969.

JEAN (W.J.), *The Royal Botanic Gardens Kew, historical and descriptive*, London, 1907.

JULLIEN (Ch.-A.), *Les voyages de découverte et les premiers établissements (XVe–XVIe siècles)*, Paris, 1948.

LA RONCIÈRE (Ch. DE), *Le Premier Voyage français autour du monde*, Revue Hebdomadaire, sept. 1907.—*Histoire de la découverte de la Terre. Explorateurs et Conquérants*, Paris, 1938.

LA BORDE (J.-B. DE), *Histoire abrégée de la mer du Sud*, 4 vol. and atlas, Paris, 1791.

MAHAN (A.T.), *The influence of sea power upon history, 1660–1783*, London, 1839.

MARKHAM (C.), *Early Spanish voyages to the Straits of Magellan*, London, 1911.

OLIVER (D.), *Les Iles du Pacifique. L'Océanie des temps primitifs à nos jours*, Paris, 1952.

OLSEN (O.), *La Conquête de la Terre. Histoire des découvertes et des explorations depuis les origines jusqu'à nos jours*, 6 vol., Paris, 1937.

PRÉVOST D'EXILES (abbé A.F.), *Histoire générale des voyages ou Nouvelle Collection de toutes les relations de voyage par mer et par terre qui ont été publiées jusqu'à présent dans les différentes langues de toutes les nations connues*, 20 vol., Paris, 1746–1770.

RAINAUD (A.), *Le Continent austral*, n.d.

RAYNAL (Abbé G.Th.), *Histoire philosophique et politique du commerce et des établissements des Européens dans les deux Indes*, Paris, 1772, 3rd ed., 1781.

SHARP (A.), *The Discovery of the Pacific Islands*, Oxford, 1960.—*Ancient voyagers in the Pacific*, London, 1957.

STEPHENS (M.), and BOSTON (H.E.), dir., *The Pacific Ocean in History*, New York, 1917.

SOTTAS (J.), *Les navigations anciennes des Malouins à la mer du Sud*, Saint-Malo, 1980.

TAYLOR (A.C.), *Le Président De Brosses et l'Australie*, Paris, 1937.

Chapter 2

Narratives of the voyages

BYRON (J.), *An account of a voyage round the world in the years 1764, 1765, and 1766*, London, 1767.—*Voyage autour du monde sur le Dolphin*, Paris, 1767.—*Voyage à la mer du Sud, complétant la relation du voyage d'Anson, avec l'extrait du 2 ième voyage de Byron autour du monde*, Paris.

CARTERET (Ph.), *Narrative of the Losts of the Wager*, London, 1746.

Carteret's voyage round the world, 1766–1769, ed. Helen Wallis, 2 vol., Hakluyt Society, Cambridge University Press, 1965.

HAWKESWORTH (J.), *Relation des voyages exécutés par le commodore Byron, le capitaine Carteret, le capitaine Wallis, le capitaine Cook . . . , rédigée d'après les journaux des différents commandants et les papiers de Banks*, 5 vol., Paris, 1774.

WALLIS (S.), *A Journal of the Second Voyage of H.M.S. Dolphin Round the World under the Command of Cap. Wallis R.N. in the years 1766, 1767 and 1768, by Her Master George Robertson*, ed. Hugh Carrington, Haklut Society, Cambridge University Press, 1948.

On Bougainville and his companions

ARAGON (marquis D'), *Un paladin au XVIIIᵉ siècle, le prince Charles de Nassau-Siegen*, Paris, 1893.

BOUGAINVILLE (L.A. DE), *Traité du calcul intégral pour faire suite à l'analyse du marquis de l'Hôpital*, Paris, 1754.—*Voyage autour du monde par la frégate du roi la Boudeuse et la flûte l'Etoile, en 1766, 1767, 1768 et 1769*, Paris, 1771.

CAP (P.A.), *Philibert Commerson, naturaliste voyageur*, Paris, 1861.

CHEVRIER (R.), *Bougainville. Voyage en Océanie*, Paris, 1946.

DIDEROT (D.), *Supplément au voyage de Bougainville*, publ. d'après le Manuscrit de Léningrad, ed. G. Chinard, Paris-Baltimore, 1935.

DORSENNE (J.), *La vie de Bougainville*, Paris, 1930.

FESCHE (C.F.P.), *La Nouvelle-Cythère. Journal de navigation inédit*, Paris, 1929.

GOEBELS (J.), *The Struggle for the Falkland Islands*, New Haven, 1927.

LACÉPÈDE (comte DE), *Discours prononcé aux funérailles de M. le sénateur comte de Bougainville, le 5 septembre 1811*.

LA RONCIERE (Ch. DE), *Le routier inédit d'un compagnon de Bougainville . . . dans La Géographie*, t. 35, 1921.—*Bougainville*, Paris, 1942.

LEFRANC (J.), *Bougainville et ses compagnons*, Paris, 1929.

MARTIN-ALLANIC (J.E.), *Bougainville navigateur*, 2 vol., Paris, 1964.

MONTESSUS DE BALLORE, *Martyrologe et Biographie de Commerson*, Chalon-sur-Saône, 1889.

OLIVER (J.J.), *Life of Ph. Commerson*, London, 1909.

PASCAL (M.), *Essai historique sur la vie et les travaux de Bougainville*, Paris, 1831.

PERNETTY (Dom A.J.), *Histoire d'un voyage aux îles Malouines fait en 1763 et 1764, avec des observations sur le détroit de Magellan et sur les Patagons*, 2 vol., Paris, 1770.

TAILLEMITTE (E.), *Il y a 200 ans . . . de Bougainville*, Paris-Papeete, 1968.—*Bougainville et ses compagnons autour du monde, 1766–1769, journaux de navigation établis et commentés par E. Taillemitte*, 2 vol., Paris, 1977.

THIERRY (M.), *Bougainville, soldat et marin*, Paris, 1930.

VIVEZ, *Voyage autour du monde (. . .) par Vivez, chirurgien-major (. . .)*, Bull. de la Soc. de Géogr. de Rochefort, 1893.

WALSH (chevalier), *Une expédition de Bougainville en 1766, journal du chevalier Walsh*, Paris, 1901.

On the discovery of Tahiti

BOVIS (E. DE), *État de la société tahitienne à l'arrivée des Européens*, Papeete, 1909.

CORNEY (B.G.), *The quest and occupation of Tahiti*. n.d.

DECHAMPS (H.), *Tahiti*, Paris, 1957.

HENRY (T.), *Tahiti aux temps anciens*, Paris, 1951.

CAILLOT (E.), *Les Polynésiens orientaux au contact de la civilisation*, Paris, 1909.

JACQUIER (H.), *Le Mirage et l'Exotisme tahitiens*, Bull. Soc. Et Océan., vol. VII.

SIMON (J.), *La Polynésie dans les lettres et l'art de l'Occident*, Paris, 1939.

Chapter 3

Narratives of Cook's 1st voyage

BANKS (J.), *Illustrations of the Botany of Capt. Cook's Voyage round the World in H.M.S. Endeavour*, 2 vol., London, 1900–1901.

Captain Cook's Journal, a Literal Transcription of the original Manuscript, by capt. W.J.L. Wharton, London, 1893.

HAWKESWORTH (J.), *An account of the voyages undertaken by the order of His present Majesty for making Discoveries in the Southern Hemisphere . . . .*, 3 vol., London, 1773.

Journal d'un voyage autour du monde, 1768–1771, (Cook, Banks et Solander), trans. by de Fréville, Paris, Saillant et Nyon, 1772.

Journal of sir Joseph Banks, during captain Cook's first voyage, ed. by sir J.D. Hooker, London, 1896.

PARKINSON (S.), *Journal of a Voyage to the South Seas in H.M.S. Endeavour*, Paris, 1787.

The Endeavour Journal of Joseph Banks, ed. by J.C. Beaglehole, 2 vol., Sydney, 1962.

The Journals of captain J. Cook, ed. by J.C. Beaglehole, 4 vol., Cambridge University Press, 1955–1961.

Voyage of governor Philipp to Botany Bay (The), London, 1879.

Narratives of Cook's 2nd voyage

COOK (J.), *A Voyage towards the South Pole and round the World. Performed in H.M.S. Resolution and Adventure in 1772–1775, in which is included captain Furneaux's narrative (. . .)*, 2 vol., London, 1777.

FORSTER (J.G.), *Voyage round the world in H.M.S. Resolution commanded by capt. Cook during the years 1772–1775*. 2 vol., London, C. White, 1777.

FORSTER (J.R.), *Observations made during a Voyage round the World*, London, G. Robinson, 1778.—*Reise um die Welt während (. . .) 1772 (. . .) 1775*, Berlin, 1784.

SPARRMANN (A.), *A Voyage round the World (. . .) on H.M.S. Resolution*, London, 1944.—*Voyage au cap de Bonne-Espérance et autour du monde avec le capitaine Cook, et principalement dans les pays des Hottentots et des Cafres*, trad. by Le Tourneur, 2 vol., Paris, Buisson, 1787.

Voyage dans l'hémisphère austral et autour du monde, fait sur l'Adventure et le Resolution en 1772–1775, écrit par J. Cook, avec la relation du capt. Furneaux et de M. Forster, 5 vol. and 1 atlas, Paris, Hôtel de Thou, 1778.

WALES (W.), *Original astronomical Observations made in a Voyage of capt. Cook and King towards the South Pole*, London, J. Nourse, 1777.

Narratives of Cook's 3rd voyage

BAYLY (W.), *The astronomical Observations made on a Voyage to the Northern Pacific Ocean, by capt. Cook and Int. King*, London, P. Elmsly, 1782.

ELLIS (W.), *An authentic Narrative of a Voyage performed by capt. Cook and capt. Clerke in His Majesty's ships Resolution and Discovery (. . .) including a faithful Account of all their Discoveries and the unfortunate Death of capt. Cook*, 2 vol. London, 1782.

LEDYARD (J.), *A Journal of capt. Cook's last Voyage. A Narrative from the Manuscript of John Ledyard*, London, 1783.

Narrative of a Voyage performed by captains Cook and Clerke, 1776–1780, illustrated by W. Ellis, 2 vol., London, 1784.

SAMWELL (D.), *A Narrative of the Death of capt. James Cook. To which are added some Particulars, concerning his Life and Character. And Observations respecting the Introduction of the Venereal Diseases into the Sandwich Islands*, London, 1786.

3ᵉ Voyage de Cook, ou voyage dans l'océan Pacifique, ordonné par le roi d'Angleterre pour faire des découvertes dans l'hémisphère nord (. . .), exécuté sous la direction des capt. Cook, Clerke et Gore sur le Resolution et le Discovery en 1776–1780, trad. by M. Demeunier, planches dessinées by M. Weber, 4 vol., Paris, Hôtel de Thou, 1785.

On Cook and his companions

CAMERON (H.), *Sir Joseph Banks. The autocrat of the philosophers (. . .)*, London, 1952.

CAMPBELL (admiral G.), *Captain Cook*, London, 1936.

CARRINGTON (H.), *Life of captain Cook*, London, 1939.

CARRUTHERS (sir J.), *Captain James Cook R.N., one hundred and fifty years after*, London, 1929.

CLARK (T.B.), *Omaï, the first Polynesian ambassador to England (. . .)*, San Francisco, 1940.

HATTEMARE (H.), *Vie et Voyages de J. Cook*, 2nd ed., Paris, 1882.

HOLMES, *Introduction to the Bibliography of capt. Cook*, London, 1936.

Narration d'Omaï. Traduit de l'otahitien, Paris, 1790.

SKELTON (R.S.), *Captain James Cook after two hundred years*, London, 1969.

Vie de (. . .) Cook, trad. de l'anglais du Dr Kippis par M. Castera, Paris, 1789.

On Cook's discoveries

DAWS (C.), *Shoal of Time. A History of the Hawaiian Islands*, New York, 1968.

ELLIS (W.), *Polynesian Researches, during a residence of nearly six years in the South Sea Islands*, 2 vol., London, 1829.

History of the British Empire, t. VII, Cambridge, 1933.

HOWITT (W.), *History of the discovery of Australia*, 2 vol., London, 1865.

KUYKENDALL (R.S.), *The Hawaiian Kingdom*, 3 vol., Honolulu, 1948–1955.

MALO (D.), *Hawaiian Antiquities*, trans.into Englist by N.B. Emerson, 2nd ed., Honolulu, 1951.

LEMONNIER (L.), *Le capitaine Cook et l'exploration de l'Océanie*, Paris, 1940.

PERSON (Y.), *La Nouvelle-Calédonie et l'Europe, 1774–1854*, Paris, 1954.

SAMWELL (D.), *Captain Cook and Hawaii*, San Francisco, 1957.

SINCLAIR (K.A.), *A History of New Zealand*, London, 1969.

SMITH (B.), *European vision of the South Pacific*, Oxford, 1960.

WARNER (O.), *Captain Cook and the South Pacific*, New York, 1963.

WILLIAMSON (W.), *Cook and the Opening of the Pacific*, 3ʳᵈ edit., London, 1946.

WOOD (G.A.), *The Discovery of Australia*, London, 1922.

WOODS (T.), *History of the discovery and exploration of Australia*, 2 vol., London, 1865.

Natural history and Cook's voyages

BODDAERT, *Elenchus animalium*, 1785.

BRITTEN (J.), *Illustrations of Australian Plants Collected in 1770 during Cook's Voyage*, London, 1900–1905.

GMELIN (J.F.), *Systema naturae de Linné*, 13th ed., 1788–1790.

LYSAGHT (A.), *Some eighteenth century bird paintings in the library of sir Joseph Banks*, Bull. of Brit. Mus. Nat. Hist., Historical 1 (6).

MARSHALL (B.J.), *The handwritings of Joseph Banks, his scientific staff and amanuenses*, Bull. of Brit. Mus. Nat. Hist., Botany series, vol. 6, n° 1, London, 1978.

MARTYN (Th.), *Le Conchyliologue universel (coquillages des mers du Sud rapportés par Byron, Wallis et Cook)*, English and French eds., 1784–1793.

MEDWAY (D.G.), *The contribution of Cook's third voyage to the ornithology of Hawaiian Islands*, Honolulu, 1981.

SHAW (G.), and SMITH (J.), *The Zoology of New Holland*, illustr. by Sowerby, London, 1794.

SMITH (J.), *The Botany of New Holland*, London, 1794.

WHITEHEAD (P.J.), *Captain Cook's role in natural history*, extr. of Australian nat. hist., vol. 16, 1964.—*Forty drawings of fishes made by the artists who accompanied captain James Cook on his three voyages to the Pacific*, London, Brit. Mus. Natur. Hist., 1968.

Chapter 4

Narratives of the voyage

BROSSARD (C.-A. DE), *Kerguelen, le découvreur et ses îles*, 2 vol., Paris, 1970.

BUFFET (H.F.), *Voyage à la découverte du port-louisien Surville.—L'Explorateur malouin Marion du Fresne.—L'Explorateur port-louisien Julien Crozet*.

CROZET (J.), *Nouveau voyage à la mer du Sud commencé sous les ordres de M. Marion*, Paris, 1783.

DUPOUY (A.), *Le Breton Yves de Kerguelen*.

FLEURIEU (P. Claret DE), *Voyage autour du monde pendant les années 1790, 1791 et 1792*, (voyage d'Étienne Marchand), Paris 1798–1800.

KERGUELEN-TRAÉMAREC (Y.J. DE), *Relation de deux voyages dans les mers australes et des Indes, faits de 1771 à 1774*, Paris, 1782.—*Histoire des événements maritimes entre la France et l'Angleterre depuis 1778 jusqu'en 1796*, Paris, 1797.

PAGAÈS, *Voyage autour du monde et vers les deux pôles par mer et par terre pendant les années 1767–1771, 1773, 1774 et 1776*.

La Pérouse's voyage

Découvertes dans la mer du Sud. Nouvelles de M. de La Pérouse jusqu'en 1794, Paris.

Journal historique du voyage de Les-

seps, depuis l'instant où il a quitté les frégates françaises de La Pérouse au port Saint-Pierre-et-Saint-Paul au Kamtchatka jusqu'à son arrivée en France, Paris, 1790.

LESSEPS (M. DE), Voyage de La Pérouse, rédigé d'après les manuscrits originaux, suivi d'un appendice renfermant tout ce que l'on a découvert depuis le naufrage jusqu'à nos jours (. . .), Paris, 1831.

Voyage de La Pérouse autour du monde pendant les années 1785, 1786, 1787 et 1788, avec la préface du contre-amiral de Brossard, Paris, 1964.

Voyage de La Pérouse autour du monde, publié conformément au décret du 22 avril 1791 et rédigé par M.L.A. Milet-Mureau, 4 vol., Paris, 1979.

On La Pérouse and his friends

BELLESORT (A.), La Pérouse, Paris, 1926.
BROSSARD (capt. de vaisseau DE), Rendez-vous avec La Pérouse à Vanikoro, Paris, 1964.
ÉTAMPES (cte J. d'), Centenaire de la mort de La Pérouse, catalogue de l'exposition. Soc. de géogr., Paris, 1888.
FLEURIOT DE LANGLE, La tragique expédition de La Pérouse et Langle, Paris, 1954.
HAPDE (A.), Expédition de La Pérouse, Paris, 1829.
MARCEL (G.), La Pérouse, récit de son voyage, expédition envoyée à sa recherche. Le capitaine Dillon, Dumont d'Urville. Reliques de l'expédition, Ed. du Centenaire, Paris, 1888.
PISIER (G.), La Pérouse an Australie, Bull. Soc. Ét. Histor., Nouvelle-Calédonie, n° 28, 1975.
SCOTT (E.), Life of La Perouse, Sydney, 1912.
VATTEMARE (H.), Vie et Voyage de La Pérouse, Paris, 1882.
VIEULES (P.M.), Centenaire de La Pérouse, Albi, 1888, supplt Albi, 1892.

D'Entrecasteaux's voyage

BENOÎT-GUYOD (A.), Au temps de la marine en bois. Sur les traces de La Pérouse, d'Entrecasteaux, Dillon, une mission de Dumont d'Urville, 4th ed., Paris, 1945.
BURNEY (J.), Memoir of the voyage of (. . .) d'Entrecasteaux (. . .), London, 1820.
Fragments d'un journal anonyme sur la Recherche. Fragments de journaux anonymes sur l'Espérance. Manusc., Serv. hydrograph. de la marine.
FRÉEMINVILLE (chevalier DE), Nouvelle Relation du voyage à la recherche de La Pérouse, Brest, 1835.
HULOT (baron E.), D'Entrecasteaux, 1737–1793, Paris, 1892.
Journaux de routes. Journal de Huon de Kermadec. Journaux de mer. Manusc., Arch. Nat.
Relation du voyage à la recherche de La Pérouse, fait par ordre de l'Assemblée constituante pendant les années 1791 . . . par le citoyen La Billardière, 2 vol., and an atlas, Paris, 1799.
Voyage D'Entrecasteaux envoyé à la recherche de La Pérouse, publié par ordre de Sa Majesté l'Empereur et Roi, (. . .), rédigé par M. de Rossel (. . .), 2 vol., Paris, 1808.

Vancouver's voyage

BROUGHTON (W.R.), Voyage de découverte dans la partie septentrionale de l'océan Pacifique dans les années 1795–1798, trad. fr. J.B.B. Eyriès, 2 vol., Paris, 1807.
VANCOUVER (G.), A Voyage of Discovery to the North Pacific Ocean and round the World, 3 vol., London, 1798.

Malaspina's voyage

CAMPORI (G.), Vita ed avventure del mar. Alessandro Malaspina, Modena, 1882.
CASELLI, C.A. de Malaspina spedizione scientifica intorno al mondo, Milano, 1929.
CUTTER (D.C.), Malaspina in California, San Francisco, 1960.
JIMENEZ DE LA ESPADA (M.), Una causa da Estado, Madrid, 1882.
NOVO Y COLSON, La vuelta al mondo par las corbetas Descubierto y Atrevida al mando de Don Alejandro Malaspina, Madrid, 1885.
ORTIZ (D.), 64 meses a bordo, Madrid, 1946.

Chapter 5

Baudin's voyage

Narratives of the voyage

BORY DE SAINT-VINCENT (J.B.G.M.), Voyage dans les quatre principales îles des mers d'Afrique, avec l'histoire de la traversée du Capitaine Baudin jusqu'au Port-Louis de l'île Maurice, 1801–1802, 3 vol., Paris, 1804.—Essai sur les îles Fortunées, Paris, 1810.
LESCHENAULT DE LA TOUR (J.-B.), Végétation de la Nouvelle-Hollande et de la Terre de Diemen, Paris, 1824.
MILBERT (J.M.), Voyage pittoresque à l'île de France, au cap de Bonne-Espérance et à l'île de Ténériffe, avec un atlas et des vues pittoresques dessinées sur les lieux et gravées en partie par l'auteur, 2 vol., Paris, 1812.
PÉRON (F.), Tableau général des colonies anglaises aux Terres australes en 1802, Paris, 1816.
PÉRON (J.), et FREYCINET (L. CL. DE), Voyage de découverte aux Terres australes exécuté sur les corvettes le Géographe, le Naturaliste et la goélette le Casuarina pendant les années 1800, 1801, 1802, 1803 et 1804, Paris, 1807–1816. Historique, par Péron, continué par Freycinet, 2 vol.—Navigation et géorgraphie, par Freycinet, Atlas historique, par Lesueur et Petit, Atlas hydrographique.—Voyage de découverte aux Terres australes (. . .), nouvelle édition augmentée par L. Cl. de Freycinet, 5 vol., Atlas historique et Atlas hydrographique, Paris, 1824.

On Baudin and his discoveries

BONPLAND (A.), Description des plantes rares de Navarre et de la Malmaison, Paris, 1812.
BOUVIER (R), et MAYNIAL (E.), Une aventure dans les mers australes; l'expédition du commandant Baudin, 1800–1803, Paris, 1947.
BUENTGEN (J.), Die Verdienste der Franzosen um die Entdeckung der australischen Küste und der Inseln des Stilles Ozeans (1783–1830), Bonn, 1907.
CUVIER (baron G.), Éloge historique de M. Baudin, Académie royale des sciences, 2 avril 1821, Paris, 1826.
LEDRU (A.P.), Voyage aux îles de Ténériffe, la Trinité, Saint-Thomas, Sainte-Croix et Porto-Rico, 30 septembre 1796 au 7 juin 1798, sous la direction du capitaine Baudin, Paris, 1810.
SCOTT (E.), Terre Napoléon, Londres, 1910.

Flinders's voyage

Narratives of the voyage

A Voyage to Terra Australis in H.M.S. Investigator, 1801–1803, by M. Flinders, 2 vol., London, 1814.
BAUER (F.L.), Illustrationes Florae Novae-Hollandiae, London, 1813–1814.
BROWN (R.), Prodromus Florae Novae-Hollandiae, London, 1810.

On Flinders and his discoveries

AITON, Hortus Kewensis, rééd. par W.T. Aiton, London, 1810–1813.
BRYANT (J.), Captain M. Flinders: his Voyages and Discoveries, London, 1928.
GOULD (J.), Mammals of Australia, 3 vol., London, 1850–1863.—Birds of Australia, 7 vol. plus 1 vol. supplement, 580 pl. couleurs, London, 1848–1869.
HOOKER (W.J.), Exotic Flora, 3 vol., Edinburgh, 1823–1827.
SCOTT (E.), The Life of captain M. Flinders, Sydney, 1914.

Chapter 6

Discoveries of the russians in the pacific

BURNEY (J.), North-Eastern Voyages. A Chronological History of North-Eastern. Voyages of Discovery; and of the Early Eastern Navigations of the Russians, London, 1819.
COXE (W.), An Account of the Russian Discoveries between Asia and America, London 1780.
GOLOVNINE, Voyage autour du monde, 2 vol., Saint Petersburg, 1822.
GOLOVNINE (V.M.), Voyage sur la chaloupe Diana de Kronstadt au Kamtchatka en 1807, 1808 et 1809; en captivité chez les Japonais en 1811, 1812 et 1813; voyage autour du monde sur la chaloupe Kamtchatka en 1817, 1818 et 1819, (in Russian), Moscow-Leningrad, 1949.
MULLER (G.F.), Voyages et découvertes faites par les Russes le long des côtes de la mer Glaciale et sur l'océan Oriental, tant vers le Japon que vers l'Amérique, 2 vol., Amsterdam, 1766.

Bellingshausen

BELLINGSHAUSEN (F.F.), Double recherche dans le sud de l'océan Glacial et voyage autour du monde en 1819, 1820 et 1821, accompli sur le Vostok et le Mirnyj (. . .), (in Russian), Moscow, 1949.
The Voyage of Captain Bellingshausen to the Antarctic Sea, Hakluyt Society, Cambridge, 1945.

Krusenstern

KRUSENSTERN (A.I. VON), Voyage autour du monde, 1803–1806, sur le Nadjejeda et le Neva commandés par de Krusenstern, trad. revue par Eyriès, 2 vol., and an atlas, Paris, 1821.
LANGSDORFF (G.H. VON), Bemerkungen auf einer Reise um die Welt in den Jahren 1803 bis 1807, 2 vol., London, 1813.
LANGSDORFF et FISCHER (F.), Plantes recueillies pendant le voyage des Russes autour du monde, Tübingen, 1810.
LISIANSKI (U.), (Lissianskoi), Description d'un voyage autour du monde, 2 vol., in-8° (in Russian), St. Petersburg,1810–1813.—A Voyage round the World, London, 1814.
TILESIUS VON TILENAU (W.G.), Naturhistorische Fruchte der ersten Kaiserlich-Russischen unter dem Kommado der Herr von Krusenstern glücklich vollbracht, St.Petersburg.

Kotzebue

1st voyage

CHAMISSO (A. VON), Voyage autour du monde, trans. by Henri Alexis Baatsch, Paris, 1981.
CHORIS (L.), Voyage pittoresque autour du monde, 1815–1818, Paris, 1822. Supplement, Paris, 1826.
KOTZEBUE (O. VON), Reise um die Welt, 2 vol., Weimar, 1821. A Voyage into the South Sea and Behring's straits, 1815–1818, trans. by H.E. Lloyd, 3 vol., London, 1821,

2nd voyage

ESCHSCHOLTZ (J.F.), System der Acalephen, 1829.—Entomographies, 1823.—Zoologischen Atlas, 1829–1833.
KOTZEBUE (O. VON), Neue Reise um die Welt in 1823, 1824, 1825 und 1826, 2 tomes en 1 vol., Weimar.—A new Voyage round the World, 1823–1826, 2 vol. London, 1830.

Lütke

LÜTKE (F.P.), Voyage autour du monde exécuté sur la corvette le Seniavine, 1826–1829. Partie historique avec atlas d'après les dessins originaux de Postels et de Kittlitz, trad. du russe par F. Boyé, 5 vol., and an atlas, Paris, 1835–1836.—Partie nautique with atlas, Saint-Petersburg, 1836.

On Chamisso and his voyage

BRUN (X.), Adelbert de Chamisso de Boncourt, Lyon, 1896.
RIEGEL (R.), Adelbert de Chamisso, sa vie et son oeuvre, 2 vol., Paris, 1934.
SCHMID (G.), Chamisso als Naturforscher. Eine Bibliographie, Leipizig, 1942.

Chapter 7

JORE (L.), L'Océan Pacifique au temps de la Restauration et de la monarchie de Juillet, 2 vol., Paris, 1959.
KOSKINEN (A.A.), Missionary Influence as a Political Factor in the Pacific Islands, Helsinki, 1953.
LAVAL (H.), Mémoires pour servir à l'histoire de Mangaréva. Ère chrétienne 1834–1871, Paris, 1968.

Freycinet

Narratives of the Voyage

ARAGO (J.), Promenade autour du monde pendant les années 1817, 1818, 1819 et 1820 sur les corvettes du roi (. . .) par J.S. Arago, dessinateur de l'Expédition, 2 vol. et atlas historique et pittoresque, Paris, 1822.
DUPERREY (L.I.), Réduction des observations de l'intensité du magnétisme terrestre, Paris, n.d.
FREYCINET (L. CL. DE SAULCES DE), Voyage autour du monde sur les corvettes de S.M. l'Uranie et la Physicienne pendant les années 1817, 1818, 1819 et 1820, Paris, 1824–1844.
FREYCINET (ROSE DE SAULCES DE), Campagne de l'Uranie. Journal de Voyage de Mme de Freycinet, d'après le ms. original annoted by Ch. Duplomb, Paris, 1927.

On Freycinet and his voyage

DEZOS DE LA ROQUETTE (J.B.), Notices historiques sur de Freycinet, lues le 15 décembre 1843, Paris, n.d.
GRILLE (F.), De Freycinet, Paris, 1853.
LA TOUR MADURE, L. de Freycinet, n.d.
MOURRAL (col.), Notice sur les expéditions

de L.-Cl. de Freycinet, 1779–1842, Grenoble, 1937.
RAULIN (G. de), Rose de Freycinet, Paris, 1944.

Duperrey

Narratives of the voyage

DUPERREY (L.I.), Voyage autour du monde exécuté par ordre du Roi sur la corvette de Sa Maj. la Coquille, pendant les années 1822, 1823, 1824 et 1825 (. . .), 7 vol. and 4 atlases—Notice sur les opérations géographiques faites pendant le voyage de la Coquille, Paris, n.d.—Observations du pendule invariable, de l'inclinasion et de la déclinaison de l'aiguille aimantée, Paris, n.d.
LESSON (R.P.), Voyage entrepris sur la Coquille, 2 vol., Paris, 1838.—Voyage médical autour du monde, 1822–1825, suivi d'un Mémoire sur les races humaines de l'Océanie, Paris, 1829.

On Duperrey's voyage

ARAGO (FR.), Rapport fait à l'Académie des sciences sur le voyage de la Coquille, Paris, n.d., (1825).
LESSON (R.P.), Histoire naturelle des Mammifères et des Oiseaux découverts après la mort de Buffon, in Compléments des oeuvres de Buffon, t. V and VI, Paris, 1829.—Centurie zoologique ou choix d'Animaux rares, nouveaux ou imparfaitement connus, Paris, 1830.—Illustrations de zoologie ou Recueil de figures d'Animaux peints d'après nature, Paris, 1832–1835.—Histoire naturelle des Oiseaux de paradis et des Épimaques, Paris, 1835.

Dumont d'Urville

Narratives of 1st voyage

DILLON (P.), Narrative and successful Result of a Voyage in the South Seas, 2 vol., London, 1829, trad. fr. by Parisot, Paris, 1830.
DUMONT D'URVILLE (J.S.C.), Voyage de la corvette l'Astrolabe exécuté pendant les années 1826, 1827, 1828, 1829 . . . , 14 vol. and 5 atlases, Paris, 1830–1835.

On Dumont D'Urville (1st voyage)

DUMONT D'URVILLE (J.S.C.), Relation de la campagne hydrographique de la gabare du roi la Chevrette dans le Levant et de la mer Noire durant l'année 1820, Journal des Voyages, Paris, 1821.—Enumeratio Plantatum quas in Insulis Archipelagi aut littoribus Ponti Euxini annis 1819—1820 collegit atque detexit, Paris, 1822.—Voyage pittoresque autour du monde, résumé général des voyages de découverte (. . .), 2 vol., Paris, 1834–1835.
FIRTH (R.), We, the Tikopia, London, 1936.
HULOT (BARON E.), LE CONTRE-AMIRAL DUMONT D'URVILLE (1790–1842), PARIS, 1892.
ROSSEL (chevalier DE), Rapport sur la navigation de l'Astrolabe, Paris, 1829.
SOUDRY DU KERVEN (Mme A.), Dumont d'Urville. Pages intimes. Paris, 1893.

H. de Bougainville

BOUGAINVILLE (H. DE), Journal de la navigation autour du globe de la frégate la Thétis et de la corvette l'Espérance pendant les années 1824, 1825, 1826, 2 vol. and an atlas, Paris, 1827.
LA TOUANNE (vicomte DE), Album pittoresque du voyage de la Thétis et de l'Espérance, Paris, 1828.

Laplace

1st voyage

LAPLACE (C.P. Th.), Voyage autour du monde par les mers de l'Inde et de la Chine (. . .) exécuté par la corvette la Favorite, 1830–1832 (. . .), 5 vol. and 2 atlases, Paris, 1833–1839.

2nd voyage

LAPLACE (C.P. Th.), Campagne de l'Artémise, 1837–1840 (. . .), 6 vol., Paris, 1841–1854.
MATHIEU (P.), Relation du voyage de la Favorite, Alger, n.d.
PARIS (Ed.), Essai sur la construction navale des peuples extra-européens.

Vaillant

VAILLANT (A.N.), Voyage autour du monde exécuté pendant les années 1836 et 1837 sur la corvette la Bonite (. . .), 15 vol. and 3 atlases.

Dupetit-Thouars

DUPETIT-THOUARS (A.), Voyage autour du monde sur la frégate la Vénus pendant les années 1836–1839, 11 vol. and 3 atlases, Paris, 1840–1864.
MOERENHOUT (J.A.), Voyage aux îles du grand Océan, contenant des documents nouveaux (. . .), Paris, 1837.—Voyage aux îles du grand Océan (. . .), 2 vol., Paris, 1942.

Chapter 8

Beechey

Narratives of the voyage

BEECHEY (F.W.), Narrative of a Voyage to the Pacific and Behring's Strait to cooperate with the Polar Expedition performed in H.M.S. Blossom . . . , 2 vol., London, 1831.
DUMONT D'URVILLE (J.S.C.), Rapport sur le voyage de Beechey, Bull. de la Soc. de Géogr., t. XV, Paris, 1831.
MONTEMONT (A.), Bibliothèque universelle des voyages autour du monde, t. 19, Beechey, Paris, 1834.
The Botany of Capt. Beechey's voyage, by sir W.J. Hooker and G.A. Walker Arnott, London, 1841.
The Geology of Capt. Beechey's voyage, by Pr Buckland and Capt. Belcher, London.
The Zoology of Capt. Beechey's voyage, compiled from the collections and notes made by capt. Beechey, by N.A. Vigors, Edw. Bennett, J.E. Gray, Richard Owen, Dr J. Richardson and George T. Lay, illustrat. with coloured plates by G. Sowerby, etc., London, 1839.

On Beechey and his voyages

BEECHEY (F.W.), Proceedings of the expedition to explore the northern coast of Africa (. . .) in 1821 and 1822 by F.W. Beechey and H.N. Beechey, London, 1828.—A Voyage of Discovery toward the North Pole performed by H.M.S. Dorothea and Trent under the command of Capt. David Buchan, 1818, (with) a summary of all the early attempts to reach the Pacific by way of the Pole (. . .), New York, 1843.—Hydrography by the late rear admiral F.W. Beechey, revised by capt. Washington, London, 1859.
Narratives of a second Expedition to the Polar Sea, in the years 1825, 1826 and 1827 by John Franklin (. . .), London, 1828.
Voyage de Bligh à Tahiti (1787–1789) et voyage du capt. Edwards pour saisir les révoltés du Bounty (1790–1792).—Second voyage de Bligh (1792–1793), in Abrégé des voyages modernes, by Eyriès.
MORRISON (J.), Journal de James Morrison, second maître à bord du Bounty, trad. fr. B. Jannez, Paris, 1966.

FitzRoy

Narratives of the voyage

Charles Darwin's Diary of the Voyage of H.M.S. Beagle, edit. from the ms by N. Barlow, Cambridge University Press 1933.
DARWIN (Ch.), Journal of Researches into the Geology and Natural History of the Countries visited (. . .), London, 1840.—Geological Observations on South America, London, 1846.—A Monograph on the sub-class Cirripedia, 2 vol., London, 1851–1854.—Voyage d'un naturaliste autour du monde, 1831–1836 par Charles Darwin.
FITZROY (R.), and KING (P.P.), Narrative of the surveying voyages of H.M.S. Adventure and Beagle between the years 1826 and 1838 describing their examination of the southern shores of South America and the Beagle's circumnavigation of the globe, 3 vol. London, 1839.
Zoology of the Voyage of H.M.S. Beagle, edited and superintended by Ch. Darwin, 5 vol., London, 1838–1843.

On Darwin
and the voyage of the Beagle

ALLEN (gr.), Ch. Darwin, trad. par P.L. Le Monnier, Paris, 1886.
Autobiography of Ch. Darwin, 1809–1882, edit. by Nora Barlow, London, 1958.
BARLOW (N. Ch.), Darwin and the Voyage of the Beagle, London, 1945.
Charles Darwin's Autobiography, with notes and letters . . . , edit. by Francis Darwin, New York, 1961.
COONE (Ch.), Admiral FitzRoy: his Facts and Failures, London, 1867.
DARWIN (Ch.), The Foundation of the Origin of Species, London, 1909.
DE BEER (G.R.), Darwin's Note Book on Transmutation of Species, London, 1960.—The Origin of Darwin's Ideas on Evolution and Natural Selection, London, 1961.
HUXLEY (J.) and KETTLEWEL (H.B.D.), Charles Darwin and his world, London n.d. (1965).
MOOREHEAD (A.), Darwin and the Beagle, London, 1969.
The Life and Letters of Ch. Darwin, edit. by his son, Francis Darwin, 3 vol., London, 1887.

Belcher

BELCHER (sir Edw.), Narrative of a Voyage round the World performed on H.M.S. Sulphur, 1836–1842, 2 vol., London, 1843.—The Last of the Arctic Voyages. Narrative of the expedition in H.M.S. Blossom (. . .) in search of Sir John Franklin during the years 1852, 1853, 1854. 2 vol., London, 1853.
BENTHAM (G.), The Botany of the Voyage of H.M.S. Sulphur, edit. by R.B. Hinds, London, 1844.
The Zoology of the Voyage of H.M.S. Sulphur, edit. by R.B. Hinds, 2 vol., London, 1843–1845.

Chapter 9

WEDDELL (J.), A Voyage towards the South Pole, performed in the years 1822–1824, London, 1825.

Dumont d'Urville—2nd voyage

DUMONT D'URVILLE (J.S.C.), Voyage au pôle Sud et dans l'Océanie sur les corvettes l'Astrolabe et la Zélée, 1837–1840, 23 vol. and 7 atlases, Paris, 1841–1854.
LE GUILLOU (dr E.J.F.), Voyage autour du monde de l'Astrolabe et de la Zélée, Paris, 1842.

Wilkes

DANA (J.D.), On Corals and Coral Islands, New York, 1872.
WILKES (Ch.), Narrative of the U.S. exploring Expedition, condensed and abridged, London, 1845.—The United States Expedition, 1838–1842. Ch. Wilkes Commander of the Exp., 20 vol. and 7 atlases, Philadelphia, 1845–1876.

Ross

ROSS (J.Cl.), Voyage of Discovery in the Southern and Antarctic Regions, 1839–1843, 2 vol., London, 1847.
The Botany of the voyage of H.M.S. Erebus and Terror (. . .), edit. by John Dalton Hooker, 6 vol., London, 1843–1859.
The Zoology of the voyage of H.M.S. Erebus and Terror (. . .), edit. by John Richardson and John Edward Gray, 2 vol., 1844–1875.

On the Discovery of the Antarctic Continent

AUBERT DE LA RÜE, Les Terres australes, Paris, 1956.
CHRISTIE (E.W.H.), The Antarctic Problem, an Historical and Political Study, London, 1951.
DEBENHAM (F.), Antarctica. History of a Continent, New York, 1961.
RICKER, Die Entstehung und Verbreitung des Antarktischen Treibreises, Leipzig, 1893.
HATHERTON (T.), Antarctica, London, 1965.
JEANNEL (R.), Au seuil de l'Antarctique, Paris, 1941.
MILL (H.R.), The Siege of the South Pole, London, 1905.
ROUCH (J.), Le Pôle Sud. Histoire des voyages antarctiques, Paris, 1921.
SOUDRY DU KERVEN (Madame A.), Dumont d'Urville. Sa vie intime pendant son troisième voyage autour du monde, Paris, 1886.

INDEX